A Short History of the Ismailis

ISLAMIC SURVEYS
General Editor
CAROLE HILLENBRAND

A Short History of the Ismailis

Traditions of a Muslim Community

Farhad Daftary

EDINBURGH UNIVERSITY PRESS

To Farimah

Edinburgh University Press
22 George Square, Edinburgh

Reprinted 1999

Typeset in Linotron Trump Mediaeval
by Koinonia, Bury, and
printed and bound in Great Britain
by The University Press, Cambridge

A CIP record for this book is available
from the British Library

ISBN 0 7486 0904 0 (hardback)
ISBN 0 7486 0687 4 (paperback)

Contents

Preface

The Ismailis represent the second largest Shīʿī Muslim community after the Twelvers (Ithnāʿasharīs), and are today scattered as religious minorities in more than twenty-five countries of Asia, Africa, Europe and North America. Despite their long history and contributions to Islamic civilisation, however, they were until recently one of the least understood Muslim communities. In fact, a multitude of medieval legends and misconceptions circulated widely about Ismaili teachings and practices, while the rich literary heritage of the Ismailis remained inaccessible to outsiders. The breakthrough in Ismaili studies had to await the recovery and study of a large number of Ismaili sources, a phenomenon that has continued unabated since the 1930s. As a result, modern scholarship in the field has already made great strides in distinguishing fact from fiction in many aspects of Ismaili history and thought.

My own interest in Ismaili studies dates back to the 1960s. Subsequently, I attempted to collect and synthesise, in as comprehensive a manner as possible at the time, the findings of modern scholarship on the complex history of the Ismailis. The results were published in *The Ismāʿīlīs: Their History and Doctrines* (Cambridge: Cambridge University Press, 1990). The present book, addressed to a wider readership, is organised quite differently, and it does not represent a condensed version of my earlier work. Here, I have adopted a topical approach within a historical framework, focusing on a selection of major themes and developments, in addition to providing historical and doctrinal overviews. In particular, the present book concentrates on the diversity of the intellectual traditions and institutions elaborated by the Ismailis, as well as their responses to the challenges and adverse circumstances which they often encountered in the course of their history.

I owe a special debt of gratitude to Neguin Yavari and Kutub Kassam who read an earlier draft of this book and made many valuable suggestions for its improvement. I would also like to thank Jan Malique who meticulously prepared the typescript for publication. Needless to add, I am solely responsible for the final product and the views expressed in it.

F.D.

Note on Transliteration, Dates and Abbreviations

The system of transliteration used in this book for the Arabic and Persian scripts is that of the new edition of *The Encyclopaedia of Islam*, with a few modifications, namely *ch* for *č*, *j* for *dj*, and *q* for *ḳ*; ligatures are also dispensed with. Diacritical marks are dispensed with for some of the dynastic and community names which occur frequently in the book and are treated as common English words in *The Concise Oxford Dictionary*. The most important of these are Abbasid for ʿAbbāsid, Fatimid for Fāṭimid, Ismaili for Ismāʿīlī, Sufi for Ṣūfī, Sunni for Sunnī, Saljuq for Saljūq, and Safawid for Ṣafawid.

The lunar years of the Islamic calendar are generally followed by the corresponding Gregorian solar years (for example, 11/632). The Islamic solar dates of the sources published in modern Iran are followed by the corresponding Christian years starting on 21 March.

The following abbreviations are used for certain periodicals and encyclopaedias cited frequently in the chapter Notes and Select Bibliography.

BIFAO	*Bulletin de l'Institut Français d'Archéologie Orientale*
BSO(A)S	*Bulletin of the School of Oriental (and African) Studies*
EI2	*The Encyclopaedia of Islam*, New edition
EIR	*Encyclopaedia Iranica*
IJMES	*International Journal of Middle East Studies*
JAOS	*Journal of the American Oriental Society*
JRAS	*Journal of the Royal Asiatic Society*
NS	New Series
WO	*Die Welt des Orients*

I

Ismaili History and Historiography: Phases, Sources and Studies

A major Shīʿī Muslim community, the Ismailis have had a long and complex history dating back to the formative period of Islam, when different communities of interpretation developed their doctrinal positions. By the time of the Abbasid revolution in 132/750, Imāmī Shīʿism, the common heritage of the major Shīʿī communities of Ithnāʿashariyya (Twelvers) and Ismāʿīliyya, had acquired a special prominence. The Imāmī Shīʿīs, who like other Shīʿī communities upheld the rights of the Prophet Muḥammad's household (*ahl al-bayt*) to the leadership of the Muslim *umma*, propounded a particular conception of divinely instituted religious authority, also recognising certain descendants of the Prophet from amongst the ʿAlids as their spiritual leaders or imams possessing the required religious authority. The Shīʿī conception of religious authority, which set the Shīʿa in general apart from the groups later designated as Sunni, came to be embodied in the central Shīʿī doctrine of the imamate expounded by the Imam Jaʿfar al-Ṣādiq and his associates. The doctrine of the imamate has retained a central position in the teachings of the Ismailis.

PHASES IN ISMAILI HISTORY

On the death of the Imam al-Ṣādiq in 148/765, his Imāmī Shīʿī following split into several groups, including those identifiable as the earliest Ismailis. The Ismailis themselves experienced several major and minor schisms in the course of their eventful history; the schisms normally revolved around the rightful succession to the imamate. By the middle of the 3rd/9th century, the Ismailis had organised a revolutionary movement against the established order under the Abbasids. In 286/899, the unified Ismaili movement was rent by its first major schism over the question of the imamate. The Ismailis now split into two rival camps, the loyal Ismailis and the dissident Qarmaṭīs. Upholding continuity in the Ismaili imamate, the loyal Ismailis acknowledged the founder of the Fatimid dynasty and his successors as their imams. The Qarmaṭīs, centred in Baḥrayn, did not recognise the Fatimid caliphs as their imams and in time they opposed the Fatimids. By the final decades of the 3rd/9th century when Ismaili *dāʿīs* or religio-political missionaries were active from the Maghrib in North Africa to Transoxania in Central Asia,

Ismailism (named after al-Ṣādiq's eldest son Ismāʿīl) had received much popular support among different social strata.

The early success of the Ismaili *daʿwa* or mission culminated in 297/909 in the establishment of an Ismaili *dawla* or state, the Fatimid caliphate, in North Africa. The Ismailis had now entered a new phase of their history. The revolutionary activities of the early Ismailis, directed by a hereditary line of central leaders, had resulted in the foundation of a state, in which the Ismaili imam was installed as caliph, rivalling the Abbasid caliph in Baghdad. The establishment of this first Shīʿī caliphate represented a serious challenge to the authority of the Abbasid caliph, the official spokesman of Sunni Islam, and the position of the Sunni *ʿulamāʾ* who legitimised the Abbasids' authority and defined Sunnism as the true interpretation of Islam. The Ismailis, who as Imāmī Shīʿī Muslims had developed their own interpretation of the Islamic message, had now in effect offered a viable alternative to Sunni "orthodoxy".

The Fatimid period was the "golden age" of Ismailism when the Ismaili imam ruled over a vast empire and Ismaili thought and literature attained their summit. The recovery of Ismaili literature in modern times attests to the rich literary heritage of the Ismailis during the Fatimid phase of their history. It was also during the first Fatimid century, designated as the "Ismaili century" of Islam by Louis Massignon (1883–1962),[1] that the Ismaili-connected Ikhwān al-Ṣafāʾ (Brethren of Purity) produced their encyclopaedic *Rasāʾil* (*Epistles*), reflecting the contemporary state of knowledge on diverse sciences and a pluralistic perception of religion and philosophy. At the same time, *dāʿī*s of the Iranian lands synthesised their theology with different philosophical traditions, giving rise to a distinctive intellectual tradition labelled as "philosophical Ismailism" by Paul Walker.[2] Other *dāʿī*s, living in Arab lands and within Fatimid dominions, produced treatises on a variety of exoteric and esoteric subjects, also developing the science of *taʾwīl* or esoteric exegesis which became the hallmark of Ismaili thought. By the second half of the 5th/11th century, the Ismailis had indeed made important contributions to Islamic thought and culture.

A new phase in Ismaili history was initiated on the death of the Fatimid caliph-imam al-Mustanṣir in 487/1094 and the ensuing Nizārī–Mustaʿlī schism in Ismailism. The succession to al-Mustanṣir was disputed between his eldest son and heir-designate Nizār, and his youngest son Aḥmad who was actually installed to the caliphate with the title of al-Mustaʿlī biʾllāh by the all-powerful Fatimid vizier al-Afḍal. Subsequently, Nizār rose in revolt to assert his claims, but he was defeated and executed in 488/1095. As a result of these events, the unified Ismaili community of the latter decades of al-Mustanṣir's reign was permanently split into two rival factions, the Nizāriyya and the Mustaʿliyya.

The Mustaʿlī Ismailis themselves split into Ḥāfiẓī and Ṭayyibī factions soon after the death of al-Mustaʿlī's son and successor al-Āmir in 524/1130. The Ḥāfiẓī Ismailis, who recognised the later Fatimids as their imams, disappeared after the collapse of the Fatimid dynasty in 567/1171. The Ṭayyibī Ismailis, who have not had any manifest imam after al-Āmir, found a permanent stronghold in Yaman. The Ṭayyibīs were henceforth led by chief *dāʿīs*. By the end of the 10th/16th century, the Ṭayyibīs themselves were subdivided into Dā'ūdī and Sulaymānī factions over the issue of the rightful succession to the office of the *dāʿī*. By that time the Indian Ṭayyibīs, known locally as Bohras and belonging mainly to the Dā'ūdī faction, had greatly outnumbered their (Sulaymānī) co-religionists in Yaman. The Ṭayyibīs in general maintained the intellectual and literary traditions of the Fatimid Ismailis, as well as a good portion of Ismaili literature of that period. The learned Ṭayyibī *dāʿīs* of Yaman themselves generated a considerable volume of Ismaili literature. Owing to frequent subdivisions in their community and extended persecutions, the Ṭayyibīs account for a minority of the Ismailis in the world today.

In contrast to the Ṭayyibī Ismailis, the Nizārī Ismailis acquired political prominence within Saljuq dominions, especially in Persia where they had a state of their own. The Nizārī state, centred at the mountain fortress of Alamūt in northern Persia, lasted some 166 years until it collapsed under the onslaught of the Mongol hordes in 654/1256. Ḥasan Ṣabbāḥ (d. 518/1124), their first leader, designed a revolutionary strategy against the Saljuqs. Ḥasan did not realise this political objective, but he did succeed in establishing and consolidating the independent Nizārī *daʿwa* and state with its territories scattered from Syria to eastern Persia.

After Ḥasan Ṣabbāḥ and his next two successors, who ruled as *dāʿīs* and *ḥujjas*, the imams' chief representatives, the Nizārī imams themselves emerged at Alamūt to lead their community of followers. The Nizārī state of the Alamūt period was thus ruled by three *dāʿīs* and five imams, generally referred to as the lords of Alamūt in the Persian sources. Preoccupied with revolutionary campaigns and constantly living in hostile surroundings, the Nizārīs did not produce a substantial literature. Their *dāʿīs* were for the most part military commanders and governors of fortresses rather than learned theologians. Nevertheless, the Nizārīs did maintain a literary tradition, also elaborating their teachings in response to changed circumstances of the Alamūt period.

Nizārī Ismailis survived the Mongol destruction of their fortresses and state, which marked the initiation of a new phase in their history. The first two post-Alamūt centuries in Nizārī history remain rather obscure. In the aftermath of the fall of Alamūt, the Nizārī imams went into hiding, losing direct contacts with their followers. Many of the Persian Ismailis who had escaped from the Mongol massacres found refuge in Central Asia, Afghanistan or India. The scattered Nizārī communities developed independently under local leaderships. It was also during the early post-Alamūt centuries that the Nizārīs of Persia and adjacent areas adopted Sufi disguise to safeguard themselves.

By the middle of the 9th/15th century, the Nizārī imams had emerged in Anjudān in central Persia, initiating what W. Ivanow has designated as the Anjudān revival in Nizārī *da'wa* and literary activities.[3] During the Anjudān revival, lasting some two centuries, the imams reasserted their central authority over the various Nizārī communities, also reviving the proselytising activities of their *da'wa*. The Nizārī *da'wa* now proved particularly successful in the Indian subcontinent where large numbers of Hindus were converted in Sind and Gujarāt; the Indian Nizārīs became locally known as Khojas. The Nizārīs of the post-Alamūt period developed distinctive literary traditions in Syria, Persia, Central Asia and India. In particular, the Nizārī Khojas developed a unique literary genre in the form of devotional hymns known as *ginān*s.

In the 1840s, the seat of the Nizārī Ismaili imamate was transferred from Persia to India, initiating the modern period in the history of the Nizārī community. Benefiting from the modernising policies and the elaborate network of institutions established by their last two imams, known internationally by their hereditary title of Aga Khan, the Nizārīs have emerged as an educated and prosperous community. Numbering several millions, the Nizārī Ismaili Muslims are currently scattered in more than twenty-five countries of Asia, Africa, Europe and North America.

EVOLUTION OF ISMAILI HISTORIOGRAPHY

Ismaili historiography, too, has had its own distinctive features and evolution, which have been closely related to the very nature of the Ismaili movement and the changing political fortunes of the Ismailis. The Ismailis were often persecuted outside the territories of their states, which necessitated the strict observance of *taqiyya* or precautionary dissimulation. And the Ismaili authors, as noted, were for the most part theologians who frequently served as their community's *dā'ī*s in hostile surroundings. Owing to their training as well as the absolute necessity of observing secrecy in their activities, the Ismaili *dāʿī*-authors were not particularly interested in compiling annalistic or other types of historical accounts. This general lack of interest in historiography is attested to by the fact that only a handful of historical works have come to light in the modern recovery of a large number of Ismaili texts. These include al-Qāḍī al-Nuʿmān's *Iftitāḥ al-daʿwa* (*Commencement of the Mission*), completed in 346/957, the earliest known historical work in Ismaili literature which covers the background to the establishment of the Fatimid caliphate. In later medieval times, only one general history of Ismailism was compiled by an Ismaili author, the *ʿUyūn al-akhbār* of Idrīs ʿImād al-Dīn (d. 872/1468), the nineteenth Ṭayyibī Mustaʿlī *dāʿī* in Yaman. This is a seven-volume history from the time of the Prophet until the commencement of the Ṭayyibī *daʿwa* in Yaman in the first half of the 6th/12th century. It is interesting to note that the pre-Fatimid period of Ismaili history in general and the opening phase of Ismailism in particular remain obscure in Ismaili historiography. There are also those brief but highly significant historical accounts of specific Ismaili events, notably the Fatimid *dāʿī* al-Nīsābūrī's *Istitār al-imām*, dealing with the settlement of the early Ismaili Imam ʿAbd Allāh al-Akbar in Salamiyya and the flight of a later imam, the future founder of the Fatimid dynasty, from Syria to North Africa.

There were, however, two periods in Ismaili history during which the Ismailis did concern themselves with historical writings, and they produced or commissioned works which may be regarded as official chronicles. During the Fatimid and Alamūt periods, the Ismailis possessed their own states and dynasties of rulers whose political events and achievements needed to be recorded by reliable chroniclers. In Fatimid times, especially after the transference of the seat of the Fatimid state from Ifrīqiya to Egypt in 362/973, numerous histories of the Fatimid state and dynasty were compiled by contemporary historians, both Ismaili and non-Ismaili. But with the exception of a few fragments, the Fatimid chronicles did not survive the downfall of the dynasty. The Sunni Ayyūbids who succeeded the Fatimids in Egypt systematically destroyed the renowned Fatimid libraries at Cairo, also persecuting Ismailis and repressing their religious literature.

Ibn Zūlāq (d. 386/996) is one of the earliest Fatimid chroniclers whose works have been completely lost. He evidently wrote several biographies of the Fatimid caliphs as well as a history of Fatimid Egypt which was continued by his descendants. The tradition of Fatimid historiography was maintained by al-Musabbiḥī (d. 420/1029), an official in the service of the Fatimids who may have been an Ismaili himself. He produced a vast history of Fatimid Egypt and its ruling dynasty, but only a small fragment of the fortieth volume of his history has survived in a unique manuscript. Fortunately, portions of the evidence compiled by these and other Fatimid chroniclers, such as al-Quḍāʿī (d. 454/1062), have been preserved by later Egyptian historians.

Aside from strictly historical sources, Ismailis of the Fatimid period also produced a few biographical works of the *sīra* genre with great historical value. Amongst the extant works of this category, mention should be made of the *Sīra* of Jaʿfar b. ʿAlī, chamberlain (*ḥājib*) to the founder of the Fatimid dynasty al-Mahdī; the *Sīra* of al-Ustādh Jawdhar (d. 363/973–4), a trusted Fatimid courtier; and the autobiography of al-Mu'ayyad fi'l-Dīn al-Shīrāzī (d. 470/1078), who held the office of chief *dāʿī* in Cairo for almost twenty years. Other biographical works, such as the one on the *dāʿī* Ibn Ḥawshab Manṣūr al-Yaman (d. 302/914) written by his son Jaʿfar, the autobiography of the *dāʿī* Abū ʿAbd Allāh al-Shīʿī (d. 298/911) quoted in al-Nuʿmān's *Iftitāḥ al-daʿwa*, and the *Sīrat al-Imām al-Mahdī* quoted by the *dāʿī* Idrīs, have not survived.

The Fatimid period was also rich in terms of archival documents of historical value, a wide variety of treatises, letters, decrees and epistles (*sijillāt*) issued through the Fatimid *dīwān al-inshā'* or chancery of state.[4] Many of these documents have survived directly, or have been quoted in later literary sources, notably the encyclopaedic manual for secretaries entitled *Ṣubḥ al-aʿshā'* compiled by al-Qalqashandī (d. 821/1418). The Geniza documents, recovered in Cairo in 1890, should also be mentioned in this context; they provide an important source of information on the socio-economic and cultural life of Fatimid Egypt.

The Nizārī Ismailis of the Alamūt period, too, maintained a historiographical tradition. They wrote a few doctrinal works and, at least in Persia, they also compiled chronicles in the Persian language recording the events of the Persian Nizārī state according to the reigns of the successive lords of Alamūt.[5] This historiographical tradition evidently commenced with a work entitled *Sargudhasht-i Sayyidnā* covering the biography of Ḥasan Ṣabbāḥ, designated as Sayyidnā (our master) by the contemporary Nizārīs, and the major events of his rule. The reign of Ḥasan's successor at Alamūt, Kiyā Buzurg-Ummīd (518–32/1124–38), was covered in another chronicle known as the *Kitāb-i Buzurg-Ummīd*. A certain Dihkhudā ʿAbd al-Malik b. ʿAlī Fashandī, who was also the commander of the Nizārī fortress of Maymūndiz near Alamūt, compiled the official chronicle for the reign of Buzurg-Ummīd's son and successor Muḥammad (532–

57/1138–62). The events of the Nizārī state during the later Alamūt period were recorded by Ra'īs Ḥasan Ṣalāḥ al-Dīn Munshī Bīrjandī, who was also a poet and secretary (*munshī*) to the Nizārī chief in Quhistān, and other chroniclers. All these official chronicles, kept at Alamūt and other Nizārī strongholds in Persia, perished in the Mongol invasions or soon afterwards during the Īlkhānid period. However, the Nizārī chronicles and other writings and documents were seen and used extensively by a group of Persian historians of the Īlkhānid period, namely, Juwaynī (d. 681/1283), Rashīd al-Dīn Faḍl Allāh (d. 718/1318), and Abu'l-Qāsim Kāshānī (d. c. 736/1335); they remain our main sources for the history of the Nizārī state in Persia.

Later Persian historians, such as Ḥamd Allāh Mustawfī (d. after 740/1339–40) and Ḥāfiẓ Abrū (d. 833/1430), who devoted separate sections of their general histories to the Persian Ismailis, based their accounts mainly on Juwaynī and Rashīd al-Dīn, as Nizārī chronicles were no longer extant in post-Mongol Persia. The Persian Ismailis of the Alamūt period are also treated in a number of contemporary Saljuq chronicles, such as the *Saljūq-nāma* of Ẓahīr al-Dīn Nīshapūrī written around 580/1184, and the *Rāḥat al-ṣudūr* of al-Rāwandī completed in 603/1206–7, all of which like other Sunni sources are extremely hostile towards the Ismailis. The Syrian Nizārīs, who unlike their Persian co-religionists did not compile chronicles, are treated in various regional histories of Syria, such as those produced by Ibn al-Qalānisī (d. 555/1160) and Ibn al-ʿAdīm (d. 660/1262).[6]

Much valuable information on the Ismailis is contained in the universal histories of Muslim authors, starting with the *Ta'rīkh* of al-Ṭabarī (d. 310/923) and its continuation by ʿArīb b. Saʿd (d. 370/980). In this category, the *Tajārib al-umam* of Miskawayh (d. 421/1030) is the most important early universal history containing information on the Ismailis. The tradition of compiling universal histories found its culmination in *al-Kāmil* of Ibn al-Athīr (d. 630/1233) which represents the peak of Muslim annalistic historiography. Ibn al-Athīr's history is rich in information on both the Fatimids and the Nizārīs of Persia and Syria.

Although generally poor in historical details, the religious literature of the Ismailis themselves is invaluable for tracing their doctrinal history at various times. The theological and philosophical treatises of the Fatimid period are indispensable not only for understanding the intellectual traditions and doctrines of Fatimid Ismailis, but also for doctrinal developments of the pre-Fatimid times when the Ismailis propagated their ideas mainly by word of mouth. In addition, some of the Ismaili texts of the Fatimid period, such as the *majālis* collections of different authors, contain historical references which are not found in other sources. The *majālis*, representing a specifically Ismaili genre of literature, were normally compiled by or for Fatimid chief *dāʿīs* for delivery in special lectures organised for Ismailis and known as the *majālis al-ḥikma* or the "sessions of wisdom". Similarly, Nizārī doctrinal developments of the Alamūt period can be studied on the basis of the meagre extant literature of that period, especially the writings of Naṣīr al-Dīn al-Ṭūsī (d. 672/1274), the accounts of the Persian historians of the Īlkhānid period, and the relevant references in certain post-Alamūt Nizārī sources.

The Nizārī tradition of historiography was discontinued upon the fall of Alamūt in 654/1256. In the unsettled conditions of the early post-Alamūt centuries, the Nizārīs engaged in limited literary activities, and they did not find ready access to the Ismaili literature of earlier times. In this particular sense, they were in effect cut off from their historical heritage, and as such a certain degree of ignorance of earlier Ismaili history came to permeate the bulk of the Nizārī literature of the post-Alamūt period. Of all the works recovered so far from the post-Alamūt literature of the Nizārīs, only one item may be classified as historical in a broad sense, namely, a hagiographical biography of Rāshid al-Dīn Sinān (d. 589/1193), the most famous Syrian *dāʿī* of the Alamūt period. As in earlier times, the doctrinal works written during the Anjudān renaissance by Persian Nizārī authors like Abū Isḥāq Quhistānī (d. after 904/1498) and Khayrkhwāh-i Harātī (d. after 960/1553) contain important historical references. The *ginān* literature of the Nizārī Khojas, developed in the post-Alamūt period in the Indian subcontinent, essentially represents the self-image of that community in a changing cultural milieu. Containing the teachings of various *pīr*s or local leaders of the community, the *ginān*s are not, however, very reliable as historical sources of information, because of the mythopoetic character of these devotional hymns which were originally transmitted orally for several centuries.

The Nizārīs of Badakhshān and the adjacent areas in the upper Oxus region have retained their distinctive literary tradition, drawing on the Persian Ismaili literature of different periods with particular reference to the writings of Nāṣir Khusraw (d. after 465/1072) as well as the Sufi traditions of Central Asia. The Ismailis of these remote regions in the Pamirs, all belonging to the Nizārī branch of Ismailism, do not seem to have produced many noteworthy authors in the post-Alamūt period, but they have preserved the bulk of the Persian Ismaili works written elsewhere. This literature is currently held in private collections, including especially those possessed by local religious leaders known traditionally as *khalīfa*s, in Shughnān, Rūshān, Ishkāshīm and other districts of the Gorno-Badakhshān province in

Tajikistan. Many of the manuscripts preserved by the Ismailis of Badakhshān in Tajikistan perished during the twentieth century as a result of persecutions by the former Soviet regime. The Nizārīs of Badakhshān, who speak a Tajik version of Persian, were obliged in the Soviet times to use only the Cyrillic alphabet, and they were not generally able to read the Persian Ismaili texts preserved in their community.

The Nizārīs of Afghan Badakhshān, too, have extensive collections of manuscripts, about which specific information is not available. The Nizārīs of Hunza, Chitral, as well as Yāsīn, Ishkoman and other districts of Gilgit, now all situated in the northern areas of Pakistan, have preserved a selection of Nizārī Ismaili works, although they themselves do not speak Persian. This literature had originally been made available to the Ismailis of these northern areas by their Badakhshānī co-religionists and neighbours. The literacy rate has been generally low in this entire region where a host of local languages and dialects such as Burushaski, Wakhī and Shinā are spoken.

The post-Alamūt Nizārī Ismailis' lack of interest in historiography persisted until more recent times. In Persia, by the opening decades of the twentieth century, only a single historical work had been produced by a Nizārī author. Permeated with anachronisms and gross inaccuracies, this was a history of Ismailism from its origins to modern times compiled by Fidā'ī Khurāsānī (d. 1342/1923).[7] The Ismailis of Badakhshān, too, do not seem to have compiled any histories of their community. However, there are references to Ismailis in certain local histories of Badakhshān.[8] The Nizārī Khojas, as noted, have elaborated their own literary tradition in the form of *ginān*s.[9] The earlier Ismaili literature, produced in Arabic and Persian, was until recently not available to the Nizārīs of the Indian subcontinent who have recorded their ginanic literature mainly in a specific Khojkī script developed by them. Drawing mainly on the *ginān*s and their oral traditions, the Nizārī Khojas compiled a few historical works in Gujarātī during the nineteenth century.

ANTI-ISMAILI WRITINGS OF OTHER MUSLIMS

Our survey of different genres of Ismaili writings attests to the rich literary heritage of the Ismailis, especially in the Fatimid period. Until the modern recovery of much of this literature, however, Ismaili texts were not generally available to those outside the community. The Ismailis and their *dā'ī*s, as noted, guarded their religious books very carefully. In fact, a good portion of Ismaili writings, dealing with esoteric subjects, was written for the benefit of the Ismailis, especially the more educationally advanced among them. On the other hand, the Fatimid and Nizārī chronicles which were not guarded secretly, perished during the 6th/12th and 7th/13th centuries. At any event, Sunni and other non-Ismaili Muslim writers, including historians who concerned themselves with the Ismailis, as in the case of the Christian Crusaders, were often not interested in acquiring accurate information about them on the basis of Ismaili sources, even if and when such sources were accessible.

In the immediate aftermath of the foundation of the Fatimid caliphate, the Sunni establishment launched what amounted to an official anti-Ismaili propaganda campaign. The aim of this prolonged campaign, fully endorsed and supported by the Abbasid caliphs, was to discredit the entire Ismaili movement from its origins so that the Ismailis could readily be condemned as *malāḥida*, heretics or deviators from the true religious path. Muslim theologians, jurists, heresiographers and historians participated in various ways in this campaign. In particular, polemicists fabricated the necessary evidence that would lend support to the condemnation of Ismailis on specific doctrinal grounds. They concocted detailed accounts of the sinister objectives, immoral doctrines and libertine practices of the Ismailis, while refuting the ʿAlid genealogy of the Ismaili imams. Polemicists also fabricated accounts in which they attributed all sorts of shocking beliefs and practices to the Ismailis; these forgeries circulated widely as genuine Ismaili treatises. The Sunni authors who were not interested in studying the internal divisions of Shīʿism and generally regarded all Shīʿī interpretations of Islam as "heterodoxies" or even "heresies", also availed themselves of the opportunity of blaming the Fatimids and indeed the entire Ismaili community for the atrocities perpetrated by the Qarmaṭīs of Baḥrayn.

By spreading these defamations and forged accounts, the polemicists and other anti-Ismaili authors gradually created, in the course of the 4th/10th century, a "black legend". Ismailism was cleverly depicted as the arch-heresy (*ilḥād*) of Islam, carefully designed by some non-ʿAlid impostors, or possibly even a Jewish magician disguised as a Muslim, bent on destroying Islam from within. By the end of the 4th/10th century, this "black legend" with its sordid details had been accepted as an accurate and reliable description of the Ismaili motives, beliefs and practices, leading to further anti-Ismaili polemics and mobilisation of the opinion of the Muslim society at large against the Ismailis. The defamatory components of this anti-Ismaili campaign continued to fire the imagination of countless generations of myriad Sunni writers throughout the medieval times.

Many of the essential components of this anti-Ismaili "black legend", relating especially to the origins of Ismailism, may be traced to a certain polemicist known as Ibn Rizām, who lived in Baghdad around the middle of the 4th/10th century. He wrote a major treatise in refutation of the Ismailis, relying on contemporary informants belonging to the anti-Fatimid Qarmaṭī circles of Iraq. Ibn Rizām's original tract has never been recovered, but it was used extensively by another anti-Ismaili polemicist, the Sharīf Abu'l-Ḥusayn Muḥammad b. ʿAlī, better known as Akhū Muḥsin. An early ʿAlid genealogist, Akhū Muḥsin wrote his anti-Ismaili work shortly after 372/982. Consisting of historical and doctrinal parts, his treatise, too, aimed at revealing the "heretical" doctrines of the Ismailis and the non-ʿAlid origins of their imams. This work has been lost, but long extracts have been preserved in the writings of three later Egyptian historians, namely, al-Nuwayrī (d. 732/1332), Ibn al-Dawādārī (d. after 736/1335) and al-Maqrīzī (d. 845/1442).

It was in Akhū Muḥsin's polemical tract that the *Kitāb al-siyāsa* (*Book of Methodology*), one of the allegedly early Ismaili works, came to be mentioned for the first time. Used by several generations of polemicists and heresiographers as a major source of information on the secret doctrines and practices of the Ismailis, this anonymously forged tract contained all the ideas needed to condemn the Ismailis as heretics on the account of their libertinism and atheism. Akhū Muḥsin claims to have read this book and quotes passages from it on the procedures that were supposedly followed by Ismaili *dāʿī*s for winning new converts and instructing them through some seven stages of initiation (*balāgh*) leading ultimately to atheism and unbelief.[10] The same book, or another forged account of Ismailism entitled *Kitāb al-balāgh*, was seen shortly afterwards by Ibn al-Nadīm who mentions it in his famous catalogue of Arabic books completed in 377/987.[11] The heresiographer al-Baghdādī even claims that the *Kitāb al-siyāsa* was sent by the founder of the Fatimid dynasty to Abū Ṭāhir al-Jannābī, the leader of the Qarmaṭī state in Baḥrayn. By this assertion al-Baghdādī not only attempted to accord authenticity to this malevolent forgery, but also made the Qarmaṭīs subservient to the Fatimids, in order further to defame the latter.[12] Needless to add that the Ismaili tradition knows these travesties only from the polemics of its enemies. At any rate, anti-Ismaili polemical writings provided a major source of information for Sunni heresiographers such as al-Baghdādī (d. 429/1037) and Ibn Ḥazm (d. 456/1064), who produced another important category of writing against the Ismailis. And the polemical and heresiographical traditions, in turn, influenced the historians, theologians and jurists who wrote on the Ismailis.

By the end of the 5th/11th century, the widespread literary campaign against the Ismailis had become quite successful throughout the central Islamic lands. The revolt of the Persian Ismailis led by

Ḥasan Ṣabbāḥ against the Saljuq Turks, the new overlords of the Abbasids, called forth another vigorous Sunni reaction against the Ismailis in general and the Nizārīs in particular. The new literary campaign, with its military counterpart, was initiated by Niẓām al-Mulk (d. 485/1092), the Saljuq vizier and virtual master of Saljuq dominions for more than two decades, with the full support of the Abbasid caliph and the Saljuq sultan. Niẓām al-Mulk devoted a long chapter in his own *Siyāsat-nāma* (*The Book of Government*) to the condemnation of the Ismailis who, according to him, aimed "to abolish Islam, to mislead mankind and cast them into perdition".[13]

The earliest polemical treatise written against the Persian (Nizārī) Ismailis and their doctrine of *taʿlīm* was produced by al-Ghazālī (d. 505/1111), the celebrated Sunni theologian, jurist and mystic. Al-Ghazālī was appointed in 484/1091 by Niẓām al-Mulk to a teaching post at the Niẓāmiyya Madrasa in Baghdad, where he was commissioned by the Abbasid caliph al-Mustaẓhir (487–512/1094–118) to write a treatise in refutation of the Bāṭinīs, another designation for the Ismailis. This book, the *Faḍā'iḥ al-Bāṭiniyya* commonly known as *al-Mustaẓhirī*, was completed shortly before al-Ghazālī left Baghdad in 488/1095. In this widely circulating book, al-Ghazālī presented his own elaborate "Ismaili" system of graded initiation and indoctrination, leading to the ultimate stage (*al-balāgh al-akbar*) of atheism.[14] Al-Ghazālī's defamations were adopted by other Sunni writers, who were also acquainted variously with the earlier "black legend". Sunni historians, including especially Saljuq chroniclers and local historians of Syria, participated actively in the renewed anti-Ismaili campaign.

By the opening decades of the 6th/12th century, the Ismailis had come under attack from new quarters. To the contentment of their Sunni enemies, the divided Ismaili community was now engaged in internal feuds. It is reported that Ḥasan Ṣabbāḥ sent secret agents to Egypt to undermine the Mustaʿlī *daʿwa* there, while the Mustaʿlīs initiated their own anti-Nizārī polemics to refute the claims of Nizār and his descendants to the imamate. In one such polemical epistle issued in 516/1122 by the Fatimid caliph al-Āmir, the Nizārīs of Syria were for the first time referred to with the abusive appellation *ḥashīshiyya*, without any explanation.[15] This term was later applied afresh to Syrian Ismailis in the earliest Saljuq chronicle containing references to the Nizārīs, the *Nuṣrat al-fatra* written in 579/1183 by ʿImād al-Dīn Muḥammad al-Kātib al-Iṣfahānī (d. 597/1201).[16] Subsequently, a few other historians, notably Abū Shāma (d. 665/1267)[17] and Ibn Muyassar (d. 677/1278),[18] also used the derogatory term *ḥashīshiyya* in reference to the Syrian Nizārīs, without actually accusing them of using hashish, a product of hemp. The Persian

Nizārīs, too, were designated as *ḥashīshī* in some Zaydī sources produced in northern Persia during the Alamūt period.[19] It is important to note that in all the Muslim sources in which the Nizārīs are referred to as *ḥashīshīs*, this term is used metaphorically and in its abusive senses of "low-class rabble" and "irreligious social outcasts". The literal interpretation of this term in reference to the Nizārīs is rooted in the fantasies of medieval Westerners and their "imaginative ignorance" of Islam and the Ismailis.

THE ASSASSIN LEGENDS OF MEDIEVAL WESTERNERS

The Fatimids and the Nizārī Ismailis found a common and formidable new enemy in the Christian Crusaders. It was in al-Mustaʿlī's reign, when Ḥasan Ṣabbāḥ was consolidating his position in Persia, that the Crusaders first appeared in the Holy Land. They easily succeeded in seizing Jerusalem, their main target, in 492/1099. The Crusaders now founded four principalities in the region and had numerous military and diplomatic encounters with the Fatimids in Egypt and the Nizārīs in Syria. By 518/1124 when Tyre (Ṣūr), too, fell into the hands of the Crusaders, the Fatimids had lost all their former possessions in the Levant. During the final decades of Fatimid rule, Egypt proper was invaded several times by the Crusader armies, forcing the Fatimids to pay tribute to the Frankish king of Jerusalem.

The Nizārīs and the Crusaders experienced numerous confrontations in Syria, which had important literary consequences and lasting repercussions in terms of the distorted image of the Nizārīs in Europe and elsewhere. Their first such encounter dates back to the opening years of the 6th/12th century. Later, the Nizārīs and the Crusaders sporadically fought each other over various strongholds in central Syria. The Syrian Nizārīs attained the peak of their power under the leadership of Rāshid al-Dīn Sinān, who was their chief *dāʿī* for some three decades from around 558/1163. It was in the time of Sinān, the original Old Man of the Mountain of Crusader fame, that occidental chroniclers of the Crusades and certain European travellers and emissaries collected details and wrote about the Nizārī Ismailis, designated as the Assassins. The term Assassin was evidently based on variants of the Arabic word *ḥashīshī* (plural, *ḥashīshiyya* or *ḥashīshīn*), applied to the Nizārīs pejoratively by other Muslims and picked up locally by the Crusaders and their European observers. At any event, Crusaders and their chroniclers, who were not interested in obtaining accurate information about the Syrian Nizārīs and other local Muslim communities, remained almost completely ignorant of Islam as a religion and its internal divisions despite protracted exposure to Muslims of the Near East. In the event, medieval Westerners themselves were responsible for fabricating and disseminating in the Latin Orient as well as in Europe a number of legends about the secret practices of the Nizārī Ismailis.

The Crusaders had been particularly impressed by the highly exaggerated reports and rumours of the Nizārī assassinations and the daring behaviour of their *fidā'īs*, the devotees who carried out these missions in public places and more often than not lost their life in the process. This explains why the legends came to revolve around the recruitment, training and indoctrination of the *fidā'īs*; fictions which were meant to provide satisfactory explanations for behaviour that would otherwise seem strange to the medieval Western mind. These so-called Assassin legends consisted of a number of separate but interrelated tales, including the "training legend", the "paradise legend", the "hashish legend" and the "death-leap legend". The legends developed in stages and finally culminated in a synthesised version popularised by Marco Polo (1254–1324). The Venetian traveller also added his own original contribution in the form of a "secret garden of paradise" where bodily pleasures were supposedly procured for the *fidā'īs* as part of their training.

Different legends were "imagined" independently and sometimes concurrently by different authors, and embellished over time. Starting with Burchard of Strassburg who visited Syria in 1175, European travellers, chroniclers and envoys to the Latin East who had something to say about the Assassins participated in this process of fabricating, propagating and legitimising the Assassin legends.[20] By the early decades of the 8th/14th century, the legends had acquired wide currency and were accepted as reliable descriptions of secret Nizārī practices, reminiscent of the manner in which the earlier anti-Ismaili "black legend" of Muslim polemicists had been treated as accurate explanation of Ismaili motives, beliefs and practices. Henceforth, the Nizārī Ismailis were portrayed in medieval European sources as a sinister order of drugged assassins bent on senseless murder and mischief.

ORIENTALIST PERSPECTIVES

By the beginning of the nineteenth century, European knowledge of the Ismailis had not essentially advanced beyond what the Crusaders and other occidental sources had transmitted on the subject. During the Renaissance, the Nizārīs were occasionally mentioned by travellers or pilgrims to the Holy Land without any new details. Meanwhile, by the middle of the 8th/14th century, the word *assassin*, instead of denoting the name of a "mysterious" community in Syria, had acquired a new meaning in Italian, French and other European languages; it had become a common noun meaning a professional murderer. With the general currency of this usage, the origin and etymology of the term Assassin was slowly forgotten, while the Assassin legends continued to maintain their popularity in Europe. Under these circumstances, the first Western monograph devoted to the subject of the Assassins and the origin of their name was published in 1603.[21] Its author, a French official at the court of King Henry IV, had combined in an utterly confused manner the accounts of a number of occidental sources with Marco Polo's narrative, but he failed to explain the etymology of the term. Henceforth, an increasing number of European philologists began to collect variants of this term occurring in medieval occidental sources, adding their peculiar etymological explanations. The Ismailis were, however, correctly identified as Shīʿī Muslims in the pioneering encyclopaedia of Western Orientalism compiled by Barthélemy d'Herbelot (1625–95).[22]

The orientalists of the nineteenth century, led by Silvestre de Sacy (1758–1838), produced more scholarly studies of the Ismailis, now utilising for the first time in Europe also historical works of Muslim authors. It was mainly on this basis, and because of the continued attraction of the long-lived Assassin legends, that de Sacy himself succeeded in finally solving the mystery of the name Assassin. In a *Memoir*, originally composed in 1809, he showed the connection of the variant forms of this name, such as *assissini* and *assassini*, to the Arabic word *hashish*, citing Abū Shāma's application of the term *ḥashīshī* (plural, *ḥashīshiyya*) to medieval Nizārīs of Syria.[23] De Sacy also produced important studies on early Ismailis as background materials in connection with his lifelong interest in the Druze religion.[24] By drawing on generally hostile Sunni sources and the fanciful accounts of the Crusaders, however, de Sacy endorsed at least partially the anti-Ismaili "black legend" of the Sunni polemicists and the Assassin legends of the Crusader circles. Indeed, de Sacy lent the weight of his own scholarship to the Ibn Rizām-Akhū Muḥsin fictitious account of early Ismailism and its alleged seven stages of initiation towards unbelief, on the one hand, and to Marco Polo's tale of how the Old Man of the Mountain of the Nizārīs secretly administered hashish to his *fidāʾī*s to inspire them with dreams of paradise, on the other.

Thus, de Sacy's studies set the stage for the investigations of the later orientalists, whose interests in the Ismailis had now been rekindled by the anti-Ismaili accounts of the then newly discovered Sunni chronicles which seemed to confirm and complement the Assassin legends found in the occidental sources. It was under such circumstances that other orientalists of the nineteenth century, such as Michael Jan de Goeje (1836–1909), produced their more strictly historical studies of the early Ismailis, the Fatimids, the Qarmaṭīs of Baḥrayn, and the Syrian and Persian Nizārīs of the Alamūt period. The most widely read among such orientalistic studies was, however, a book written by Joseph von Hammer-Purgstall (1774–1856). Focusing on the Persian Nizārīs of the Alamūt period, this Austrian orientalist-diplomat had accepted Marco Polo's narrative in its entirety as well as all the defamations heaped on the Ismailis by their Sunni enemies. This book achieved great success in Europe and continued to be treated as the standard history of the Nizārīs until the 1930s.[25] Westerners also retained the habit of referring to the Nizārī Ismailis as the Assassins, a misnomer rooted in a medieval pejorative designation, even though the name had now become a common noun meaning murderer in European languages.

Meanwhile, the ongoing progress in Islamic studies did not lead to any significant improvement in the scholarly investigation of the Shīʿa in general, and the Ismailis in particular. The utterly distorted images of the Ismailis painted by Sunni polemicists and heresiographers, as well as the occidental legends of the Assassins, had indeed proved seminal.

MODERN PROGRESS IN ISMAILI STUDIES

The breakthrough in Ismaili studies had to await the recovery and study of genuine Ismaili texts on a large scale. A few Ismaili sources of Syrian provenance had already surfaced in Europe during the nineteenth century, and some fragments of these writings were edited and studied there. In 1898, Paul Casanova (1861–1926), who later published important studies on the Ismailis, announced his discovery at the Bibliothèque Nationale, Paris, of a fragment of the *Rasā'il Ikhwān al-Ṣafā'*, also recognising for the first time in Europe the Ismaili origin of this encyclopaedic compendium.[26] More Ismaili manuscripts preserved in the remote regions of Yaman and Central Asia were recovered in the opening decades of the twentieth century, and they were subsequently added to the collections of the Ambrosian Library in Milan and the Asiatic Museum in St Petersburg. By 1922, when the first Western bibliography of Ismaili works was published,[27] knowledge of European scholarly circles about Ismaili literature still remained extremely limited.

Modern scholarship in Ismaili studies was actually initiated in the 1930s in India, where significant collections of Ismaili manuscripts had been preserved in the Ismaili Bohra community. This long-awaited breakthrough resulted from the efforts of a few Indian Ismaili scholars and the Russian orientalist Wladimir Ivanow (1886–1970), who had by then settled in Bombay. In an unprecedented development, three learned Ismaili Bohras who had received their university education in England, namely, Zāhid ʿAlī (1888–1958), Ḥusayn F. al-Hamdānī (1901–62) and Asaf A. A. Fyzee (1899–1981), now began to produce the first truly scholarly studies of Ismailism drawing on their ancestral collections of manuscripts. These pioneers of modern Ismaili studies also collaborated with Ivanow, who through his own connections with the Nizārī Ismaili Khoja community, gained access also to Nizārī literature preserved in Central Asia, Persia, Afghanistan and elsewhere. Consequently, Ivanow compiled the first detailed catalogue of Ismaili works, citing some 700 separate titles attesting to the hitherto unknown richness and diversity of Ismaili literature and literary traditions.[28] The publication of this catalogue in 1933 provided a scientific frame for further research in the field, heralding an entirely new era in Ismaili studies.

Ismaili scholarship received a major impetus through the establishment in 1933 of the Islamic Research Association, which was effectively transformed in 1946 to the Ismaili Society of Bombay under the patronage of Sulṭān Muḥammad Shāh, Aga Khan III (1877–1957), the forty-eighth imam of the Nizārī Ismailis. Ivanow played a key role in the creation of both these institutions whose publications were devoted mainly to his own Ismaili works.[29] By 1963, when Ivanow published a second expanded edition of his Ismaili catalogue,[30] progress in Ismaili scholarship had been astonishing. In addition to many pioneering studies, numerous Ismaili texts had now begun to be critically edited, providing the ground for further progress. In this connection, particular mention should be made of the Nizārī texts edited by Ivanow himself; the Fatimid and later texts edited with contextualising introductions by Henry Corbin (1903–78), published simultaneously in Paris and Tehran in his Bibliothèque Iranienne series; the Fatimid texts edited by the Egyptian scholar Muḥammad Kāmil Ḥusayn (1901–61) and published in his Silsilat Makhṭūṭāṭ al-Fāṭimiyyīn series, and the Ismaili texts of Syrian provenance published by ʿĀrif Tāmir, an Ismaili scholar from Salamiyya. Meanwhile, a new generation of scholars, notably Bernard Lewis, Samuel M. Stern (1920–69), Wilferd Madelung and Abbas Hamdani, made valuable contributions to modern Ismaili studies. Here, Marshall G. S. Hodgson (1922–68), who produced the first scholarly monograph on the Nizārīs of the Alamūt period, deserves particular attention.

Progress in Ismaili studies has proceeded at a steady pace during the last few decades through the efforts of yet another generation of specialists such as Ismail K. Poonawala, Heinz Halm, Paul E. Walker and Azim A. Nanji. Ismaili scholarship promises to continue unabated as more obscure issues in Ismaili history and thought are clarified and as Ismaili manuscripts continue to be recovered from different sources. The accelerated modern recovery and study of Ismaili literature is well represented in Poonawala's monumental bibliography published in 1977, which identifies some 1,300 titles attributed to more than 200 authors.[31]

To date, the largest single collection of Nizārī Ismaili manuscripts written in Persian has been recovered from Shughnān, Rūshān and other districts of Badakhshān in Tajikistan.[32] The vast Arabic manuscript collections of the Bohra libraries at Sūrat and Bombay (Mumbai), which remain under the strict control of the leader of the Dā'ūdī Ṭayyibī community, have not been generally accessible to scholars. The largest number of Ismaili manuscripts in any one location in the West, comprised of more than 1,200 titles in Arabic, Persian, Gujarātī and other Indic languages, is to be found at the Institute of Ismaili Studies Library in London.[33] Established in 1977 under the patronage of H. H. Prince Karim Aga Khan IV, the present imam of the Nizārī Ismailis, the Institute of Ismaili Studies is currently making its own contributions to Ismaili scholarship through monographs published in its Ismaili Heritage series, as well as other programmes of research, publications and acquisition of manuscripts.

NOTES

1. L. Massignon, "Mutanabbī devant le siècle Ismaélien de l'Islam", in *Al-Mutanabbi: Recueil publié à l'occasion de son millénaire* (Beirut, 1936), p. 1.
2. P. E. Walker, *Early Philosophical Shiism: The Ismaili Neoplatonism of Abū Ya'qūb al-Sijistānī* (Cambridge, 1993), pp. 13 ff., 61.
3. W. Ivanow, *Brief Survey of the Evolution of Ismailism* (Leiden, 1952), p. 29.
4. See Abū Tamīm Ma'add al-Mustanṣir bi'llāh, *al-Sijillāt al-Mustanṣiriyya*, ed. 'Abd al-Mun'im Mājid (Cairo, 1954); Ḥusain F. al-Hamdānī, "The Letters of al-Mustanṣir bi'llāh", BSOS, 7 (1934), pp. 307–24; Jamāl al-Dīn al-Shayyāl (ed.), *Majmū'at al-wathā'iq al-Fāṭimiyya* (Cairo, 1958); S. M. Stern, *Fāṭimid Decrees* (London, 1964), and his *Coins and Documents from the Medieval Middle East* (London, 1986), articles V, VI, VII.
5. F. Daftary, "Persian Historiography of the Early Nizārī Ismā'īlīs", *Iran, Journal of the British Institute of Persian Studies*, 30 (1992), pp. 91–7.
6. Claude Cahen, *La Syrie du Nord à l'époque des Croisades* (Paris, 1940), pp. 33–93, and B. Lewis, "Sources for the History of the Syrian Assassins", *Speculum*, 27 (1952), pp. 475–89, reprinted in B. Lewis, *Studies in Classical and Ottoman Islam (7th–16th Centuries)* (London, 1976), article VIII.
7. Muḥammad b. Zayn al-'Ābidīn, Fidā'ī Khurāsānī, *Kitāb-i hidāyat al-mu'minīn al-ṭālibīn*, ed. A. A. Semenov (Moscow, 1959; reprinted, Tehran, 1362/1983).
8. See, for instance, Mīrzā Sang Muḥammad Badakhshī and Mīrzā

Faḍl ʿAlī Beg Surkh Afsar, *Taʾrīkh-i Badakhshān*, ed. A. N. Boldyrev (Leningrad, 1959); ed. M. Sutūda (Tehran, 1367/1988), and Ghurbān Muḥammad-Zāda and Muḥabbat Shāh-Zāda, *Taʾrīkh-i Badakhshān*, ed. A. A. Yigāna (Moscow, 1973).

9. Ali S. Asani, "The Ginān Literature of the Ismailis of Indo-Pakistan: Its Origins, Characteristics and Themes", in D. L. Eck and F. Mallison (eds), *Devotion Divine: Bhakti Traditions from the Regions of India* (Groningen and Paris, 1991), pp. 1–18.
10. The Arabic text of this book, together with an English translation, is partially reconstructed by S. M. Stern on the basis of quotations preserved by al-Nuwayrī, al-Baghdādī and others; see his "The Book of the Highest Initiation and Other anti-Ismāʿīlī Travesties", in S. M. Stern, *Studies in Early Ismāʿīlism* (Jerusalem and Leiden, 1983), pp. 56–83.
11. Ibn al-Nadīm, *Kitāb al-fihrist*, ed. M. R. Tajaddud (2nd edn, Tehran, 1973), pp. 238, 240; English trans. B. Dodge, *The Fihrist of al-Nadīm* (New York, 1970), vol. 1, pp. 462ff., 471.
12. Abū Manṣūr ʿAbd al-Qāhir b. Ṭāhir al-Baghdādī, *al-Farq bayn al-firaq*, ed. M. Badr (Cairo, 1328/1910), pp. 277–9; English trans. A. S. Halkin, *Moslem Schisms and Sects*, part II (Tel Aviv, 1935), pp. 130–2.
13. Niẓām al-Mulk, *Siyar al-mulūk* (*Siyāsat-nāma*), ed. H. Darke (2nd edn, Tehran, 1347/1968), p. 311; English trans. H. Darke, *The Book of Government or Rules for Kings* (2nd edn, London, 1978), p. 231.
14. Abū Ḥāmid Muḥammad al-Ghazālī, *Faḍāʾiḥ al-Bāṭiniyya*, ed. ʿAbd al-Raḥmān Badawī (Cairo, 1964), especially pp. 21–36.
15. Abū ʿAlī al-Manṣūr al-Āmir bi-Aḥkām Allāh, *Īqāʿ ṣawāʿiq al-irghām*, in al-Āmir, *al-Hidāya al-Āmiriyya*, ed. A. A. A. Fyzee (Bombay, etc., 1938), pp. 27, 32, reprinted in al-Shayyāl (ed.), *Majmūʿat al-wathāʾiq*, pp. 233, 239.
16. This history has survived only in an abridged version prepared by al-Fatḥ b. ʿAlī al-Bundārī, *Zubdat al-nuṣra*, ed. M. Th. Houtsma (Leiden, 1889), pp. 169, 195.
17. Abū Shāma, *Kitāb al-rawḍatayn fī akhbār al-dawlatayn* (Cairo, 1287–8/1870–1), vol. 1, pp. 240, 258.
18. Ibn Muyassar, *Akhbār Miṣr*, ed. A. Fuʾād Sayyid (Cairo, 1981), p. 102.
19. See W. Madelung (ed.), *Arabic Texts Concerning the History of the Zaydī Imāms of Ṭabaristān, Daylamān and Gīlān* (Beirut, 1987), pp. 146, 329.
20. For a survey of these legends, and their authorship and early development, see F. Daftary, *The Assassin Legends: Myths of the Ismaʿilis* (London, 1994), especially pp. 88–127.
21. Denis Lebey de Batilly, *Traicté de l'origine des anciens Assasins porte-couteaux* (Lyons, 1603), reprinted in C. Leber (ed.), *Collection des meilleurs dissertations, notices et traités particuliers relatifs à l'histoire de France* (Paris, 1838), vol. 20, pp. 453–501.
22. See the entries "Fathemia", "Ismaelioun", "Malahedoun", and "Schiah", in Barthélemy d'Herbelot de Molainville, *Bibliothèque orientale* (Paris, 1697).
23. A. I. Silvestre de Sacy, "Mémoire sur la dynastie des Assassins, et sur l'étymologie de leur nom", *Mémoires de l'Institut Royal de France*, 4 (1818), pp. 1–84; English trans., "Memoir on the Dynasty

of the Assassins, and on the Etymology of their Name", in Daftary, *Assassin Legends*, pp. 136–88.

24. Silvestre de Sacy, *Exposé de la religion des Druzes* (Paris, 1838), vol. 1, introduction pp. 1–246.
25. J. von Hammer-Purgstall, *Die Geschichte der Assassinen* (Stuttgart and Tübingen, 1818); French trans. J. Hellert and P. A. de la Nourais, *Histoire de l'ordre des Assassins* (Paris, 1833); English trans. O. C. Wood, *The History of the Assassins* (London, 1835; reprinted, New York, 1968).
26. P. Casanova, "Notice sur un manuscrit de la secte des Assassins", *Journal Asiatique*, 9 série, 11 (1898), pp. 151–9.
27. L. Massignon, "Esquisse d'une bibliographie Qarmaṭe", in T. W. Arnold and R. A. Nicholson (eds), *A Volume of Oriental Studies Presented to Edward G. Browne* (Cambridge, 1922), pp. 329–38, reprinted in L. Massignon, *Opera Minora*, ed. Y. Moubarac (Paris, 1969), vol. 1, pp. 627–39.
28. W. Ivanow, *A Guide to Ismaili Literature* (London, 1933). See also P. Kraus, "La Bibliographie Ismaëlienne de W. Ivanow", *Revue d'Etudes Islamiques*, 6 (1932), pp. 483–90.
29. F. Daftary, "Bibliography of the Publications of the late W. Ivanow", *Islamic Culture*, 45 (1971), pp. 56–67, and 56 (1982), pp. 239–40, and "Anjoman-e Esmā'īlī", EIR, vol. 2, p. 84.
30. W. Ivanow, *Ismaili Literature: A Bibliographical Survey* (Tehran, 1963).
31. I. K. Poonawala, *Biobibliography of Ismā'īlī Literature* (Malibu, Calif., 1977). Professor Poonawala has informed the author that in the course of preparing a revised edition of his bibliography he has been able to identify a significant number of additional Ismaili titles.
32. A. Berthels and M. Baqoev, *Alphabetic Catalogue of Manuscripts found by 1959–1963 Expedition in Gorno-Badakhshan Autonomous Region*, ed. B. G. Gafurov and A. M. Mirzoev (Moscow, 1967).
33. A. Gacek, *Catalogue of Arabic Manuscripts in the Library of the Institute of Ismaili Studies* (London, 1984–5), vol. 1. Catalogues of the Institute's Persian manuscripts and its ginanic collection have not yet been published.

2

Origins and Early History: Shīʿīs, Ismailis and Qarmaṭīs

The Prophet Muḥammad laid the foundations of a new religion which was portrayed as the seal of the great revealed religions of the Abrahamic tradition. Thus, Islam from early on claimed to have completed and superseded the messages of Judaism and Christianity, whose adherents were accorded a special status among the Muslims as the "people of the book" (*ahl al-kitāb*). The unified and nascent Muslim community (*umma*) of the Prophet's time was, however, soon divided into numerous rival communities and groupings, as the Muslims now disagreed on a number of fundamental issues. The standard text of the Qur'an itself, the principal source of the sacred law of Islam (*sharīʿa*) to which Muslims would turn for divine guidance, was not committed to writing for several decades after the death of the Prophet in 11/632, while the doctrinal positions of various Muslim communities were elaborated gradually over several centuries.

DIVERSITY IN EARLY ISLAM

Modern scholarship has indeed shown that the early Muslims lived, at least during the first three centuries of their history, in an intellectually dynamic and fluid milieu. The formative period of Islam was essentially characterised by a multiplicity of communities of interpretation and schools of thought, and a diversity of views on the major religio-political issues faced by the early Muslims. At the time, the Muslims were confronted by many gaps in their religious knowledge and understanding of Islam, revolving around issues such as the attributes of God, nature of authority, and definitions of true believers and sinners. It was under such circumstances that different religious communities and schools of thought formulated their doctrines in stages and gradually acquired their names and distinctive identities. In this intellectually effervescent ambience, in which ordinary individuals as well as theorists moved readily from one community to another, Muslims engaged in lively discourses on a variety of theological, juristic and political issues. In terms of political loyalties, which remained closely intertwined with theological perspectives, diversity in early Islam ranged widely from the stances of those, later designated as Sunnis, who endorsed the actual course of events, notably the historical caliphate and the authority-power structure that had actually evolved in the Muslim society, to various religio-political opposition communities, notably the Khawārij and the Shīʿa, who aspired towards the establishment of new orders.

The Sunni Muslims of medieval times, or rather their religious scholars (*ʿulamāʾ*), painted a picture of early Islam that is at great variance with the findings of modern scholarship on the subject. According to this perspective, Islam from early on represented a monolithic phenomenon with a well-articulated doctrinal basis, from which different groups then deviated over time. Sunni Islam was, thus, portrayed by its exponents as the "true" interpretation of Islam, while all non-Sunni Muslim communities, especially the Shīʿī ones among them, who had "deviated" from the right path, were accused of *ilḥād* or heresy. The same narrow sectarian perspectives and classifications of the medieval Sunnis and their heresiographers were adopted by the nineteenth-century orientalists, who studied Islam primarily on the basis of Sunni sources and perceptions. As a result, the orientalists, too, endorsed the normativeness of Sunnism which was now distinguished from non-Sunni interpretations of Islam with the aid of terms such as "orthodoxy" and "heterodoxy", borrowed inappropriately from their own Christian experience.

In the meantime, the Shīʿa had developed an idealised model of "true" Islam, grounded in a particular interpretation of certain Qur'anic verses and events of early Islamic history, as well as a distinctive conception of religious authority vested in the Prophet's family. There had also developed disagreements within the Shīʿa regarding the identity of the legitimate leaders or imams of the community. As a result, the Shīʿa subdivided into a number of major communities, notably the Ithnāʿasharīs or Twelvers, the Zaydīs and the Ismailis, and several minor groupings. There were also those Shīʿī communities like the Kaysāniyya, who did not survive even though they occupied a majoritarian position during the formative period of Shīʿism. At any rate, each Shīʿī community possessed a distinct and idealised self-image, rationalising its claims and legitimising the authority of its line of imams. In such a milieu of diversity and conflicting communal interpretations, abundantly manifested in the heresiographical tradition of the Muslims, general consensus could not be established regarding the definition of "true" Islam, as different religio-political regimes were legitimised in different states by their *ʿulamāʾ* who, in return, were accorded a privileged social status among the elite of the society. Thus defined, "true" Islam in effect merely represented the "official" Islam, which varied widely from region to region, from the Sunnism of the Abbasid caliphate and the Khārijism of North Africa to the Ismaili Shīʿism of the Fatimid caliphate and the Zaydī Shīʿism of territorial states in Yaman and northern Persia, among other "official" versions of Islam. Needless to add that many of the original and fundamental disagreements among the Sunnis, Shīʿīs and other Muslims continue to persist today, and will probably never be satisfactorily explained and resolved by modern scholarship.

ORIGINS OF SHIʿISM

The origins of Islam's main divisions, Sunnism and Shīʿism, may be traced to the crisis of succession to the Prophet Muḥammad who as the "seal of the prophets" (*khātim al-anbiyāʾ*) could not be succeeded by another prophet (*nabī*). A successor was, however, needed to assume his functions as leader of the Islamic community and state, ensuring the continued unity of the Muslim *umma* under a single leader. In practice, this choice was resolved by a group of leading Muslim notables who chose Abū Bakr as the successor to the Messenger of God (*khalīfat rasūl Allāh*), hence the word *caliph* in Western languages. In so doing, Muslims had also founded the distinctive Islamic institution of the caliphate. The precise nature of the authority of Abū Bakr and his immediate successors remains obscure. It has now become clear, however, that from its inception the historical caliphate embodied not only political but also religious aspects of the leadership of the community. At any given time, myriad groups were engaged in formulating differing conceptions of religio-political authority and the caliph's moral responsibility towards the community. Abū Bakr (11–13/632–4) and his next two successors, ʿUmar (13–23/634–44) and ʿUthmān (23–35/644–56), belonging to the influential Meccan tribe of Quraysh, were among the earliest converts to Islam, and Companions of the Prophet. Only the fourth caliph, ʿAlī b. Abī Ṭālib (35–40/656–61), who occupies a unique position in the annals of Shīʿism, belonged to the Prophet's own clan of Banū Hāshim within the Quraysh. ʿAlī was also closely related to the Prophet, being his cousin and son-in-law, bound in matrimony to the Prophet's daughter Fāṭima.

Upon the Prophet's death, a small group in Medina held that ʿAlī was better qualified than any other candidate to succeed the Prophet. This minority group in time expanded and became generally designated as the *Shīʿat ʿAlī*, "party of ʿAlī", or simply as the Shīʿa. It is the fundamental belief of the Shīʿa, including the major Shīʿī communities of the Ithnāʿashariyya and Ismāʿīliyya, that the Prophet himself had designated ʿAlī as his successor, a designation or *naṣṣ* instituted through divine command and revealed by the Prophet at Ghadīr Khumm shortly before his death. ʿAlī himself was convinced of the legitimacy of his claim to leadership. Consequently, ʿAlī's partisans were obliged to protest against those, the Muslim majority, who ignored this designation. According to the Shīʿa, it was this very protest that originally separated the partisans of ʿAlī from the rest of the Muslim community.[1]

The Shīʿa also held a particular conception of religious authority that set them apart from other Muslims. From early on, the partisans of ʿAlī had come to believe that the Islamic message contained inner truths that could not be understood directly through human reason. They had, thus, recognised the need for a religiously authoritative guide, or imam as the Shīʿa have preferred to call their spiritual teacher and leader. In addition to being a guardian of Islamic revelation and leader of the community, as perceived by the majority of the Muslims, the Shīʿa thus saw in the succession to the Prophet a key spiritual function as well. As such, the successor was also entitled to a religious mandate for elucidating the message of Islam. A person with such qualifications, according to the Shīʿa, could belong only to the Prophet's family (*ahl al-bayt*), whose members alone could provide the legitimate channel for explaining and interpreting the teachings of Islam. Soon, the Shīʿa disagreed among themselves regarding the precise definition and composition of the *ahl al-bayt*, causing irrevocable internal subdivisions. It was not until after the Abbasid revolution that the *ahl al-bayt* came to be defined to include only ʿAlī and Fāṭima and certain members of their progeny.

These Shīʿī views on the origins of Shīʿism contain distinctive doctrinal elements that cannot be entirely attributed to the early Shīʿa, especially the original partisans of ʿAlī. Be that as it may, the Shīʿa from early on emphasised the hereditary attributes of individuals and the importance of the imam's kinship to the Prophet as prerequisites for possessing the required religious knowledge (*ʿilm*) and authority. Later, the Shīʿa also held that after ʿAlī the leadership of the Muslim community was the exclusive prerogative of ʿAlids, descendants of ʿAlī belonging to the *ahl al-bayt*. The earliest Shīʿī ideas and currents of thought eventually found their full formulation and consolidation in the central Shīʿī doctrine of the imamate.

Pro-ʿAlī sentiments and Shīʿī inclinations persisted in ʿAlī's lifetime, finding a particular stronghold in the garrison town of Kūfa on the Euphrates, whose Arab soldier-tribesmen were predominantly members of south Arabian tribes. Kūfa, the scene of many events in the early history of Shīʿism, had also served as ʿAlī's temporary capital during his brief and turbulent caliphate. During this period of civil war and strife in the community, ʿAlī's caliphal authority was particularly challenged by Muʿāwiya b. Abī Sufyān, the powerful governor of Syria, who eventually succeeded in installing his aristocratic

Meccan clan of Banū Umayya to the leadership of the Muslim community. The prolonged hostilities between ʿAlī and Muʿāwiya also led to the emergence of the Khawārij, who later opposed both the Shīʿa and the Sunnis.

On ʿAlī's murder in 40/661, Muʿāwiya was speedily recognised as the new caliph by the majority of the Muslims, except the Shīʿa and the Khawārij. Muʿāwiya founded the first dynasty in Islam, the Umayyads, who stayed in power for nearly a century (41–132/661–750). By Muʿāwiya's time, the unified Muslim *umma* of the first decades of Islamic history had clearly split into several parties with differing interpretations as to the rightful leadership (caliphate or imamate) of the community and the leader's moral responsibilities. These factions gradually developed doctrinal positions and acquired distinct identities as separate communities of interpretation. The partisans of Muʿāwiya, who repudiated the caliphate of ʿAlī, also included the upholders of the principles of the early caliphate, notably the rights of the non-Hāshimid early Companions of the Prophet to the caliphate. The partisans of ʿAlī, the *Shīʿat ʿAlī*, who now referred to themselves also as the *Shīʿat ahl al-bayt*, repudiated Muʿāwiya's claims to leadership; they aimed to re-establish the rightful imamate in the community through the Hāshimids, members of the Prophet's clan, and more particularly through ʿAlī's sons. The Khawārij, who adopted highly uncompromising positions in opposition to other communities, adhered to strict Islamic egalitarianism, maintaining that any meritorious Muslim of any ethnic or tribal origin could be chosen through popular election as the legitimate leader or imam of the community. They aimed to establish a form of "Islamic democracy", in which authority and leadership would not be based on tribal or hereditary considerations.

EARLY HISTORY OF SHĪʿISM: THE KAYSĀNIYYA AND THE IMĀMIYYA

The early Shīʿa, centred in Kūfa, survived ʿAlī's murder and numerous subsequent tragic events under the Umayyads. After ʿAlī, the Shīʿa recognised his eldest son al-Ḥasan as their new imam. However, al-Ḥasan, who had also been acclaimed briefly as caliph in Kūfa, refrained from any political activity after his abdication from the caliphate and his peace settlement with Muʿāwiya. On al-Ḥasan's death in 49/669, the Shīʿa revived their aspirations for restoring the caliphate to ʿAlids, now headed by their next imam, al-Ḥusayn, second son of ʿAlī and Fāṭima. They persistently invited al-Ḥusayn to their midst in Kūfa to rise in rebellion against the Umayyads; and he finally responded to these summons. The tragic martyrdom of the Prophet's grandson and his companions at Karbalāʾ near Kūfa, where they were massacred by an Umayyad army in 61/680, played an important role in the consolidation of the Shīʿī ethos; it also led to the formation of radical trends among the Shīʿa. The earliest of such trends became manifest in the movement of al-Mukhtār who won control of Kūfa in an open revolt in 66/685. Aiming to avenge al-Ḥusayn's murder, al-Mukhtār launched his own movement in the name of ʿAlī's third son and al-Ḥusayn's half-brother Muḥammad, known as Ibn al-Ḥanafiyya because his mother hailed from the tribe of Banū Ḥanīfa. Al-Mukhtār proclaimed Ibn al-Ḥanafiyya as the Mahdi, "the divinely guided one", the messianic saviour imam and restorer of true Islam who would establish justice on earth and deliver the oppressed from tyranny.

The new eschatological concept of the imam-Mahdi proved particularly appealing to the *mawālī*, the non-Arab converts to Islam who under the Umayyads were treated as second-class Muslims, an intermediary category between Arab Muslims and non-Muslim subjects of the Islamic state. As a large and underprivileged social class concentrated in Kūfa and other urban milieus, and aspiring for the establishment of an order based on the egalitarian precepts of Islam, the *mawālī* provided a significant recruiting ground for any movement opposed to the exclusively Arab hegemony of the Umayyads and their social structure. Starting with the movement organised by al-Mukhtār and through the appeal of the concept of the Mahdi, however, the *mawālī* became particularly involved in Shīʿism. Indeed, they swarmed in large numbers to the side of al-Mukhtār, calling themselves the *Shīʿat al-Mahdī* or the "party of the Mahdi". The success of al-Mukhtār proved short-lived owing to the emergence of a strong coalition against him, representing the interests of the Umayyads and other Arab tribal aristocracies. However, al-Mukhtār's movement survived his demise in 67/687 and the death in 81/700 of Ibn al-Ḥanafiyya who personally had not played an active part in this movement; and it continued to occupy a central role in early Shīʿism until the Abbasid revolution, under the general name of Kaysāniyya.

Initially, Shīʿism represented a unified movement or community with limited membership. The Shīʿa, consisting then mainly of Arab Muslims, had during this initial period of some fifty-odd years recognised successively ʿAlī, al-Ḥasan and al-Ḥusayn as their imams. But from the time of al-Mukhtār's movement, different Shīʿī communities and groupings, consisting of both Arabs and *mawālī*, came to coexist, each one having its own line of imams and propounding its own ideas. Furthermore, the Shīʿī imams now came not only from the major branches of the extended ʿAlid family, namely, the Ḥusaynids (descendants of al-Ḥusayn b. ʿAlī), the Ḥanafids (descendants of Muḥammad b. al-Ḥanafiyya) and, later, the Ḥasanids (descendants of al-Ḥasan b. ʿAlī), but also from other branches of the Prophet's clan of Banū Hāshim. This was because the Prophet's family, whose sanctity was supreme for the Shīʿa, was then still defined broadly in its old Arabian tribal sense.

In this fluid setting, Shīʿism developed mainly in terms of two main branches or trends, the Kaysāniyya and the Imāmiyya, each with its own internal groupings; and, later, another ʿAlid movement led to the foundation of yet another major Shīʿī community, the Zaydiyya. There were also those Shīʿī *ghulāt*, individual theorists with small groups of followers, who existed in the midst or on the fringes of the major Shīʿī communities.

A radical branch, in terms of both doctrine and policy, evolved out of al-Mukhtār's movement and accounted for the bulk of the Shīʿa until shortly after the Abbasid revolution. This branch, breaking away from the religiously moderate attitudes of the early Kūfan Shīʿa, was generally designated as the Kaysāniyya by heresiographers who have been responsible for coining the names of numerous early Muslim communities. The Kaysāniyya, comprised of a number of interrelated groups recognising various Ḥanafid ʿAlids and other Hāshimids as their imams, elaborated some of the doctrines that came to distinguish the radical wing of early Shīʿism. For instance, they condemned the first three caliphs before ʿAlī as usurpers and also held that the community had gone astray by accepting their rule. They considered ʿAlī and his three sons, al-Ḥasan, al-Ḥusayn and Muḥammad, as their four original imams, successors to the Prophet, who had been divinely appointed and were endowed with supernatural attributes. Certain aspects of the intellectual heritage of the Kaysāniyya were later absorbed into the teachings of the main Shīʿī communities of the early Abbasid times, including the Ithnāʿasharīs or Twelvers and the Ismailis.

The Kaysānī groups drew mainly on the support of the superficially Islamicised *mawālī* in southern Iraq, Persia and elsewhere. Drawing on diverse pre-Islamic traditions, the *mawālī* played an important role in transforming Shīʿism from an Arab party of limited size and doctrinal basis to a dynamic movement. Many of the Kaysānī doctrines were propounded by the so-called *ghulāt* or "exaggerators", who were accused by the more moderate Shīʿīs of later times of exaggeration (*ghuluw*) in religious matters. In addition to their condemnation of the caliphs before ʿAlī, the commonest feature of the ideas propagated by the early Shīʿī *ghulāt* was the attribution of superhuman qualities, or even divinity, to imams. The early *ghulāt* speculated on a host of issues and were responsible for emphasising certain ideas, including spiritual interpretations of the Day of Resurrection (*qiyāma*), Paradise and Hell. Many also held a cyclical view of the religious history of mankind, with prophets ushering in new eras. The Shīʿī *ghulāt*, like other contemporary Muslims, also concerned themselves with the status of the true believer. Emphasising the acknowledgement of the rightful Shīʿī imam of the time as the most important religious obligation of the true believer, the role of the then developing *sharīʿa* became less significant for the Kaysānī Shīʿīs and their *ghulāt*. Consequently, they were often accused of advocating *ibāḥa* or antinomianism.

By condemning the early caliphs before ʿAlī, and the Umayyads, as usurpers of the rights of ʿAlī and his descendants and aiming to restore the actual leadership of the Muslim *umma* to ʿAlids, the Kayasāniyya also pursued an activist anti-establishmentarian policy. Several Kaysānī groups, often led by *ghulāt* ideologues, agitated against the Umayyad regime in or around Kūfa. As these Kaysānī revolts were poorly organised and their centres of activity were too close to the seats of caliphal power, however, they all proved abortive. By the end of the Umayyad period, the main body of the Kaysāniyya, known as the Hāshimiyya, had transferred their allegiance to the Abbasid family, who had been cleverly conducting an anti-Umayyad campaign on behalf of an anonymous member of the *ahl al-bayt* with much Shīʿī appeal. At any rate, the Abbasids, descendants of the Prophet's uncle al-ʿAbbās, inherited the party and the *daʿwa* or missionary organisation of the Hāshimiyya, which served as the main instruments of their eventual victory over the Umayyads.

Meanwhile, there had appeared another major branch or faction of Shīʿism, later designated as the Imāmiyya. This faction, the early common heritage of the Ismailis and the Twelver Shīʿīs, recognised a particular line of Ḥusaynid ʿAlid imams and remained completely removed from any oppositional political activity. In fact, the Imāmiyya adopted a quiescent policy in the political field while doctrinally they subscribed to some of the radical views of the Kaysāniyya, such as the condemnation of ʿAlī's predecessors in the caliphate. The Imāmīs, who like other Shīʿīs of the Umayyad times were centred in Kūfa, traced the imamate through al-Ḥusayn b. ʿAlī's sole surviving son ʿAlī b. al-Ḥusayn (d. 95/714), with the honorific epithet of Zayn al-ʿĀbidīn (the Ornament of the Pious). It was with Zayn al-ʿĀbidīn's son Muḥammad al-Bāqir that the Ḥusaynid line of ʿAlid imams and the Imāmī community distinguished themselves among the early Shīʿa. Like his father, the Imam al-Bāqir refrained from political activity and concerned himself solely with the religious aspects of his mandate. In particular, he developed the rudiments of some of the ideas which later became the legitimist principles of Imāmī Shīʿism. Above all, he propounded the attributes and functions of imams as spiritual guides of the community. He is also credited with introducing the important principle of *taqiyya*, or precautionary dissimulation of one's true belief under adverse circumstances, a principle which was later adopted by both the Ismailis and the Twelvers.[2]

In spite of many difficulties, including the alternative claims of other contemporary ʿAlids to the imamate, al-Bāqir succeeded during his imamate of almost twenty years to increase his following. He was also the first Ḥusaynid imam to attract a few *ghulāt* thinkers to his circle of partisans; these included al-Mughīra b. Saʿīd (d. 119/737) and Abū Manṣūr al-ʿIjlī (d. 124/742), who later founded important groups of their own. The origins of religious elitism among the Shīʿa may in fact be traced to these two early Shīʿī *ghulāt* groups; they also laid the foundations of religious militancy in dealing with religio-political adversaries. In addition, the Imam al-Bāqir acquired a number of adherents from among the famous traditionists and jurists of the time.

Al-Bāqir's imamate coincided with the rise of different legal and theological schools in Islam. Under these circumstances, competing Shīʿī groups sought the guidance of their imam as an authoritative guide. Al-Bāqir was in fact the first imam of the Ḥusaynid line to perform this role, and his partisans regarded him as the sole legitimate religious authority of the time. He has been mentioned as a reporter of *ḥadīth* or the Prophetic traditions, particularly of those supporting the ʿAlid-Shīʿī cause and derived from ʿAlī b. Abī Ṭālib. However, al-Bāqir and his son and successor Ja"far al-Ṣādiq interpreted the law on their own authority, without much recourse to *ḥadīth* reported by earlier authorities. In Shīʿism, it may be noted, *ḥadīth* is reported on the authority of the imams and it includes their sayings in addition to the Prophetic traditions. Having established a distinctive identity for Imāmī Shīʿism, Abū Jaʿfar Muḥammad b. ʿAlī al-Bāqir died around 114/732, a century after the death of the Prophet.

JAʿFAR AL-ṢĀDIQ'S IMAMATE, ABU'L-KHAṬṬĀB AND ISMĀʿĪL

The Imāmiyya expanded significantly and became a major religious community during the long and eventful imamate of al-Bāqir's son and successor Jaʿfar al-Ṣādiq, the foremost scholar and teacher among the Ḥusaynid imams. On al-Bāqir's death, his Shīʿī partisans split into several groups, but a majority recognised his eldest son Abū ʿAbd Allāh, later called al-Ṣādiq (the Trustworthy), as their new imam designated as such by his father. Al-Ṣādiq's rise to prominence occurred rather gradually during this turbulent period, when the Abbasids finally succeeded in uprooting the Umayyads. During the first twenty years of his imamate, however, the Imāmiyya were still overshadowed by the Kaysāniyya, including especially the revolutionary Hāshimiyya-ʿAbbāsiyya who were then actively conducting an anti-Umayyad campaign.

In the earlier years of al-Ṣādiq's imamate the oppositional movement of Zayd b. ʿAlī, al-Bāqir's half-brother and al-Ṣādiq's uncle, was launched from Kūfa. In close affinity to the views of the Khawārij, Zayd seems to have taught the need for a just imam and the community's duty to remove an unjust ruler. Furthermore, he is reported to have stated that if an imam wished recognition, he would have to assert his claims publicly and sword in hand if necessary. In other words, Zayd did not attach any significance to a hereditary imamate and to passive policies, nor was he prepared to accept the eschatological notions associated with the Mahdiship of an imam. The observance of *taqiyya*, too, was rather foreign to Zayd's activist policies. Doctrinally, however, Zayd adopted a compromising stance, reflecting the moderate position of the early Kūfan Shīʿa. He asserted that though ʿAlī was the most excellent (*al-afḍal*) to succeed the Prophet, nevertheless the allegiance given to the earlier caliphs, who were less excellent (*al-mafḍūl*), remained valid. This view, repudiated by the later Zaydīs, won Zayd the general sympathy of many non-Shīʿī Muslims. The combination of Zayd's militant policy and his otherwise conservative teachings appealed to many Shīʿīs as well. At any rate, Zayd's movement survived his abortive uprising in Kūfa in 122/740, and the Zaydīs succeeded by the second half of the 3rd/9th century to establish two states, one in Yaman and another one in the Caspian provinces in northern Persia, a region known as Daylam in medieval times.

The Ḥasanid ʿAlid movement of Muḥammad al-Nafs al-Zakiyya (the Pure Soul), too, began to acquire importance during the earlier years of al-Ṣādiq's imamate. This movement had been launched earlier by Muḥammad's father, ʿAbd Allāh, a grandson of al-Ḥasan b. ʿAlī b. Abī Ṭālib. ʿAbd Allāh, head of the Ḥasanid family, had designated his son Muḥammad from the time of his birth for the role of the Mahdi. Lacking proper organisation, this Ḥasanid movement was readily overtaken by that of the Abbasids who later, in 145/762, crushed the revolts of al-Nafs al-Zakiyya and his brother Ibrāhīm.

In the meantime, the Abbasids had learned important lessons from all the abortive revolts against the Umayyads. They paid particular attention to the organisational aspects of their own religio-political *daʿwa*, establishing secret headquarters in Kūfa while concentrating their activities in the remote province of Khurāsān. Numerous *dāʿīs* preached the revolutionary message of the Abbasid movement, which was launched in the name of the *ahl al-bayt* with much appeal to the Shīʿa and the Persian *mawālī*. After several decades of activities, the Abbasids finally succeeded in 132/750 to the caliphate, remaining effectively or nominally in power for almost five centuries until 656/1258.

The Abbasid revolution marked a turning point in early Islam, initiating many socio-political and economic changes in the established order, including the disappearance of distinctions between the Arab Muslims and the *mawālī*. However, the Abbasid victory proved a source of utter disillusionment for the Shīʿa who had all along expected an ʿAlid to succeed to the caliphate. The Shīʿa became further disappointed when the Abbasids, soon after their accession, began to persecute their former Shīʿī supporters and many of the ʿAlids. In time, the Abbasid caliph in fact became the spiritual spokesman of Sunni Islam, lending support to the elaboration of Sunni interpretations of the Islamic message. With these developments, those remaining Kaysānī Shīʿīs who had not joined the Abbasid party sought to align themselves with alternative Shīʿī communities. In Khurāsān and other eastern lands of the caliphate, many of such alienated Shīʿīs attached themselves to the groups generically termed the Khurramiyya (or Khurramdīniyya), espousing anti-Abbasid and anti-Arab ideas. In Iraq, however, they rallied to the side of Jaʿfar al-Ṣādiq or Muḥammad al-Nafs al-Zakiyya, who were then the main ʿAlid claimants to the imamate. And with the demise of the activist movement of al-Nafs al-Zakiyya, the quiescent Jaʿfar al-Ṣādiq emerged as the main rallying point for the allegiance of Shīʿīs of diverse backgrounds other than the Zaydīs who followed their own imams.

Maintaining the Imāmī tradition of political pacifism, Jaʿfar al-Ṣādiq had gradually acquired widespread reputation as a religious scholar. He was a reporter of *ḥadīth*, and later was cited as such also in the chains of authorities (*isnād*) accepted by Sunnis; he taught *fiqh* or jurisprudence and has been credited with founding, after the work of his father, the Imāmī Shīʿī school of religious law or *madhhab*, named Jaʿfarī after him. Jaʿfar al-Ṣādiq was accepted as a teaching authority not only by his Shīʿī partisans but by a wider circle which included many of the piety-minded Muslims of Medina, permanent home to ʿAlids, and Kūfa where the bulk of the Imāmiyya was located. By the final decade of his imamate, al-Ṣādiq had acquired a noteworthy group of thinkers and associates around himself which included some of the most eminent jurist-traditionists as well as theologians of the time, such as Hishām b. al-Ḥakam (d. 179/795), the foremost representative of Imāmī *kalām* or scholastic theology. As a result of the intense intellectual activities of the Imam al-Ṣādiq and his learned associates, the Imāmiyya now came to possess a distinctive body of ritual as well as theological and legal doctrines.

Building on the foundations laid by his father, the Imam al-Ṣādiq, assisted by his associates, elaborated the basic conception of the doctrine of the imamate, which was essentially retained by the later Ithnāʿasharī and Ismaili Shīʿīs.[3] This central doctrine of Imāmī Shīʿism was based on belief in the permanent need of mankind for a divinely guided, sinless and infallible (*maʿṣūm*) imam who, after the Prophet Muḥammad, would act as the authoritative teacher and guide of men in all their spiritual affairs. The imam, who can practise *taqiyya* when necessary, is entitled to temporal leadership as much as to religious authority; his mandate, however, does not depend on his actual rule. The doctrine further taught that the Prophet himself had designated ʿAlī as his legatee or *waṣī* and successor, by an explicit designation or *naṣṣ* under divine command. After ʿAlī, the imamate was to be transmitted from father to son by *naṣṣ* among the descendants of ʿAlī and Fāṭima, and after al-Ḥusayn, it would continue in the Ḥusaynid line until the end of time. This Ḥusaynid ʿAlid imam, the sole legitimate imam at any given point in time, is in possession of a special knowledge or *ʿilm*, and has perfect understanding of the exoteric (*ẓāhir*) and esoteric (*bāṭin*) meanings of the Qur'an and the message of Islam. Indeed, the world could not exist without such an imam who is the proof of God (*ḥujjat Allāh*) on earth. Recognition of the true imam of the time and obedience to him were the absolute duties of every believer.

This doctrine enabled the Imam al-Ṣādiq to consolidate Shīʿism after its numerous earlier defeats, on a quiescent basis, as it no longer required the imam to rebel against the established regime to assert his claims. In other words, the institutions of the imamate and the caliphate were henceforth doctrinally separated from one another. It was on the basis of his *ʿilm*, divinely inspired and transmitted through the *naṣṣ* of the previous imam, that the rightful imam became the sole authorised source of religious guidance even if he did not rule as caliph. As in the case of *naṣṣ*, the imam's *ʿilm* was traced back in the Ḥusaynid ʿAlid line to the Prophet himself. By elaborating a conception of the imamate based on the twin and interrelated principles of *naṣṣ* and *ʿilm*, and emphasising the practice of *taqiyya*, Jaʿfar al-Ṣādiq presented an entirely new interpretation of the imam's functions and attributes.

The Imam al-Ṣādiq, too, attracted a few *ghulāt* thinkers to his circle of associates, but kept the speculations of the more extremist elements of his following within tolerable bounds. The foremost member of this group was Abu'l-Khaṭṭāb al-Asadī, the most prominent of all early Shī'ī *ghulāt*. The imam had originally appointed Abu'l-Khaṭṭāb as his chief representative in Kūfa, centre of the Imāmī Shī'īs. However, Abu'l-Khaṭṭāb propagated extremist ideas about the imam in addition to other exaggerated views. In time, Abu'l-Khaṭṭāb acquired his own disciples, the Khaṭṭābiyya, adopting a revolutionary policy in contradistinction to the imam's quiescent stance. As a result, the imam was obliged to denounce and refute him. Soon afterwards in 138/755, Abu'l-Khaṭṭāb and his band of supporters, who had gathered in the mosque of Kūfa for rebellious purposes, were attacked and massacred by the forces of the city's watchful governor.

On Abu'l-Khaṭṭāb's death, the Kūfa-based Khaṭṭābiyya split into several small groups. Some of the Khaṭṭābīs now rallied to the side of the Imam al-Ṣādiq's eldest son Ismā'īl, apparently a supporter of Abu'l-Khaṭṭāb's activist policy. This is reported by the later Imāmī heresiographers al-Nawbakhtī (d. after 300/912) and al-Qummī (d. 301/913–14), who in fact identify the nascent Ismā'īliyya with the Khaṭṭābiyya. This identification may also have been due to parallels between certain Ismaili teachings and ideas originally propagated by Abu'l-Khaṭṭāb and the early Khaṭṭābīs.[4] In this connection, Abu'l-Khaṭṭāb is reported to have taught that at all times there must be a speaker-prophet (*nāṭiq*) and a silent one (*ṣāmit*). The early Khaṭṭābīs also relied on the *bāṭinī ta'wīl* or esoteric interpretation of Qur'anic passages, and were preoccupied with cyclicism and hierarchism. On the other hand, the Khaṭṭābīs upheld the divinity of the imams on the basis of the divine light (*nūr*) inherited by them, which never found any expression in the Imāmī doctrine of the imamate maintained by the Ismailis. In fact, in the earliest Ismaili literature containing references to the Khaṭṭābiyya, Abu'l-Khaṭṭāb is denounced as a heretic and his followers are condemned in strong terms.[5]

Few biographical details are available on Ismā'īl b. Ja'far.[6] Ismā'īl and his full brother 'Abd Allāh were the eldest sons of the Imam al-Ṣādiq by his first wife Fāṭima, a granddaughter of al-Ḥasan b. 'Alī b. Abī Ṭālib. Born during the initial years of the second Islamic century, Ismā'īl was some twenty-five years older than his half-brother Mūsā al-Kāẓim who was born in 128/745–6. There is sufficient evidence indicating that Ismā'īl had close relations with the more activist circles in his father's following. In fact, it is reported that he participated in at least one anti-Abbasid plot in 138/755.[7] There were evidently also contacts between Ismāʿīl and Abu'l-Khaṭṭāb. This association is alluded to in the enigmatic Persian treatise known as *Umm al-kitāb*, which states that the Ismaili religion was founded by the disciples of Abu'l-Khaṭṭāb, who sacrificed their lives for Ismāʿīl.[8] However, recent scholarship has revealed that the *Umm al-kitāb*, preserved by the Ismailis of Central Asia, does not contain the doctrines of the early Ismailis or the Khaṭṭābīs; it was in fact originally produced in Arabic by one of the Kūfan Shīʿī *ghulāt* groups of the 2nd/8th century known as the Mukhammisa (the Pentadists).

According to the majority of the sources, both Ismaili and non-Ismaili, the Imam al-Ṣādiq had originally designated Ismāʿīl as his successor by the rule of *naṣṣ*. There cannot be any doubt regarding the historicity of this designation, which provides the basis of the Ismaili claims. However, matters become rather confused as Ismāʿīl apparently predeceased his father, and as several of al-Ṣādiq's sons laid claim to his heritage. According to the Ismaili religious tradition and as reported in some of their sources, Ismāʿīl survived his father and succeeded him in due course. But most sources relate that he died before his father, the latest date mentioned being 145/762–3; they also add how during Ismāʿīl's funeral procession in Medina the Imam al-Ṣādiq made several attempts to show the face of his dead son to witnesses, though some of the same sources also indicate that Ismāʿīl was later seen in Baṣra.[9] At any rate, in the accounts of Ismāʿīl's death and burial, al-Manṣūr (136–58/754–75) is named as the ruling Abbasid caliph. Al-Bharūchī, an Indian Ismaili author, relates visiting Ismāʿīl's tomb in the Baqīʿ cemetery in Medina in 904/1498; his grave still existed there in 1302/1885, but it was later destroyed by the Wahhābīs along with the graves of his father and other imams located in that cemetery.[10]

Having established a solid doctrinal foundation for Imāmī Shīʿism, Abū ʿAbd Allāh Jaʿfar b. Muḥammad al-Ṣādiq, the last imam recognised by both the Ithnāʿasharīs and the Ismailis, died in 148/765. The dispute over his succession led to historic divisions in Imāmī Shīʿism, also marking the emergence of the Ismailis.

THE EARLIEST ISMAILIS

Jaʿfar al-Ṣādiq, as noted, had originally designated his eldest son Ismāʿīl as his successor. However, as related in the majority of the sources, Ismāʿīl was not present in Medina or Kūfa at the time of his father's death. At any rate, three of the Imam al-Ṣādiq's other sons now simultaneously claimed his succession. As a result, the Imāmī Shīʿīs split into six groups, two of which may be identified as the earliest Ismailis. While some of al-Ṣādiq's followers denied his death and awaited his return as the Mahdi, the majority of the Imāmī Shīʿīs acknowledged his eldest surviving son, ʿAbd Allāh al-Afṭaḥ, the full brother of Ismāʿīl, as their new imam; they became known as the Afṭaḥiyya. When ʿAbd Allāh died a few months later, the bulk of his supporters turned to his half-brother Mūsā al-Kāẓim, later counted as the seventh imam of the Twelvers, who had already received the allegiance of a group of the Imāmiyya. Another small Imāmī group recognised the imamate of Muḥammad b. Jaʿfar, known as al-Dībāj, who revolted unsuccessfully against the Abbasids in 200/815 and died soon afterwards.

Two other splinter groups issued from the Imāmiyya in 148/765. Numerically insignificant and based in Kūfa, these earliest Ismaili groups supported the claims of Ismāʿīl b. Jaʿfar and his son Muḥammad. It seems that these groups had come into existence earlier as pro-Ismāʿīl or proto-Ismaili factions of the Imāmiyya, but they separated from other Imāmī Shīʿīs only on al-Ṣādiq's death. According to al-Nawbakhtī and al-Qummī, who wrote shortly before 286/899 and remain our main authorities on the earliest Ismailis,[11] one splinter group denied the death of Ismāʿīl in his father's lifetime. They maintained that Ismāʿīl was the true imam after al-Ṣādiq and that he would eventually return as the Mahdi. Designated as "al-Ismāʿīliyya al-khāliṣa"or the "pure Ismāʿīliyya" by al-Nawbakhtī and al-Qummī, the members of this group further held that the Imam al-Ṣādiq had announced Ismāʿīl's death merely as a ruse to protect him from the persecutions of the Abbasids who were annoyed by his political activities. The second pro-Ismāʿīl group, designated by al-Nawbakhtī and al-Qummī as the Mubārakiyya, affirmed Ismāʿīl's death during the lifetime of his father and now recognised his son Muḥammad as their imam. They held that the Imam al-Ṣādiq had personally designated Muḥammad as the rightful successor to Ismāʿīl, after the latter's death. Furthermore, the Mubārakiyya held that the imamate could no longer be transferred from brother to brother after the case of al-Ḥasan and al-Ḥusayn, sons of ʿAlī b. Abī Ṭālib; and this is why they could not accept the claims of Ismāʿīl's brothers. At any rate, it is clear that the Mubārakiyya, named after Ismāʿīl's epithet al-Mubārak (the Blessed One), had come into existence in Ismāʿīl's lifetime and they were originally his supporters. The Mubārakiyya may be taken to represent one of the original designations of the nascent Ismāʿīliyya.

As in the case of Ismāʿīl, little is known about the life and career of Muḥammad b. Ismāʿīl, the seventh imam of the Ismailis. The relevant biographical details contained in early Ismaili sources have been collected by the *dāʿī* Idrīs.[12] Muḥammad was the eldest son of Ismāʿīl and the eldest grandson of the Imam al-Ṣādiq. Born around 120/738, he was about twenty-six years old at the time of al-Ṣādiq's death. Muḥammad became the eldest male member of al-Ṣādiq's family on the death of his uncle ʿAbd Allāh al-Afṭaḥ in 149/766; he was older than his uncle Mūsā by about eight years. Soon after the recognition of Mūsā's imamate by the majority of the Imāmiyya, Muḥammad b. Ismāʿīl left Medina for the East and went into hiding to avoid Abbasid persecution, initiating the *dawr al-satr* or period of concealment in early Ismaili history. Henceforth, Muḥammad acquired the epithet of al-Maktūm (the Hidden One), in addition to al-Maymūn (the Fortunate One). However, he maintained his contacts with the Kūfa-based Mubārakiyya. Muḥammad seems to have spent the latter part of his life in Khūzistān, in southwestern Persia, where he had some followers. He died not too long after 179/795 during the caliphate of the celebrated Hārūn al-Rashīd (170–93/786–809).

No details are available on the early relations between "al-Ismāʿīliyya al-khāliṣa" and the Mubārakiyya. On the basis of what is reported by al-Nawbakhtī and al-Qummī, however, subsequent developments in the history of the earliest Ismailis can be summarised as follows. On the death of Muḥammad b. Ismāʿīl, the Mubārakiyya split into two groups. A majority, identified by Imāmī heresiographers as the immediate predecessors of the dissident Qarmaṭīs, refused to accept Muḥammad b. Ismāʿīl's death. They acknowledged him as their seventh and last imam, awaiting his imminent return as the Mahdi or *qāʾim* (riser) – terms which were basically synonymous in their early usage by the Ismailis and other Shīʿīs. A second group, very small and extremely obscure, affirmed Muḥammad b. Ismāʿīl's death and now began to trace the imamate in his progeny. Thus, by the time of Muḥammad b. Ismāʿīl's death, the earliest Ismailis were comprised of three distinct groups. Almost nothing is known with certainty regarding the subsequent history of these groups, and their interrelations, until shortly after the middle of the 3rd/9th century, when a unified Ismaili movement emerged on the historical stage.

THE *DAʿWA* OF THE 3RD/9TH CENTURY

Drawing on different categories of sources, notably Ismaili writings and traditions of the early Fatimid period, the heresiographical works of Imāmī scholars and even the anti-Ismaili tracts of Sunni polemicists, modern scholarship has to a large extent succeeded in clarifying the circumstances leading to the emergence of an Ismaili movement in the 3rd/9th century. It seems certain that for almost a century after Muḥammad b. Ismāʿīl, a group of leaders, originally well placed within the nascent Ismāʿīliyya, worked secretly and systematically for the creation of a unified and expanding Ismaili movement. Initially attached to one of the earliest Ismaili groups, these leaders were in all probability the imams of that obscure sub-group issued from the Mubārakiyya who maintained continuity in the imamate in the progeny of Muḥammad b. Ismā'īl.

Be that as it may, these leaders whose Fatimid 'Alid genealogy was in due course acknowledged by the Ismailis, did not for three generations claim the imamate openly. This was a precautionary tactic to safeguard themselves against Abbasid persecution. In fact, the true identities of these leaders remained known only to a handful of trusted associates. There was, however, another – much more important – reason why these leaders did not initially claim the imamate. As a tactical measure, 'Abd Allāh, the first among them, organised his campaign around the central doctrine of the bulk of the earliest Ismailis, namely, those who had issued from the Mubārakiyya and recognised Muḥammad b. Ismā'īl as their Mahdi. This doctrine, of course, did not allow for any imams after the Mahdi, then in occultation (*ghayba*). Organising a revolutionary movement in the name of a hidden imam who could not be pursued by Abbasid agents must have had its obvious advantages. And this ingenious stratagem continued to serve as the central teaching of the early Ismailis until the year 286/899 when the then leader of the movement, 'Abd Allāh al-Mahdī, felt secure enough to abandon the disguising measures of his predecessors.

The existence of such a group of early Ismaili leaders is indeed confirmed by both the official view of the later Fatimid Ismailis regarding the pre-Fatimid phase of their history, and the hostile Ibn Rizām-Akhū Muḥsin account of the same period. On the basis of this evidence it is clear that the leaders in question represented a sole group, members of the same family who succeeded one another on a hereditary basis. This is further corroborated by the fact that despite some minor variations, the names of these leaders ('Abd Allāh, Aḥmad, al-Ḥusayn or Muḥammad, and finally 'Abd Allāh al-Mahdī) are almost identical in the accounts of the later Fatimid Ismailis,[13] and in the lists traceable to Akhū Muḥsin and his source, Ibn Rizām,[14] although the Ismaili sources ultimately trace the 'Alid ancestry of 'Abd Allāh, the first leader after Muḥammad b. Ismā'īl, to the Imam al-Ṣādiq, while in the hostile polemics the same 'Abd Allāh is portrayed as a non-'Alid, son of a certain Maymūn al-Qaddāḥ.

Modern scholarship has shown that the Qaddāḥid ancestry attributed to the leaders of the early Ismailis and, therefore, to their descendants and successors in the Fatimid dynasty had been motivated by the anti-Fatimid designs of polemicists, who wrote soon after the establishment of the Fatimid caliphate. By correctly identifying the personalities of Maymūn al-Qaddāḥ and his son ʿAbd Allāh, who lived in the 2nd/8th century and were closely associated with the Imams al-Bāqir and al-Ṣādiq, W. Ivanow succeeded once and for all to demolish the myth of ʿAbd Allāh b. Maymūn al-Qaddāḥ, or Ibn al-Qaddāḥ, as the founder of Ismailism and the progenitor of the Ismaili imams.[15] As noted, al-Maymūn (the Fortunate One) was in fact one of the epithets or code-names of Muḥammad b. Ismāʿīl himself, whose followers were evidently also known as the Maymūniyya. This may explain why Ibn Rizām, the originator of this myth, decided to identify the ʿAlid ʿAbd Allāh b. Muḥammad b. Ismāʿīl (al-Maymūn), who could in fact be referred to as ʿAbd Allāh b. al-Maymūn, with the non-ʿAlid ʿAbd Allāh b. Maymūn al-Qaddāḥ, who lived almost a century earlier and personally had nothing to do with Ismailism.

Ismaili tradition, corroborated by the Ibn Rizām-Akhū Muḥsin account, recognised three generations of leaders between Muḥammad b. Ismāʿīl and ʿAbd Allāh al-Mahdī, founder of the Fatimid state and the last of the leaders during the *dawr al-satr* in early Ismaili history. The first of these leaders, a shrewd strategist, as noted, was ʿAbd Allāh, designated in later Ismaili sources as al-Akbar (the Elder), probably in order to distinguish him from ʿAbd Allāh al-Mahdī. The Ismaili *dāʿī* Aḥmad b. Ibrāhīm al-Nīsābūrī, who flourished in the second half of the 4th/10th century, relates important details on ʿAbd Allāh al-Akbar and his successors down to ʿAbd Allāh al-Mahdī.[16] It is also interesting to note that al-Nīsābūrī's account of ʿAbd Allāh al-Akbar is corroborated in its basic outline by what has been related on the authorities of Ibn Rizām and Akhū Muḥsin. Both sources agree that ʿAbd Allāh came originally from the vicinity of Ahwāz in Khūzistān, where Muḥammad b. Ismāʿīl had spent the latter years of his life. Eventually ʿAbd Allāh settled down in ʿAskar Mukram, then a prosperous town about forty kilometres north of Ahwāz. Today the ruins of ʿAskar Mukram, situated to the south of Shūshtar, are known as Band-i Qīr. ʿAbd Allāh lived as a wealthy merchant in ʿAskar Mukram where he owned two houses. It was from there that he decided to organise an expanding Ismaili movement, sending *dāʿīs* to different districts in and around Khūzistān. Soon, ʿAbd Allāh encountered hostile reactions to his activities, obliging him to flee Khūzistān.

Subsequently, ʿAbd Allāh proceeded secretly to the nearby town of Baṣra, where he stayed for some time with his distant cousins, descendants of ʿAqīl b. Abī Ṭālib, ʿAlī's brother; at the time, ʿAbd Allāh may even have claimed an ʿAqīlid ancestry, as is reported in anti-Ismaili sources. In Baṣra, too, he was soon harassed by opponents. At some unknown date in the first half of the 3rd/9th century, ʿAbd Allāh was once again forced to flee. This time he went into hiding in Syria where he initially found refuge in a Christian monastery in the hills of the Jabal al-Summāq, near Maʿarrat al-Nuʿmān. It was there that a group of ʿAbd Allāh's *dāʿīs*, who had been searching for him in different localities, finally re-established contact with their leader. At the time, the ancient town of Salamiyya, situated at the edge of the Syrian desert some thirty-five kilometres southeast of Ḥamā, was being resettled by Muḥammad b. ʿAbd Allāh b. Ṣāliḥ, an Abbasid in charge of the locality. The Ismaili *dāʿīs* now acquired a plot of land in Salamiyya for ʿAbd Allāh al-Akbar, who settled there permanently posing as a prosperous Hāshimid merchant. In Salamiyya, ʿAbd Allāh's true identity remained known only to a handful of relatives and close associates. He built a sumptuous palace for himself in Salamiyya, which served as the secret headquarters of the Ismaili *daʿwa* for several decades until the year 289/902. ʿAbd Allāh al-Akbar died in Salamiyya, at an unknown date soon after 261/874. Around 400/1009, the Fatimids constructed a domed mausoleum over his grave which still exists and is locally known as the *maqām al-imām*.[17]

The sustained efforts of ʿAbd Allāh al-Akbar to reorganise and reinvigorate the Ismaili movement had begun to bear concrete fruit by the early 260s/870s, when numerous *dāʿīs* appeared in southern Iraq and other regions. It was in 261/874 that Ḥamdān Qarmaṭ was converted to Ismailism by al-Ḥusayn al-Ahwāzī, an important *dāʿī* who had accompanied ʿAbd Allāh to Salamiyya and was then dispatched to Iraq. Ḥamdān organised the *daʿwa* in the Sawād or the rural environs of Kūfa, his native locality, as well as in other districts of southern Iraq. Ḥamdān's chief assistant was his brother-in-law ʿAbdān, originally from Ahwāz. A learned theologian, ʿAbdān trained numerous *dāʿīs*, including Abū Saʿīd al-Ḥasan b. Bahrām al-Jannābī, a native of the port of Jannāba (Persian, Gannāva) on the northern shore of the Persian Gulf, and the future founder of the Qarmaṭī state of Baḥrayn. Ḥamdān and ʿAbdān rapidly won the allegiance of the Ismailis of southern Iraq in addition to converting an increasing number of villagers in the Sawād of Kūfa; soon they all became generally known as the Qarāmiṭa (singular, Qarmaṭī), after their first local leader. Later, the same term was applied in a derogatory sense to Ismailis of other regions.

At the time, there was a single Ismaili movement, centrally directed from Salamiyya. The Ismailis now referred to their religio-political campaign and movement simply as *al-daʿwa* (the mission) or *al-daʿwa al-hādiya* (the rightly guiding mission), in addition to using expressions such as *daʿwat al-ḥaqq* (summons to the truth) or *dīn al-ḥaqq* (religion of the truth); they also referred to themselves as *ahl al-ḥaqq* (people of the truth). The united Ismailis, as noted, then rallied around the doctrine of the Mahdiship of Muḥammad b. Ismāʿīl.[18]

Centred on the expectation of the imminent emergence of the Mahdi who would establish the rule of justice in the world, the Ismaili movement of the 3rd/9th century had a great deal of messianic appeal for underprivileged groups of diverse social backgrounds. The Mahdi would deliver a multitude of oppressed and discontented groups from the inequities of the social order established under the Abbasids, usurpers of the legitimate ʿAlid rights to leadership. Among such groups mention may be made of landless peasantry and bedouin tribesmen whose interests were set apart from those of the prospering urban classes. Indeed, the Ismaili *daʿwa* now appeared as a movement of social and religious protest against the Abbasids and their order, including especially the privileged urban classes and the centralised administration of their state. The Ismaili *dāʿī*s also capitalised on regional grievances. On the basis of such a well-designed strategy, the religio-political message of the Ismaili *daʿwa* spread in different regions and among different social strata. The *dāʿī*s were initially more successful in non-urban milieus, removed from the administrative centres of the Abbasid caliphate. This explains the early success of Ismailism among rural inhabitants and bedouin tribesmen of the Arab lands, notably in southern Iraq, eastern Arabia (Baḥrayn) and Yaman. In contrast and in the Iranian lands, especially in the Jibāl, Khurāsān and Transoxania, the *daʿwa* was primarily addressed to the ruling classes and the educated elite.

The early Ismaili movement achieved particular success among those Imāmī Shīʿīs of Iraq and elsewhere who had hitherto acknowledged Mūsā al-Kāẓim and certain of his descendants as their imams. These Imāmīs shared a theological heritage with the Ismailis, especially the Imāmī doctrine of the imamate, while many amongst them had become gradually disillusioned with the quietist policies of their own imams. For a while during the imamate of Mūsā al-Kāẓim's son and successor, ʿAlī al-Riḍā (d. 203/818), later son-in-law and heir apparent of the Abbasid caliph al-Ma'mūn (198–218/813–33), there had even arisen some hope for a lasting peace settlement between the Abbasids and that particular branch of the Fatimid ʿAlids. Be that as it may, the Imāmīs too had witnessed several schisms, resulting in a multiplicity of groups in their community and rival claimants to the imamate. It was under such circumstances that the main Imāmī group, later designated as Ithnāʿashariyya (Twelvers),[19] faced a major crisis in 260/874. In that year, on the death of their eleventh imam, al-Ḥasan al-ʿAskarī, and the simultaneous disappearance of his infant son Muḥammad, the Imāmīs were left without an imam and in a state of utter disarray and confusion. A large number of such discontented Imāmīs responded to the summons of the Ismaili *daʿwa* spreading in their midst.

It is not coincidental that the revolutionary movement of the Ismailis appeared on the historical stage after the middle of the 3rd/9th century. By that time, important developments had taken place both at the centre of caliphal power in Iraq and in the provincial territories, initiating the fragmentation of the Abbasid state. As a result of the complex problems created by Turkish slave soldiers and their commanders who had come to play an increasingly important role in the central affairs of the state, the Abbasids' caliphal authority and their control over the outlying provinces had weakened. This made it possible for new political powers, based on military force, to assert themselves on the fringes of the caliphate. The Ṣaffārids, based in Sīstān, were the first such major military power to appear in the eastern lands of the caliphate; they established a dynasty in 247/861 and separated vast territories from the Abbasid domains. A few years later in 250/864, Zaydī ʿAlid rule was established in the Caspian provinces of northern Persia. In North Africa, too, various local dynasties accorded only nominal allegiance to the Abbasids. The black slaves, known as the Zanj, working on the marshlands of Baṣra, launched their insurrectional activities close to the seat of Abbasid power in Iraq. The Zanj terrorised southern Iraq for fifteen years (255–70/869–83), seriously distracting the attention of Abbasid officials at Baghdad.

It was under such circumstances that Ḥamdān embarked on anti-Abbasid activities in Iraq. His rapid success is attested by the fact that references to the Qarmaṭīs began to appear soon after 261/874; and by 267/880, when Ḥamdān attempted in vain to join forces with the Zanj, the Qarmaṭīs had indeed become quite numerous in Iraq. Aside from the narratives traceable to Ibn Rizām and Akhū Muḥsin,[20] valuable details on the early history of the Ismaili (Qarmaṭī) movement in Iraq have been preserved by al-Ṭabarī (d. 310/923) who had access to Qarmaṭī informants.[21] At this time, Ḥamdān acknowledged the authority of the central leader of the Ismaili movement in Salamiyya, with whom he corresponded but whose identity remained a guarded secret; Ḥamdān had established his own secret headquarters in Kalwādhā near Baghdad.

Ḥamdān and ʿAbdān were instructed from Salamiyya to propagate their mission in the name of the Mahdi Muḥammad b. Ismāʿīl. In fact, in order to prepare for the emergence of the Mahdi, in 277/890

Ḥamdān built a fortified *dār al-hijra*, or abode of migration, near Kūfa for the Qarmaṭīs, where they also gathered supplies of weapons and other provisions. This abode was to serve for the Qarmaṭīs as the nucleus of a new society, as Medina had served the Prophet Muḥammad in the aftermath of his emigration from Mecca. It would also serve as a base of operations for launching assaults against the Abbasids. Similar *dār al-hijra*s were later founded for other early Ismaili communities in Yaman, Baḥrayn, North Africa and elsewhere. The Qarmaṭī leaders of Iraq also instituted an elaborate system of taxation to raise the required financial resources for their activities; these taxes ostensibly included the *khums* or fifth, set aside for the Mahdi.

Meanwhile, Ismaili *dāʿī*s had appeared in other regions. Ḥamdān and ʿAbdān had extended their activities to areas adjacent to southern Iraq, notably Fārs in southern Persia where Abū Saʿīd al-Jannābī and ʿAbdān's brother al-Ma'mūn operated as *dāʿī*s. Abū Saʿīd was later sent to eastern Arabia, then known as Baḥrayn, where he campaigned successfully among the bedouin tribesmen and the local Persian community. Originally belonging to a prominent Imāmī family in Kūfa, Ibn Ḥawshab, later known as Manṣūr al-Yaman, was converted by ʿAbdān and then sent to initiate the *daʿwa* in Yaman, where he arrived in 268/881 accompanied by his chief collaborator Ibn al-Faḍl, another one of the early *dāʿī*s who had converted from Imāmī Shīʿism. As a result of the rapid success of these *dāʿī*s, the Ismaili mission was preached publicly in Yaman by 270/883; and by 293/905–6, when Ibn al-Faḍl occupied Ṣanʿā', almost all of Yaman had been brought under the control of the Ismailis.[22] Yaman also served as a base for the spread of the *daʿwa* to adjoining areas as well as remote lands. For instance, in 270/883, Ibn Ḥawshab sent his relative al-Haytham to Sind (in today's Pakistan), initiating the *daʿwa* on the Indian subcontinent. And in 280/893, on Ibn Ḥawshab's instructions Abū ʿAbd Allāh al-Shīʿī was already active among the Kutāma Berbers of the Lesser Kabylia mountains in the Maghrib (in present-day Algeria). The *dāʿī* Abū ʿAbd Allāh too, had originally belonged to the Imāmī community of Kūfa; he and his elder brother, Abu'l-ʿAbbās, were converted in Iraq by the *dāʿī* Abū ʿAlī. Ibn Ḥawshab sent other *dāʿī*s to Yamāma, Egypt and Baḥrayn to propagate Ismailism.

The initiation of the *daʿwa* in the west-central and northwestern parts of Persia, the region designated generally as the Jibāl by the Arabs, also dates to the early 260s/870s. Khalaf al-Ḥallāj was the first *dāʿī* of the Jibāl, sent there by the central leader of the Ismaili movement. Khalaf established himself in the area of Rayy (to the south of modern-day Tehran), where an important Imāmī community already existed; and it continued to serve for a long time as the headquarters of the *da'wa* in the Jibāl. Under Khalaf's successors, the *da'wa* spread to Qumm – another important Imāmī centre in Persia – Kāshān, Hamadān and other towns of the Jibāl. However, the efforts of these *dā'ī*s to mobilise rural support for insurrectional purposes proved futile; the successes of the Ismailis of Iraq were not to be repeated in Persia. The *dā'ī*s of the Jibāl soon adopted a new policy, targeting the elite and the ruling classes. After its initial success in the Jibāl, the same policy was adopted by the *dā'ī*s of Khurāsān and Transoxania. Ghiyāth, the third *dā'ī* of Rayy, extended the *da'wa* to Khurāsān on his own initiative. His chief deputy was the learned theologian-philosopher Abū Ḥātim Aḥmad b. Ḥamdān al-Rāzī, who in time became the chief *dā'ī* of Rayy, his native land. Abū Ḥātim further extended the Ismaili (Qarmaṭī) mission to Ādharbāyjān, in northwestern Persia, and to various provinces of Daylam in northern Persia, including Gīlān, Ṭabaristān and Gurgān. Abū Ḥātim succeeded in converting several Daylamī *amīr*s as well as the governor of Rayy.

The Ismaili mission was officially established in Khurāsān during the last decade of the 3rd century/903–13. Ghiyāth, as noted, had already propagated Ismailism there, but now a certain Abū 'Abd Allāh al-Khādim was dispatched as the first *dā'ī* of Khurāsān; he established his secret headquarters at Nīshāpūr. One of the later chief *dā'ī*s of Khurāsān, al-Ḥusayn b. 'Alī al-Marwazī, was an eminent *amīr* in the service of Sāmānids and as such, he readily extended the *da'wa* to the districts under his control, including Maymana, Harāt, Gharjistān and Ghūr; he also transferred the provincial *da'wa* headquarters from Nīshāpūr to Marw al-Rūdh (present-day Bālā Murghāb in northern Afghanistan). Al-Ḥusayn al-Marwazī's successor as chief *dā'ī* of Khurāsān was the Central Asian Muḥammad b. Aḥmad al-Nasafī. A highly learned theologian-philosopher, al-Nasafī introduced a form of Neoplatonism into Ismaili thought. He moved his base of operations to his native town of Nakhshab (Arabic, Nasaf) and then to Bukhārā, the Sāmānid capital (in present-day Uzbekistan), whence he propagated the *da'wa* within Transoxania. Al-Nasafī's success was crowned by his conversion of the Sāmānid *amīr* Naṣr II b. Aḥmad (301–31/914–43), as well as his vizier and other dignitaries at the Sāmānid court. However, al-Nasafī's success was short-lived. In the aftermath of the revolt of the Turkish soldiers, who deposed Naṣr, the *dā'ī* al-Nasafī and his associates were executed in Bukhārā in 332/943. Their co-religionists too were severely persecuted under Naṣr's son and successor Nūḥ I (331–43/943–54), who appeased the Sunni *'ulamā'* and called for a *jihād* or holy war against the Qarmaṭī "heretics". Despite these setbacks, the *da'wa* survived in Khurāsān and

Early Imāmī and Ismaili Imams

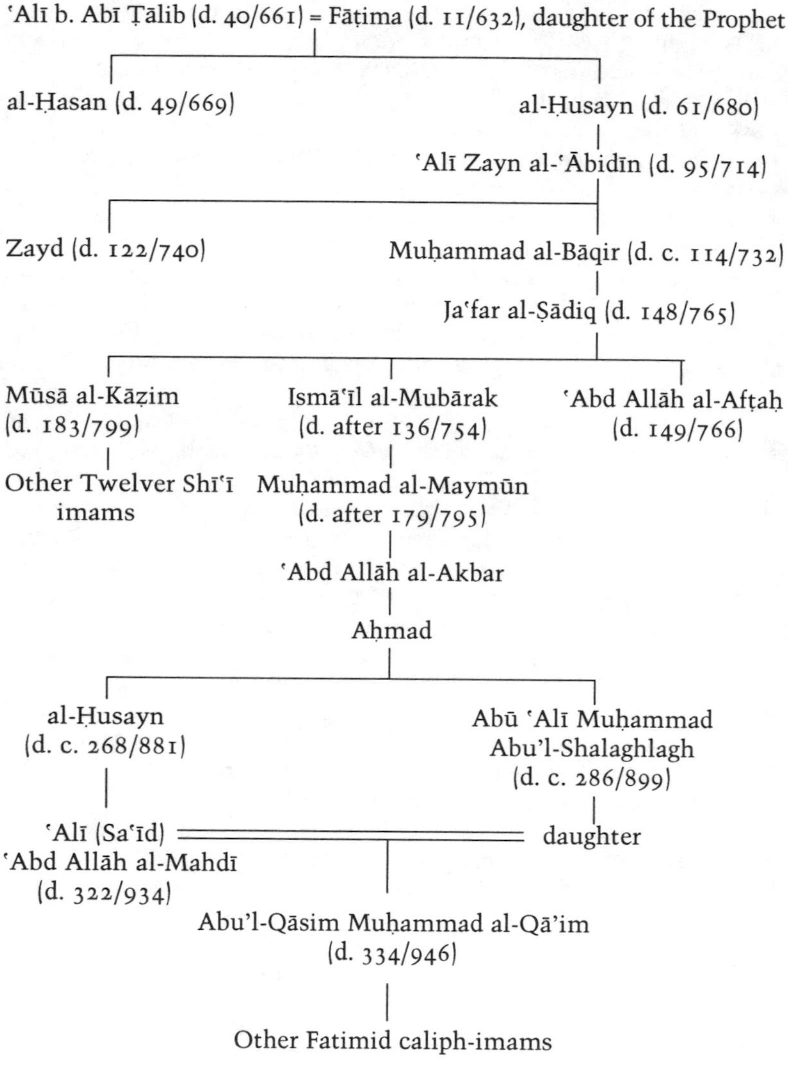
'Alī b. Abī Ṭālib (d. 40/661) = Fāṭima (d. 11/632), daughter of the Prophet
al-Ḥasan (d. 49/669)
al-Ḥusayn (d. 61/680)
'Alī Zayn al-'Ābidīn (d. 95/714)
Zayd (d. 122/740)
Muḥammad al-Bāqir (d. c. 114/732)
Ja'far al-Ṣādiq (d. 148/765)
Mūsā al-Kāẓim (d. 183/799)
Ismā'īl al-Mubārak (d. after 136/754)
'Abd Allāh al-Afṭaḥ (d. 149/766)
Other Twelver Shī'ī imams
Muḥammad al-Maymūn (d. after 179/795)
'Abd Allāh al-Akbar
Aḥmad
al-Ḥusayn (d. c. 268/881)
Abū 'Alī Muḥammad Abu'l-Shalaghlagh (d. c. 286/899)
'Alī (Sa'īd) 'Abd Allāh al-Mahdī (d. 322/934)
daughter
Abu'l-Qāsim Muḥammad al-Qā'im (d. 334/946)
Other Fatimid caliph-imams

Transoxania under the leadership of other *dāʿī*s, including especially Abū Yaʿqūb Isḥāq b. Aḥmad al-Sijistānī.[23]

In the meantime, ʿAbd Allāh al-Akbar had died in Salamiyya at an unknown date after 261/874. He was succeeded in the leadership of the Ismaili movement by his son Aḥmad, about whom almost nothing is known. Aḥmad had two sons, al-Ḥusayn and Muḥammad, also known as al-Ḥakīm and Abu'l-Shalaghlagh. According to Ismaili tradition, Aḥmad was in turn succeeded by al-Ḥusayn, who seems to have re-established a foothold in ʿAskar Mukram. Al-Ḥusayn died prematurely around 268/881, when his son ʿAlī, the future Fatimid caliph ʿAbd Allāh al-Mahdī, was only eight years old and left in the care of his paternal uncle Muḥammad. At any rate, on al-Ḥusayn's death the leadership of the movement fell for many years into the hands of Muḥammad b. Aḥmad, guardian and spiritual father to his nephew ʿAlī (ʿAbd Allāh); hence the *kunya* Abū ʿAlī. In time, Muḥammad gave one of his daughters to ʿAlī; and it was out of this marriage that al-Qā'im, the second Fatimid caliph-imam, was born in Salamiyya in 280/893. There are indications that Muḥammad b. Aḥmad attempted several times, in vain, to usurp the leadership for his own sons. However, ʿAlī (ʿAbd Allāh) himself eventually took charge of the affairs of the Ismaili *daʿwa* in 286/899, or shortly earlier, on the death of his uncle Muḥammad b. Aḥmad. The new leader, henceforth referred to as ʿAbd Allāh al-Mahdī, immediately proceeded to issue new instructions to his *dāʿī*s, reflecting a drastic change in the *daʿwa* policy.

It was in reaction to the new policy that the Ismaili movement of the 3rd/9th century was split into two rival factions, the loyal Ismailis and the dissident Qarmaṭīs.

THE SCHISM OF 286/899 AND ITS CONSEQUENCES

By the early 280s/890s, a unified Ismaili movement had completely replaced the earlier Kūfa-based splinter groups. The leaders of this newly organised *daʿwa*, as noted, made every effort to conceal their identity, propagating a revolutionary messianic message in the name of the hidden Imam-Mahdi Muḥammad b. Ismāʿīl whose advent was eagerly anticipated. In 286/899, soon after ʿAbd Allāh al-Mahdī's accession to leadership, Ḥamdān detected significant changes in the written instructions received from Salamiyya. Consequently, he dispatched his lieutenant, ʿAbdān, on a fact-finding mission. It was only after arriving at the headquarters of the Ismaili *daʿwa* in Salamiyya that ʿAbdān learned of the recent accession of ʿAbd Allāh, whom he met in due course. To his astonishment, ʿAbdān discovered that instead of acknowledging the Mahdiship of Muḥammad b. Ismāʿīl, the new leader now claimed the imamate for himself and his ancestors, the same individuals who had actually organised and led the Ismaili movement after Muḥammad b. Ismāʿīl. On receiving ʿAbdān's report, Ḥamdān renounced his allegiance to the central leadership in Salamiyya, and ordered his subordinate *dāʿī*s in Iraq to suspend all activities in their districts. Soon after, Ḥamdān disappeared, while ʿAbdān was murdered at the instigation of Zikrawayh b. Mihrawayh, a major *dāʿī* in Iraq who had remained loyal to Salamiyya. The sources indicate that all these events occurred in the year 286/899.[24]

ʿAbd Allāh al-Mahdī's reform is also explained in his already-noted letter addressed to the Ismaili community of Yaman. In this letter, written after al-Mahdī's accession to the Fatimid caliphate and preserved in an isolated instance by Jaʿfar b. Manṣūr al-Yaman, an Ismaili scholar, ʿAbd Allāh in fact attempts to reconcile his reform with the actual course of events in earlier Ismaili history, divulging for the first time some of the missionary tactics of his predecessors. As explained in this letter, and corroborated by the few surviving early Ismaili sources,[25] the central leaders of the Ismaili movement before ʿAbd Allāh al-Mahdī had actually assumed the rank of *ḥujja*, proof or full representative, of the absent Imam-Mahdi Muḥammad b. Ismāʿīl. And it was through the *ḥujja* that the Ismailis could establish contact with the hidden imam. By his reform ʿAbd Allāh had, thus, elevated the ranks of himself and his predecessors from *ḥujja*s of the expected Mahdi to imams, also explaining that the individuals in question had all along secretly regarded themselves as the legitimate imams from the progeny of Jaʿfar al-Ṣādiq, but they had not divulged this for security reasons.

These points are elaborated in various ways in ʿAbd Allāh's letter, which explains that as a form of *taqiyya* his predecessors had assumed different pseudonyms such as Mubārak (the Blessed One) and Maymūn (the Fortunate One), also disguising themselves as the *ḥujja*s of the absent imam in order to escape Abbasid persecution. ʿAbd Allāh, who himself used the code-name of Saʿīd (the Happy One), further states that the earlier belief in the Mahdiship of Muḥammad b. Ismāʿīl had in fact been a misunderstanding. The leaders before him, he emphasises, had been so successful in their *taqiyya* practices that the Ismailis themselves had come to believe in the Mahdiship of Muḥammad b. Ismāʿīl, conceived merely as one of these dissimulating measures. The name Muḥammad b. Ismāʿīl, he now reveals, was a code-name referring to every true imam in the progeny of Jaʿfar al-Ṣādiq, rather than to his particular grandson who actually bore that name. The Mahdiship of Muḥammad b. Ismāʿīl was a collective nomenclature encompassing the Mahdiship of all the legitimate imams in Ja'far al-Ṣādiq's progeny. 'Abd Allāh's letter also contained some controversial statements regarding his own 'Alid genealogy, which need not concern us here, especially since they were not confirmed by his successors in the Fatimid dynasty.

The reform of 'Abd Allāh al-Mahdī split the unified Ismaili movement into two rival factions. One faction remained loyal to the central leadership, accepting 'Abd Allāh's explanation that the Ismaili imamate had been handed down among his ancestors. These loyal Ismailis, later known as Fatimid Ismailis, thus maintained the doctrine of continuity in the imamate, later adopted as the official Fatimid Ismaili doctrine. Accordingly the Fatimid Ismailis recognised three hidden imams (*al-a'imma al-mastūrīn*) between Muḥammad b. Ismā'īl and 'Abd Allāh al-Mahdī. This loyalist camp included the bulk of the Ismailis of Yaman and those communities loyal to the central leadership and founded in North Africa, Egypt and Sind by *dā'ī*s sent by Ibn Ḥawshab. The reform was, on the other hand, rejected by a faction of the community. The dissidents retained their original belief in the Mahdiship of Muḥammad b. Ismā'īl. Henceforth, the term Qarāmiṭa came to be applied specifically to the dissident Ismailis, who did not acknowledge as imams 'Abd Allāh al-Mahdī and his predecessors, as well as his successors in the Fatimid dynasty. Before long, leaders of various Qarmaṭī communities claimed the Mahdiship for themselves or others, with catastrophic results for Qarmaṭism in general. The dissident Qarmaṭī faction comprised the communities in Iraq, Baḥrayn and most of those situated in the Iranian lands.[26] It should be noted, however, that pockets of dissidence existed for some time in Yaman, while loyal groups were to be found alongside the dissident Qarmaṭī communities of Iraq and the eastern Iranian lands.

In Iraq, the Qarmaṭīs were left in a state of confusion following the disappearance of Ḥamdān and the demise of 'Abdān. Soon, 'Īsā b. Mūsā, a relative of 'Abdān, rose to a position of leadership among them and revived the Qarmaṭī *da'wa* in southern Iraq in the name of the hidden Mahdi. In 313/925, Abbasid officials in Baghdad found white clay seals on several captured Qarmaṭīs bearing the expression "*Muḥammad ibn Ismā'īl al-imām al-mahdī walī Allāh*".[27] However, Qarmaṭism does not seem to have survived in Iraq long after the middle of the 4th/10th century. 'Īsā b. Mūsā and other Qarmaṭī *dā'ī*s of Iraq ascribed their own writings to 'Abdān, perhaps in order to stress doctrinal continuity.[28] In Baḥrayn, Abū Sa'īd al-Jannābī sided with Ḥamdān and 'Abdān, and later he claimed to represent the expected Mahdi. Abū Sa'īd in fact established his rule over Baḥrayn in the same eventful year 286/899; he founded the independent Qarmaṭī state of Baḥrayn which survived until 470/1077.

Abū Sa'īd was murdered in 300/913, and subsequently several of his sons rose to the leadership of the Qarmaṭī state in Baḥrayn. Under his youngest son Abū Ṭāhir Sulaymān (311–32/923–44), the Qarmaṭīs of Baḥrayn became notorious for their raids into Iraq and their regular pillaging of the Meccan pilgrim caravans. Abū Ṭāhir's ravaging activities culminated in his attack on Mecca during the pilgrimage season in 317/930, when the Qarmaṭīs massacred the pilgrims and committed numerous desecrating acts in the most sacred places of Islam for a whole week. They also dislodged the Black Stone (*al-ḥajar al-aswad*) from the corner of the Ka'ba and carried it to al-Aḥsā', their new capital in Baḥrayn where Abū Ṭāhir had already begun to build a *dār al-hijra*. This sacrilegious act, presumably committed in preparation for the coming of the Qarmaṭīs' Mahdi, shocked the entire Muslim world and provided a unique opportunity for Ibn Rizām and other anti-Ismaili polemicists to condemn Ismailism as a conspiracy to destroy Islam; they also alleged that Abū Ṭāhir had secretly received his instructions from 'Abd Allāh al-Mahdī who was then reigning as the first Fatimid caliph in North Africa.

Modern scholarship has shown, however, that the Qarmaṭīs of Baḥrayn were at the time, like other Qarmaṭī communities, predicting the imminent appearance of the Mahdi and did not acknowledge the first Fatimid caliph, or any of his successors, as their imams. In fact, on the basis of certain astrological calculations the Qarmaṭīs had been predicting the advent of the Mahdi for the year 316/928; an event which according to contemporary Qarmaṭī doctrine would end the era of Islam and its law and initiate the final era in the history of mankind. This explains why Abū Ṭāhir sacked Mecca and then recognised the expected Mahdi in a young Persian, to whom he handed over the rule in 319/931. The Persian Mahdi, however, turned out to be a restorer of Persian religion. He abolished the *sharī'a* and Islamic worship, also condemning all prophets recognised in Islam. After some eighty days, when the Mahdi undertook the execution of Qarmaṭī notables of Baḥrayn, Abū Ṭāhir was finally obliged to seize and kill him, admitting that the Mahdi had been an impostor. The obscure episode of the "Persian Mahdi" seriously demoralised the Qarmaṭīs, also weakening the influence of the Qarmaṭī leaders of Baḥrayn over other Qarmaṭī communities. After this disastrous episode the Qarmaṭīs of Baḥrayn reverted to their former beliefs, and their leaders, once again, claimed to be acting on the orders of the hidden Mahdi. They eventually returned the Black Stone to its original place in Mecca in 339/950, for a large ransom paid by the Abbasids and not, as alleged by anti-Ismaili sources, in response to the Fatimid caliph's request.

The Ismailis of Yaman initially remained loyal to ʿAbd Allāh al-Mahdī. By 291/904, or possibly earlier, Ibn Ḥawshab's junior associate, Ibn al-Faḍl, displayed signs of disloyalty. In 299/911, after occupying Ṣanʿāʾ, Ibn al-Faḍl openly renounced his allegiance to ʿAbd Allāh, declared war on Ibn Ḥawshab, and possibly even claimed the Mahdiship for himself. However, he failed to coerce and win the collaboration of Ibn Ḥawshab who remained loyal until his death in 302/914. With Ibn al-Faḍl's demise in 303/915, the Qarmaṭī movement in Yaman disintegrated rapidly.

In Persia, Qarmaṭism continued to spread after 286/899. The *dāʿī*s of Rayy did not recognise the imamate of ʿAbd Allāh al-Mahdī, awaiting the return of Muḥammad b. Ismāʿīl as the expected Mahdi. Abū Ḥātim al-Rāzī, too, prophesied the Mahdi's advent for the year 316/928. As Abū Ḥātim's predictions did not materialise, he encountered serious hostilities from his co-religionists and was obliged to seek refuge with an *amīr* in Ādharbāyjān. He died there shortly afterwards in 322/934. Later, some rulers of Ādharbāyjān and Daylam, belonging to the Musāfirid (or Sallārid) dynasty, adhered to Qarmaṭism and recognised the Mahdiship of Muḥammad b. Ismāʿīl; this is attested by some rare Musāfirid coins dating from the year 343/954–5. In Khurāsān and Transoxania, too, dissident Qarmaṭism persisted after the establishment of the Fatimid state. The *dāʿī* al-Nasafī affirmed the Mahdiship of Muḥammad b. Ismāʿīl in his major treatise entitled *Kitāb al-maḥṣūl,* which soon acquired a prominent status within various Qarmaṭī circles.

In the meantime, the loyal *dāʿī* Zikrawayh b. Mihrawayh embarked on an adventurous campaign on behalf of ʿAbd Allāh al-Mahdī. Zikrawayh had gone into hiding following the events of the year 286/899, possibly in fear of reprisals by ʿAbdān's supporters. From 288/901, he sent several of his sons as *dāʿī*s to the Syrian desert where large numbers of bedouins were soon converted, especially from amongst the Banū Kalb who controlled the Samāwa region between Palmyra and the Euphrates.[29] There are different medieval and modern interpretations of Zikrawayh's intentions and activities. However, H. Halm has argued convincingly on the basis of diverse sources that Zikrawayh and his sons initially remained loyal to the Ismaili leader in Salamiyya, aiming to establish a Fatimid state for ʿAbd Allāh al-Mahdī without having received his prior authorisation.[30] This premature campaign in fact compromised al-Mahdī's position, since Zikrawayh's zealous sons revealed his true identity and summoned their bedouin followers to go to Salamiyya and pay homage to the imam. Indeed, it was to escape capture by the Abbasid agents that ʿAbd Allāh al-Mahdī secretly and hastily left Salamiyya in

289/902, at the height of Zikrawayh's success. Accompanied by his young son and future successor al-Qā'im, the chief *dā'ī* Fīrūz and a few attendants, al-Mahdī first went to Ramla, in Palestine, where he stayed for some time awaiting the outcome of Zikrawayh's adventures. Ja'far b. 'Alī, al-Mahdī's chamberlain (*ḥājib*), has left a valuable autobiographical account of this historic journey, which ended several years later in North Africa, and al-Mahdī's installation to the Fatimid caliphate.[31]

Initially Zikrawayh's sons and their army of Ismaili bedouins, who called themselves "the Fāṭimīs" (Fāṭimiyyūn), enjoyed much success in Syria. By 290/903, they captured Salamiyya, Ḥimṣ and several other towns of the Orontes region where they established a short-lived state in the name of 'Abd Allāh al-Mahdī. In these Ismaili-controlled towns, it was in the name of the Ismaili imam, and not the Abbasid caliph, that for the first time the *khuṭba* was read and coins minted. Zikrawayh's sons now established contacts with al-Mahdī in Ramla and attempted in vain to persuade him to return to Salamiyya and assume power. The Ismaili leader was not yet prepared to confront the Abbasids, and his prudence was soon justified. In 291/903, the Ismaili bedouins were routed almost completely by a major Abbasid army sent against them. It was in the immediate aftermath of this disastrous defeat that al-Ḥusayn b. Zikrawayh, then leading the bedouins, turned in anger against 'Abd Allāh al-Mahdī. He destroyed al-Mahdī's palace in Salamiyya, also killing his relatives and servants who had stayed behind. In 291/904, al-Ḥusayn was captured by the Abbasid troops and sent to the caliph in Baghdad, where he was interrogated under torture and revealed the identity and whereabouts of the Ismaili imam before being executed. Thereupon, the Abbasids launched a widespread search for 'Abd Allāh al-Mahdī who had meanwhile gone to Egypt. Following the demise of his sons, Zikrawayh himself emerged from hiding and attempted to revive his campaign, which had by now appropriated the characteristics of dissident Qarmaṭism. He was finally defeated in 294/907 in battle by the government troops in Iraq and died in captivity of his wounds.

EARLY ISMAILI DOCTRINES

The basic framework of an Ismaili system of religious thought was laid during the pre-Fatimid phase of Ismaili history. In fact, the Ismaili intellectual traditions had already acquired distinctive forms and expressions by 286/899 when Ismailism split into rival factions. As only a handful of Ismaili texts have survived from this early period, and as the literature of the Qarmaṭīs has disappeared almost completely, it is not possible to trace the development of early Ismailism in any great detail. Indeed, modern scholars still disagree on certain of its aspects. It is nevertheless possible to sketch a skeletal account of the fundamental intellectual traditions and the central teachings of the early Ismailis. These were expounded by the unified Ismaili movement during 261–86/874–99. Subsequently, the early doctrines were further developed by the Fatimid Ismailis who also modified or discarded aspects of early Ismailism, while the Qarmaṭīs followed a separate course.

The early Ismailis emphasised a fundamental distinction between the exoteric (*ẓāhir*) and the esoteric (*bāṭin*) aspects of the sacred scriptures, religious commandments and prohibitions. Earlier Shīʿī groups living in the 2nd/8th century in southern Iraq, including some of the Shīʿī *ghulāt*, had already formulated certain doctrines on the basis of this distinction which, however, found its greatest application in the Ismaili system of thought. Accordingly, the early Ismailis held that the revealed scriptures, including especially the Qur'an, and the laws laid down in them, had their apparent or literal meaning, the *ẓāhir*, which had to be distinguished from their inner meaning or true spiritual reality (*ḥaqīqa*), hidden in the *bāṭin*. They further held that the *ẓāhir*, or the religious laws enunciated by prophets, underwent periodical change while the *bāṭin*, containing the spiritual truths (*ḥaqā'iq*), remained immutable and eternal. These hidden truths were made apparent through *ta'wīl* or esoteric exegesis, the process of educing the *bāṭin* from the *ẓāhir* which amounted to leading the explainable ideas back to their origins. Although similar processes of exegeses or hermeneutics existed in earlier Judaeo-Christian as well as Gnostic traditions, the immediate antecedents of Ismaili *ta'wīl*, also known as *bāṭinī ta'wīl*, may be traced to the Shīʿī milieus of the 2nd/8th century in Iraq.

The early Ismailis further taught that in every age, the esoteric world of spiritual reality could be accessible only to the elite (*khawāṣṣ*) of mankind, as distinct from the common people (*ʿawāmm*) who were merely capable of perceiving and understanding the *ẓāhir*, the apparent meaning of the revelations. Accordingly, in the era of Islam, initiated by the Prophet Muḥammad, the eternal truths of religion could be explained only to those who had been properly initiated into the Ismaili community and recognised the teaching authority of the Prophet Muḥammad's *waṣī*, ʿAlī b. Abī Ṭālib, and the legitimate imams who succeeded him (as they represented the sole sources of *ta'wīl* in the era of Islam). The centrality of *ta'wīl* for the early Ismailis is attested by the fact that the bulk of their literature is comprised of the *ta'wīl* genre of writing which seeks justification for Ismaili doctrines in Qur'anic verses.

Initiation into Ismailism, known as *balāgh*, took place after the novice had taken an oath of allegiance, known as *ʿahd* or *mīthāq*. The initiates were bound by their oath to keep secret the *bāṭin*, imparted to them by a hierarchy (*ḥudūd*) of teachers authorised by the imam. The *bāṭin* was thus not only hidden but also secret, and its knowledge had to be kept away from the uninitiated common people, the non-Ismailis who were not capable of understanding it. Initiation into the Ismaili community was gradual, also involving the payment of certain dues for receiving instructions. The *Kitāb al-ʿālim wa'l-ghulām* (*Book of the Teacher and the Pupil*), one of the few surviving early texts attributed to Ibn Ḥawshab Manṣūr al-Yaman or his son Jaʿfar, contains valuable details on this process of initiation;[32] but there is no evidence of any system of fixed (seven or more) initiation stages, as claimed by anti-Ismaili polemicists.

By exalting the *bāṭin* and the truths (*ḥaqā'iq*) contained therein, the early Ismailis came to be regarded by the rest of the Muslim society as the most representative Shīʿī community expounding esotericism in Islam, hence their common designation as the Bāṭiniyya. It should, however, be noted that this designation was often used abusively by anti-Ismaili sources which accused the Ismailis in general of ignoring the *ẓāhir*, or the commandments and prohibitions of Islam. The available evidence, including the fragmentary texts of the Ismaili oath of allegiance,[33] clearly shows that the early Ismailis were not exempted in any sense from adhering to the *sharīʿa* and its rituals and prescriptions. On the contrary, early Ismaili teachings did accord equal significance to both the *ẓāhir* and the *bāṭin* and their inseparability, ideas that were later fully elaborated in the Ismaili teachings and texts of the Fatimid period. Such accusations of *ibāḥa* or antinomianism levelled against the early Ismailis seem to have been rooted in the hostilities of their enemies, who also blamed the entire Ismaili movement for the anti-Islamic views and practices of the Qarmaṭīs, especially those of Baḥrayn. Sunni polemicists deliberately and groundlessly attributed to the early Ismailis certain views propounded by the early Shīʿī *ghulāt*, who evidently taught that the prescriptions of the *sharīʿa* no longer applied to those Muslims who knew and obeyed the rightful imam of the time.

The Ismailis taught that the eternal truths (*ḥaqā'iq*) hidden in the *bāṭin*, in fact, represented the true message common to Judaism, Christianity and Islam. The truths of the monotheistic religions recognised in the Qur'an had, however, been veiled by different exoteric laws as required by changing temporal circumstances. Fully aware of their "ecumenical" approach, the early Ismailis developed the broader implications of these truths in terms of a gnostic system of thought, a system that represented an elegant and distinctly Ismaili esoteric world of spiritual reality. The two main components of this system were a cyclical history of revelation and a gnostic cosmological doctrine.

By the early 280s/890s, the Ismailis had already developed a cyclical interpretation of time and the religious history of mankind, which they applied to the Judaeo-Christian revelations as well as certain other pre-Islamic religions. They had a particular, semi-cyclical and semi-linear, conception of time. They conceived of time as a progression of successive cycles or eras with a beginning and an end. On the basis of their eclectic temporal view, reflecting Greek, Judaeo-Christian and Gnostic influences as well as Shīʿī eschatological ideas, the Ismailis developed a view of religious history in terms of the eras of different prophets recognised in the Qur'an. This view was also combined with their doctrine of the imamate which had been essentially inherited from the earlier Imāmī Shīʿīs.

According to their cyclical view, the Ismailis believed that the religious history of mankind proceeded through seven prophetic eras (*dawrs*) of various durations, each one inaugurated by a speaker or enunciator (*nāṭiq*) of a divinely revealed message which in its exoteric (*ẓāhir*) aspect contained a religious law, *sharīʿa*. The *nāṭiq*s of the first six eras of human history were Adam, Noah (Nūḥ), Abraham (Ibrāhīm), Moses (Mūsā), Jesus (ʿĪsā) and Muḥammad. These *nāṭiq*s had announced the outer (*ẓāhir*) aspects of each revelation with its rituals, commandments and prohibitions, without explaining details of its inner (*bāṭin*) meaning. For that purpose, each *nāṭiq* was succeeded by a legatee (*waṣī*), also called the silent one (*ṣāmit*) and later the foundation (*asās*), who revealed only to the elite the esoteric truths (*ḥaqā'iq*) contained in the inner (*bāṭin*) dimension of that era's message. The first six *waṣī*s of human history were Seth (Shīth), Shem (Sām), Ishmael (Ismāʿīl), Aaron (Hārūn), Simon Peter (Shamʿūn al-Ṣafā') and ʿAlī b. Abī Ṭālib. In every era, each *waṣī* was, in turn, succeeded by seven imams, also called *atimmā'* (singular, *mutimm*, completer), who guarded the true meaning of the divine scriptures and laws in both their *ẓāhir* and *bāṭin* aspects. The seventh imam (or *mutimm*) of every era would rise in rank to become the *nāṭiq* of the following era, abrogating the *sharīʿa* of the previous era and proclaiming a new one. This pattern would change only in the seventh, final *dawr* of history.

In the sixth *dawr*, the era of Islam, Muḥammad b. Ismāʿīl was the seventh imam who had gone into concealment as the Mahdi. On his return, he would become the seventh *nāṭiq*, initiating the final era. However, unlike the previous speakers, Muḥammad b. Ismāʿīl would not bring a new *sharī'a* to replace the sacred law of Islam. Instead, as is expected in the final eschatological age, his mission would consist of fully revealing to all mankind the hitherto hidden esoteric truths of all the preceding revelations. Muḥammad b. Ismā'īl would, thus, unite in himself the ranks of *nāṭiq* and *waṣī*, also being the last of the imams, the eschatological Imam-Mahdi. In the final, millenarian age of pure spiritual knowledge, the *ḥaqā'iq* would be completely freed from all their veils and symbolisms. In the messianic age of the Mahdi, there would no longer be any distinction between the *ẓāhir* and the *bāṭin*, the letter of the law and its inner spirituality. On his advent, heralding the end of time, Muḥammad b. Ismā'īl would rule in justice before the physical world is consummated.[34]

It was in the light of such doctrines, rooted in a syncretic and ecumenical worldview, that the early Ismailis developed their system of thought, a system that appealed not only to Muslims belonging to different communities of interpretation and social strata but also to a diversity of non-Islamic religious communities. Of all the Muslim communities only the Ismailis accommodated so comprehensively and overtly, in their cyclical scheme of history, the Judaeo-Christian traditions as well as a variety of other pre-Islamic religions, notably Zoroastrianism and Mazdakism which were at the time still enjoying some prominence in the Iranian world. In this connection it is interesting to note that many of the so-called Khurramiyya or Khurramdīniyya groups active in the Iranian lands during the early Abbasid centuries were attracted to the Ismaili movement. These groups, scattered from Ādharbāyjān to Khurāsān and Central Asia, amalgamated Islamic teachings with Iranian religious traditions and sentiments, and politically they shared with the Ismailis a common enmity towards the Abbasids. The propagation of the Mahdiship of Muḥammad b. Ismā'īl, as noted, made its key contribution in giving the early Ismaili *da'wa* a great deal of messianic appeal in Muslim milieus, especially amongst the Imāmī Shī'īs. Deliverance in this world and salvation in the hereafter would, thus, be almost guaranteed upon proper initiation into Ismailism. It was on the basis of such teachings that a unified Ismaili movement developed rapidly after the middle of the 3rd/9th century.

'Abd Allāh al-Mahdī's doctrinal reform introduced important modifications to the cyclical view of history propounded by the early Ismailis. In fact, after the schism of 286/899, while the dissident Qarmaṭīs continued to adhere to the earlier scheme, the loyal Fatimid Ismaili camp developed a different conception of the sixth era of religious history, the era of Islam. By introducing continuity in the imamate, 'Abd Allāh al-Mahdī had allowed for more than one heptad of imams in the era of Islam. In effect, the seventh era, earlier defined as the spiritual age of the Mahdi, had now completely lost its messianic appeal for the Fatimid Ismailis. The final age, whatever its nature, was henceforth postponed indefinitely into the future; and the functions of the Mahdi or *qā'im* who would initiate the Day of Resurrection (*yawm al-qiyāma*) at the end of time, were similar to those envisaged by other Muslim communities.

The Qarmaṭīs, by contrast, retained their original belief in the Mahdiship of Muḥammad b. Ismā'īl and his role as the seventh *nāṭiq*. After the schism of 286/899, they made specific predictions about his advent. Indeed, the Qarmaṭīs were intensely preoccupied with such prophesies and the circumstances of the seventh era which would supersede the era of Islam. For instance, al-Nasafī in his *Kitāb al-maḥṣūl* conceived of that era as an age without a religious law. He also seems to have maintained that the era of Islam had ended with the first coming of Muḥammad b. Ismā'īl. In other words, according to the Qarmaṭī *dā'ī* al-Nasafī, the seventh era had already commenced in his time. The Qarmaṭīs' sack of Mecca and the disastrous episode of the "Persian Mahdi" in Baḥrayn should also be viewed in this context. All these developments, of course, proved catastrophic for the Qarmaṭī movement, undermining its chances for lasting success in the Muslim world. As noted, they were also seized upon by Sunni polemicists to accuse the entire Ismaili movement of libertinism and antinomianism.

The second main component of the early Ismaili *ḥaqā'iq* system was a cosmology. Developed during the second half of the 3rd/9th century, this cosmological doctrine seems to have been propagated orally in Ismaili circles. At any rate, the original cosmology is not elaborated in any known early Ismaili text. More than any other modern scholars, S. M. Stern and H. Halm have partially reconstructed and studied the original cosmology of the Ismailis on the basis of fragmentary evidence contained in later writings, notably a treatise by Abū 'Īsā al-Murshid, a Fatimid *dā'ī* and judge in Egypt of the time of the caliph-imam al-Mu'izz (341–65/953–75), certain references in Fatimid sources and allusions found in some contemporary Zaydī texts produced in Yaman.[35] According to Stern and Halm, the pre-Fatimid cosmology, representing essentially a gnostic cosmological myth, was espoused by the entire Ismaili movement until it was superseded in the 4th/10th century by a new cosmology of Neoplatonic provenance.

According to this early cosmological doctrine, God existed when there was no space, no eternity and no time. Through His intention (*irāda*) and will (*mashī'a*), He first created a light (*nūr*) and addressed it with the Qur'anic creative imperative *kun* (Be!), thus calling creation into being. Through duplication of its two letters, *kāf* and *nūn*, *kun* acquired its feminine form and became *kūnī*. On God's command (*amr*), Kūnī, the first creature, also called the preceder (*sābiq*), created from its light the second creature called Qadar (determination), to act as vizier and assistant to her. Qadar, also known as the follower (*tālī*), represented the male principle, in contradistinction to Kūnī as the female principle. Kūnī and Qadar were, thus, the first two principles of creation, identified with the Qur'anic terms "pen" (*qalam*) and "tablet" (*lawḥ*). Through Kūnī, God brought into being (*kawwana*) all things, and, through Qadar, He determined (*qaddara*) them; such ideas, derived on the basis of certain Qur'anic verses, were grossly misrepresented by the Zaydī authors of the early 4th/10th century, who report that at the time the Ismailis (Qarmaṭīs) of Yaman considered Kūnī and Qadar as their gods.[36]

The Arabic names of the primal pair, Kūnī and Qadar, were comprised of seven consonantal letters, also called the higher letters (*al-ḥurūf al-ʿulwiyya*); they were interpreted as the archetypes of the seven *nāṭiq*s and their messages, beginning with K for Adam and ending with R for Mahdi or *qā'im*. It was out of the original heptad of letters that all other letters and names emerged, and with the names there simultaneously appeared the very things they signified. God's creative activity by the intermediacy of the primal pair first brought forth the beings of the spiritual world, the pleroma. Corresponding to the seven *nāṭiq*s, Kūnī created from its light the seven Cherubim (*karūbiyya*), giving them esoteric names (*asmā' bāṭina*) whose meaning can only be understood by the "friends of God" (*awliyā' Allāh*) and the sincere believers who follow them, namely, the Ismailis. Then, on Kūnī's order, Qadar created and named twelve spiritual beings (*rūḥāniyya*) out of its light. The names of several spiritual beings are well known from Islamic angelology, including Riḍwān (guardian of Paradise), Mālik (angel of Hell), and the two funerary angels Munkar and Nakīr. The spiritual beings act as intermediaries between Qadar, in which Kūnī is veiled for creation, and the speaker-prophets and imams of human history. The first three spiritual beings – called Jadd (good fortune), Fatḥ (triumph) and Khayāl (imagination) – identified with the archangels Jibrā'īl (Gabriel), Mīkā'īl (Michael) and Isrāfīl (Sepraphiel), played a leading role in mediating between the spiritual world and the religious hierarchy in the physical world. These three spiritual beings, in fact, formed an important pentad with Kūnī and Qadar, linking the cosmology of the early Ismailis with their cyclical view of the religious history of mankind. This cosmological doctrine also accounted for the creation of the lower physical world. The material world, too, was created through the mediation of Kūnī and Qadar, starting with the creation of air and water, identified esoterically with Qur'anic terms "throne" (*ʿarsh*) and "chair" (*kursī*), and, then, of the seven skies, the earth, the seven seas and so on.

In this cosmology there are numerous parallelisms between the spiritual and the physical worlds; almost everything in the higher world corresponds to something in the lower world, such as correspondences between Kūnī and the sun, Qadar and the moon, the seven Cherubim and the seven skies, and the twelve spiritual beings and the twelve signs of the zodiac. The early Ismaili cosmology also had a key soteriological purpose. Man, who appears at the end of the process of creation, is far from his origin and from his Creator. This cosmology, thus, aimed to show the way for removing this distance and bringing about man's salvation. It could be achieved only if man acquired knowledge (Greek, *gnosis*) of his origin and the causes for his distance from God, a knowledge that has to be imparted from above by God's messengers (*nāṭiq*s), as recognised in the Qur'an.

The pre-Fatimid cosmology of the Ismailis contains all the essential characteristics of a gnostic system. Reminiscent of the system of the ancient Gnostics in which the first of God's creatures is usually feminine, here too the original Qur'anic creative command *kun* is transformed into its feminine form, *kūnī*. The progressive creation first of the spiritual and then of the physical world, and man's distance from God and his salvation through knowledge communicated to him by messengers, are other key features of this gnostic system. Indeed, many of its mythological themes and concepts, symbolic numbers and hermeneutic speculations have parallels in the systems of earlier Gnostics, such as the Samaritan and Mandaean systems developed in southern Iraq where the earliest Ismailis also flourished. It is clear that the early Ismailis derived many of their cosmological terminologies from the Qur'an and the Islamic tradition in general; there are also some Judaeo-Christian influences, such as the ultimate provenance of the Cherubim. More cannot be said, in our present state of knowledge, on the specific sources of the early Ismaili cosmology, which to a large extent seems to represent an original model.

The Muslim adversaries of the Ismailis from early on attempted to depict their doctrines as anti-Islamic, rooted extensively in non-Islamic traditions. Some of them even viewed Ismailism as an Iranian conspiracy, based on pre-Islamic beliefs and designed to subvert Islam from within. W. Madelung has well summed up the findings of modern scholarship here by stating that the claim of anti-Ismaili polemicists and heresiographers that Ismailism was rooted in various dualist religions, such as Zoroastrianism, Manichaeism, Mazdakism and the Khurramdīniyya, is not borne out by its early doctrines; Kūnī and Qadar do not reflect a cosmic dualism of light and darkness, or good and evil, as in some of these earlier religious traditions.[37] The available evidence does in fact show that the Ismailis had founded an Islamic gnostic tradition of their own, a tradition in which cosmology was closely connected to soteriology and a specific view of sacred history. In this system, man's salvation ultimately depended on his knowledge of God, the creation and his own origins, a knowledge that had been periodically made accessible to him afresh through special messengers.

NOTES

1. A modern exposition of a quintessentially Shī'ī account of the origins of Shī'ism, in the English language, is contained in Sayyid Muḥammad Ḥusayn Ṭabāṭabā'ī, *Shī'ite Islam*, ed. and tr. S. H. Nasr (London, 1975), especially pp. 39–73, 173–90. See also S. Husain M. Jafri, *Origins and Early Development of Shī'a Islam* (London, 1979), pp. 27–79, and W. Madelung, "Shī'a", EI2, vol. 9, pp. 420–4. More recently, Heinz Halm has produced a summary account of the relevant issues in his *Shiism*, tr. J. Watson (Edinburgh, 1991), pp. 1–28. The issues surrounding the succession to the Prophet and 'Alī's legitimate claims to leadership are thoroughly investigated afresh in a scholarly fashion in W. Madelung's *The Succession to Muḥammad: A Study of the Early Caliphate* (Cambridge, 1997).
2. E. Kohlberg, "Some Imāmī-Shī'ī Views on Taqiyya", JAOS, 95 (1975), pp. 395–402, reprinted in his *Belief and Law in Imāmī Shī'ism* (Aldershot, 1991), article III. Many interesting ideas on the early development of Imāmī Shī'ism are contained in M. A. Amir-Moezzi, *The Divine Guide in Early Shi'ism: The Sources of Esotericism in Islam*, tr. D. Streight (Albany, NY, 1994), especially pp. 5–97.
3. See Abū Ja'far Muḥammad b. Ya'qūb al-Kulaynī, *al-Uṣūl min al-kāfī*, ed. 'A. A. al-Ghaffārī (Tehran, 1388/1968), vol. 1, pp. 168–548, containing the earliest Shī'ī *ḥadīth*s on the imamate reported mainly from Ja'far al-Ṣādiq; many of the same Imāmī *ḥadīth*s are reiterated in al-Qāḍī al-Nu'mān, *Da'ā'im al-Islām*, ed. A. A. A. Fyzee (Cairo, 1951–61), vol. 1, pp. 1–98; see also Jafri, *Origins*, pp. 235–300, and M. Momen, *An Introduction to Shi'i Islam* (New Haven, 1985), pp. 147–60.
4. Al-Ḥasan b. Mūsā al-Nawbakhtī, *Kitāb firaq al-Shī'a*, ed. H. Ritter (Istanbul, 1931), pp. 37–41, 58–60; Sa'd b. 'Abd Allāh al-Qummī, *Kitāb al-maqālāt wa'l-firaq*, ed. M. J. Mashkūr (Tehran, 1963), pp. 50–5, 63–4, 81–2; H. Corbin, "Une liturgie Shī'ite du Graal", in *Mélanges d'histoire des religions offerts à Henri Puech* (Paris, 1974), especially pp. 83–93, reprinted in H. Corbin, *L'Iran et la philosophie* (Paris, 1990), pp. 190–207, and H. Halm, *Die islamische Gnosis* (Zurich and Munich, 1982), pp. 199–217.
5. Al-Nu'mān, *Da'ā'im*, vol. 1, pp. 49–50, and his *Kitāb al-majālis wa'l-musāyarāt*, ed. al-Ḥabīb al-Faqī et al. (Tunis, 1978), pp. 84–5.
6. Al-Qāḍī al-Nu'mān, *Sharḥ al-akhbār*, ed. S. M. al-Ḥusaynī al-Jalālī

(Qumm, 1409–12/1988–92), vol. 3, pp. 302, 309–10; Ja'far b. Manṣūr al-Yaman, *Sarā'ir wa-asrār al-nuṭaqā'*, ed. M. Ghālib (Beirut, 1984), pp. 256–7, 258; Idrīs 'Imād al-Dīn, *'Uyūn al-akhbār wa-funūn al-āthār*, ed. M. Ghālib (Beirut, 1973–84), vol. 4, pp. 332–50; Abū 'Amr Muḥammad b. 'Umar al-Kashshī, *Ikhtiyār ma'rifat al-rijāl*, as abridged by Muḥammad b. al-Ḥasan al-Ṭūsī, ed. Ḥ. al-Muṣṭafawī (Mashhad, 1348/1969), pp. 217–18, 321, 325–6, 354–6, 376–82, 390, and F. Daftary, "Esmā'īl b. Ja'far al-Ṣādeq", EIR, vol. 8, pp. 625–6.

7. Al-Kashshī, *Ikhtiyār*, pp. 244–5, and Aḥmad b. 'Alī al-Najāshī, *Kitāb al-rijāl* (Bombay, 1317/1899), pp. 81–2.
8. *Umm al-kitāb*, ed. W. Ivanow, in *Der Islam*, 23 (1936), text p. 11; Italian trans. P. Filippani-Ronconi, *Ummu'l-Kitāb* (Naples, 1966), p. 23. See also Halm, *Die islamische Gnosis*, pp. 113–98.
9. Al-Nu'mān, *Sharḥ*, vol. 3, p. 309; Ja'far b. Manṣūr al-Yaman, *Sarā'ir*, pp. 262–3; Idrīs 'Imād al-Dīn, *Zahr al-ma'ānī*, ed. M. Ghālib (Beirut, 1991), pp. 200–1; his *'Uyūn*, vol. 4, p. 334, and Muḥammad b. Muḥammad al-Mufīd, *Kitāb al-Irshād: The Book of Guidance*, tr. I. K. A. Howard (London, 1981), p. 431.
10. Ḥasan b. Nūḥ al-Bharūchī, *Kitāb al-azhār*, in 'Ādil al-'Awwā (ed.), *Muntakhabāt Ismā'īliyya* (Damascus, 1958), pp. 234–5, and Muḥammad Ḥusayn Farāhānī, *Safar-nāma*, ed. Ḥ. Farmān-Farmā'īyān (Tehran, 1342/1963), p. 288; English trans., *A Shī'ite Pilgrimage to Mecca 1885–1886*, ed. and tr. H. Farmayan and E. L. Daniel (Austin, 1990), p. 274.
11. Al-Nawbakhtī, *Kitāb firaq al-Shī'a*, pp. 57–8, 60–1, and al-Qummī, *Kitāb al-maqālāt*, pp. 80–1, 83. See also Abū Ḥātim al-Rāzī, *Kitāb al-zīna*, part 3, ed. 'Abd Allāh S. al-Sāmarrā'ī, in his *al-Ghuluw wa'l-firaq al-ghāliya* (Baghdad, 1988), pp. 287–9; Idrīs, *Zahr al-ma'ānī*, pp. 199ff., and F. Daftary, "The Earliest Ismā'īlīs", *Arabica*, 38 (1991), pp. 220ff.
12. Idrīs, *'Uyūn*, vol. 4, pp. 351–6, also his *Zahr al-ma'ānī*, pp. 204–8; English trans. in W. Ivanow, *Ismaili Tradition Concerning the Rise of the Fatimids* (London, etc., 1942), pp. 240–8. See also al-Kulaynī, *al-Uṣūl*, vol. 1, pp. 485–6, and al-Kashshī, *Ikhtiyār*, pp. 263–5.
13. The earliest Ismaili reference to this genealogy may be found in Aḥmad b. Ibrāhīm al-Nīsābūrī, *Istitār al-imām*, ed. W. Ivanow, in *Bulletin of the Faculty of Arts, University of Egypt*, 4, part 2 (1936), p. 95; English trans. Ivanow, in his *Ismaili Tradition*, p. 162. See also 'Abd Allāh al-Mahdī's letter addressed to the Ismaili community of Yaman, as edited and translated into English by Ḥusayn F. al-Hamdānī in his *On the Genealogy of Fatimid Caliphs* (Cairo, 1958), text p. 10. A better translation of this letter, together with a complex hypothesis on the genealogy of the Fatimids, is contained in A. Hamdani and F. de Blois, "A Re-Examination of al-Mahdī's Letter to the Yemenites on the Genealogy of the Fatimid Caliphs", JRAS (1983), pp. 173–207.
14. Ibn al-Nadīm, *Kitāb al-fihrist*, p. 238; tr. Dodge, *The Fihrist*, vol. 1, pp. 462–4; Ibn al-Dawādārī, *Kanz al-durar*, vol. 6, ed. Ṣ. al-Munajjid (Cairo, 1961), pp. 17–20; Aḥmad b. 'Alī al-Maqrīzī, *Itti'āẓ al-ḥunafā' bi-akhbār al-a'imma al-Fāṭimiyyīn al-khulafā'*, ed. J. al-Shayyāl and M. Ḥ. M. Aḥmad (Cairo, 1967–73), vol. 1, pp. 22–6; al-Maqrīzī's *Kitāb al-muqaffā al-kabīr*, ed. M. al-Ya'lāwī (Beirut, 1987), pp. 56–9, 70, 73–81, and Shihāb al-Dīn Aḥmad b. 'Abd al-Wahhāb al-

Nuwayrī, *Nihāyat al-arab fī funūn al-adab*, vol. 25, ed. M. J. ʿA. al-Ḥīnī et al. (Cairo, 1984), p. 189.

15. W. Ivanow, *The Alleged Founder of Ismailism* (Bombay, 1946), and his *Ibn al-Qaddah* (2nd edn, Bombay, 1957). See also H. Halm, "ʿAbdallāh b. Maymūn al-Qaddāḥ", EIR, vol. 1, pp. 182–3, and W. Madelung, "Maymūn b. al-Aswad al-Ḳaddāḥ", EI2, vol. 6, p. 917.
16. Al-Nīsābūrī, *Istitār al-imām*, ed. Ivanow, pp. 93–107; English trans. in Ivanow, *Ismaili Tradition*, pp. 157–83.
17. See H. Halm, "Les Fatimides à Salamya", *Revue des Etudes Islamiques*, 54 (1986), especially pp. 141–9, and J. H. Kramers and F. Daftary, "Salamiyya", EI2, vol. 8, pp. 921–3.
18. Modern scholarship on the central doctrine of the early Ismailis dates back to the pioneering studies of S. M. Stern and W. Madelung; see in particular Stern's "Ismāʿīlīs and Qarmaṭians", in *L'Elaboration de l'Islam* (Paris, 1961), pp. 99–108, reprinted in his *Studies*, pp. 289–98, and Madelung's "Das Imamat in der frühen ismailitischen Lehre", *Der Islam*, 37 (1961), especially pp. 43–65.
19. In the 4th/10th century, the Imāmīs formulated their doctrine of the twelve imams, starting with ʿAlī b. Abī Ṭālib and ending with Muḥammad b. al-Ḥasan, recognised as the Mahdi whose emergence is still awaited. With this doctrine, Twelver Shīʿism began to be distinguished from the earlier Imāmī Shīʿism. Owing to the prominence of the Twelver Shīʿīs, however, the terms Imāmiyya and Ithnāʿashariyya gradually became synonymous while the Ismailis, too, have continued to use the term Imāmī in reference to their own community. See E. Kohlberg, "From Imāmiyya to Ithnāʿashariyya", BSOAS, 39 (1976), pp. 521–34, reprinted in his *Belief and Law*, article XIV.
20. As preserved in al-Nuwayrī, *Nihāyat al-arab*, vol. 25, pp. 189ff.; Ibn al-Dawādārī, *Kanz*, vol. 6, pp. 44ff., and al-Maqrīzī, *Ittiʿāẓ*, vol. 1, pp. 151ff.
21. Muḥammad b. Jarīr al-Ṭabarī, *Taʾrīkh al-rusul waʾl-mulūk*, ed. M. J. de Goeje et al. (Leiden, 1879–1901), III, pp. 2124ff.; English trans., *The History of al-Ṭabarī*: Volume XXXVII, *The ʿAbbāsid Recovery*, tr. Philip M. Fields (Albany, NY, 1987), pp. 169ff.
22. Al-Qāḍī al-Nuʿmān, *Iftitāḥ al-daʿwa*, ed. W. al-Qāḍī (Beirut, 1970), pp. 32–54; ed. F. Dachraoui (Tunis, 1975), pp. 2–26; H. Halm, "Die Sīrat Ibn Ḥaušab: Die ismailitische *daʿwa* im Jemen und die Fatimiden", WO, 12 (1981), pp. 107–35, and his "Ebn Ḥawšab", EIR, vol. 8, pp. 28–9.
23. The most detailed account of the initiation of the Ismaili *daʿwa* in the Jibāl and Khurāsān is contained in Niẓām al-Mulk, *Siyar al-mulūk*, pp. 282–95, 297–305; English trans. Darke, *Book of Government*, pp. 208–18, 220–6. The best modern treatment of the subject is to be found in S. M. Stern, "The Early Ismāʿīlī Missionaries in North-West Persia and in Khurāsān and Transoxania", BSOAS, 23 (1960), pp. 56–90, reprinted in his *Studies*, pp. 189–233.
24. Al-Nuwayrī, *Nihāyat al-arab*, vol. 25, pp. 227–32; Ibn al-Dawādārī, *Kanz*, vol. 6, pp. 65–8; al-Maqrīzī, *Ittiʿāẓ*, vol. 1, pp. 167–8, and Ibn Ḥawqal, *Kitāb ṣūrat al-arḍ*, ed. J. H. Kramers (2nd edn, Leiden, 1938–9), p. 295; French trans. J. H. Kramers and G. Wiet, *Configuration de la terre* (Paris, 1964), vol. 2, p. 289. See also Madelung, "Das Imamat", pp. 59–65, 69ff., and F. Daftary, "A Major Schism in the

Early Ismāʿīlī Movement", *Studia Islamica*, 77 (1993), pp. 123–39.

25. Jaʿfar b. Manṣūr al-Yaman, *Kitāb al-kashf*, ed. R. Strothmann (London, etc., 1952), pp. 97–9, 102 ff. See also Madelung, "Das Imamat", pp. 254–8.
26. On the subsequent history of some of these Qarmaṭī communities, especially the Qarmaṭīs of Baḥrayn, and their relations with the Fatimids, see W. Madelung, "Fatimiden und Baḥrainqarmaṭen", *Der Islam*, 34 (1959), pp. 34–88; English trans., "The Fatimids and the Qarmaṭīs of Baḥrayn", in F. Daftary (ed.), *Mediaeval Ismaʿili History and Thought* (Cambridge, 1996), pp. 21–73, a landmark in modern Ismaili studies; W. Madelung, "Ḳarmaṭī", EI2, vol. 4, pp. 660–5, and F. Daftary, "Carmatians", EIR, vol. 4, pp. 823–32.
27. Ibn al-Jawzī, *al-Muntaẓam fī ta'rīkh al-mulūk wa'l-umam*, ed. F. Krenkow (Hyderabad, 1357–62/1938–43), vol. 6, p. 195.
28. See Poonawala, *Biobibliography*, pp. 31–3, 45–6. Amongst such books, erroneously attributed to ʿAbdān, mention may be made of the *Kitāb shajarat al-yaqīn*, ed. ʿĀrif Tāmir (Beirut, 1982) which, as Walker has now shown, was in fact produced by a certain Abū Tammām, an obscure Qarmaṭī author who flourished in Khurāsān in the first half of the 4th/10th century. See Paul E. Walker, "Abū Tammām and his *Kitāb al-Shajara*: A New Ismaili Treatise from Tenth-Century Khurasan", JAOS, 114 (1994), pp. 343–52, and his "An Ismaʿili Version of the Heresiography of the Seventy-two Erring Sects", in Daftary, *Mediaeval Ismaʿili History*, pp. 161–77.
29. A detailed account of the activities of Zikrawayh and his sons is contained in al-Ṭabarī, *Ta'rīkh*, III, pp. 2218–26, 2230–2, 2237–46, 2255–66, 2269–75; English trans., *The History of al-Ṭabarī*: Volume XXXVIII, *The Return of the Caliphate to Baghdad*, tr. F. Rosenthal (Albany, NY, 1985), pp. 113–23, 126–9, 134–44, 157–68, 172–9. See also al-Nuwayrī, *Nihāyat al-arab*, vol. 25, pp. 246–76; Ibn al-Dawādārī, *Kanz*, vol. 6, pp. 69–90, and al-Maqrīzī, *Ittiʿāẓ*, vol. 1, pp. 168–79.
30. H. Halm, "Die Söhne Zikrawaihs und das erste fatimidische Kalifat (290/903)", WO, 10 (1979), pp. 30–53, and his *The Empire of the Mahdi: The Rise of the Fatimids*, tr. M. Bonner (Leiden, 1996), pp. 66–88, 183–90.
31. This autobiographical work, an eyewitness account of al-Mahdī's flight from Salamiyya to Sijilmāsa, was dictated later to Muḥammad b. Muḥammad al-Yamānī. The text of the *Sīrat al-Ḥājib Jaʿfar b. ʿAlī* was edited by W. Ivanow in *Bulletin of the Faculty of Arts, University of Egypt*, 4, part 2 (1936), pp. 107–33; English trans. in Ivanow, *Ismaili Tradition*, pp. 184–223; French trans. M. Canard, "L'Autobiographie d'un chambellan du Mahdī ʿObeidallāh le Fāṭimide", *Hespéris*, 39 (1952), pp. 279–324, reprinted in his *Miscellanea Orientalia* (London, 1973), article V.
32. The Arabic text of the *Kitāb al-ʿālim wa'l-ghulām* is included in M. Ghālib (ed.), *Arbaʿ kutub ḥaqqāniyya* (Beirut, 1983), pp. 13–75; and its abridged English translation, entitled "The Book of the Teacher and the Pupil", may be found in W. Ivanow, *Studies in Early Persian Ismailism* (2nd edn, Bombay, 1955), pp. 61–86. See also H. Corbin, "Un Roman initiatique Ismaélien", *Cahiers de Civilisation Médiévale*, 15 (1972), pp. 1–25, 121–42, and his "L'Initiation Ismaélienne ou l'ésotérisme et le Verbe", *Eranos Jahrbuch*, 39

(1970), pp. 41–142, reprinted in H. Corbin, *L'Homme et son ange* (Paris, 1983), pp. 81–205.

33. See H. Halm, "The Isma'ili Oath of Allegiance (*'ahd*) and the 'Sessions of Wisdom' (*majālis al-ḥikma*) in Fatimid Times", in Daftary, *Mediaeval Isma'ili History*, pp. 91–8.

34. Ibn Ḥawshab Manṣūr al-Yaman, *Kitāb al-rushd wa'l-hidāya*, ed. M. Kāmil Ḥusayn, in W. Ivanow (ed.), *Collectanea*: vol. 1 (Leiden, 1948), pp. 185–213; English trans. Ivanow, "The Book of Righteousness and True Guidance", in his *Studies*, pp. 29–59; Ja'far b. Manṣūr al-Yaman, *Kitāb al-kashf*, pp. 14ff., 103–4, 109–10, 113–14, 132–3, 138, 143, 150, 169–70. See also H. Corbin, "Le Temps cyclique dans le Mazdéisme et dans l'Ismaélisme", *Eranos Jahrbuch*, 20 (1951), pp. 149–217; English trans. in H. Corbin, *Cyclical Time and Ismaili Gnosis*, tr. R. Manheim and J. W. Morris (London, 1983), pp. 1–58; Paul E. Walker, "Eternal Cosmos and the Womb of History: Time in Early Ismaili Thought", IJMES, 9 (1978), pp. 355–66; H. Halm, "Dawr", EI2, Supplement, pp. 206–7, and F. Daftary, "Dawr", EIR, vol. 7, pp. 151–3.

35. S. M. Stern, "The Earliest Cosmological Doctrines of Ismā'īlism", in his *Studies*, pp. 3–29; H. Halm, *Kosmologie und Heilslehre der frühen Ismā'īlīya* (Wiesbaden, 1978), especially pp. 18–127, and his "The Cosmology of the Pre-Fatimid Ismā'īliyya", in Daftary, *Mediaeval Isma'ili History*, pp. 75–83. See also Ian R. Netton, *Allāh Transcendent: Studies in the Structure and Semiotics of Islamic Philosophy, Theology and Cosmology* (London, 1989), pp. 203–9.

36. The relevant Zaydī references are cited in C. van Arendonk, *Les Débuts de l'Imamat Zaidite au Yémen*, tr. J. Ryckmans (Leiden, 1960), pp. 330–4.

37. W. Madelung, *Religious Trends in Early Islamic Iran* (Albany, NY, 1988), p. 95, and his "Cosmogony and Cosmology: vi. In Isma'ilism", EIR, vol. 6, pp. 322–3.

3

The Fatimid Age: Dawla *and* Da'wa

OVERVIEW

The Fatimid period is often represented as the golden age of Ismailism, an "interlude" in Ismaili history. The foundation of the Fatimid caliphate in 297/909 in North Africa doubtless marked the crowning success of the early Ismailis. The religio-political *da'wa* of the Ismā'īliyya had finally led to the establishment of a state or *dawla* headed by the Ismaili imam. This was no small achievement. The leader of a secret revolutionary movement, having tactfully evaded confrontation with the military forces of the Abbasids, had been installed to a new Shī'ī caliphate. The establishment of the Fatimid caliphate represented not only a great success for the Ismailis, who had come to possess for the first time an important state under the leadership of their imam, but for the entire Shī'a as well. Not since the time of 'Alī had the Shī'a witnessed the succession of an 'Alid from the *ahl al-bayt* to the actual leadership of an important Muslim state. Fatimid victory, therefore, heralded the fulfilment of a long-awaited Shī'ī ideal, frustrated and postponed for more than two centuries by numerous defeats and setbacks.

The Ismaili imam had always claimed to possess sole legitimate religious authority as the divinely appointed and infallible spiritual guide of the Muslims; with the Abbasids, like the Umayyads before them, never more than usurpers, depriving the rightful 'Alid imams of their claims to leadership of the *umma*. With Fatimid victory in North Africa, however, events took a drastic turn in that remote corner of the Muslim world. By acquiring political power, and then transforming his nascent *dawla* into a flourishing and vast empire, the Ismaili imam presented his Shī'ī challenge to Abbasid hegemony and Sunni interpretations of Islam. Ismailism, too, now found its long-neglected place among the state-sponsored communities of interpretation in Islam. Henceforth, the Ismaili Fatimid caliph-imam could act as the spiritual spokesman of Shī'ī Islam in general, much like the Abbasid caliph had been the mouthpiece of Sunni Islam. And the situation of the Fatimids remained unchanged even after the coming to power, in the 320s/930s, of the Shī'ī Būyids (Buwayhids), not only because the Būyids themselves lacked 'Alid ancestry and did not lay any claims to religious authority, but more importantly because they permitted the now helpless Abbasid caliph to stay in power nominally as the titular head of Sunni Islam. When in the middle of the 5th/11th century the zealous Sunni Saljuqs replaced the Shīʿī Būyids as masters of the Abbasid caliphate, the status of the caliph in Baghdad as the titular head of Sunni Islam was not only reaffirmed but strengthened.

In the course of the Fatimid interlude, the Ismailis were permitted to practise their faith openly and without fearing persecution within Fatimid dominions, while outside the boundaries of their state they were obliged to observe *taqiyya* as before. In fact, with the establishment of the Fatimid *dawla*, the need had arisen for promulgating a state religion and a legal code, even though Ismailism was never to be imposed on Fatimid lands. Ismaili law, which had not existed during the earlier underground phase of Ismailism, was codified during the early Fatimid period. The Fatimid Ismailis now came to possess their own *madhhab* or school of religious law, similarly to the principal Sunni systems of jurisprudence and the Jaʿfarī system of the Imāmī (Twelver) Shīʿīs.

In line with their universal claims, the Fatimid caliph-imams did not abandon *daʿwa* activities on assuming power. Aiming to extend their authority and rule over the entire Muslim *umma* and others, they in fact retained a network of *dāʿī*s, operating on their behalf as religio-political missionaries both within and outside Fatimid dominions. The Fatimid caliph-imams particularly concerned themselves with the affairs of their *daʿwa* after transferring the seat of the state to Egypt; the conquest of Egypt itself in 358/969 represented an intermediary stage in the Fatimids' strategy of eastern expansion. Cairo, founded as a royal city by the Fatimids, became the headquarters of their complex hierarchical *daʿwa* organisation. Supreme leadership of the Ismaili *daʿwa* and the Fatimid *dawla* were the prerogatives of the Fatimid caliph-imam. Special institutions of learning and teaching were set up for the training of *dāʿī*s and instructing ordinary Ismailis. Educated as theologians, the Fatimid *dāʿī*s were at the same time the scholars and authors of their community, producing what were to become the classical texts of Ismaili literature dealing with a multitude of exoteric and esoteric subjects. The *dāʿī*s of the Fatimid period elaborated distinctive intellectual traditions. In particular, certain *dāʿī*s of the eastern, Iranian lands amalgamated Ismaili theology with different philosophical traditions into elegant and complex metaphysical systems of thought. Some of these Iranian *dāʿī*s ranked among the foremost Muslim philosophers of their time. It was indeed during this period that Ismailis made their most lasting contributions to Islamic theology and philosophy in general and to Shīʿī thought in particular. Modern recovery of their literature abundantly attests to the richness and diversity of the literary and intellectual heritage of the Ismailis of the Fatimid period.

The organisation of the Fatimid state remained relatively simple during its North African period, 297–362/909–73. But in Egypt, the Fatimids developed complex administrative and financial systems, drawing on centralised models adopted earlier by the Abbasids. The central administration of the Fatimids, headed by the caliph and his vizier, was comprised of a number of *dīwān*s, ministries or departments, including the *dīwān al-amwāl*, the ministry of finance, the *dīwān al-jaysh*, the department of the army, and the *dīwān al-inshā'*, the chancery of state responsible for issuing and handling various types of official documents. Fatimid officials, in administrative, financial, military, judicial as well as religious institutions were organised in strict hierarchies in terms of their rank, insignia and order of precedence in public ceremonies. The Fatimids, in fact, developed an elaborate system of rituals and ceremonials, with corresponding symbols and processional characteristics.[1]

With occasional exceptions, the Fatimids pursued a policy of tolerance towards other religious and ethnic communities, a record hardly challenged under any other Muslim dynasty of the medieval period, not to mention the contemporary European experience. The Fatimid officials, including viziers, were generally selected on the basis of merit and qualification without any particular regard to religious affiliation or ethnic background. This policy explains why it was possible for several Christians, including Armenians, to succeed to the Fatimid vizierate, with numerous Jewish secretaries working in the Fatimid chancery. It was also not unusual for Sunni jurists to head the Fatimid judiciary as supreme judge (*qāḍī al-quḍāt*). All this, of course, contributed to the resiliency and efficiency of the Fatimid administrative system. However, the Fatimids' liberal ethnic policy of utilising the services of Berbers, Turks, Sūdānīs, Daylamīs and Arabs led to unsurmountable rivalries and factionalism in the army and administration, eventually providing a major cause of unrest and disorder in Fatimid Egypt.

The Fatimids established a vast network of trade and commerce after settling down in Egypt. In rivalry with the Abbasids who used the Persian Gulf for trading purposes, the Fatimids successfully developed another trade route to India passing through the Red Sea. In fact, they soon came to control all international trade between the Indian Ocean and the Mediterranean. As a result, the Fatimid treasury received substantial revenues, second only to its land tax (*kharāj*) income, from the customs duties levied on imports of spices and luxury goods from India, China and other parts of Asia. Fatimid commercial activities were at times accompanied, or perhaps even strongly motivated, by religious considerations and designs. In particular, Fatimid trade with western India resulted in the extension of the *da'wa* to Gujarāt under the initial leadership of the Ṣulayḥids of Yaman who acknowledged Fatimid suzerainty.

In Egypt the Fatimid caliphate acquired a substantial economic base, supported not only by trade and commerce but by a flourishing agricultural sector, dependent on the Nile, and a variety of domestic productive activities.[2] At the same time, items of high quality and artistic value produced in workshops and establishments throughout Fatimid Egypt, including woollen fabrics, linen, ceramics and items of glassware, retained permanent export markets in medieval Europe. The Fatimid *dā'ī*-author and traveller Nāṣir Khusraw, who visited Cairo during 439–41/1047–50, has left a vivid account of the enviable conditions in Egypt and the splendour of the Fatimid capital with its 20,000 shops and numerous bazaars, caravanserais and bathhouses, as well as its fine houses and gardens, all of which were eclipsed by the Fatimid palace with its high encircling walls; he also reports with astonishment that the drapers, moneychangers and jewellers of Egypt did not lock their shops due to the high degree of peace and safety prevailing in that country.[3] Indeed, political stability and economic prosperity enabled the Fatimid regime to mobilise the resources required to sustain the operations of its public administration, armies (*juyūsh*), and its vast fleet sailing throughout the Mediterranean. For much of the 5th/11th century, Fatimid Egypt was a major sea power, competing with the Byzantine empire from Sicily to the northern shores of Syria. However, high military expenditures eventually took their toll leading to a gradual deterioration of state finances and rioting by factions of the army.

In Egypt, the Fatimids patronised intellectual activities. They founded major libraries in Cairo, and, through their efforts, the Fatimid capital became a flourishing centre of Islamic scholarship, sciences, art and culture, in addition to playing a prominent role in international trade and commerce. All in all, the Fatimid period marked not only a glorious age in Ismaili history, but also one of the greatest eras in Egyptian and Islamic histories; and, as such, a milestone in the development of Islamic civilisation.

The Fatimids were not destined to realise their universal ideals. But they did manage, at least for a while, to have their suzerainty acknowledged from North Africa and Egypt to the Ḥijāz, Palestine and Syria. In the Ḥijāz, they supplanted the Abbasids as protectors of

Dynasty of the Fatimid Caliph-Imams (297–567/909–1171)

1. al-Mahdī (297–322/909–34)
2. al-Qā'im (322–34/934–46)
3. al-Manṣūr (334–41/946–53)
4. al-Mu'izz (341–65/953–75)
5. al-'Azīz (365–86/975–96)
6. al-Ḥākim (386–411/996–1021)
7. al-Ẓāhir (411–27/1021–36)
8. al-Mustanṣir (427–87/1036–94)
9. al-Musta'lī (487–95/1094–1101)
10. al-Āmir (495–524/1101–30)
11. al-Ḥāfiẓ
    as regent (524–6/1130–2)
    as caliph (526–44/1132–49)
12. al-Ẓāfir (544–9/1149–54)
13. al-Fā'iz (549–55/1154–60)
14. al-'Āḍid (555–67/1160–71)

Numbers designate the succession order of the Fatimid caliphs. The caliphs from al-Mahdī to al-Mustanṣir were recognised as imams by the contemporary Fatimid Ismailis and, subsequently, by all the Nizārī and Musta'lī Ismailis. After al-Mustanṣir, the Nizārīs and Musta'līs acknowledged different lines of imams; the Nizārīs did not recognise any of the later Fatimid caliphs as their imams. Al-Musta'lī and al-Āmir were recognised as imams by all Musta'lī Ismailis; the later Fatimid caliphs (11–14) were recognised as imams only by the Ḥāfiẓī Musta'lī Ismailis.

the holy cities of Mecca and Medina; and for one brief but memorable year, 450–1/1058–9, the *khuṭba* at the Friday sermon in Baghdad was recited in the name of the Fatimid caliph. Confronted with a multitude of internal and external difficulties, the Fatimid caliphate had already stumbled on a steady path of decline by the second half of the 5th/11th century, almost one century before its final demise. By then, however, Fatimid *dāʿīs* working in the central and eastern lands of Islam, from Syria to Central Asia, had achieved lasting successes. They had won the allegiance of a growing number of converts, in both urban and rural areas, throughout the Abbasid domain, including areas under the control of the Būyids, Saljuqs, Ṣaffārids, Ghaznawids and other dynasties emerging in the East. These converts acknowledged the Fatimid caliph as the rightful imam of the time. All surviving dissident Qarmaṭīs outside of Baḥrayn, too, had by then switched their allegiance to the Fatimid Ismaili *daʿwa*. It was essentially thanks to successes of Fatimid *dāʿīs*, such as Abū Yaʿqūb al-Sijistānī, Ḥamīd al-Dīn al-Kirmānī and Nāṣir Khusraw, as well as many lesser known ones, that Ismailism outlived the downfall of the Fatimid dynasty and caliphate, also surviving the challenges posed by the Sunni revival of the 5th/11th and 6th/12th centuries.

On the death of al-Mustanṣir in 487/1094, the Ismailis permanently subdivided into the Nizārī and Mustaʿlī factions, named after al-Mustanṣir's sons who claimed his heritage. Henceforth, the Nizārī and Mustaʿlī Ismailis followed separate lines of imams, and reunification was never achieved in the aftermath of this schism. The Nizārīs, as we shall see, acquired a territorial state in Persia and Syria, and enjoyed political prominence until the Mongols destroyed that state in 654/1256. By 526/1132, the Mustaʿlī Ismailis themselves were split into the Ṭayyibī and Ḥāfiẓī branches. Only the Ḥāfiẓī Mustaʿlīs recognised the later Fatimids as their imams.

The final phase of the Fatimid caliphate, 487–567/1094–1171, was a turbulent one. Reduced to Egypt proper, the Fatimid state was now almost continuously beset by political and economic crises worsened by intense factionalism and disorder within the Fatimid armies. The later Fatimids all died prematurely, and were no more than puppets in the hands of their viziers, who since the time of Badr al-Jamālī (d. 487/1094) held the effective reins of power in the Fatimid state. Ironically, it was left to the last Fatimid vizier Ṣalāḥ al-Dīn, Saladin of the occidental sources, to terminate Fatimid rule in 567/1171.

FOUNDATION AND CONSOLIDATION OF THE FATIMID CALIPHATE

ʿAbd Allāh al-Mahdī, as noted, had left Salamiyya in 289/902, shortly before the eruption of the devastating activities of Zikrawayh's sons and the Syrian bedouins. Soon afterwards al-Mahdī's identity and whereabouts became known to the Abbasids who launched a widespread chase to capture him. Consequently, the Ismaili leader once again fled from his temporary refuge in Ramla, capital of Palestine. Al-Mahdī's chamberlain Ja'far has left a detailed account of the remainder of his master's fateful journey. Early in 291/904 al-Mahdī's small party arrived in Egypt, then under the quasi-autonomous rule of the Ṭūlūnids. There, al-Mahdī was received by the chief local *dā'ī* Abū 'Alī, who had been spreading the *da'wa* in Egypt for some time. Ibn Ḥawqal, the well-informed geographer and traveller of the second half of the 4th/10th century who may have been in the service of the Fatimids, oddly reports that the *dā'ī* Abū 'Alī was none other than Ḥamdān Qarmaṭ.[4] If this contention is taken seriously, then it implies that subsequent to the schism of 286/899 Ḥamdān had switched back his allegiance once again to al-Mahdī and served him under a new identity.

Be that as it may, al-Mahdī stayed for about a year in the Ṭūlūnid capital of Fusṭāṭ or Old Cairo, retaining his earlier disguise as a Hāshimid merchant. In 292/905, the same Abbasid army that had defeated the bedouin converts of Zikrawayh's sons in Syria, another Ṭūlūnid dominion, was dispatched to Egypt to re-establish direct Abbasid rule. These developments made al-Mahdī's stay in Egypt untenable. Instead of heading to Yaman, as evidently expected all along by his travelling companions, the imam now decided to go to the Kutāma country in the Maghrib, where the *dā'ī* Abū 'Abd Allāh al-Shī'ī had already achieved much success. Al-Mahdī was probably deterred from going to Yaman, where a loyal Ismaili community headed by Ibn Ḥawshab Manṣūr al-Yaman awaited him, to avoid risking serious confrontations with the intensified Abbasid chase. It is also possible that dissident Qarmaṭī outbursts had already broken out in that part of southern Arabia, making the imam's settlement even more dangerous; this is attested by the fact that the chief *dā'ī* Fīrūz deserted the imam in Egypt and joined Ibn al-Faḍl, who soon became leader of the Qarmaṭī movement in Yaman.

At any rate, al-Mahdī now attached himself to a caravan of merchants travelling to the Maghrib. In Tripoli, he dispatched the *dā'ī* Abu'l-'Abbās ahead to the Kutāma country to inform Abū 'Abd Allāh, the younger brother of Abu'l-'Abbās, of his imminent arrival. However, the identity of Abu'l-'Abbās was discovered in Qayrawān (Kairouan) where he was seized and imprisoned by the Aghlabid rulers of Ifrīqiya, then instructed by their Abbasid overlords to search for the Ismaili imam and his companions. Once again, al-Mahdī was obliged to change his plans. Accompanied only by his son, al-Qā'im, and the faithful chamberlain Jaʿfar, al-Mahdī joined another caravan and, passing through southern Ifrīqiya in Shawwāl 292/August 905, he finally arrived at the remote town of Sijilmāsa (today's Rissani in southeastern Morocco). An important trading route on the Saharan fringes, Sijilmāsa was then ruled by the Khārijī Berber family of Banū Midrār. Al-Mahdī lived quietly for four years (292–6/905–9) in this prosperous town as one of the locality's many merchant residents, also maintaining contact with the *dāʿī* Abū ʿAbd Allāh who was now preparing to launch the final, military phase of his operations in the Maghrib.

Abū ʿAbd Allāh al-Ḥusayn b. Aḥmad, known as al-Shīʿī due to his religious persuasion, had been active as a *dāʿī* among the Kutāma Berbers of the Lesser Kabylia, in present-day eastern Algeria, since 280/893. Initially, he established himself in Īkjān, near Mīla, and propagated Ismailism in the name of the Mahdi. Subsequently, he transferred his headquarters to Tāzrūt, where he built a *dār al-hijra* for the Berber converts. Tāzrūt, a few kilometres to the southwest of Mīla, remained the seat of the *daʿwa* in the Maghrib for almost ten years; it was from there that the *dāʿī* al-Shīʿī converted the bulk of the Kutāma Berbers, also transforming the Kutāma tribal confederation into a disciplined army. The Kutāma warriors acquired much booty in the course of their raids and campaigns which, as in the case of the early Islamic wars of conquest, served as an important inducement for them to fight for the victorious *dāʿī*.

Shīʿī Islam had never taken deep root in the Maghrib, where the Berbers generally adhered to diverse schools of Khārijism while Qayrawān itself, founded as a garrison town and inhabited by Arab warriors, was the bastion of Mālikī Sunnism. Under such circumstances, the newly converted Berbers' understanding of Ismailism, which at the time still lacked a distinctive school of law, must have been rather superficial. It is reported that Abū ʿAbd Allāh exercised full authority in the affairs of his followers and enforced the *sharīʿa*, not without difficulty, on the Berbers who had their customary law. Adopting a simple lifestyle and displaying an exemplary behaviour, he treated the occasionally unruly and greedy Kutāma with utter strictness, meting out punishments (*ḥudūd*) as specified in the Qur'an for various offences. The *dāʿī* personally taught the Kutāma initiates, who addressed one another as brethren (*ikhwān*), Ismaili doctrines in regularly held lectures. These lectures were known as the "sessions of wisdom" (*majālis al-ḥikma*), since esoteric Ismaili doctrine was already referred to as "wisdom" (*ḥikma*). Abū ʿAbd Allāh instructed his subordinate *dāʿī*s to hold similar sessions in the areas under their individual jurisdiction, also insisting on the participation of women in these Ismaili lectures.[5]

By 290/903, Abū ʿAbd Allāh had commenced his conquest of Ifrīqiya, covering today's Tunisia and eastern Algeria. The Sunni Aghlabids had ruled over this part of the Maghrib, and Sicily, since 184/800 as vassals of the Abbasids. After seizing the entire Kutāma region, Abū ʿAbd Allāh embarked on systematic offensives against Ṭubna and other major towns of Ifrīqiya. By 296/908, the Kutāma army had achieved much success, effectively signalling the fall of Qayrawān, the Aghlabid capital. Under the circumstances, Ziyādat Allāh III, the last Aghlabid ruler, hastily abandoned the palace city of Raqqāda, in the suburbs of Qayrawān, and fled to Egypt. Thereupon, the palaces of Raqqāda were looted for a few days by the inhabitants of Qayrawān. On 1 Rajab 296/25 March 909, one day after the Kutāma warriors had taken possession of the Aghlabid palaces, Abū ʿAbd Allāh himself entered Raqqāda, and immediately received a delegation of the notables of Qayrawān who had come to congratulate the *dāʿī*'s victory. Abū ʿAbd Allāh and the Kutāma chiefs now took up residence in Raqqāda.

Acting as al-Mahdī's deputy, Abū ʿAbd Allāh al-Shīʿī governed Ifrīqiya for almost a whole year. One of his first deeds was to issue a general guarantee of amnesty and safe-conduct (*amān*) for the people of Qayrawān, also celebrating the victory of the "helpers of the truth" (*anṣār al-ḥaqq*), as his Ismaili Kutāma Berbers were called. He immediately appointed new governors to every city, and introduced the Shīʿī form of *adhān* or call to prayer. In the *khuṭba* at the Friday sermon, too, he added the blessings on the *ahl al-bayt;* but withheld the name of al-Mahdī, who was still in Sijilmāsa. Abū ʿAbd Allāh's newly struck coins heralded the arrival of God's proof (*ḥujjat Allāh*), reflecting the earlier Imāmī Shīʿī tradition of using the terms *ḥujja*, or *ḥujjat Allāh*, and *imām* synonymously. Abū ʿAbd Allāh's chief assistant was his brother Abu'l-ʿAbbās Muḥammad, freed in the meantime from prison in Qayrawān. A learned *dāʿī* of high intellectual calibre, Abu'l-ʿAbbās held public disputations with the leading Mālikī Sunni jurists (*faqīhs*) of Qayrawān in that city's Great Mosque, expounding the Shīʿī foundations of the new regime and the legitimate rights of the *ahl al-bayt* to leadership of the Muslim *umma*. The ground was thus being rapidly laid also doctrinally for the establishment of a new Shīʿī caliphate.

Having secured his control over Ifrīqiya, Abū ʿAbd Allāh set off at the head of his army towards Sijilmāsa, in Ramaḍan 296/June 909, to hand over the reins of power to al-Mahdī. On his way, he caused the downfall of yet another local dynasty of the Maghrib, the Khārijī Rustamids of Tāhart in western Algeria. Abū ʿAbd Allāh arrived in Sijilmāsa some two months later. Al-Mahdī, who had been shortly earlier placed under house arrest by the Midrārid *amīr* there, was then set free and permitted to unite with his *dāʿī*. The Kutāma readily took control of Sijilmāsa, where al-Mahdī was acclaimed as caliph in special ceremonies that lasted several days in Dhu'l-Ḥijja 296/August 909. With these events, the period of concealment (*dawr al-satr*) in early Ismailism came to an end.

In Muḥarram 297/October 909, al-Mahdī set off for Ifrīqiya and made his triumphant entry into Raqqāda on 20 Rabīʿ II 297/4 January 910. On the same day, he was acclaimed as ruler by the notables of Qayrawān and the Kutāma Berbers. On the following day, Friday 21 Rabīʿ II 297/5 January 910, the *khuṭba* was pronounced for the first time in all the mosques of Qayrawān in the name of ʿAbd Allāh Abū Muḥammad, mentioning his full titles, namely, *al-imām al-mahdī bi'llāh* (the imam rightly guided by God) and *amīr al-mu'minīn* (commander of the faithful).[6] At the same time, a manifesto was read out from the pulpits announcing that the imamate had finally come to be vested in the *ahl al-bayt*. As one of the first acts of the new regime, the jurists of Ifrīqiya were instructed to give their legal opinions in accordance with the Shīʿī principles of jurisprudence, paying particular attention to the teachings of the Imam Jaʿfar al-Ṣādiq. The Ismaili teaching sessions for men and women, initiated by Abū ʿAbd Allāh, also continued under the direction of Aflaḥ b. Hārūn al-Malūsī, an Ismaili Kutāma Berber appointed as the judge of Raqqāda. The Shīʿī caliphate of the Fatimids now officially commenced in distant Ifrīqiya. The new dynasty came to be known as Fatimid (Fāṭimiyya), derived from the Prophet's daughter Fāṭima, to whom al-Mahdī and his successors traced their ʿAlid ancestry.

The first four Fatimid caliph-imams, ruling from Ifrīqiya, encountered numerous difficulties whilst consolidating their power. In addition to the continued animosity of the Abbasids, and the Umayyads of Spain, who as rival claimants to the caliphate had their own designs for North Africa, the Fatimids had numerous military encounters with the Byzantines in Sicily and elsewhere. Closer to home, the early Fatimids were obliged to devote much of their energy to subduing the rebellions of the Khārijī Berbers, especially those belonging to the Zanāta confederation, and the hostilities of the Sunni inhabitants of Qayrawān and other cities of Ifrīqiya led by their influential Mālikī jurists. All this made it extremely difficult for the early Fatimids to secure control over any region of the Maghrib, beyond the heartland of Ifrīqiya, for any extended period.

The first challenge to al-Mahdī issued from an entirely unexpected quarter, however. The *dāʿī* Abū ʿAbd Allāh had enjoyed absolute authority in the Maghrib, and had made himself popular with the Kutāma Berbers. But the arrival of the imam resulted in a drastic curtailment of the *dāʿī*'s authority and freedom to initiate policies. Soon, disagreements developed between the caliph-imam and the *dāʿī*. Aside from the limits now imposed on Abū ʿAbd Allāh's authority, there were also policy differences at issue, especially regarding taxation matters. It was under such circumstances that about a year after his accession al-Mahdī discovered that Abū ʿAbd Allāh and his brother were conspiring against him in alliance with certain Kutāma chieftains. In 298/911, al-Mahdī reacted swiftly and had the conspirators executed. The demise of the architect of Fatimid victory was, indeed, reminiscent of the fate of Abū Muslim al-Khurāsānī in the aftermath of the Abbasid revolution. In both cases, revolutionary *dāʿī*s who had paved the way for the installation of new dynasties proved incapable of adjusting themselves to the post-revolutionary aims and policies of their masters, affirming that the requirements of a successful *daʿwa* differed from the exigencies of a *dawla*. Al-Mahdī acted with equal speed and resolve to subdue a Kutāma revolt that erupted after Abū ʿAbd Allāh's demise. He was now the undisputed leader of the new regime, and the various clans of Kutāma Berbers henceforth served the Fatimids loyally as the backbone of their armies.

Soon after his accession, al-Mahdī proclaimed his son, who had accompanied him on the long journey from Salamiyya, as his heir-designate. That al-Mahdī's successor bore the name Abu'l-Qāsim Muḥammad b. ʿAbd Allāh, the Prophet's name, attests to the lasting importance of early Ismaili ideas and expectations relating to the appearance of the Mahdi or *qā'im*, ideas which had circulated in some form also among the Ismaili Berbers of the Maghrib. In this connection it may be recalled that according to Shīʿī traditions, the name of the Mahdi or *qā'im*, the restorer of true Islam from among the *ahl al-bayt*, was expected to be precisely identical with the Prophet's name. The choices of the regnal titles al-Mahdī bi'llāh and al-Qā'im bi-Amr Allāh for the first Fatimid caliph-imam and his successor indicate that the expectations of the emergence of the eschatological Mahdi and circumstances of his rule were still widespread among the Ismaili Berbers at the time of al-Mahdī's accession. The earlier changes in al-Mahdī's name from ʿAlī and Saʿīd to ʿAbd Allāh, and in al-Qā'im's name from ʿAbd al-Raḥmān to Muḥammad, allowing al-Qā'im to bear the Prophet's name, should be seen in the same context. Meanwhile, the Qarmaṭīs had retained their belief in the Mahdiship of Muḥammad b. Ismāʿīl; they did not recognise their expected Mahdi in the founder of the Fatimid dynasty.

As an expression of Fatimid universalism, al-Mahdī from early on concerned himself with extending his dominions eastwards. The conquest of Egypt, then ruled by the Ikhshīdids who recognised Abbasid suzerainty, would represent the first phase in that eastern strategy of conquest which occupied the Fatimids intermittently for half a century before success was finally achieved in 358/969. By 308/921, al-Mahdī had settled in his new eponymous capital city of Mahdiyya. He had personally selected the site of this royal city on the coastline of Ifrīqiya. The oldest Fatimid architectural structures are still preserved in the modern-day small town of Mahdiyya in Tunisia, including especially the mosque built there by al-Mahdī. As successors to the Aghlabids, the Fatimids inherited their fleet as well as the island of Sicily in southern Italy. Thus, from early on, the Fatimid state was also a sea power with Mahdiyya serving as a naval base equipped with a shipyard. Fatimid fleets operated extensively throughout the Mediterranean, where they vied with Byzantium for supremacy. The Fatimids appointed governors to Sicily (Ṣiqilliyya), who played an important role in transmitting Islamic culture to Europe. From 336/948, Fatimid Sicily was ruled for almost one century by the semi-independent vassal dynasty of the Kalbids. It was eventually lost to the Normans in 463/1070.

Having laid the foundations of Fatimid rule, extended in his time from present-day Algeria and Tunisia to the Libyan coast of Tripolitania, ʿAbd Allāh al-Mahdī died in 322/934, and was succeeded by his son al-Qā'im. The second Fatimid caliph-imam continued his father's policies of consolidation. It was in his reign that the prolonged revolt of the Khārijī Berbers erupted and almost succeeded in bringing about the downfall of the new dynasty.

Drawing on a variety of regional, tribal and religious conflicts, this Khārijī revolt was organised and led by Abū Yazīd Makhlad b. Kaydād, from an important branch of the Zanāta Berbers who had their rivalries with the Ṣanhāja Berbers, Fatimid supporters. Known as "the man on the donkey" (*ṣāḥib al-ḥimār*), because of his preference for riding on a donkey, while in Fatimid sources he was referred to as the *Dajjāl*, the great deceiver of the Islamic tradition, Abū Yazīd eventually succeeded to the leadership of the Nukkārī Ibāḍī community of the Khārijīs in the Maghrib. Departing from the moderate teachings of the Ibāḍī Khārijīs, however, he propagated as a matter of policy the assassination of religio-political adversaries together with their women and children. Abū Yazīd launched his anti-Fatimid revolt in 332/943 and his Khārijī Zanāta Berbers swiftly overran Ifrīqiya seizing Qayrawān, whose Sunni inhabitants had initially lent their support to the rebels. In due course, Abū Yazīd besieged Mahdiyya itself, but failed to storm the Fatimid capital. It was in the midst of this revolt that al-Qā'im died in 334/946 and was succeeded by his son Abū Ṭāhir Ismāʿīl, who adopted the regnal title of al-

Manṣūr bi'llāh. Al-Manṣūr personally took the field for several years against Abū Yazīd, who had meanwhile been abandoned by the Sunni inhabitants of Ifrīqiya due to the ravaging excesses of his unruly Khārijī fighters. In 336/947, al-Manṣūr decisively defeated Abū Yazīd and uprooted the remnants of his movement.[7] Having saved the Fatimid state, al-Manṣūr died prematurely in 341/953, at the age of thirty-nine, after a brief reign of only seven years.

Al-Manṣūr, the first Fatimid caliph-imam to have been born in Ifrīqiya, built a new city named Manṣūriyya, after himself. The royal city of Manṣūriyya, situated near the village of Ṣabra to the south of Qayrawān, served as the Fatimid capital from 337/948, when al-Manṣūr settled there, until al-Manṣūr's son and successor al-Mu'izz transferred the seat of the state to the newly founded city of Cairo in 362/973. Manṣūriyya, with its palaces, al-Azhar Mosque and gates, served as a model for Cairo. In subsequent times, Manṣūriyya was abandoned and left to be used as a quarry by the inhabitants of Qayrawān; today nothing remains of this Fatimid capital except what modern archaeological excavations have unearthed of its original circular layout and other foundational structures.

FATIMID ACHIEVEMENTS UNDER AL-MU'IZZ

Fatimid rule was firmly established in North Africa only during the reign of the fourth Fatimid caliph-imam Abū Tamīm Ma'add al-Mu'izz li-Dīn Allāh (341–65/953–75). Taking advantage of the pacification and stability of the state, secured largely by the loyalty of the Kutāma and Ṣanhāja Berbers, al-Mu'izz was able to pursue successful policies of war and diplomacy, resulting in territorial expansion and peaceful relations with the local dynasties in North Africa. His overall aim, however, was to extend the universal authority and hegemony of the Fatimids *vis-à-vis* their major rivals, namely, the Umayyads of Spain, the Byzantines and above all, the Abbasids. The sources abound in their praises of al-Mu'izz's statesmanship and diplomatic skills. He was also an organiser and contributed significantly to the development of the state's political, administrative and financial institutions. All in all, al-Mu'izz played a crucial role in transforming the Fatimid caliphate from a regional power into a great empire as well as "promoting the rise of intellectual and artistic life and initiating the development of a brilliant civilisation which reached its full flowering on the banks of the Nile".[8]

Al-Mu'izz was well versed in literary and scholarly matters and himself composed a number of epistles,[9] in addition to scrutinising the writings of al-Qāḍī al-Nu'mān (d. 363/974), the foremost Ismaili jurist of the Fatimid period. He was also the first member of his dynasty to concern himself specifically with the propagation of Ismailism outside Fatimid dominions; and he attempted, with some success, to win the allegiance of dissident Qarmaṭīs of the eastern lands. The policies of al-Muʿizz, including those pertaining to theological and juristic issues, are amply documented in the works of al-Qāḍī al-Nuʿmān and in the biography of Jawdhar (d. 362/973), a servant and confidant to the first four Fatimid caliph-imams.[10]

While the Sunni polemicists intensified their anti-Ismaili campaign after the establishment of the Fatimid caliphate, claiming the Ismailis did not observe the *sharīʿa* since they had found access to its hidden meaning, the Fatimids from early on concerned themselves increasingly with legalistic matters. In fact, Ismaili literature of the Fatimid period in various ways underlines the inseparability of the *ẓāhir* and the *bāṭin*, the external commandments and prohibitions of the law and their inner spiritual significance. However, the early Fatimids confronted a fundamental practical problem in that there did not exist a distinctly Ismaili school of jurisprudence. Earlier, the dissimulating Ismailis belonged to a covert revolutionary movement, observing the law of the land wherever they lived. The process of codifying Ismaili law started in al-Mahdī's reign when the precepts of Shīʿī law were put into practice. It is reported that Aflaḥ b. Hārūn al-Malūsī, the first chief judge (*qāḍī al-quḍāt*) of the Fatimid state under al-Mahdī, composed a few treatises on *fiqh* or jurisprudence. In this connection, it is interesting to note that from the time of Aflaḥ, the Fatimid chief judge was also often placed in charge of the affairs of the *daʿwa* as chief *dāʿī* (*dāʿī al-duʿāt*). Thus, responsibilities for explaining and enforcing the *ẓāhir* or the letter of the law and interpreting its *bāṭin* or inner meaning, were united in one and the same person under the overall guardianship and guidance of the imam of the time.

The promulgation of an Ismaili *madhhab* resulted mainly from the efforts of al-Qāḍī Abū Ḥanīfa al-Nuʿmān b. Muḥammad b. Manṣūr al-Tamīmī, better known as al-Qāḍī al-Nuʿmān, officially commissioned by al-Muʿizz to prepare legal compendia.[11] Al-Nuʿmān started serving the Fatimids in different capacities from the time of al-Mahdī, and in 337/948 he was appointed by al-Manṣūr to the highest judicial office of the Fatimid state. In 343/954, al-Muʿizz confirmed al-Nuʿmān's status as chief judge, also authorising the learned jurist to hold the "sessions of wisdom" every Friday after the noon prayers.[12] Al-Nuʿmān codified Ismaili law by systematically collecting the firmly established legal *ḥadīths* transmitted from the *ahl al-bayt*, drawing on the Imāmī works of al-Kulaynī and other earlier authorities. The results of his initial endeavours appeared in a massive compendium entitled *Kitāb al-īḍāḥ*, which has not survived except for one small fragment. Subsequently, he produced several abridgements of the *Īḍāḥ*, treated as semi-official compendia by the Fatimids. His efforts culminated in the compilation of the *Daʿāʾim al-Islām* (*The Pillars of Islam*), which was read carefully by al-Muʿizz and endorsed as the official code of the Fatimid state. Al-Muʿizz, in fact, urged everyone to study and copy the *Daʿāʾim*, also read regularly in the weekly *majālis al-ḥikma*.[13] Similarly to the Sunnis and non-Ismaili Shīʿī communities, the Ismailis, too, had now come to possess a system of law and jurisprudence, also delineating an Ismaili paradigm of governance.

As developed by al-Nuʿmān, Ismaili law accorded special importance to the central Shīʿī doctrine of the imamate. This doctrine finds a clear expression in the *Daʿāʾim al-Islām*'s opening chapter on *walāya*, which deals with the necessity of acknowledging the rightful imam of the time and provides Islamic legitimation for an ʿAlid state ruled by the family of the Prophet.[14] As a result, the authority of the infallible ʿAlid imam and his teachings became the third principal source of Ismaili law, after the Qur'an and the *sunna* of the Prophet which are accepted as the first two sources by all Muslim communities. Thus, al-Nuʿmān elaborated the *ẓāhirī* doctrinal basis of the Fatimids' legitimacy as ruling imams, also lending support to their universal claims. Al-Qāḍī al-Nuʿmān, as noted, drew on numerous earlier sources, both Shīʿī and Sunni, for collecting and sifting *ḥadīth* and developing the Fatimid legal code. As a result, strong Imāmī (Twelver) and Zaydī Shīʿī influences are present in the legal system elaborated in the *Daʿāʾim al-Islām*, which also tended to reconcile certain differences between the doctrines of the Ismailis and those upheld by the Mālikī Sunni school of jurisprudence prevailing in Ifrīqiya.[15] In a sense, al-Nuʿmān, guided closely by al-Muʿizz, recognised the minoritarian status of the Ismailis in North Africa and attempted a legalistic rapprochement with Sunni Islam, presumably aiming to reduce the precarious isolation of the Ismailis as a ruling class in the midst of predominantly non-Ismaili surroundings. Al-Nuʿmān was also the founder of a distinguished family of chief judges in the Fatimid state, but, subsequently, there did not occur any noteworthy developments in Ismaili law. The *Daʿāʾim al-Islām* has continued throughout the centuries to be used by the Ṭayyibī Mustaʿlī Ismailis as their principal authority in legal matters. On the other hand, the Nizārī Ismailis have been guided in their legalistic affairs by current imams.

Al-Muʿizz concerned himself with intensifying *daʿwa* activities outside Fatimid dominions, also aiming to win the allegiance of dissident Qarmaṭīs. In addition to preparing the ideological ground for Fatimid rule, al-Muʿizz's *daʿwa* policy was based on a number of more specific religio-political objectives. The Qarmaṭī propaganda circulating in Baḥrayn, Iraq and the Iranian lands generally undermined the Fatimid *daʿwa*, exacerbating the already dire predicament of the Fatimid *dāʿī*s. It was primarily owing to the teachings and practices of the Qarmaṭīs that Ismailis were accused in Sunni polemics of irreligiosity and lawlessness, especially after the Qarmaṭīs' sack of Mecca. There is evidence suggesting that the Qarmaṭī doctrines had also undesirable effects on the beliefs of certain Ismaili communities of the eastern lands which had hitherto acknowledged the imamate of the Fatimids. Finally, al-Muʿizz must have been aware of the military advantages of winning the formidable armies of the Qarmaṭīs of Baḥrayn to his side, a military coalition that would have greatly enhanced Fatimid chances of dealing with the Abbasids and their supporters.

In order to attain these objectives, al-Muʿizz attempted a tactful rapprochement with the Qarmaṭīs, and evidently recognised common aspects of their teachings upheld by the majority of the early Ismailis.[16] In particular, al-Muʿizz once again acknowledged Muḥammad b. Ismāʿīl as the Mahdi or *qāʾim*, but with a modified interpretation of his role. Since Muḥammad b. Ismāʿīl had appeared in an era of concealment (*satr*), he had been unable to accomplish the task of revealing the inner meaning of religious laws. This function, however, had been taken over by his deputies or *khulafāʾ*, who were his descendants. Initially, these deputies, too, had remained hidden, but starting with ʿAbd Allāh al-Mahdī they became manifest, and they would continue to rule until the end of the physical world. At any rate, Muḥammad b. Ismāʿīl himself was no longer expected to return as the *qāʾim*, as his deputies, the Fatimid caliph-imams, had already appropriated his functions.

The *daʿwa* strategy of al-Muʿizz proved to be rather successful, as the Fatimid cause was taken up actively outside the confines of the Fatimid state. However, al-Muʿizz was only partially successful in winning over the Qarmaṭī circles and neutralising their propaganda. In particular, the *dāʿī* Abū Yaʿqūb al-Sijistānī, hitherto belonging to the dissident Ismaili camp, was won over to the Fatimid side. As a result, large numbers of al-Sijistānī's followers in Khurāsān, Sīstān (Arabicised, Sijistān), Makrān and Central Asia, switched their allegiance to the Fatimid Ismaili imam. Al-Sijistānī was executed as a "heretic" by the Ṣaffārid *amīr* of Sīstān, Khalaf b. Aḥmad (352–93/963–1003), not long after 361/971. Fatimid Ismailism also gained a strong foothold in Sind, where Ismailism has survived to our times.

Around 347/958, through the efforts of a Fatimid *dāʿī* who had converted a local ruler, an Ismaili principality was established in Sind, with its seat at Multan (in present-day Pakistan) serving as a *dār al-hijra* for the Ismailis of that part of the Indian subcontinent. Large numbers of Hindus converted to Ismailism in this principality, where the *khuṭba* was read in the name of al-Muʿizz. Ismaili rule in Sind lasted until 396/1005 when Sultan Maḥmūd of Ghazna invaded Multan and persecuted the Ismailis. However, Fatimid Ismailism survived in Sind, and later received the protection of the Ismaili dynasty of the Sūmras, independent rulers based in Thatta, for almost three centuries.[17] On the other hand, Qarmaṭism persisted in certain parts of Persia, notably in Daylam and Ādharbāyjān, as well as in Iraq. Above all, al-Muʿizz did not succeed in winning the support of the Qarmaṭīs of Baḥrayn, who launched incursions into Palestine and Syria in 353/964 and thereafter posed an effective obstacle to the successful implementation of al-Muʿizz's eastward expansion.

In the meantime, al-Muʿizz had been making meticulous plans for the conquest of Egypt, an erstwhile and hitherto unrealised Fatimid desideratum. At the time, Egypt was beset by numerous economic and political crises; and, in 357/968 with the death of Kāfūr, effective ruler on behalf of the enfeebled Ikhshīdid dynasty, conditions deteriorated into anarchy. As part of the Fatimid design for subjugating Egypt, numerous *dāʿīs*, notably Abū Jaʿfar Aḥmad b. Naṣr, a wealthy merchant who spread the cause of the Fatimids in the Ikhshīdid capital of Fusṭāṭ, intensified their activities. They promised peace and prosperity under the Fatimids, then the most powerful rulers of North Africa and capable of delivering the Egyptians from their misery. Having acquired effective independence from the Abbasids, the Ikhshīdid regime could no longer be expected to receive assistance from the caliph in Baghdad whose own position was now being undermined by the Qarmaṭīs of Baḥrayn. It was under such circumstances that the last nominal ruler of Ikhshīdid Egypt, who had precariously established himself in Fusṭāṭ after Kāfūr's death, summoned al-Muʿizz to Egypt. Needless to add that the Fatimid response was swift.

Jawhar, a Fatimid freedman of Slav origins who had risen in ranks in his long service to the dynasty, was to lead the Egyptian expedition on al-Muʿizz's behalf. Jawhar had earlier proven his military and administrative capabilities in subduing rebellious local rulers throughout the Maghrib. The Fatimid army marched out of Raqqāda, after a special ceremony attended by al-Muʿizz, in Rabīʿ I 358/February 969, and arrived in Egypt some four months later. Jawhar did not encounter any resistance in Egypt. He set up camp outside of Fusṭāṭ, about two kilometres north of the Mosque of Ibn Ṭūlūn, and immediately entered into peace negotiations with a delegation of notables, including the capital's chief judge Abū Ṭāhir al-Dhuhlī, the *dāʿī* Abū Jaʿfar, and the heads of the Ḥasanid and Ḥusaynid ʿAlids of Egypt who had acknowledged the ʿAlid descent of the Fatimid caliph-imams. Jawhar issued a proclamation of safe-conduct (*amān*), guaranteeing the restoration of the true *sunna* of the Prophet and the safety of the pilgrimage routes, among other things. Later, the Fatimids gradually introduced the Ismaili *madhhab*, necessitating changes in the external aspects of certain rituals. But they never attempted forced conversion of their subjects and the bulk of Egyptians remained Sunni, belonging to the Shāfiʿī *madhhab*, in addition to a large community of Christian Copts. Prior to the Fatimid arrival, the Shīʿa represented a minority in Egypt, and their minoritarian status remained unchanged throughout the two centuries of Fatimid rule.

Jawhar ruled over Egypt as Fatimid viceroy for four years until 362/973. As the Fatimids had done after their takeover of power in Ifrīqiya, Jawhar essentially retained the administrative and judiciary officials of the previous regime, including the vizier Ibn al-Furāt and the chief judge Abū Ṭāhir al-Dhuhlī. However, a Kutāma Berber was attached as supervisor to every high official of the state. All this, of course, made the transition to Fatimid rule and the revival of the economy more readily attainable. In line with the eastern strategy of the Fatimids, in Muḥarram 359/November 969 Jawhar dispatched the main body of the Fatimid army for the conquest of Palestine and Syria. However, Fatimid success in Syria proved transitory. The Qarmaṭīs of Baḥrayn, in alliance with the Būyids and other powers, defeated the Fatimids in Damascus in 360/971, the first of numerous Fatimid setbacks in Syria. Encouraged by his victory and impressive coalition of allies, al-Ḥasan al-Aʿṣam, a nephew of Abū Ṭāhir al-Jannābī and commander of Qarmaṭī forces in most campaigns, then invaded Egypt itself and proceeded to the gates of Fusṭāṭ, but was forced to retreat in 361/971. These events marked the initiation of numerous military encounters between the Fatimids and the Qarmaṭīs of Baḥrayn, delaying the establishment of Fatimid hegemony over Palestine and Syria for several more decades.

Meanwhile, Jawhar's camp site outside of Fusṭāṭ rapidly developed into a city, initially called Manṣūriyya like its namesake in Ifrīqiya where al-Muʿizz was then still residing. Al-Muʿizz himself had supervised the plan of the new city which, like its North African predecessor, was given northern and southern gates called Bāb al-Futūḥ and Bāb al-Zawīla, respectively, as well as a mosque named al-Azhar. Jawhar also built two palaces, for the caliph-imam and his heir-designate, separated by a wide space. Special lodgings and buildings were erected for government departments and the Fatimid army. By the summer of 361/972, al-Muʿizz was prepared for the transference of the seat of the Fatimid state to Egypt. Before leaving for Egypt, he appointed Buluggīn as governor of Ifrīqiya and the entire Maghrib. Buluggīn, son of the *amīr* of Ṣanhāja Zīrī b. Manād who had lost his life in his faithful service to the Fatimids, was to found the Zīrid dynasty of the Maghrib.

Accompanied by the entire Fatimid family, Ismaili notables, Kutāma chieftains, as well as the Fatimid treasuries, with al-Qāḍī al-Nuʿmān riding on his side, al-Muʿizz crossed the Nile and took possession of the royal palaces in his new capital in Ramaḍān 362/June 973. He had also brought with him the coffins of his predecessors, al-Mahdī, al-Qā'im and al-Manṣūr. Al-Muʿizz's new capital was renamed "al-Qāhira al-Muʿizziyya" (the Victorious One of al-Muʿizz), al-Qāhira (Cairo) for short. With this transference ended the North African phase of the Fatimid caliphate (297–362/909–73). But Egypt itself, as noted, represented only an intermediary step in the eastern strategy that was to take the Fatimids to Baghdad. This longer-term goal was now once again reiterated by the Fatimid court poet and panegyrist Ibn Hāni' al-Andalusī (d. 362/973) in his glorification of the Fatimid conquest of Egypt.

Al-Muʿizz's rule in Egypt lasted just over two years, mainly devoted to the elaboration of Fatimid governance in Cairo and repelling further Qarmaṭī incursions. He died in his new capital in 365/975, having transformed the Fatimid *dawla* into an empire with a reinvigorated *daʿwa* apparatus. His mausoleum, in which his predecessors and successors as well as other members of the Fatimid family were also buried, was decorated with ornamental stuccos and wall-hangings, including a splendid one made of blue silk and gold depicting the regions of the world with their cities, commissioned by al-Muʿizz himself in 353/964.[18]

PHILOSOPHICAL ISMAILISM OF THE IRANIAN *DĀʿĪS*

By the end of the 3rd/9th century, much of the intellectual heritage of antiquity was accessible to the Muslims. This resulted from the great translation movement into Arabic of numerous texts of Greek wisdom. The works of Plato (Aflāṭūn), Aristotle (Arisṭūṭālīs), Galen (Jālīnūs), Ptolemy (Baṭlamiyūs) and many other Greek sages were initially translated into Syriac-Aramaic mainly by the Christian scholars of Mesopotamia and Syria who, then, translated the same materials into Arabic. After the sporadic efforts of the Umayyad period, this translation movement was officially sponsored by the early Abbasids, especially by the caliph al-Ma'mūn (198–218/813–33) who established at his palace in Baghdad the House of Wisdom (Bayt al-Ḥikma) with a library where translations were undertaken systematically by a team of scholars. At any rate, the Muslims now became closely acquainted not only with different branches of Greek sciences, such as medicine, physics, mathematics and astronomy, but also with logic and metaphysics, transporting Hellenising influences to the Islamic sciences and other traditions of learning.

In philosophy, along with the works of the great Greek masters, the writings of the authors of the so-called Neoplatonic school were also translated into Arabic with commentaries from the 3rd/9th century on. These Arabic Neoplatonic materials were to have seminal impact on the development of Islamic philosophy in general and the Ismaili thought of the Fatimid period in particular. Neoplatonism, a term coined by modern historians of philosophy, was founded by Plotinus (d. AD 270), known to Muslims as the Shaykh al-Yūnānī, who re-worked Plato in an original manner. After the contributions of a number of Plotinus's disciples, Neoplatonic philosophy received its major systematisation at the hands of the Athenian Proclus (d. AD 485).

Muslims did not generally distinguish among the various schools of Greek philosophy, but they did consider Aristotle as its foremost representative. This explains their attribution of numerous pseudepigrapha to Aristotle, and the early popularity of these pseudo-Aristotelian texts in Muslim intellectual milieus. By the 4th/10th century, there appeared several Arabic treatises containing Neoplatonic doctrines rooted in the teachings of Plotinus and other Greek philosophers. Although a number of these Neoplatonic works were translated into Arabic under the correct names of their original Greek authors, a majority bore false attributions, preponderantly to Aristotle. Foremost among the Neoplatonic materials in Arabic, which disseminated Neoplatonism among the Muslims and also influenced the Ismaili (Qarmaṭī) *dāʿīs* of the Iranian lands, was a paraphrase of portions of Plotinus's principal work, the *Enneads*. Existing in "longer" and "shorter" versions, this treatise circulated as Aristotle's *Theology* (Arabic, *Uthūlūjiyā*). The Ismaili *dāʿīs* and other Muslim scholars also had at their disposal the *Kalām fī maḥḍ al-khayr* (*Discourse on the Pure Good*), another important pseudo-Aristotelian work which was in fact a paraphrase of Proclus's *Elements of Theology*. When medieval Europe began in the 6th/12th century to find access to texts on Greek sciences and philosophy through translations from their Arabic versions, the *Kalām* became famous in its Latin version under the title of *Liber de causis* (*Book of Causes*).[19]

The pseudo-Aristotelian writings, and other Arabic translations of Greek philosophical texts, circulated among the educated classes and their Neoplatonic doctrines proved particularly appealing to a diversity of Muslim thinkers, who adopted and adapted them in the course of the 4th/10th century. In this context, mention may be made of individuals as divergent as Abū Sulaymān al-Sijistānī, the Muslim logician and philosopher living in Baghdad in the second half of that century, and Isḥāq b. Sulaymān al-Isrā'īlī, better known as Isaac Israeli, the earliest Jewish Neoplatonist scholar who was also physician to the first Fatimid caliph-imam al-Mahdī in North Africa and died shortly before 320/932. There were also the Baṣra-based Ikhwān al-Ṣafā', or the Brethren of Purity, who secretly produced their encyclopaedic *Rasā'il* or *Epistles* on a wide range of subjects during the 4th/10th century. The members of this group, too, with their obscure Ismaili affiliation, had come under the influence of Neoplatonism. However, the Ikhwān al-Ṣafā', who similarly to the contemporary Ismaili (Qarmaṭī) *dā'ī*s of the Iranian lands aimed to harmonise religion and philosophy, did not have any discernible impact on Ismaili thought of the Fatimid period; it was only in the 6th/12th century that the *Rasā'il* were introduced into the literature of the Ṭayyibī Musta'lī Ismaili *da'wa* in Yaman and, thereafter, were commented upon by the Ṭayyibī *dā'ī*s.[20]

The diffusion of the Arabic texts of Greek wisdom led to the development of a distinctive philosophical tradition in the Muslim world. Initiated by al-Kindī (d. after 256/870), the early success of this philosophical tradition found its full application in the works of al-Fārābī (d. 339/950), widely known as the "second teacher" (*al-mu'allim al-thānī*) of philosophy in the Islamic world after Aristotle, and Ibn Sīnā (d. 428/1037), or Avicenna of the medieval Europeans. Both of these great Muslim philosophers or *falāsifa* hailed from the eastern Iranian world, adopting a variegated synthesis of Aristotelian metaphysics with Neoplatonic doctrines. Neoplatonism was particularly attractive to the intellectual circles of Nīshāpūr and other cities of Khurāsān and Transoxania. Ibn Sīnā's father and brother, ranking among the educated Ismailis of Central Asia, had become acquainted with Neoplatonic doctrines in Bukhārā in the course of their Ismaili instructions. Ibn Sīnā was himself familiar with Ismaili tenets and the *Rasā'il Ikhwān al-Ṣafā'*.

The pseudo-Aristotelian texts and their Neoplatonic philosophy had also attracted the attention of the learned Ismaili (Qarmaṭī) *dā'ī*s of the Iranian lands. It was in the course of the 4th/10th century that these *dā'ī*s set about to harmonise Ismaili Shī'ī theology with Neoplatonic philosophy. This amalgam of reason and revelation, or philosophy and theology, led to the development of a unique intellectual tradition of philosophical theology within Ismailism, with a variant modern appellation as philosophical Ismailism. Muḥammad al-Nasafī, the chief *dāʿī* of Khurāsān and Transoxania, was evidently the earliest of the Iranian *dāʿī*s to introduce Neoplatonic philosophy into his theology and system of thought. He, and other *dāʿī*s of the eastern Iranian lands, wrote for the ruling elite and the educated classes of society, aiming to attract them intellectually and win their support for the *daʿwa*. This may explain why these *dāʿī*s expressed their theology in terms of the then most modern and intellectually fashionable philosophical terminologies and themes, without compromising the essence of their religious message revolving around the central Shīʿī doctrine of the imamate.

It was under such circumstances that Muḥammad al-Nasafī, Abū Ḥātim al-Rāzī, and most importantly Abū Yaʿqūb al-Sijistānī, drawing on a type of "Neoplatonism" then current among the educated circles of certain regions of Persia and Central Asia, wrote on various philosophical themes generally absent in the writings of al-Qāḍī al-Nuʿmān and other contemporary Ismaili authors operating in Arab lands and North Africa. The Iranian *dāʿī*s elaborated complex metaphysical systems of thought with a distinct Neoplatonised emanational cosmology, representing the earliest tradition of philosophical theology in Shīʿism. Sharing a common interest in philosophy, they also became involved in a long-drawn theological debate. The *dāʿī* al-Nasafī's main work, *Kitāb al-maḥṣūl* (*Book of the Yield*), written around 300/912 and representing the earliest work of a *dāʿī* to incorporate Greek philosophical materials, has not survived. It is known, however, that it circulated widely for a while in diverse circles. The *Maḥṣūl* was criticised by al-Nasafī's contemporary *dāʿī* of Rayy, Abū Ḥātim al-Rāzī, who wrote his *Kitāb al-iṣlāḥ* (*Book of the Correction*) to correct aspects of al-Nasafī's teachings. Abū Ḥātim's *al-Iṣlāḥ* called forth a rejoinder from al-Nasafī's successor in Khurāsān, al-Sijistānī. He wrote a book entitled *Kitāb al-nuṣra* (*Book of the Support*) specifically to defend aspects of al-Nasafī's views against the criticisms of the *dāʿī* of Rayy. It is, however, mainly on the basis of al-Sijistānī's numerous extant writings that modern scholars have begun to study the origins and early development of philosophical Ismailism, with its cosmology, as elaborated during the 4th/10th century.[21]

In the Neoplatonised Ismaili cosmology, fully discussed in al-Sijistānī's *Kitāb al-yanābīʿ* (*Book of the Wellsprings*) and other writings, God is described as absolutely transcendent, beyond human comprehension, beyond any name or attribute, beyond being and non-being, and therefore unknowable. This conception of God, reminiscent of the ineffable One of Greek Neoplatonists, was also in close agreement with the fundamental Islamic principle of *tawḥīd*, affirming the absolute unity of God. For Plotinus and his school, creation emanates directly and involuntarily from the One. However, in the system of the Iranian *dāʿīs*, God brings creation into being through His command (*amr*) or word (*kalima*), in an act of extra-temporal, primordial origination (*ibdāʿ*) out of nothing or *ex nihilo*. Hence, God is the originator or the *mubdiʿ*; and His command or word act as intermediary between Him and His creation. The universal intellect (*ʿaql*) is the first originated being (*al-mubdaʿ al-awwal*), produced out of nothing through God's volition. Intellect is eternal, motionless and perfect, both potentially and actually. From the intellect proceeds, through emanation (*inbiʿāth*), the soul or the universal soul (*nafs*). Soul is deficient and requires the benefits of intellect in order to achieve perfection. Intellect and soul are also referred to as preceder (*sābiq*) and follower (*tālī*), the original dyad or roots (*aṣlān*) of the pleroma. The Iranian *dāʿīs* continued the emanational chain of their cosmology all the way to the genesis of man, while recognising that God had created everything in the spiritual and physical worlds all at once (*dafʿatan wāḥidatān*). The various parts of the universe, however, became only gradually manifested through the process of causation and emanation.

The desire of soul to attain perfection is the cause of its mobility and activity. And from the movement of soul comes into being, through emanation, prime matter (*hayūlā*) and form (*ṣūra*), which provide the foundations of the material world. The order of creation then proceeded as follows: from soul emanated the seven spheres and their stars. Through the revolution of the spheres the four simple elements (*mufradāt*), humidity, dryness, cold and heat, were produced. These elements were then mixed to form the four composite elements (*murakkabāt*), namely, earth, water, air and ether (fire). Out of the mixture of the composites, plants developed with their vegetative soul (*al-nafs al-nāmiya*), whence animals with their sentient soul (*al-nafs al-ḥissiyya*) were produced. And finally, from the latter man with his rational soul (*al-nafs al-nāṭiqa*) came forth. The Iranian *dāʿīs* identified certain basic concepts of this cosmology with Qur'anic terms. Thus, intellect was identified with "pen" (*qalam*) and "throne" (*ʿarsh*), while soul was equated with "tablet" (*lawḥ*) and "chair" (*kursī*).

The Ismaili theologian-philosophers of the Iranian world also propounded a doctrine of salvation as part of their cosmology. Indeed, al-Sijistānī's Neoplatonic philosophy and his Ismaili theology, as in the systems of his Ismaili (Qarmaṭī) predecessors, were closely related to a soteriological vision of the cosmos in which man appears as a microcosm with individual human souls as parts of the universal soul. Al-Sijistānī's doctrine of salvation, elaborated in purely spiritual terms, bears a close affinity to Plotinus's ideas on mystical union between man and the One. Drawing extensively on various Neoplatonic and gnostic motifs, al-Sijistānī's doctrine of salvation is, as expected, also closely related to his doctrine of soul and the Ismaili cyclical view of the sacred history of mankind. This soteriological vision can be explained in terms of descending and ascending scales or paths with their related hierarchies. The descending scale traces creation from God's command through an emanational hierarchy, to the world of material reality and the genesis of man. As a counterpart, the ascending scale maps the rise of man's soul to the higher, spiritual world in quest of salvation. The doctrine of salvation, thus, forms the necessary counterpart to the cosmological doctrine in the metaphysical system of al-Sijistānī, as in the case of other Ismaili theologian-philosophers of the "Iranian school".

The ultimate goal of man's salvation is the human soul's progression out of a purely mundane, physical existence towards his Creator, in quest of a spiritual reward in an eternal, paradisal afterlife. This ascending quest along a ladder of salvation involves purification of man's soul, which depends on guidance provided by the terrestrial hierarchy of the Ismaili *da'wa*; because only authorised members of this hierarchy are in a position to reveal the "right path" along which God guides those who seek the truth and whose souls on the Day of Judgement will be rewarded spiritually. In every era of human history, the terrestrial hierarchy consists of the law-announcing speaker (*nāṭiq*) of that era and his rightful successors. In the era of Islam, the guidance required for salvation is provided by the Prophet Muḥammad, his *waṣī* 'Alī, and the Ismaili imams. In this system, man's salvation depends on his acquisition of a particular type of knowledge through a unique source or wellspring of wisdom. This knowledge can be imparted only through the guidance of religious authorities, sole possessors of the true, inner meaning of revelation in any prophetic era, who provide its authoritative interpretation or *ta'wīl*. And it is only through perfection of individual souls that the actually defective universal soul can realise its own perfection, which is tantamount to restoring perfection to the pleroma. History, thus, becomes the record of the universal soul's quest for perfection, and also the record of human achievement as man is called upon to assist in the perfection of the universal soul.

In evaluating intellectual contributions of the "Iranian school" of philosophical Ismailism, themes of theology and philosophy need to be considered side by side, even though al-Sijistānī and his Ismaili predecessors would not have considered themselves as Muslim philosophers or *falāsifa*. These proponents of philosophical Ismailism produced original syntheses of religious and philosophical themes, amalgamating Islamic revelation and its Ismaili interpretation with reason and free enquiry. Yet, it is important to bear in mind that they used philosophy in a subservient manner and in service of their religious quest, which ultimately required the guidance of the Ismaili imam and the hierarchy of teachers authorised by him in the *da'wa* organisation. Al-Sijistānī and other proponents of philosophical Ismailism, thus, remained devout *dā'ī*-theologians propagating the central Shī'ī doctrine of the imamate. However, the philosophical superstructures of their systems enhanced the intellectual appeal of their message. This explains why their writings circulated widely in Persia and Central Asia, in both Ismaili and non-Ismaili intellectual circles. Some non-Ismaili scholars, like Abū Manṣūr al-Māturīdī (d. 333/944), the Sunni theologian of Transoxania and founder of the Māturīdiyya school of *kalām* theology, and Abu'l-Qāsim al-Bustī, the Zaydī Mu'tazilī scholar of Persia, even commented upon aspects of the systems of thought developed by al-Nasafī and his school, and preserved fragments of these Ismaili (Qarmaṭī) works in their writings.[22]

As noted, the Fatimid *da'wa* headquarters in Ifrīqiya did not contribute to the development of early philosophical Ismailism of Iranian *dā'ī*s. The Neoplatonic cosmology of these eastern *dā'ī*s was, however, endorsed eventually by the Fatimid caliph-imam al-Mu'izz. The new cosmology was generally advocated by Fatimid *dā'ī*-authors, in preference to the earlier mythological cosmology of Ismailis, at least until the time of Nāṣir Khusraw, the last major Iranian proponent of philosophical Ismailism who drew extensively on al-Sijistānī's writings in elaborating his own metaphysical system in the middle of the 5th/11th century.

The Neoplatonised Ismaili cosmology went through further transformation, representing a third stage in the medieval development of Ismaili cosmology, at the hands of the *dā'ī* Ḥamīd al-Dīn Aḥmad b. 'Abd Allāh al-Kirmānī, perhaps the most learned philosopher of the entire Fatimid period. Al-Kirmānī was fully acquainted with Aristotelian and Neoplatonic philosophies as well as the metaphysical systems of Muslim philosophers, notably al-Fārābī and Ibn Sīnā, the latter a contemporary. He also knew Hebrew and Syriac languages and was familiar with the Hebrew text of the Old Testament, the Syriac version of the New Testament, as well as other Judaeo-Christian sacred scriptures. Al-Kirmānī acted as an arbiter in the prolonged debate that had earlier taken place among the *dāʿīs* al-Nasafī, al-Rāzī and al-Sijistānī. He reviewed this debate from the viewpoint of the Fatimid *daʿwa* in his *Kitāb al-riyāḍ* (*Book of the Meadows*), and in particular upheld the views of al-Rāzī against those of al-Nasafī in affirming the indispensability of both the *ẓāhir* and the *bāṭin* of the law.[23] This explains why Abū Ḥātim al-Rāzī's *al-Iṣlāḥ* was the only early text related to this debate that was selected for preservation by the Fatimid *daʿwa*. All this also points to the rich variety of intellectual traditions espoused by the early *dāʿīs*, and the high degree of freedom they enjoyed in scientific enquiries.

Al-Kirmānī harmonised Ismaili theology with a diversity of philosophical traditions in developing his elaborate metaphysical system expounded in the *Rāḥat al-ʿaql* (*Repose of the Intellect*), his major philosophical treatise completed in 411/1020 for advanced adepts.[24] In fact, al-Kirmānī's thought represents a unique syncretic tradition within the Iranian school of philosophical Ismailism. His cosmology was partially based on al-Fārābī's Aristotelian cosmic system, and also took account of some of Abū Ḥātim al-Rāzī's objections to the school of al-Nasafī. Regarding God's unknowability and transcendence, or His absolute unconnectedness with His creation, al-Kirmānī adopted a yet more uncompromising position compared to the stances of his Ismaili predecessors, denying the hypostatic role of any mediator (*wāsiṭa*) such as the divine word or command between God and the first created being, because they too would compromise the principle of *tawḥīd* and God's transcendence. He was also opposed to the views of Muslim philosophers like Ibn Sīnā who regarded God as a "necessary existent" (*wājib al-wujūd*), a conception that would again compromise God's transcendence since it could apply only to a "created being".

In his cosmology, al-Kirmānī replaced the Neoplatonic dyad of intellect (*ʿaql*) and soul (*nafs*) in the spiritual world, adopted by his Ismaili predecessors, by a system of ten separate intellects, or archangelical hypostases, in partial adaptation of al-Fārābī's school of philosophy. In his system, the first intellect, or the first originated being, is identical with the very act of origination (*ibdāʿ*); it is perfect in its essence, motionless and stable. These attributes signify the complete tranquillity or repose (*rāḥa*) of the first intellect; hence the designation *Rāḥat al-ʿaql*. The first intellect is also the cause (*ʿilla*) of all beings, corresponding to the One of Plotinus and other Greek Neoplatonists, and the "necessary existent" of the *falāsifa*. The first intellect becomes the point of departure for the emanation (*inbiʿāth*) of remaining intellects and all other beings. The second and third intellects are emanated from the higher and lower relations of the first intellect. The remaining seven intellects, symbolically identified with the seven higher letters (*al-ḥurūf al-ʿulwiyya*) of the original Ismaili cosmology, are issued from the second intellect, the first emanated being. Al-Kirmānī's ideas on the third intellect, representing archetypes of matter (*hayūlā*) and form (*ṣūra*) seem to have been without antecedent among his Ismaili predecessors and Muslim philosophers. Celestial bodies and the corporeal world are formed through the third intellect. The physical world consists of nine celestial spheres, the seven spheres of the planets and the sublunar world. Each sphere is related to one of the intellects; and the tenth or active intellect (*al-ʿaql al-faʿʿāl*) governs the sublunar world as a demiurge. Al-Kirmānī, then, explains at great length the generation of the four elements (*arkān*), the realms of minerals, plants and animals, and finally, of man as a microcosm reflecting in his essence the macrocosm.

Al-Kirmānī's system, too, culminates in a soteriological doctrine, centred around the salvation of man's soul through the attainment of spiritual knowledge provided by authoritative guidance of prophets and their legitimate successors. In al-Kirmānī's metaphysical system, there are numerous correspondences between celestial and terrestrial hierarchies, and between the ten separate intellects of the higher world and the ranks or *ḥudūd* of the complete terrestrial *daʿwa* organisation, ranging from *nāṭiq*, *waṣī* (or *asās*) and imam to *bāb* (or *dāʿī al-duʿāt*), *ḥujja*, and different ranks of *dāʿī* and his assistant or *ma'dhūn*.[25] Many aspects of al-Kirmānī's system still puzzle modern scholars. Clearly, he used his diverse sources creatively and elaborated an original synthesis. At the same time, he represents continuity in terms of the pivotal tenets of Ismailism, and as in the case of his Ismaili predecessors, it is the authoritative guidance of the Prophet Muḥammad and his successors, the imams, that reigns supreme in his system. For unknown reasons, however, at least his cosmology failed to be generally adopted by the Fatimid *daʿwa*, but it later provided the doctrinal basis for the fourth and final stage in the medieval evolution of Ismaili cosmology at the hands of Ṭayyibī Mustaʿlī *dāʿī*s of Yaman.

FATIMID ISMAILI *DAʿWA* AND *DĀʿĪ*S: CAIRO AND THE "ISLANDS"

In this section we shall briefly discuss aspects of the Ismaili *daʿwa* propagated on behalf of the Fatimid caliph-imams, especially after the transference of the seat of the *dawla* to Cairo. From 362/973, the Fatimid capital in Egypt served as the central headquarters of a *daʿwa* organisation that developed rapidly disseminating its religio-political messages through a network of *dāʿī*s operating both within and outside of Fatimid dominions. The latter regions, situated beyond the confines of the Fatimid state, were known to the Fatimid Ismailis as the *jazāʾir* (singular, *jazīra*), literally the "islands". The term *daʿwa* itself referred to both the "organisation" of the Fatimid Ismaili religio-political mission, with its elaborate hierarchical ranks, as well as the functioning of that organisation, especially the missionary activities of *dāʿīs* who represented the *daʿwa* in different localities. Fatimid Ismailis also developed certain traditions of teaching and learning, including especially the distinctive institution known as the "sessions of wisdom" (*majālis al-ḥikma*), closely connected to their *daʿwa* activities. Indeed, provision of systematic instruction in Ismaili doctrines for the initiates was, from early on, an important concern of the Fatimid Ismaili *daʿwa*.

The organisation and functioning of Ismaili *daʿwa* were, for obvious reasons, normally among the most closely guarded secrets of Ismailism, and the Fatimid period was no exception. It is, therefore, not surprising that the relatively extensive Ismaili literature of the Fatimid period is silent on the subject. Information on intricacies of the Fatimid Ismaili *daʿwa* would probably have been available only to the *daʿwa*'s central administration, supervised by the Fatimid caliph-imam himself, and possibly also to some of the high-ranking *dāʿīs*. The Fatimid *dāʿīs* themselves, particularly those active in hostile surroundings outside the Fatimid state, such as in Yaman, Iraq, Persia, Sind and Central Asia, operated in secrecy. They took every precaution not to divulge details of their clandestine activities in their writings. All this secrecy and lack of information provided fertile grounds for fantastic myths fabricated by enemies of the Ismailis about their *daʿwa* and policies pursued by the *dāʿīs*. But now, by piecing together a variety of relevant details scattered in Fatimid Ismaili sources as well as in a few well-informed contemporary chronicles, illustrated best in the works of al-Maqrīzī, modern scholarship has finally succeeded in understanding the broad outlines of the Fatimid Ismaili *daʿwa* organisation and some of its major practices and institutions.

The Fatimid caliph-imams, as noted, never abandoned their aspirations for ruling over the entire Muslim *umma*. In other words, they aimed to be recognised as imams by all Muslims. Its attainment was the central responsibility of the Fatimid *daʿwa* organisation. This explains the retention of the Ismaili *daʿwa* after the founding of the Fatimid *dawla*, and its continued designation as *al-daʿwa al-hādiya*, or the rightly guiding summons. Fatimid *dāʿīs* were responsible for summoning people everywhere to the rightful imam of the time. Those cognisant of the summons were known in the *daʿwa* terminology as respondents or *mustajībs*.

The term *dāʿī*, literally meaning "summoner", was used by several Muslim groups, including the earliest Abbasids, the early Muʿtazila, and the Zaydiyya, to designate their religio-political propagandists or missionaries. But it acquired its widest application in connection with the Ismāʿīliyya, though the early Ismailis (Qarmaṭīs) in Persia sometimes used other appellations such as *janāḥ* (plural, *ajniḥa*). In spite of occasional variations in nomenclature, and the fact that several categories of *dāʿī*s existed at any particular time in any region, the term *dāʿī* (plural, *duʿāt*) came to be applied generically to any authorised representative of *al-daʿwa al-hādiya* of the Ismailis, a missionary responsible for spreading Ismailism through winning new suitable converts, or followers for the Ismaili imam; he was also responsible as a teacher for preaching Ismaili doctrines to the new converts. During the Fatimid period, the *dāʿī* served also as an unofficial agent of the Fatimid state, promoting the Fatimid cause secretly outside their dominions, much in the same way as Abū ʿAbd Allāh al-Shīʿī had done in North Africa. However, any institutional ties between the Fatimid *dawla* and the Ismaili *daʿwa* of the time remain little understood. Suffice it to say that in the person of the Fatimid caliph-imam, a collaborative relationship was made possible between these two religio-political spheres of activity.

Despite the central importance of his role, however, very little seems to have been written by Ismailis of the Fatimid period, or indeed any other time, on the subject of the *dāʿī*. The prolific al-Qāḍī al-Nuʿmān, who himself headed the Fatimid *daʿwa* organisation for some time, devoted only a short chapter in one of his books to explaining the apprenticeship, qualifications and virtues of an ideal *dāʿī*.[26] This text falls into the *adab* genre in Arabic, dealing with etiquette or proper codes of conduct in different social contexts. Al-Nuʿmān reiterates that the *daʿwa*, a divine task, was above all a teaching activity and that *dāʿī*s were teachers who promoted the appeal of their message through their exemplary behaviour. A more detailed, though still general, description of an ideal *dāʿī* is contained in the only known exclusively Ismaili work of the genre produced by Aḥmad b. Ibrāhīm al-Nīsābūrī, a *dāʿī* and author who flourished under the caliph-imams al-ʿAzīz and al-Ḥākim. Although not extant, this unique text is preserved extensively in later Ismaili works.[27]

According to al-Nīsābūrī, a *dāʿī* was appointed only by the imam's permission (*idhn*). Reflecting contemporary realities, when *dāʿī*s often operated in remote and hostile areas and were unable to establish frequent contacts with the central headquarters of the *daʿwa*, al-Nīsābūrī further explains that they enjoyed a high degree of autonomy, receiving only general instructions from the central authorities.

Under such circumstances, only persons of high educational qualifications combined with extraordinary moral and intellectual attributes, as well as organisational abilities, could rise to found and lead Ismaili communities in particular regions. In so far as religious education is concerned, the *dāʿī* was to have sufficient knowledge of both the *ẓāhir* and the *bāṭin*, or the *sharīʿa* as well as its Ismaili interpretation (*ta'wīl*). If operating outside the Fatimid state, the *dāʿī* was also expected to act as a judge of binding adjudication for his community, whose members were discouraged from appealing to local non-Ismaili judges. The *dāʿī* was, thus, often trained in jurisprudence, in addition to being knowledgeable in the Qur'an and *ḥadīth*. The ideal *dāʿī* was also expected to be well versed in a diversity of other, non-religious subjects, such as philosophy and history, as well as the teachings of non-Islamic religions. In addition, he was required to be familiar with the languages and customs of the region in which he was to operate, so that he could perform his duties properly and inconspicuously. In sum, the paradigmatic *dāʿī* was a highly learned and cultured individual.

The Fatimids devoted particular attention to the training of their *dāʿīs*, and founded a variety of institutions to that end. Many of the Fatimid Ismaili *dāʿīs* became eminent scholars in theology, philosophy, jurisprudence and other exoteric and esoteric fields of learning, making important contributions to Islamic thought and culture. They also produced the bulk of Ismaili literature of the Fatimid period in Arabic, the scholarly and religious language of the period. Of all the major *dāʿī*-authors of the Fatimid period, Nāṣir Khusraw was the only one to produce the corpus of his writings in Persian. The *dāʿī* was expected to take special care in selecting his associates, including his subordinate *dāʿīs* and assistants, for whose training he was personally responsible.

Information on the actual methods used by Fatimid *dāʿīs* for winning new converts (*mustajībs*) and educating them is extremely sparse. Our few sources do, however, state that the *dāʿī* had to be personally acquainted with individual initiates, who were selected with special regard to their intellectual capabilities. Never aiming at mass proselytisation, the *dāʿī* was to address himself to one prospective *mustajīb* at a time, subsequent to a careful process of evaluation and selection. The act of initiation itself was perceived as the spiritual rebirth of the adept. Many Sunni sources, influenced especially by the anti-Ismaili polemical tradition, mention a seven-stage process of initiation into Ismailism, often giving each stage a distinctive designation.[28] Extant Ismaili literature does not support any such fixed graded system, though a certain degree of gradualism in the initiation and education of converts was inevitable. Indeed, al-Nīsābūrī does state that the *dāʿī* was expected to instruct the *mustajīb* in a gradual manner, not divulging too much at any given time. The *dāʿī* often held regular teaching sessions for the new converts and other Ismailis in his own house, and he organised his lectures on the basis of the capabilities and aptitude of his student initiates, moving from simpler and exoteric subjects to more complex and esoteric ones. All this, of course, demanded refined pedagogical skills, as conversion and teaching were equally important in his activity.

It was the duty of the *dāʿī* to administer to the initiate an oath of allegiance (*ʿahd* or *mīthāq*) to the Ismaili imam of the time, which also involved a pledge on the part of the *mustajīb* to maintain the secrecy of his learning. It was only after this oath that the initiate underwent a gradual course of instruction. The funds required by the *dāʿī* for the performance of his duties were raised locally from members of his community. He collected on behalf of the imam a number of dues such as the alms tax (*zakāt*) and the one-fifth (*khums*), paid by all Shīʿī Muslims, as well as certain Ismaili-specific dues, including especially the *najwā* paid by every new convert for receiving instruction. The *dāʿī* normally kept a portion of these funds to finance his *daʿwa* activities, sending the remainder to the imam to whom he was ultimately accountable. For this purpose, the *dāʿī* used trustworthy couriers, who brought back general instructions from *daʿwa* headquarters. These couriers, especially those going to the Fatimid capital from remote *daʿwa* regions such as Badakhshān, also brought back Ismaili books for the *dāʿī*s, keeping them abreast of the latest intellectual developments within Ismailism.

The Ismailis' high esteem for learning resulted in distinctive traditions and institutions under the Fatimids. The Fatimid *daʿwa*, as noted, was particularly concerned with educating converts and teaching them the *ḥikma* or "wisdom", as Ismaili esoteric doctrine has been known. Consequently, a variety of lectures or "teaching sessions", generally designated as *majālis* (singular, *majlis*), were organised under the auspices of the Fatimid state. These sessions, with increasing formalisation and specialisation, served different pedagogical purposes and, as such, addressed different audiences, especially in the Fatimid capital. There were, however, basically two types of teaching sessions, namely, public lectures for large audiences on Ismaili law and other exoteric subjects, and private lectures on Ismaili esoteric doctrines reserved exclusively for the benefit of the Ismaili initiates.[29]

The Fatimid *majālis* were initiated early in North Africa in the time of the *dāʿī* Abū ʿAbd Allāh al-Shīʿī, who lectured to the Kutāma Berbers on the virtues of the *ahl al-bayt* and the legitimate ʿAlid imams. This is, indeed, how the *dāʿī* gradually succeeded in converting the Kutāma. He also organised exclusive Ismaili sessions for teaching the "wisdom" (*ḥikma*) to initiated Berbers, including their women.[30] After Abū ʿAbd Allāh, the caliph-imam al-Mahdī appointed Aflaḥ b. Hārūn to leadership of the *daʿwa*, although the expression *dāʿī al-duʿāt* had not yet come into use. A Kutāma Berber belonging to the Malūsa clan, Aflaḥ also effectively headed the judiciary, and as such was chief *qāḍī* or *qāḍī al-quḍāt* of the Fatimid state. From that time until much later in Egypt, the chief *qāḍī* of the Fatimid empire was at the same time in charge of the *daʿwa* as chief *dāʿī* or *dāʿī al-duʿāt*. In other words, responsibilities for the *sharīʿa* and its Ismaili interpretation were vested in the same person. This serves to underline overwhelming Fatimid concern for maintaining a balance between the *ẓāhir* and the *bāṭin* of religion. The "teaching sessions" were systematised by al-Qāḍī al-Nuʿmān, chief *qāḍī* and chief *dāʿī* who also played a key role in codifying Ismaili law.

Ismailism had been adopted as the official *madhhab* of the Fatimid state, and its legal doctrines were applied by the judiciary. The *sharīʿa*, as interpreted by Ismaili jurisprudence, thus, provided the legal basis for the daily life of the Muslim subjects of Fatimids. However, the Ismaili legal code was new and its precepts had to be explained to Ismailis as well as other Muslims. This was effectively accomplished in regular public sessions, held by al-Qāḍī al-Nuʿmān on Fridays, after the midday prayers when large numbers would gather for the occasion. In Ifrīqiya, these sessions were originally held in the Great Mosque of Qayrawān, and later in the Mosque of al-Azhar in Manṣūriyya. For these sessions on law, al-Nuʿmān used his own legal works, especially the *Daʿāʾim al-Islām*.[31]

The teaching sessions related to the *bāṭin*, known as the "sessions of wisdom" (*majālis al-ḥikma*), on the other hand, catered to the Ismaili initiates, who referred to themselves as the *awliyāʾ Allāh*, or simply as the *awliyāʾ*, namely, the "friends of God" or the "saintly". To control the privacy of these sessions, they were held at the Fatimid palace, in a special hall, also called *majlis*. Al-Nuʿmān himself held the *majālis al-ḥikma* following the public *ẓāhirī* sessions on Fridays. The lectures delivered by al-Nuʿmān, and later by his successors, were approved by the imam beforehand. Only the imam was the source and repository of the *ḥikma*; the *dāʿī* was merely the imam's mouthpiece through whom the initiates received their instruction in Ismaili esoteric doctrines. Some of al-Nuʿmān's lectures prepared for the *majālis al-ḥikma* were collected in his *Taʾwīl al-daʿāʾim*, which is the *bāṭinī* companion to his *ẓāhirī* legal compendium, the *Daʿāʾim al-Islām*.

The convening of public and private teaching sessions, together with other general practices of the *daʿwa*, were maintained after the Fatimids settled in Cairo. In fact, the *majālis* gradually developed into an elaborate programme of instruction for a variety of audiences. After al-Nuʿmān, his sons and grandsons succeeded to the office of chief *qāḍī*; they were at the same time in charge of the *daʿwa*, as they held the "sessions of wisdom" in the Fatimid palace in Cairo. From the time of al-Ḥākim, however, responsibility for the headship of the judiciary and the *daʿwa* were vested in different persons, with the chief *qāḍī* taking precedence in status and in ceremonials over the chief *dāʿī*.

In Cairo, public sessions on Ismaili law were held at the great mosques of the Fatimid capital, namely, al-Azhar, ʿAmr and later the Mosque of al-Ḥākim. In line with earlier custom, they were normally conducted after the Friday prayers, when excerpts from the exoteric works of al-Qāḍī al-Nuʿmān, especially his *Daʿāʾim al-Islām* and his abridged book, *Kitāb al-iqtiṣār*, were read to large audiences. The credit for using al-Azhar as a teaching centre on law, from 378/988 onwards, belongs to Ibn Killis, the first official vizier of the Fatimids, though earlier others had effectively discharged the duties of that office in the Fatimid state. A capable administrator, Ibn Killis also played an important part in establishing and consolidating Fatimid rule in Egypt. Subsequently, Ibn Killis served al-ʿAzīz in different capacities until his appointment to the vizierate in 367/977; he held that post, with the exception of two brief periods, until his death in 380/991. Egypt enjoyed an extended period of economic prosperity under Ibn Killis; he was also instrumental in the extension of Fatimid rule to Syria under al-ʿAzīz. A polymath in his own right, Ibn Killis became an accomplished jurist, composing a treatise on Ismaili jurisprudence, *al-Risāla al-wazīriyya*, based on the pronouncements of the caliph-imams al-Muʿizz and al-ʿAzīz. To master Ismaili jurisprudence was a remarkable achievement for a recent convert from Judaism.

The private *majālis al-ḥikma* were held in Cairo for the Ismaili initiates who had already taken the oath of allegiance and secrecy. These tightly controlled sessions, also referred to as the *majālis al-daʿwa*, were held on Fridays as well as Thursdays in special sections of the Fatimid palace, a practice established earlier in Ifrīqiya. As before, the texts read at the "sessions of wisdom" received the prior approval and authorisation of the imam. Many of these *majālis* on Ismaili doctrine prepared by, or for, various chief *dāʿīs* were, in due course, collected and committed to writing. This all-important Fatimid tradition of learning culminated in the *Majālis al-*

Mu'ayyadiyya, a collection of 800 lectures of al-Mu'ayyad fi'l-Dīn al-Shīrāzī, *dāʿī al-duʿāt* for almost twenty years under al-Mustanṣir.

By the time of al-Ḥākim, different types of teaching sessions were organised for different categories of participants, including the initiates (*awliyā'*) proper; the courtiers (*khāṣṣa*) and high officials as well as the staff of the Fatimid palace, and the ordinary people of Cairo. A separate session was held for women at al-Azhar, while the royal and noble women received their instruction at the palace. These valuable details are preserved by al-Maqrīzī, who had access to the contemporary chronicle of al-Musabbiḥī (d. 420/1029), the well-informed Fatimid court historian who flourished under al-Ḥākim and may have been an Ismaili himself. Doubtless not all the sessions mentioned by al-Musabbiḥī were of the specific *majālis al-ḥikma* genre; several of them seem to have been of an introductory nature designed to provide general instruction and create an interest in the Ismaili faith. Fatimid *dāʿī*s working within the confines of the state, and at least some of the major ones active in the "islands", appear to have held similar sessions, though of a more limited nature, for the exclusive education of Ismaili initiates. For instance, the *dāʿī* al-Kirmānī, who operated in Iraq and parts of Persia, refers to his collection of *majālis* delivered in Baghdad and Baṣra.[32] In Cairo, the sessions for the Ismailis were used for collecting various types of dues, including especially the *najwā* paid in gratitude for the favour of confidential instruction. Wealthy Ismailis made donations over and above the sums paid by all adepts. Lists of all the contributions were regularly compiled by a special scribe, the *kātib al-daʿwa*, appointed by the chief *dāʿī*.

Another of the major institutions of learning founded by the Fatimids was the Dār al-ʿIlm, the House of Knowledge, sometimes also called the Dār al-Ḥikma. Established in 395/1005 by the caliph-imam al-Ḥākim in the Fatimid palace, a variety of religious and non-religious subjects, ranging from the Qur'an, *ḥadīth* and jurisprudence (*fiqh*) to logic, grammar, philology, astronomy and mathematics, were taught at this institution, which was also equipped with a major library. In time, the manuscript collections of this library grew to several hundred thousand volumes. Functioning as a true academy, the Dār al-ʿIlm was used by scholars of different religious persuasions, and its library was accessible to everyone. Many Fatimid *dāʿī*s received at least part of their training at the Dār al-ʿIlm, which also variously served the Fatimid Ismaili *daʿwa*.[33] Jurists and other scholars, as well as scribes and librarians worked at the Dār al-ʿIlm, drawing salaries from the Fatimid treasury or that institution's endowment (*waqf*) established privately by al-Ḥākim himself. The chief *dāʿī* al-

Mu'ayyad resided in the Dār al-ʿIlm, and conducted the affairs of the *daʿwa* from there. In later Fatimid times, the Dār al-ʿIlm was moved to a new location and it more closely served the needs of the *daʿwa*. These traditions and institutions of learning, including the *majālis al-ḥikma* and the Dār al-ʿIlm, were retained until the downfall of the Fatimid state in 567/1171.

Information on the organisation of the Fatimid Ismaili *daʿwa*, and its hierarchical ranks (*ḥudūd*), is rather scarce, especially for the "islands" where the *daʿwa* was conducted in utmost secrecy. The *daʿwa* was under the overall guidance of the person of the Ismaili imam, who authorised its policies and teachings. The chief *dāʿī* (*dāʿī al-duʿāt*) acted as the administrative head of the *daʿwa* organisation. He was closely supervised by the imam, and assisted by a number of subordinate *dāʿī*s in the discharge of his duties. The chief *dāʿī* also appointed the provincial *dāʿī*s of the Fatimid empire. These *dāʿī*s were stationed in several localities in Egypt, the main cities of the Fatimid provinces, including Ascalon, Ramla, Acre, Tyre and Damascus, and also in the rural areas of the empire, such as the Jabal al-Summāq in Syria. The provincial *dāʿī*s represented the *daʿwa* and the chief *dāʿī*, operating alongside the local *qāḍī*s, representatives of the chief *qāḍī* (*qāḍī al-quḍāt*). The chief *dāʿī* also played a key role in selecting *dāʿī*s for the "islands". The appointment of all Fatimid *dāʿī*s, however, had to be approved by the imam. The chief *dāʿī*, as noted, was also responsible for organising the *majālis al-ḥikma* and preparing lectures delivered by him at these gatherings. Not much else is known about the functions of the chief *dāʿī*. Even the title of *dāʿī al-duʿāt*, used frequently in non-Ismaili sources, rarely appears in those Ismaili texts of the Fatimid period which refer to the *daʿwa* organisation. Instead, they use the term *bāb* (gate), or sometimes *bāb al-abwāb* in reference to the administrative head of the *daʿwa*, gateway to the imam's "wisdom" (*ḥikma*) and the Ismaili teachings emanating from that unique source.

Organised in a strictly hierarchical fashion, the Fatimid *daʿwa* developed over time and reached its full elaboration under the caliph-imam al-Mustanṣir.[34] The *daʿwa* terminology evolved, with differing nomenclatures used in Fatimid provinces and the "islands". Be that as it may, the *daʿwa* organisation and its hierarchy of ranks (*ḥudūd*) alluded to in various Ismaili texts of the Fatimid period seem to have applied to an idealised or utopian situation when the Ismaili imam would rule the entire world, and not to any actual system. According to this scheme, the world, notably the region falling outside Fatimid jurisdiction, was divided into twelve "islands" (*jazīras*) for the purposes of propagating the *daʿwa*. Delineated along a combination of geographic and ethnographic considerations, these "islands" included Rūm (Byzantium); Daylam, used synonymously with Persia; Sind and Hind (India); Ṣīn (China); and regions inhabited by Arabs, Nubians, Khazars, Slavs and the Zanj (Africans), among others.[35] Other classifications, too, seem to have been observed in practice. Nāṣir Khusraw, for instance, makes numerous references to Khurāsān as a distinct *jazīra*, a fact corroborated by Ibn Ḥawqal who adds that Balūchistān, in eastern Persia, belonged to that same "island".[36] This *jazīra* also included neighbouring regions in Afghanistan and Transoxania. Amongst other regions evidently serving as *jazīra*s in Fatimid times, mention may be made of Yaman and Iraq (including central and western parts of Persia).

Each "island" was placed under the overall charge of a high-ranking *dāʿī* known as *ḥujja* (proof, guarantor), also called *naqīb*, *lāḥiq* or *yad* (hand) in the early Fatimid period. The highest representative of the *daʿwa* in any "island", the *ḥujja* was assisted by a number of subordinate regional and local *dāʿī*s of varying ranks, including the *dāʿī al-balāgh* who seems to have acted as liaison between the *ḥujja*'s headquarters in a *jazīra* and the central *daʿwa* headquarters in the Fatimid capital. The *dāʿī*s, in turn, had their own assistants, designated as *ma'dhūn*. The lowest-ranking official in the hierarchy was *al-ma'dhūn al-mukāsir*, eventually called the *mukāsir* (breaker), whose duty was to attract prospective converts and to "break" their attachments to previous persuasions. The ordinary Ismaili initiates, the *mustajībs* or respondents who referred to themselves as *awliyā*', did not occupy a rank at the bottom of the *daʿwa* hierarchy. Belonging to the *ahl al-daʿwa*, or "people of the mission", they represented the elite (*khāṣṣa* or *khawāṣṣ*) as compared to common (non-Ismaili) Muslims, the *ʿāmmat al-Muslimīn* or simply the *ʿawāmm*. The *dāʿī* al-Kirmānī's idealised depiction distinguishes seven *daʿwa* ranks – corresponding to those of the celestial hierarchy – from *bāb* (or *dāʿī al-duʿāt*) to *mukāsir*, after *nāṭiq*, *asās* (or *waṣī*) and imam.[37]

The Fatimid *daʿwa* was propagated openly within the empire. But with the exception of Syria, where a diversity of Shīʿī traditions had coexisted throughout the centuries, the success of the *daʿwa* in Fatimid dominions, stretching from North Africa to Palestine and parts of Syria, was both very limited and transitory. In North Africa, the spread of Ismailism had always been effectively checked by Mālikī Sunnism and Khārijism. In Ifrīqiya, the Zīrids who governed as viceroys of the Fatimids after their departure, soon succumbed to pressure by Mālikī jurists, massacring minority Ismaili communities of Qayrawān, Mahdiyya and other cities. Ismailism had practically disappeared from North Africa when the fourth Zīrid ruler, al-Muʿizz

b. Bādīs, formally renounced his allegiance to the Fatimids in 440/1048. Henceforth, the *khuṭba* was read in different principalities of North Africa for the Abbasids. The Ismailis remained a minority in historically Sunni Egypt, with a negligible Shīʿī population.

It was in non-Fatimid territories, the *jazīra*s, that the Fatimid *daʿwa* achieved lasting success. Many of these "islands", scattered from Central Asia to Yaman, were already well acquainted with Shīʿī traditions, including Ismailism, and responded positively to the summons of the learned and skillful Fatimid *dāʿī*s. By the time of al-Mustanṣir's long reign, a dynamic and unified Ismaili movement had been established in these "islands". The dissident Qarmaṭīs had by this time either disappeared or switched their allegiance to the Fatimids. Unity proved short-lived in the Ismaili community, however. In 487/1094, the Ismailis split into Nizārī and Mustaʿlī branches. That Ismailism survived this schism and the downfall of the Fatimid dynasty is testimony to the achievements of the *dāʿī*s operating in the "islands". Here, we can only summarise aspects of this record of success.

The Fatimid *daʿwa* was systematically intensified in the East, especially in Iraq and Persia, under al-Ḥākim. In Iraq, where anti-Shīʿī pressures intensified following the demise of the Shīʿī Būyids, the Fatimid *dāʿī*s continued to undermine the Abbasids. They now concentrated their efforts on a number of local *amīr*s and influential tribal chiefs, with whose support they aspired to uproot the caliph in Baghdad. Foremost among the *dāʿī*s of this period operating in the "islands" was Ḥamīd al-Dīn al-Kirmānī. Born in the Persian province of Kirmān, he spent the greater part of his life as a *dāʿī* in Iraq. The title *ḥujjat al-ʿIrāqayn*, the *ḥujja* (or chief *dāʿī*) of both Iraqs, which is often added to his name, implies that al-Kirmānī was also active in west-central parts of Persia. The activities of al-Kirmānī and other *dāʿī*s in Iraq soon led to concrete results for the Fatimid *daʿwa*. In 401/1010, for instance, Qirwāsh b. al-Muqallad (391–442/1001–50), the ʿUqaylid ruler of Mawṣil, Kūfa and other towns in Iraq, acknowledged Fatimid suzerainty and had the *khuṭba* read in the name of al-Ḥākim. Other local chieftains of Iraq, too, came forth in support of the Fatimids. Alarmed by these developments, the Abbasid caliph al-Qādir (381–422/991–1031) swiftly adopted retaliatory measures to check the spread of Ismailism within the very seat of his realm. In addition to intimidating the refractory *amīr*s by military threats, al-Qādir launched a vigorous anti-Fatimid polemical campaign. In 402/1011, he assembled a number of Muslim scholars at his court and commanded them to declare in a written document that al-Ḥākim and his predecessors lacked genuine Fatimid ʿAlid ancestry. This so-called Baghdad manifesto was then read in mosques throughout the Abbasid domain. He also commissioned several polemical works to discredit the Ismailis and refute their doctrines.

Al-Ḥākim's reign also witnessed the genesis of what was to become known as the Druze religion. A number of *dāʿīs* who had come to Cairo from Persia and Central Asia, notably al-Akhram, Ḥamza and al-Darzī (al-Darazī), now began to propagate, under obscure circumstances, certain extremist ideas regarding al-Ḥākim and his imamate. Drawing on the traditions of early Shīʿī *ghulāt* and eschatological expectations of early Qarmaṭīs (Ismailis), these *dāʿīs* founded a new religious movement, proclaimed the end of the era of Islam and the abrogation of its *sharīʿa*. By around 410/1019, Ḥamza and al-Darzī (Persian, "the tailor") were also publicly declaring the divinity of al-Ḥākim. It was after al-Darzī that adherents of this movement later became known as Darziyya or Durūz (Darzīs); hence their general designation as Druzes. The new movement rapidly attracted a following in Cairo, encouraging its founders to boldly urge the chief *dāʿī* and other leaders of the *daʿwa* to join them and recognise al-Ḥākim's divinity. This was the first serious internal crisis confronting the Fatimid *daʿwa* and its leadership.

Contrary to the claims of some later Sunni authors, there is no evidence suggesting that al-Ḥākim himself in any way encouraged or supported the extremist doctrines upheld by founders of the Druze movement. Indeed, he never laid claims to divinity in any of his numerous edicts; and the leadership of the *daʿwa* organisation in Cairo was in fact categorically opposed to this movement and denounced the new doctrine in special decrees. It was under such circumstances that the *dāʿī* al-Kirmānī was invited to Cairo by the chief *dāʿī*, Qut Tegin (Khuttakīn) al-Ḍayf, to refute officially the new doctrine from a theological standpoint. Al-Kirmānī stayed in Cairo for a few years around 405/1014, and composed a number of tracts reiterating the Ismaili Shīʿī doctrine of the imamate in refutation of the new doctrine. For instance, in his *al-Risāla al-wāʿiẓa*, written in 408/1017 in response to a pamphlet by al-Akhram, al-Kirmānī explicitly rejects the idea that al-Ḥākim possessed divine attributes, equating such ideas with *kufr* (infidelity).[38] Al-Kirmānī also found it necessary to emphasise that the era of Islam and the validity of its *sharīʿa* would continue under al-Ḥākim's countless successors until the end of time.

The writings of al-Kirmānī circulated widely and were evidently successful in preventing the extremist Druze ideas from influencing the inner circles of the *daʿwa* organisation, but the movement had already acquired momentum and popular appeal. Its adherents survived severe persecution under al-Ḥākim's successor al-Ẓāhir, and later found a permanent stronghold in Syria. Meanwhile, the new doctrine found another lease of life when al-Ḥākim disappeared mysteriously in 411/1021 in one of his customary nocturnal outings. He had evidently fallen victim to a conspiracy and his body was never recovered. But the leaders of the Druze movement interpreted al-Ḥākim's disappearance as a voluntary, superhuman act initiating his *ghayba* or occultation. The Druzes eventually developed their body of doctrine and sacred scriptures, reflecting mainly Ḥamza's teachings. A highly closed and secretive community, still awaiting the reappearance of al-Ḥākim, the Druzes are today mainly scattered in Syria and Lebanon.[39]

The Fatimid *da'wa* was propagated successfully in the eastern lands even after the Sunni Saljuqs had replaced the Shī'ī Būyids as overlords of the Abbasids in 447/1055. The Saljuqs regarded themselves as the new champions of Sunni Islam and as such they also aimed to uproot the Fatimids. In spite of the Saljuqs' actively hostile stance, by the middle of the 5th/11th century, the Fatimid *dā'ī*s had managed to win many Ismaili converts in Iraq, and different parts of Persia, notably Fārs, Kirmān, Iṣfahān, Rayy and other areas of the Jibāl. In Fārs, the *da'wa* was intensified under the *dā'ī* al-Mu'ayyad fi'l-Dīn al-Shīrāzī, who had succeeded his father as the chief local *dā'ī*. The most prominent *dā'ī* of al-Mustanṣir's period, al-Mu'ayyad was born in Shīrāz, capital of Fārs, around 390/1000; his father was influential in the Būyid circles of Fārs. In 429/1037, al-Mu'ayyad entered the service of the Būyid *amīr* Abū Kālījār Marzubān (415–40/1024–48) who ruled over Fārs and Khūzistān. The subsequent decades in al-Mu'ayyad's career are well documented in his autobiography.[40] He soon succeeded in converting Abū Kālījār and many of his courtiers as well as a large number of the Daylamī soldiers in Būyid service. Al-Mu'ayyad's success in Fārs naturally met with hostile Abbasid reaction, obliging the *dā'ī* to emigrate permanently to Fatimid Egypt. He arrived in Cairo in 439/1047, and established close relations with the chief *dā'ī*, al-Qāsim b. 'Abd al-'Azīz, a great-grandson of al-Qāḍī al-Nu'mān and the last of his descendants to hold high office under the Fatimids. Henceforth, al-Mu'ayyad played an active part in the affairs of the Fatimid *dawla* and Ismaili *da'wa*. In 450/1058, al-Mustanṣir appointed him chief *dā'ī*, a post he held, with the exception of a brief period, for twenty years until shortly before his death in 470/1078. In that capacity, al-Mu'ayyad established closer contacts with *da'wa* leaderships in several *jazīra*s, especially in the Iranian world and Yaman.

The recovery of al-Mu'ayyad's autobiography has revealed the central role this *dā'ī* played as an intermediary between the Fatimids and the Turkish military commander al-Basāsīrī, who briefly led the

Fatimid cause in Iraq against the Saljuqs. Taking advantage of the chaotic conditions of the final years of Būyid rule, when the Saljuq leader Ṭughril was preoccupied with subduing dissent in his camp, al-Basāsīrī managed to seize several cities in Iraq. He then appealed to al-Mustanṣir for support to conquer Baghdad in his name. Al-Mu'ayyad was dispatched to Syria and Iraq in 447/1055 by the Fatimid regime to deliver crucial material and financial support to al-Basāsīrī. For some three years, al-Mu'ayyad advised al-Basāsīrī, also negotiating with a number of local tribal *amīrs* to win their allegiance to the Fatimid caliph. *Daʿwa* activities had now intensified in Iraq under the supervision of al-Mu'ayyad, who planned all of al-Basāsīrī's policies and alliances. In 448/1057, al-Basāsīrī inflicted a heavy defeat on the Saljuqs, who had entered Baghdad a year earlier. The Fatimids were now once again acknowledged by the ʿUqaylids of Iraq.

In Dhu'l-Qaʿda 450/December 1058, al-Basāsīrī crowned his successes by entering Baghdad. He immediately instituted the Shīʿī form of *adhān* and had the *khuṭba* read for al-Mustanṣir. The Abbasid caliph al-Qā'im (422–67/1031–75) was placed under the charge of the ʿUqaylid *amīr*, while the Abbasid caliphal insignia were sent to Cairo. The Fatimids appeared to have finally – albeit ephemerally – attained their perennial goal. Abandoned by Cairo, where a new vizier no longer wanted to support him, and confronted by the full military force of Ṭughril, who had meanwhile suppressed the rebellion in his family, al-Basāsīrī was obliged to surrender Baghdad in Dhu'l-Qaʿda 451/December 1059. He was then chased and killed by the Saljuqs. Thus ended the episode of al-Basāsīrī who, under al-Mu'ayyad's guidance, established Fatimid suzerainty for a whole year over the Abbasid capital.

In the meantime, the Fatimid *daʿwa* continued in many parts of Persia, now incorporated into the Saljuq sultanate. By the early 460s/1070s, the Persian Ismailis of the Saljuq dominions owned the authority of a single chief *dāʿī*, ʿAbd al-Malik b. ʿAṭṭāsh, with secret headquarters at Iṣfahān, the main Saljuq capital. A learned scholar, ʿAbd al-Malik seems to have been the very first *dāʿī* to organise the various Ismaili communities in Persia, and possibly in Iraq, under his leadership. But his supervision was not extended to certain parts of Khurāsān, Badakhshān and adjacent regions in Central Asia. In these eastern parts of the Iranian world, too, the *daʿwa* enjoyed increasing success after the downfall of the Sāmānids in 395/1005, when the newly emerging Turkish Qarakhānid and Ghaznawid dynasties divided former Sāmānid territories between them. This is attested by the fact that in 436/1044 Bughrā Khān, ruler of the eastern Qarakhānid kingdom, ordered a general massacre of Ismailis who had been converted by *dāʿīs* operating throughout his dominions. The Fatimid *daʿwa* had been successful also in the western Qarakhānid dominions, in Bukhārā, Samarqand, Farghāna and elsewhere in Transoxania.[41]

Nāṣir Khusraw was one of the most prominent *dāʿīs* of al-Mustanṣir's time playing a key role in propagating Ismailism in the remote eastern regions of the Iranian world. A learned theologian, philosopher, traveller and a renowned poet of the Persian language, Nāṣir Khusraw was born in 394/1004 near Balkh, which at the time was part of the district of Marw in Khurāsān. He belonged to a family of government officials and landowners. In his youth, Nāṣir held administrative posts at Marw (now in Turkmenistan) under the Ghaznawids and their Saljuq successors. Around 437/1045, Nāṣir Khusraw experienced a spiritual upheaval, probably caused by his conversion to Ismailism. Thereupon, he resigned from his post and set off on a long journey for the apparent reason of making the *ḥajj* pilgrimage to Mecca. But this seven-year journey, narrated vividly in his *Safar-nāma* (*Travelogue*), in fact took Nāṣir to the Fatimid capital where he arrived in 439/1047, in the same year as al-Mu'ayyad. Nāṣir stayed in Cairo for some three years and was trained as a *dāʿī*. During this period, he succeeded in seeing the caliph-imam al-Mustanṣir, and also established close relations with al-Mu'ayyad, who was to remain his mentor at the central headquarters of the Fatimid *daʿwa*. Later, Nāṣir dedicated several of his poems to al-Mu'ayyad.

In 444/1052, Nāṣir Khusraw returned to Balkh (near today's Mazār-i Sharīf in northern Afghanistan), and began his career as a *dāʿī*, or according to himself as the *ḥujja* of Khurāsān. He set up his secret headquarters at Balkh, from where he extended the *daʿwa* to Nīshāpūr and other districts of Khurāsān; he also spread Ismailism to Ṭabaristān (Māzandarān) and other Caspian provinces in northern Persia, which he visited personally. By 452/1060, the hostility of the Sunni *ʿulamāʾ* who denounced Nāṣir as a heretic (*mulḥid*) and destroyed his house, obliged the *dāʿī* to flee to the remote valley of Yumgān in Badakhshān.[42] There, amidst the Pamir mountains, he sought refuge with Abu'l-Maʿālī ʿAlī b. al-Asad, an autonomous Ismaili *amīr* of Badakhshān. Nāṣir's obscure period of exile in Yumgān lasted until his death, which occurred at an unknown date after 465/1072. Like other *dāʿīs* operating in the "islands", Nāṣir maintained his contacts with the *daʿwa* headquarters in Cairo, receiving books and general instructions.

It was mostly during his period of exile that Nāṣir Khusraw extended the *daʿwa* throughout Badakhshān (divided in modern times by the Oxus or Āmū Daryā between Afghanistan and Tajikistan). At any rate, the Ismailis of Badakhshān and their offshoot community in the Hindu Kush region, now situated in Hunza and other northern areas of Pakistan, regard Nāṣir Khusraw as the founder of their communities, and refer to him with high esteem as Pīr or Shāh Sayyid Nāṣir. It was in Yumgān that Nāṣir produced the bulk of his poetry as well as his philosophico-theological writings, including the *Jāmiʿ al-ḥikmatayn*, his last known work completed in 462/1070 at the request of his Ismaili protector.[43] The Ismailis of Badakhshān, who later adhered to Nizārī Ismailism, have preserved Nāṣir's genuine and spurious works, all written in Persian. Nāṣir Khusraw's mausoleum remains today in the vicinity of Fayḍābād, the capital of Afghan Badakhshān.

The Fatimid *daʿwa* achieved another of its major successes closer to Cairo, in Yaman where Ismailism had persisted in a subdued form throughout the 4th/10th century. During this period, when the *daʿwa* was led secretly by a succession of *dāʿī*s after Ibn Ḥawshab Manṣūr al-Yaman, Yaman was ruled by a number of independent local dynasties including that of the Zaydī imams. By the time of al-Mustanṣir's accession, the headship of the Yamani *daʿwa* had fallen into the hands of ʿAlī b. Muḥammad al-Ṣulayḥī, an important chieftain of the powerful Banū Hamdān in the mountainous region of Ḥarāz. In 429/1038, the *dāʿī* ʿAlī al-Ṣulayḥī rose in Ḥarāz marking the effective foundation of the Ṣulayḥid dynasty, ruling over different parts of Yaman as vassals of the Fatimids for almost a century until 532/1138. Receiving much help from the Banū Hamdān and other Yamani tribes, ʿAlī successfully embarked on a career of conquest in Yaman, instituting the *khuṭba* in the name of the Fatimids in many localities. His successes culminated in the defeat of the Zaydīs and seizure of Ṣanʿāʾ, which he adopted as capital. By 455/1063, ʿAlī al-Ṣulayḥī had subjugated all of Yaman. Later, through the efforts of the Ṣulayḥids, Fatimid sovereignty came to be recognised in other parts of Arabia, including ʿUmān and Baḥrayn where the Qarmaṭī state finally collapsed in 470/1077.

The foundation of the Ṣulayḥid dynasty ushered in a new, open phase in the history of Yamani Ismailism, under the close supervision of Fatimid Cairo. ʿAlī al-Ṣulayḥī headed the Ismaili *daʿwa* as well as the Ṣulayḥid *dawla* in Yaman. Subsequently, this arrangement went through several modifications, leading to an entirely independent status for the head of the Yamani *daʿwa*.[44] In 454/1062, the *dāʿī* ʿAlī sent Lamak b. Mālik al-Ḥammādī, the then chief *qāḍī* of Yaman, on a diplomatic mission to Cairo. Lamak spent some five years in the Fatimid capital, staying with the chief *dāʿī* al-Muʾayyad at the Dār al-ʿIlm. Al-Muʾayyad instructed the Yamani *qāḍī* in Ismaili doctrines, as he had done for Nāṣir Khusraw a decade earlier. Lamak returned to

Yaman with a valuable collection of Ismaili books soon after ʿAlī al-Ṣulayḥī's death in 459/1067. Lamak was now appointed as chief *dāʿī* of Yaman, while ʿAlī al-Ṣulayḥī's son, Aḥmad al-Mukarram, succeeded his father merely as head of the Ṣulayḥid state. The extremely close Ṣulayḥid–Fatimid relations, maintained under ʿAlī al-Ṣulayḥī's successors, are well attested to by numerous letters and epistles (*sijillāt*) sent from the Fatimid chancery to the Ṣulayḥids.

From the latter part of Aḥmad al-Mukarram's rule, during which time the Ṣulayḥids lost much of northern Yaman to Zaydīs, effective authority in the Ṣulayḥid state was exercised by al-Mukarram's consort, al-Malika al-Sayyida Ḥurra. Noted for her beauty, courage, piety and independent character, al-Sayyida was a most remarkable queen. One of her first acts was to transfer the seat of the Ṣulayḥid state from Ṣanʿāʾ to Dhū Jibla, where she built a new palace and transformed the old one into a mosque. It is a testimony to the queen al-Sayyida's capabilities that upon her assumption of political power she also came to play an increasingly important role in the *daʿwa* affairs, which culminated in her appointment as the *ḥujja* of Yaman by al-Mustanṣir shortly after the death of her husband in 477/1084. This represented the first application of the rank of *ḥujja*, or indeed any high rank in the *daʿwa* hierarchy, to a woman.[45]

The Ṣulayḥids also played a crucial part in the renewed efforts of the Fatimids to spread the Ismaili *daʿwa* on the Indian subcontinent, where Ismailism had survived the persecutions of Sultan Maḥmūd of Ghazna. Around 460/1067, a new Ismaili community was founded in Gujarāt by *dāʿī*s sent from Yaman. The Ṣulayḥids themselves supervised the selection and dispatch of these *dāʿī*s with the approval of al-Mustanṣir. The imam personally charged the queen al-Sayyida with the affairs of the *daʿwa* in western India.[46] The *daʿwa* in Gujarāt maintained close ties with Yaman, and the Ismaili community founded there in the second half of the 5th/11th century evolved into the present Ṭayyibī Bohra community.

The caliph-imam al-Mustanṣir's long reign of almost sixty years witnessed numerous domestic vicissitudes with the Fatimid empire now on the decline. Racial rivalries in Fatimid armies provided a major source of unrest in Egypt. Factional fighting among the Berber, Turkish, Daylamī and African regiments came to a head in 454/1062, when Fatimid troops engaged in open warfare near Cairo. Later, Nāṣir al-Dawla, commander of the victorious Turkish troops, rebelled against al-Mustanṣir and had the *khuṭba* pronounced in the name of the Abbasids in Alexandria and elsewhere in lower Egypt. Meanwhile, Egypt was plagued by a series of crises, food shortages and famine due to low water levels of the Nile for seven consecutive years (457–64/1065–72). The atrocities of the Turkish troops eventually led to a complete breakdown of law and order. The Fatimid palaces and libraries in Cairo, too, were looted by unruly Turkish guards in 461/1068–9.

It was under such chaotic circumstances that al-Mustanṣir finally appealed to Badr al-Jamālī, an Armenian general in the service of the Fatimids in Syria, for help. Badr arrived in Cairo in 466/1074, quelling the Turkish rebellion with his Armenian troops. Soon, he monopolised political power, as he assumed leadership of the civil, judicial and religious administrations, in addition to being "commander of the armies" (*amīr al-juyūsh*), his best-known title. Indeed, during his long vizierate of twenty years, Badr was virtual ruler of the Fatimid state and it was mainly through his efforts that Egypt enjoyed peace and relative prosperity in the remaining years of al-Mustanṣir's reign. Despite Badr's attempts to revive Fatimid authority in Syria and Palestine, however, they effectively lost these regions to the newly arriving Turkish tribes. In 471/1078–9, Damascus became the capital of a Saljuq principality based in Syria. And by the end of al-Mustanṣir's rule, of the former Fatimid possessions in Syria and Palestine only Ascalon and a few coastal towns such as Acre and Tyre still remained intact. In North Africa by then, Fatimid dominions were practically reduced to Egypt proper.

Badr al-Jamālī, founder of a powerful dynasty of Fatimid viziers, died in 487/1094, having arranged for the succession of his son al-Afḍal. A few months later, in Dhu'l-Ḥijja 487/December 1094, Abū Tamīm Ma'add al-Mustanṣir bi'llāh, eighth Fatimid caliph and eighteenth Ismaili imam, died in Cairo. The dispute over his succession led to a permanent schism in the Ismaili community with lasting consequences for Ismailism.

THE NIZĀRĪ–MUSTA'LĪ SCHISM OF 487/1094

The unified Ismaili *da'wa* of al-Mustanṣir's period split into two branches upon his death in 487/1094. Al-Mustanṣir had initially designated his eldest surviving son Abū Manṣūr Nizār (437–88/1045–95) as his successor, following the Shī'ī rule of the *naṣṣ*. Abu'l-Qāsim Shāhanshāh, better known by his title of al-Afḍal, who a few months earlier had succeeded his father Badr al-Jamālī as the all-powerful Fatimid vizier and "commander of the armies", however, had other plans. Aiming to strengthen his own dictatorial position, al-Afḍal favoured the candidacy of Nizār's much younger half-brother Abu'l-Qāsim Aḥmad (467–95/1074–1101), who was entirely dependent on him. At the time, the youthful Aḥmad was also married to al-Afḍal's sister. Al-Afḍal moved swiftly and, on the day after al-Mustanṣir's death, placed Aḥmad on the Fatimid throne with the caliphal title of al-Mustaʿlī bi'llāh. Supported by the Fatimid armies, al-Afḍal quickly obtained for al-Mustaʿlī the allegiance of all the notables of the Fatimid court and *daʿwa* leaders in Cairo. There are conflicting accounts of this important event. Later, the Mustaʿlī Ismaili leadership circulated different versions of the circumstances, including a deathbed designation, by decree of which al-Mustanṣir had allegedly nominated al-Mustaʿlī as his heir apparent.[47] It remains historically true, however, that al-Mustanṣir never revoked Nizār's succession rights and that al-Mustaʿlī was placed on the Fatimid throne through al-Afḍal's machinations which amounted to a palace *coup*. This explains why Nizār refused to endorse al-Afḍal's designs and fled to Alexandria in revolt early in 488/1095.

Nizār received much local support in Alexandria, the centre of certain military factions suppressed by Badr al-Jamālī. His cause was taken up there by the city's governor and its Ismaili *qāḍī*. Soon thereafter, he was declared caliph, entitled al-Muṣṭafā li-Dīn Allāh, and received the allegiance of the Alexandrians. The declaration of Nizār as caliph as well as imam in Alexandria is attested to by the discovery of a gold dinar in 1994. Minted in AH 488, this unique find is now preserved in the collections of the Institute of Ismaili Studies Library, London. Nizār was initially successful in his encounter with al-Afḍal's forces. By the end of 488/1095, however, al-Afḍal personally took the field against Nizār, whose coalition of supporters had meanwhile faltered, and forced him to surrender. Nizār was taken to Cairo, where he was executed.

The dispute over al-Mustanṣir's succession permanently split the Ismailis into two rival factions, later designated as the Nizāriyya (Nizārī) and the Mustaʿliyya (Mustaʿlī). The imamate of al-Mustaʿlī, installed to the Fatimid caliphate, was acknowledged by the official *daʿwa* establishment in Cairo, as well as the Ismaili communities of Egypt, Yaman and western India. These Ismailis, who depended on the Fatimid regime and later traced the imamate in al-Mustaʿlī's progeny, maintained their relations with Cairo, serving hereafter as headquarters to the Mustaʿlī Ismaili *daʿwa*.

The situation was quite different in the eastern lands where the Fatimids no longer exercised political influence. By 487/1094, Ḥasan Ṣabbāḥ had emerged as leader of the Ismailis of Persia. The responsibility in the Saljuq domains for taking sides in the Nizārī-Mustaʿlī conflict now rested with Ḥasan who showed no hesitation in supporting Nizār. Ḥasan, in fact, founded the independent Nizārī *daʿwa*, severing his ties with the Fatimid regime and the *daʿwa* headquarters in Cairo. In this decision, Ḥasan was supported by the entire Ismaili community of Persia as well as that of Iraq. Nizār also had partisans in Egypt, but they were quickly suppressed by al-Afḍal. The original reaction of the Syrian Ismailis to the succession dispute remains obscure. Both factions were present in Syria, despite its relatively small Ismaili community. As a former dominion with close ties to the central government, the bulk of the Syrian Ismailis initially probably endorsed the actual course of events in Egypt, acknowledging al-Mustaʿlī. By the 510s/1120s, however, the Mustaʿlī Ismaili community of Syria was overtaken by an expanding Nizārī community and was, in time, entirely subsumed by it. The Ismailis of Central Asia seem to have remained uninvolved in the Nizārī–Mustaʿlī schism for quite some time. It was much later in the Alamūt period that the Ismailis of Badakhshān and other parts of Central Asia openly accorded their allegiance to the Nizārī *daʿwa*.

LATER FATIMIDS AND EARLY MUSTAʿLĪ ISMAILISM

The Fatimid state, reduced almost entirely to Egypt proper and devoid of its earlier grandeur, survived for another seventy-seven precarious years after the Nizārī–Mustaʿlī schism of 487/1094. These final decades were marked by the rapid decline of what remained of the Fatimid caliphate until its total and uneventful collapse. Al-Mustaʿlī and the later Fatimids, generally powerless in the hands of their viziers and scheming military commanders, continued to be recognised as imams in Egypt, Syria, Yaman and Gujarāt by the Mustaʿlī Ismailis, split into Ṭayyibī and Ḥāfiẓī factions.

Al-Afḍal remained the effective ruler of the Fatimid state during al-Mustaʿlī's brief reign (487–95/1094–1101). It was in this period that the Crusaders appeared in the Near East to wrest control of the Holy Land from Muslims. In 492/1099, they occupied Jerusalem, their primary target, after defeating a Fatimid army led by al-Afḍal near Ascalon. The Crusaders now established permanent states and settlements in the Near East and entered into war and diplomacy with Muslim rulers.

On al-Mustaʿlī's premature death in 495/1101, al-Afḍal placed his five-year-old son on the throne with the caliphal title of al-Āmir bi-Aḥkām Allāh, while himself retaining the reins of state. Despite al-Afḍal's efforts, the greater part of Palestine and the Syrian coastal towns now fell into the hands of the Crusaders, who had prolonged encounters with the Nizārī Ismailis of Syria. Egypt was temporarily invaded in 511/1117 by Baldwin I, king of the Latin state of Jerusalem. On al-Afḍal's murder in 515/1121, probably at the instigation of the Fatimid caliph himself, al-Āmir personally took charge of the deteriorating affairs of the Fatimid state until he, too, was assassinated in 524/1130. The majority of the sources relate that his assassins were Nizārī *fidā'īs* or devotees who at the time carried out such missions on behest of their leaders. Al-Āmir had made numerous attempts officially to refute the claims of Nizār, his uncle, and his descendants to the imamate.

The Fatimid caliph al-Musta'lī, as noted, had been recognised as imam by the *da'wa* headquarters in Cairo and by the Ismailis of Egypt, and the bulk of the community in Syria. In Yaman, owing to the close relations then existing between the Ṣulayḥids and the Fatimid regime, the queen al-Sayyida, too, had supported the imamate of al-Musta'lī. As a result of al-Sayyida's decision to retain her ties with Cairo, the entire Ismaili community of Yaman, and that of Gujarāt dependent on it, also joined the Musta'lī camp. And on al-Musta'lī's death, all Musta'lī Ismailis acknowledged al-Āmir as their new imam. In her decision to side with the Musta'lī cause, the aged Ṣulayḥid queen was fully supported by the *dā'ī* Lamak, the executive head of the Yamani *da'wa*, and his son and successor Yaḥyā who took charge of the affairs of the *da'wa* on his father's death around 491/1098. On Yaḥyā b. Lamak's death in 520/1126, his assistant *da'ī*, al-Dhu'ayb b. Mūsā al-Wādi'ī al-Hamdānī, became executive head of the *da'wa* in Yaman; his appointment had received the prior approval of both the deceased *dā'ī* and the Ṣulayḥid queen. The Ṣulayḥid state itself was now in turmoil, however. In addition to incessant pressures from the Zaydīs and other local dynasties, al-Sayyida's authority had been challenged by a number of tribal chiefs. As a result, the Ṣulayḥids eventually lost Ṣan'ā' to a new Hamdānid dynasty supported by the refractory chiefs.

The assassination of al-Āmir confronted the Musta'lī Ismailis with a new crisis that was to split their community into Ḥāfiẓī and Ṭayyibī factions.[48] The Fatimid caliphate, too, was on the verge of disintegration, marked by an almost uninterrupted chain of dynastic, religious, political and military crises. According to the Ṭayyibī Musta'lī tradition, a son, named al-Ṭayyib, had been born to al-Āmir a few months before his death. This tradition is supported by an epistle of al-Āmir sent to the Ṣulayḥid queen of Yaman. The historicity of al-Ṭayyib's birth is also attested by Ibn Muyassar,[49] among other chroniclers. At any rate, al-Ṭayyib was immediately designated as al-Āmir's heir. However, on al-Āmir's death power was assumed by his cousin, Abu'l-Maymūn 'Abd al-Majīd, a grandson of al-Mustanṣir, who was then the eldest member of the Fatimid family.

'Abd al-Majīd ruled officially as regent, managing to conceal the existence of al-Ṭayyib about whose subsequent fate nothing is known. Shortly after, Abū 'Alī Aḥmad, nicknamed Kutayfāt, son of al-Afḍal b. Badr al-Jamālī, was installed to the vizierate by the army, while ʿAbd al-Majīd stayed in power as regent or the *walī ʿahd al-Muslimīn*. Soon after assuming the vizierate, in what is undoubtedly the most confusing event in the entire history of the Fatimid dynasty, Kutayfāt imprisoned ʿAbd al-Majīd and proclaimed the sovereignty of the twelfth imam or the Mahdi of the Ithnāʿashariyya, in occultation since 260/874. Kutayfāt, now a Twelver Shīʿī, issued coins in Cairo naming himself as representative (*nāʾib*) of the hidden imam. This may have been an ingenious – albeit temporary – solution to the problem of succession to the Fatimid caliphate and imamate in the absence of legitimate claimants.

In 526/1131 Kutayfāt was overthrown and killed in yet another *coup* organised by supporters of the Fatimid dynasty. ʿAbd al-Majīd was released from prison and restored to power. Initially, he once again ruled as regent, but three months later, in Rabīʿ II 526/February 1132, he was proclaimed caliph and imam with the title of al-Ḥāfiẓ li-Dīn Allāh; and Ismailism was reinstated as the official religion of the Fatimid state. The irregular succession of al-Ḥāfiẓ, whose father had not ruled before him, was legitimised in an epistle issued by the Fatimid chancery, claiming that al-Āmir had personally designated his cousin al-Ḥāfiẓ as his successor in the same manner that the Prophet had appointed his cousin ʿAlī to leadership of Muslims at Ghadīr Khumm.[50] This document provided a "legitimising" foundation on which Fatimid rule was to continue precariously for another four decades.

The proclamation of al-Ḥāfiẓ as imam caused a major split in the Mustaʿlī Ismaili community. As in the case of the Nizārī–Mustaʿlī schism, it was endorsed by the *daʿwa* headquarters in Cairo, and, hence, it also received the support of most Mustaʿlī Ismailis in Egypt and Syria, who were dependent on the Fatimid regime. These Ismailis, recognising al-Ḥāfiẓ and the later Fatimids as their imams, became known as the Ḥāfiẓiyya. The situation was quite different in Yaman, where a bitter contest rooted in power politics ensued within the Mustaʿlī community. As a result, the Mustaʿlī Ismailis of Yaman themselves were split into two factions. The Zurayʿids of ʿAdan, and some of the Hamdānids of Ṣanʿāʾ, who had won their independence from the Ṣulayḥids, now supported the Ḥāfiẓī cause. In fact, the Zurayʿids became chief *dāʿī*s of the Ḥāfiẓī *daʿwa* in Yaman. On the other hand, the Ṣulayḥid queen, already somewhat disillusioned with Cairo, championed the cause of al-Ṭayyib, recognising him as al-Āmir's successor to the imamate. These Mustaʿlī Ismailis of Yaman, as well as some minority groups in Egypt and Syria, were initially known as the Āmiriyya, but later, after the establishment of the independent Ṭayyibī *daʿwa*, were designated as the Ṭayyibiyya. Thus, by 526/1132, the unified Ismaili *daʿwa* and community of al-Mustanṣir's time was permanently divided into the rival Nizārī, Ḥāfiẓī and Ṭayyibī factions that were to remain irreparably hostile towards one another.

Like al-Ḥāfiẓ, the later Fatimid caliphs, too, were recognised as imams by the Ḥāfiẓī Mustaʿlī Ismailis. And the earlier Fatimid Ismaili traditions continued to be maintained in Egypt. These included the central *daʿwa* apparatus in Cairo, and the appointment of a *dāʿī al-duʿāt* and a *qāḍī al-quḍāt*, as well as the delivery of the "sessions of wisdom". However, Ḥāfiẓī *daʿwa* activities were now almost exclusively limited to Fatimid Egypt and parts of Yaman. The Dār al-ʿIlm, too, was still operative with close ties to *daʿwa* activities. This institution had been moved to a new building in Cairo, outside the Fatimid palace, in 526/1132, from where it continued to function until it was closed down on the fall of the Fatimid dynasty. Ḥāfiẓī theologians of this period must have concerned themselves with literary activities. However, the Ḥāfiẓī *daʿwa* did not survive the collapse of the Fatimid state when Ḥāfiẓī Ismailism soon disappeared completely and there were no longer any Ḥāfiẓī communities left to preserve their literature.

In the closing decades of Fatimid rule, Egypt was beset by all types of internal and external difficulties whilst the youthful caliphs remained helpless spectators. The penultimate Fatimid caliph, al-Fā'iz, succeeded his father al-Ẓāfir (544–9/1149–54) at the age of five. When he died childless some five years later in 555/1160, the dynasty and the Ḥāfiẓī imamate were faced with yet another serious problem of succession. Ibn Ruzzīk, the Fatimid vizier and absolute master of the state, placed another grandson of al-Ḥāfiẓ on the throne with the title of al-ʿĀḍid li-Dīn Allāh. Destined to be the seal of his dynasty, al-ʿĀḍid was only nine years old at the time.

Al-ʿĀḍid's nominal reign represented the most turbulent and confusing period of Fatimid history. Power remained concentrated in the hands of several short-lived viziers, who continuously intrigued against one another. The Franks, too, resumed their invasions, establishing a virtual protectorate over Egypt. Under the circumstances, Shāwar, a Fatimid vizier who had been deposed in 558/1163, took refuge at the court of Nūr al-Dīn in Syria, seeking help from the Zangid ruler for regaining the vizierate. Nūr al-Dīn, with his own expansionist ambitions, sent Shāwar back to Egypt accompanied by an expedition commanded by Asad al-Dīn Shīrkūh. On this expedition Shīrkūh took along his nephew, Ṣalāḥ al-Dīn b. Ayyūb (Saladin), the future founder of the Sunni Ayyūbid dynasty.

Shāwar was restored to the Fatimid vizierate, but later in the course of a third Zangid expedition, again led by Shīrkūh, he was arrested and killed in 564/1169. Thereupon, al-ʿĀḍid was obliged to appoint Shīrkūh to the vizierate, and when Shīrkūh died a few months later, he was succeeded by Saladin who had accompanied his uncle to Cairo. Saladin, the last of the Fatimid viziers, systematically prepared the ground for deposing the Fatimid dynasty and suppressing Ismailism in Egypt, objectives sought by Nūr al-Dīn. Saladin formally put an end to Fatimid rule when on 7 Muḥarram 567/10 September 1171 he had the *khuṭba* read in Cairo in the name of the reigning Abbasid caliph, symbolising the return of Egypt to the fold of Sunni Islam. A few days later, al-ʿĀḍid, the fourteenth and final Fatimid caliph-imam, died after a brief illness. The Fatimid *dawla* had, thus, come to a close after 262 years. On Nūr al-Dīn's death in 569/1174, Saladin proclaimed the independent Ayyūbid dynasty, which was to rule over Egypt, Syria, Yaman and other parts of the Near East for almost three centuries.

On al-ʿĀḍid's death, numerous members of the Fatimid family were placed in permanent captivity in various locations in Cairo. The immense treasures of the Fatimids, including their vast libraries, were pillaged or sold. Saladin severely persecuted the Ismailis of Egypt, also suppressing the Ḥāfiẓī *daʿwa* organisation and all the Fatimid Ismaili traditions and institutions; the Dār al-ʿIlm was transformed into a hospital. For a while longer, however, al-ʿĀḍid's son Dā'ūd (d. 604/1207) as well as other Fatimids laid claims to the Ḥāfiẓī imamate. Some of these pretenders also rose in revolts in Egypt, attracting limited local support.[51] By the end of the 7th/13th century, Ḥāfiẓī communities had disintegrated completely in Egypt and Syria. With these developments, Ismailism of any form disappeared permanently from Egypt. Meanwhile, in Yaman too, Ḥāfiẓī Ismailism did not survive the downfall of its Zurayʿid and Hamdānid supporters in the wake of the Ayyūbid conquests of southern Arabia in 569/1173. Henceforth, Mustaʿlī Ismailism survived only in its Ṭayyibī form.

The Ṣulayḥid queen al-Sayyida had meanwhile become leader of the Ṭayyibī faction in Yaman. She severed her ties with Cairo and the Fatimid regime, similarly to what Ḥasan Ṣabbāḥ had done earlier in Persia on al-Mustanṣir's death. The queen al-Sayyida, as noted, held the real power in Ṣulayḥid Yaman, also controlling the affairs of the *daʿwa* there and in Gujarāt. In her decision, the queen was fully endorsed by the *dāʿī* al-Dhu'ayb, then executive head of the Yamani *daʿwa*. Nothing is known about the fate of al-Ṭayyib, probably murdered secretly on al-Ḥāfiẓ's order. According to a Yamani Ṭayyibī tradition, however, al-Āmir had placed his infant son in the custody of a group of trusted *dāʿīs* who, in due course, managed to hide him, and made it possible for the Ṭayyibī imamate to continue in his progeny. The Ṭayyibī Mustaʿlī Ismailis are, indeed, of the opinion that their imamate in the current period of *satr*, initiated by al-Ṭayyib's concealment, has been handed down among his descendants down to the present time.

From 526/1132 until her death in 532/1138, al-Malika al-Sayyida made every effort to consolidate the Ṭayyibī *daʿwa*. It was soon after 526/1132 that the Ṣulayḥid queen declared al-Dhu'ayb as *al-dāʿī al-muṭlaq*, or *dāʿī* with absolute authority, to conduct and supervise the *daʿwa* on behalf of the hidden imam, al-Ṭayyib. This marked the foundation of the independent Ṭayyibī *daʿwa*, henceforth called *al-daʿwa al-Ṭayyibiyya*. Having earlier broken off relations with the Fatimid regime, she also made the new Ṭayyibī *daʿwa* independent of the Ṣulayḥid regime, a measure that was to ensure the survival of Ṭayyibī Ismailism under the leadership of a *dāʿī muṭlaq*. Al-Dhu'ayb's successors have retained this title down to the present day.[52]

Al-Dhu'ayb was initially assisted by al-Khaṭṭāb b. al-Ḥasan, who belonged to a family of the chieftains of al-Ḥajūr, another Hamdānī clan. An important Ismaili author and poet, al-Khaṭṭāb's loyalty to the Ṣulayḥid queen and his military services to the Ismaili cause in Yaman contributed significantly to the early success of the Ṭayyibī *daʿwa*.[53] On al-Khaṭṭāb's death in 533/1138, a year after the queen had died, al-Dhu'ayb appointed Ibrāhīm b. al-Ḥusayn al-Ḥāmidī, of the Ḥāmidī clan of the Banū Hamdān, as his new assistant or *ma'dhūn*, the second highest rank in the Ṭayyibī *daʿwa* hierarchy. On al-Dhu'ayb's death in 546/1151, Ibrāhīm al-Ḥāmidī (d. 557/1162) succeeded to the headship of the Ṭayyibī *daʿwa* as the second *dāʿī muṭlaq*. Ibrāhīm introduced the *Rasā'il Ikhwān al-Ṣafā'* into the religious literature of the Ṭayyibīs of Yaman. Drawing extensively on al-Kirmānī's *Rāḥat al-ʿaql*, he also formulated a new synthesis in the doctrinal domain, and, in fact, founded the specifically Ṭayyibī *ḥaqā'iq* system of thought. This system, first expounded in Ibrāhīm's major work entitled *Kanz al-walad* (*The Child's Treasure*), combines al-Kirmānī's metaphysical structure, especially its cosmological doctrine of the ten separate intellects, with gnostic mythical elements. The Neoplatonic cosmology introduced into Ismaili thought by the Iranian *dāʿīs* thus received final modification at the hands of the Ṭayyibī Mustaʿlī *dāʿīs* in Yaman.[54]

Al-Dhu'ayb, al-Khaṭṭāb and Ibrāhīm al-Ḥāmidī were in fact the earliest leaders of the Ṭayyibī *daʿwa* who, under the guidance and protection of the Ṣulayḥid queen, consolidated Ṭayyibī Mustaʿlī Ismailism in Yaman. The Ṭayyibī *daʿwa* was independent of both the

Fatimid regime as well as the Ṣulayḥid state, and this explains why it survived their downfall. The Ṭayyibī community of Yaman also managed to preserve the bulk of Ismaili literature of the Fatimid times. It was under such circumstances that Ṭayyibī Ismailism spread successfully in Yaman, and later in Gujarāt. In time, the overwhelming majority of Ṭayyibī Ismailis came to be situated in the Indian subcontinent where they have been known as Bohras.

NOTES

1. The subject of Fatimid ceremonials and their significance is treated at length in Paula Sanders's *Ritual, Politics, and the City in Fatimid Cairo* (Albany, NY, 1994), also containing references to the earlier studies of M. Canard and others.
2. For a number of important studies by Claude Cahen on the economic history of Fatimid Egypt, see his *Makhzūmiyyāt: Etudes sur l'histoire économique et financière de l'Egypte médiévale* (Leiden, 1977).
3. Nāṣir Khusraw, *Safar-nāma*, ed. M. Dabīr Siyāqī (5th edn, Tehran, 1356/1977), pp. 74–99; English trans. W. M. Thackston, Jr., *Nāṣer-e Khosraw's Book of Travels (Safarnāma)* (Albany, NY, 1986), pp. 44–57.
4. Ibn Ḥawqal, *Kitāb ṣūrat al-arḍ*, p. 96; French trans., *Configuration*, vol. 1, p. 94. Professor W. Madelung, who in 1994 presented a paper on this issue to a conference held at St Petersburg, is now (letter to the author dated 22 July 1996) of the opinion that Ibn Ḥawqal's information may well be reliable; see also Madelung's "The Fatimids and the Qarmaṭīs of Baḥrayn", p. 55 n. 28.
5. The propagation of the *da'wa* in the Maghrib and Abū 'Abd Allāh's activities there, culminating in the establishment of the Fatimid caliphate, are treated at length in al-Nu'mān's *Iftitāḥ al-da'wa*, ed. al-Qāḍī, pp. 71–222; ed. Dachraoui, pp. 47–257, drawing extensively on the *Sīra* of Abū 'Abd Allāh which has not survived; and in Idrīs, *'Uyūn al-akhbār*, vol. 5, pp. 44–88. See also T. Nagel, *Frühe Ismailiya und Fatimiden im lichte der Risālat Iftitāḥ ad-Da'wa* (Bonn, 1972), pp. 11–48; F. Dachraoui, *Le Califat Fatimide au Maghreb, 296–365 H./909–975 Jc.* (Tunis, 1981), pp. 57–122, and Halm, *Empire of the Mahdi*, pp. 9–128.
6. Al-Nu'mān, *Iftitāḥ al-da'wa*, ed. al-Qāḍī, pp. 249–50; ed. Dachraoui, pp. 293–4.
7. On this revolt and its underlying causes, see Idrīs, *'Uyūn al-akhbār*, vol. 5, pp. 172–318; al-Maqrīzī, *Itti'āẓ*, vol. 1, pp. 75–89; G. Marçais, *La Berbérie Musulmane et l'Orient au moyen-âge* (Paris, 1946), pp. 131–56; H. Halm, "Der Mann auf dem Esel: Der Aufstand des Abū Yazīd gegen die Fatimiden nach einem Augenzeugenbericht", WO, 15 (1984), pp. 144–204, and his *Empire of the Mahdi*, pp. 298–325.
8. F. Dachraoui, "al-Mu'izz li-Dīn Allāh", EI2, vol. 7, p. 489.
9. Poonawala, *Biobibliography*, pp. 68–70.
10. See, for instance, al-Nu'mān's *Kitāb al-majālis*, and Abū 'Alī Manṣūr al-'Azīzī al-Jawdharī, *Sīrat al-ustādh Jawdhar*, ed. M. Kāmil Ḥusayn and M. 'A. Sha'īra (Cairo, 1954), pp. 87–148; French trans. M. Canard, *Vie de l'ustadh Jaudhar* (Algiers, 1958), pp. 127–255. See also Idrīs, *'Uyūn al-akhbār*, vol. 6, pp. 9–204, and his *Ta'rīkh*

al-khulafā' al-Fāṭimiyyīn bi'l-Maghrib, ed. M. al-Ya'lāwī (Beirut, 1985), pp. 523–739, and al-Maqrīzī, *Itti'āẓ*, vol. 1, pp. 93–150, 186–235.

11. Asaf A. A. Fyzee, "Qadi an-Nu'man: The Fatimid Jurist and Author", JRAS (1934), pp. 1–32; and the following works by I. K. Poonawala: "Al-Qāḍī al-Nu'mān's Works and the Sources", BSOAS, 36 (1973), pp. 109–15; "A Reconsideration of al-Qāḍī al-Nu'mān's *Madhhab*", BSOAS, 37 (1974), pp. 572–9; *Biobibliography*, pp. 48–68, and F. Dachraoui, "al-Nu'mān", EI2, vol. 8, pp. 117–18.
12. Al-Nu'mān, *Kitāb al-majālis*, pp. 386–8, 435–6, 487, 546.
13. Ibid., p. 306.
14. Al-Qāḍī al-Nu'mān, *The Book of Faith*, tr. A. A. A. Fyzee (Bombay, 1974), containing a translation of the *Kitāb al-walāya*, and A. Nanji, "An Ismā'īlī Theory of *Walāyah* in the *Da'ā'im al-Islām* of Qāḍī al-Nu'mān", in D. P. Little (ed.), *Essays on Islamic Civilization Presented to Niyazi Berkes* (Leiden, 1976), pp. 260–73.
15. W. Madelung, "The Sources of Ismā'īlī Law", *Journal of Near Eastern Studies*, 35 (1976), pp. 29–40, reprinted in his *Religious Schools and Sects in Medieval Islam* (London, 1985), article XVIII, and I. K. Poonawala, "Al-Qāḍī al-Nu'mān and Isma'ili Jurisprudence", in Daftary, *Mediaeval Isma'ili History*, pp. 117–43.
16. See S. M. Stern, "Heterodox Ismā'īlism at the Time of al-Mu'izz", BSOAS, 17 (1955), pp. 10–33, reprinted in his *Studies*, pp. 257–88; Madelung, "Das Imamat", pp. 86–101, and Daftary, *The Ismā'īlīs*, pp. 176–80.
17. S. M. Stern, "Ismā'īlī Propaganda and Fatimid Rule in Sind", *Islamic Culture*, 23 (1949), pp. 298–307, reprinted in his *Studies*, pp. 177–88; A. Hamdani, *The Beginnings of the Ismā'īlī Da'wa in Northern India* (Cairo, 1956), pp. 3–16, and Halm, *Empire of the Mahdi*, pp. 385–92.
18. See al-Maqrīzī, *Itti'āẓ*, vol. 2, pp. 292–3.
19. On these Neoplatonic texts and their influences on early Ismaili thinkers, see P. Kraus, "Plotin chez les Arabes", *Bulletin de l'Institut d'Egypte*, 23 (1940–1), pp. 263–95, reprinted in P. Kraus, *Alchemie, Ketzerei, Apokryphen im frühen Islam*, ed. R. Brague (Hildesheim, 1994), pp. 313–45; S. Pines, "La Longue récension de la Théologie d'Aristote dans ses rapports avec la doctrine Ismaélienne", *Revue des Etudes Islamiques*, 22 (1954), pp. 7–20; S. M. Stern, "Ibn Ḥasdāy's Neoplatonist", *Oriens*, 13–14 (1960–1), especially pp. 58–98, reprinted in his *Medieval Arabic and Hebrew Thought* (London, 1983), article VII; R. C. Taylor, "The *Kalām fī maḥḍ al-khair* (*Liber de causis*) in the Islamic Philosophical Milieu", and F. W. Zimmermann, "The Origins of the so-called *Theology of Aristotle*", both in J. Kraye et al. (eds), *Pseudo-Aristotle in the Middle Ages: The Theology and Other Texts* (London, 1986), pp. 37–52 and 110–240, and Walker, *Early Philosophical Shiism*, pp. 37–44.
20. On the Ikhwān al-Ṣafā' and their *Rasā'il*, see Ian R. Netton, "The Brethren of Purity (Ikhwān al-Ṣafā')", in S. H. Nasr and O. Leaman (eds), *History of Islamic Philosophy* (London, 1996), vol. 1, pp. 222–30; Y. Marquet, "Ikhwān al-Ṣafā'", EI2, vol. 3, pp. 1071–6, and Daftary, *The Ismā'īlīs*, pp. 246–9, 650–1, where additional references are given.
21. For a comprehensive study of the metaphysical systems of the Iranian

dāʿīs, as elaborated especially by al-Sijistānī, see Walker, *Early Philosophical Shiism*, pp. 67–142, and his *Abū Yaʿqūb al-Sijistānī: Intellectual Missionary* (London, 1996), pp. 26–103. See also Netton, *Allāh Transcendent*, pp. 210–22, and Azim Nanji, "Ismāʿīlī Philosophy", in Nasr and Leaman (eds), *History of Islamic Philosophy*, vol. 1, pp. 144–54. Only one of al-Sijistānī's books, the *Kitāb al-yanābīʿ*, containing the major themes of his metaphysical system, has been translated into English; see Paul E. Walker, *The Wellsprings of Wisdom: A Study of Abū Yaʿqūb al-Sijistānī's Kitāb al-Yanābīʿ* (Salt Lake City, 1994), pp. 37–111; for the Arabic text and a partial French translation of this work, see H. Corbin (ed. and tr.), *Trilogie Ismaélienne* (Tehran and Paris, 1961), text pp. 1–97, translation pp. 5–127.

22. See Abū Manṣūr Muḥammad b. Muḥammad al-Māturīdī, *Kitāb al-tawḥīd*, ed. F. Kholeif (Beirut, 1970), pp. 3–27, 63–4; Halm, *Kosmologie*, pp. 129–38, 222–4, with excerpts from al-Bustī's *Min kashf asrār al-Bāṭiniyya*, and S. M. Stern, "Abu'l-Qasim al-Bustī and his Refutation of Ismāʿīlism", JRAS (1961), pp. 14–35, reprinted in his *Studies*, pp. 299–320.
23. Ḥamīd al-Dīn al-Kirmānī, *Kitāb al-riyāḍ*, ed. ʿĀrif Tāmir (Beirut, 1960), pp. 176–212; see also Madelung, "Das Imamat", pp. 101–14.
24. Ḥamīd al-Dīn al-Kirmānī, *Rāḥat al-ʿaql*, ed. M. Kāmil Ḥusayn and M. Muṣṭafā Ḥilmī (Cairo, 1953); ed. M. Ghālib (Beirut, 1967). For a thorough study of al-Kirmānī's metaphysical system, including his cosmology, see Daniel de Smet, *La Quiétude de l'intellect: Néoplatonisme et gnose Ismaélienne dans l'œuvre de Ḥamīd ad-Dīn al-Kirmānī (Xe/XIes.)* (Louvain, 1995).
25. See al-Kirmānī, *Rāḥat al-ʿaql*, ed. Ḥusayn and Ḥilmī, pp. 134–9, 224–5, and H. Corbin, "Epiphanie divine et naissance spirituelle dans la gnose Ismaélienne", *Eranos Jahrbuch*, 23 (1954), pp. 178–84; English trans., "Divine Epiphany and Spiritual Birth in Ismailian Gnosis", in his *Cyclical Time*, pp. 90–5, and Netton, *Allāh Transcendent*, pp. 222–9.
26. Al-Qāḍī al-Nuʿmān, *Kitāb al-himma fī ādāb atbāʿ al-a'imma*, ed. M. Kāmil Ḥusayn (Cairo, 1948), pp. 136–40.
27. A facsimile edition of al-Nīsābūrī's lost treatise *al-Risāla al-mūjaza al-kāfiya fī ādāb al-duʿāt*, as preserved in Ḥasan b. Nūḥ al-Bharūchī's unpublished *Kitāb al-azhār*, vol. 2, is contained in Verena Klemm, *Die Mission des fāṭimidischen Agenten al-Mu'ayyad fī d-dīn in Šīrāz* (Frankfurt, etc., 1989), pp. 206–77. This text also provided the basis of W. Ivanow's pioneering article on the subject, "The Organization of the Fatimid Propaganda", *Journal of the Bombay Branch of the Royal Asiatic Society*, NS, 15 (1939), especially pp. 18–35.
28. See, for instance, al-Nuwayrī, *Nihāyat al-arab*, vol. 25, pp. 195–225; al-Baghdādī, *al-Farq*, pp. 282ff.; tr. Halkin, pp. 138ff., and al-Ghazālī, *Faḍā'iḥ al-Bāṭiniyya*, pp. 21–32.
29. Al-Maqrīzī, *Kitāb al-mawāʿiẓ wa'l-iʿtibār bi-dhikr al-khiṭaṭ wa'l-āthār* (Būlāq, 1270/1853–4), vol. 1, pp. 390–1, and vol. 2, pp. 341–2; ed. A. Fu'ād Sayyid (London, 1995), pp. 91–4, and Ibn al-Ṭuwayr, *Nuzhat al-muqlatayn fī akhbār al-dawlatayn*, ed. A. Fu'ād Sayyid (Beirut, 1992), pp. 110–12. For the best modern studies of these teaching sessions, see Heinz Halm's "The Ismaʿili Oath of Allegiance (*ʿahd*) and the 'Sessions of Wisdom' (*majālis al-ḥikma*) in Fatimid

Times", pp. 98–112, and his *The Fatimids and their Traditions of Learning* (London, 1997), especially pp. 23–9, 41–55.

30. Al-Nuʿmān, *Iftitāḥ al-daʿwa*, ed. al-Qāḍī, pp. 73, 76, 130, 140; ed. Dachraoui, pp. 49, 53, 128, 146.
31. See al-Nuʿmān, *Kitāb al-majālis*, pp. 86, 104, 209, 224, 231, 265, 305–6, 343, 344, 348, 386, 387–8, 434, 467, 487, 499, 511, 512, 545–6.
32. Al-Kirmānī, *Kitāb al-riyāḍ*, p. 108.
33. Al-Maqrīzī, *al-Khiṭaṭ*; ed. Būlāq, vol. 1, pp. 458–60; ed. Sayyid, pp. 300–4, and Halm, *The Fatimids*, pp. 71–7.
34. On the Fatimid Ismaili *daʿwa* and its evolution, see S. M. Stern, "Cairo as the Centre of the Ismāʿīlī Movement", in *Colloque international sur l'histoire du Caire* (Cairo, 1972), pp. 437–50, reprinted in his *Studies*, pp. 234–56; A. Hamdani, "Evolution of the Organisational Structure of the Fāṭimī Daʿwah", *Arabian Studies*, 3 (1976), pp. 85–114; P. E. Walker, "The Ismaili Daʿwa in the Reign of the Fatimid Caliph al-Ḥākim", *Journal of the American Research Center in Egypt*, 30 (1993), pp. 161–82; Daftary, *The Ismāʿīlīs*, pp. 224–32, and his "Dāʿī", EIR, vol. 6, pp. 590–3.
35. Al-Qāḍī al-Nuʿmān, *Ta'wīl al-daʿā'im*, ed. M. Ḥ. al-Aʿẓamī (Cairo, 1967–72), vol. 2, p. 74, and vol. 3, pp. 48–9, and al-Sijistānī, *Ithbāt al-nubuwwāt*, ed. ʿĀrif Tāmir (Beirut, 1966), p. 172.
36. Nāṣir Khusraw, *Zād al-musāfirīn*, ed. M. Badhl al-Raḥmān (Berlin, 1341/1923), p. 397, and Ibn Ḥawqal, *Ṣūrat al-arḍ*, p. 310.
37. Al-Kirmānī, *Rāḥat al-ʿaql*, ed. Ḥusayn and Ḥilmī, pp. 134–9; ed. Ghālib, pp. 249–57. See also R. Strothmann (ed.), *Gnosis Texte der Ismailiten* (Göttingen, 1943), pp. 82, 174–7; Nāṣir Khusraw, *Shish faṣl*, ed. and tr. W. Ivanow (Leiden, 1949), text pp. 34–6, translation pp. 74–7, and his *Wajh-i dīn*, ed. G. R. Aʿvānī (Tehran, 1977), p. 255.
38. Al-Kirmānī, *Majmūʿat al-rasā'il al-Kirmānī*, ed. M. Ghālib (Beirut, 1983), pp. 134–47.
39. For further details and sources on the Druze religion, see D. R. W. Bryer, "The Origins of the Druze Religion", *Der Islam*, 52 (1975), pp. 47–84, 239–62, and 53 (1976), 5–27, and Nejla M. Abu-Izzeddin, *The Druzes: A New Study of their History, Faith and Society* (Leiden, 1993). More recent developments in the Druze community are covered in Kais M. Firro, *A History of the Druzes* (Leiden, 1992).
40. Al-Mu'ayyad fi'l-Dīn al-Shīrāzī, *Sīrat al-Mu'ayyad fi'l-Dīn dāʿī al-duʿāt*, ed. M. Kāmil Ḥusayn (Cairo, 1949); see also Klemm, *Die Mission*, especially pp. 2–63, 136–92.
41. Al-Maqrīzī, *Ittiʿāẓ*, vol. 2, pp. 191–2; Ibn al-Athīr, *al-Kāmil fi'l-ta'rīkh*, ed. C. J. Tornberg (Leiden, 1851–76), vol. 9, pp. 211, 358, and vol. 10, pp. 122 ff., 165–6, and V. V. Barthhold, *Turkestan down to the Mongol Invasion*, ed. C. E. Bosworth (3rd edn, London, 1968), pp. 251, 304–5, 316–8.
42. Nāṣir Khusraw, *Zād al-musāfirīn*, pp. 3, 402, and his *Dīwān*, ed. M. Mīnuvī and M. Muḥaqqiq (Tehran, 1353/1974), pp. 162, 234, 287, 436; partial English trans. P. L. Wilson and G. R. Aavani, *Forty Poems from the Divan* (Tehran, 1977), pp. 73, 113.
43. Nāṣir Khusraw, *Jāmiʿ al-ḥikmatayn*, ed. H. Corbin and M. Muʿīn (Tehran and Paris, 1953), pp. 16–17; French trans. I. de Gastines, *Le Livre réunissant les deux sagesses* (Paris, 1990), p. 48.
44. A. Hamdani, "The Dāʿī Ḥātim Ibn Ibrāhīm al-Ḥāmidī (d. 596 H./

AD 1199) and his Book *Tuḥfat al-Qulūb*", *Oriens*, 23–4 (1970–1), pp. 270–9.

45. The earliest account of the Ṣulayḥids, and the contemporary Ismaili *da'wa* in Yaman, is contained in 'Umāra b. 'Alī al-Ḥakamī, *Ta'rīkh al-Yaman*, ed. and tr. Henry C. Kay, in his *Yaman, its Early Mediaeval History* (London, 1892), text pp. 1–102, translation pp. 1–137. Our chief Ismaili authority here is Idrīs, *'Uyūn al-akhbār*, vol. 7, which is still in manuscript form. For the best modern account of the Ṣulayḥids, see Ḥusayn F. al-Hamdānī, *al-Ṣulayḥiyyūn wa'l-ḥaraka al-Fāṭimiyya fi'l-Yaman* (Cairo, 1955), pp. 62–231.
46. Al-Mustanṣir, *al-Sijillāt*, pp. 167–9, 203–6, and al-Hamdānī, "Letters of al-Mustanṣir", pp. 321, 324.
47. In particular, see the epistle of the Fatimid caliph al-Āmir, issued in 516/1122, entitled *al-Hidāya al-Āmiriyya*, ed. Fyzee, pp. 3–26, reprinted in al-Shayyāl (ed.), *Majmū'at al-wathā'iq*, text pp. 203–30, commentaries pp. 47–67. This epistle is analysed in S. M. Stern, "The Epistle of the Fatimid Caliph al-Āmir (al-Hidāya al-Āmiriyya) – its Date and its Purpose", JRAS (1950), pp. 20–31, reprinted in his *History and Culture in the Medieval Muslim World* (London, 1984), article X.
48. The best modern study of the Fatimid dynasty after al-Āmir, and the Ḥāfiẓī-Ṭayyibī schism, is contained in S. M. Stern, "The Succession to the Fatimid Imam al-Āmir, the Claims of the Later Fatimids to the Imamate, and the Rise of Ṭayyibī Ismailism", *Oriens*, 4 (1951), pp. 193–255, reprinted in his *History and Culture*, article XI; see also Daftary, *The Ismā'īlīs*, pp. 256–97, where references to the sources are cited.
49. Ibn Muyassar, *Akhbār Miṣr*, pp. 109–10.
50. This epistle is preserved in al-Qalqashandī, *Ṣubḥ al-a'shā* (Cairo, 1331–8/ 1913–20), vol. 9, pp. 291–7, reprinted in al-Shayyāl (ed.), *Majmū'at al-wathā'iq*, text pp. 249–60, commentaries pp. 71–102.
51. The fullest account of these pro-Fatimid revolts, and the tragic fate of the surviving members of the Fatimid dynasty who remained in captivity for several generations until 671/1272, is provided in Paul Casanova, "Les Derniers Fāṭimides", *Mémoires de la Mission Archéologique Française du Caire*, 6 (1897), pp. 415–45.
52. The earliest history of the Ṭayyibī *da'wa* in Yaman is related by Ḥātim b. Ibrāhīm, the third *dā'ī muṭlaq*, in his unpublished *Tuḥfat al-qulūb*. The *dā'ī* Idrīs, too, has the relevant information, with biographical details of the earlier *dā'*īs, in the seventh volume of his *'Uyūn al-akhbār* and in his *Nuzhat al-afkār*, which still remain in manuscript form. See also Abbas Hamdani, "The Dā'ī Ḥātim", pp. 279ff.; his "The Ṭayyibī-Fāṭimid Community of the Yaman at the Time of the Ayyūbid Conquest of Southern Arabia", *Arabian Studies*, 7 (1985), pp. 151–60, and F. Daftary, "Sayyida Ḥurra: The Ismā'īlī Ṣulayḥid Queen of Yemen", in Gavin R. G. Hambly (ed.), *Women in the Medieval Islamic World* (New York, 1998), pp. 117–30.
53. Ismail K. Poonawala, *al-Sulṭān al-Khaṭṭāb* (Cairo, 1967), especially pp. 29–95, and his *Biobibliography*, pp. 133–7.
54. See Ibrāhīm b. al-Ḥusayn al-Ḥāmidī, *Kitāb kanz al-walad*, ed. M. Ghālib (Wiesbaden, 1971). The Ṭayyibī *ḥaqā'iq* system, with its cosmological doctrine and mythical "drama in heaven", is expounded

also in numerous writings of the later Ṭayyibī authors; see, for instance, ʿAlī b. Muḥammad b. al-Walīd (d. 612/1215), *Kitāb al-dhakīra fi'l-ḥaqīqa*, ed. M. Ḥ. al-Aʿẓamī (Beirut, 1971), and al-Ḥusayn b. ʿAlī b. al-Walīd (d. 667/1268), *al-Mabda' wa'l-maʿād*, ed. and tr. Corbin, in his *Trilogie Ismaélienne*, text pp. 99–130, translation pp. 148–200, containing a summary of the subject by the eighth *dāʿī muṭlaq*. The nineteenth *dāʿī*, Idrīs ʿImād al-Dīn (d. 872/1468), was the last great Yamani exponent of the Ṭayyibī *ḥaqā'iq* system; see especially his *Zahr al-maʿānī*, pp. 33–106. H. Corbin devoted numerous studies to Ṭayyibī thought, including its cosmology, eschatology, soteriology and cyclical hierohistory; see his *Cyclical Time*, pp. 37–58, 65ff., 76ff., 103ff., 116ff., 173–81, and *History of Islamic Philosophy*, tr. L. Sherrard (London, 1993), pp. 79–93. For the writings of Yamani Ṭayyibī authors until Idrīs, see Poonawala, *Biobibliography*, pp. 133–75.

4

The Alamūt Period in Nizārī Ismaili History

OVERVIEW

By 487/1094, Ḥasan Ṣabbāḥ, who preached the Fatimid *da'wa* within Saljuq dominions in Persia, emerged as the undisputed leader of the Persian Ismailis. Ḥasan already followed an independent policy against the Saljuq Turks. In fact, his seizure of the mountain fortress of Alamūt in northern Persia in 483/1090 signalled the initiation of an open revolt against the Saljuqs as well as the foundation of what was to become the Nizārī Ismaili state. It was under such circumstances that in al-Mustanṣir's succession dispute, Ḥasan upheld the cause of Nizār and severed his relations with the Fatimid regime and the *da'wa* headquarters in Cairo which had lent their support to al-Musta'lī. By this decision, Ḥasan Ṣabbāḥ had, in fact, founded the independent Nizārī *da'wa* on behalf of the Nizārī imam who then was inaccessible.

The Nizārī state, centred at Alamūt and with territories in different parts of Persia and Syria, lasted for some 166 years until it collapsed in 654/1256 under the onslaught of the Mongol hordes. This initial phase in Nizārī history was marked by numerous political vicissitudes. A capable organiser and dedicated to his cause, Ḥasan Ṣabbāḥ designed a revolutionary strategy aimed at uprooting the Saljuq Turks, whose rule was detested throughout Persia. He did not achieve his target, nor did the Saljuqs succeed in dislodging the Nizārīs from their mountain strongholds. But Ḥasan did manage to found and consolidate the independent Nizārī *da'wa* and state. By around 514/1120, a stalemate had in effect developed between the Nizārīs and the Saljuqs; and the Nizārī state survived despite the incessant hostilities of the Saljuqs and their successors until the arrival of the Mongols. At the same time, *dā'ī*s dispatched from Alamūt organised an expanding Nizārī community in Syria. The Syrian Nizārīs, too, possessed a network of mountain fortresses, and pursued complex policies towards various Muslim powers as well as the Crusaders in politically fragmented Syria.

Ḥasan Ṣabbāḥ (d. 518/1124) and his next two successors at Alamūt ruled as *dā'ī*s of Daylam and *ḥujja*s, or chief representatives, of the Nizārī imams who then were concealed and inaccessible to their followers. Subsequently, starting with Ḥasan *ʿalā dhikrihiʾl-salām*, Nizārī imams emerged at Alamūt to take charge of the affairs of their state and community. The Nizārī Ismaili state, *daʿwa* and community of the Alamūt period were, thus, led by three *dāʿī*s (and *ḥujja*s) and five imams, who are generally referred to as the lords (*khudāwands*) of Alamūt in Persian sources.

Nizārī Ismaili Rulers at Alamūt (483–654/1090–1256)

As *dāʿī*s and *ḥujja*s:
1. Ḥasan Ṣabbāḥ (483–518/1090–1124)
2. Kiyā Buzurg-Ummīd (518–32/1124–38)
3. Muḥammad b. Buzurg-Ummīd (532–57/1138–62)

As imams:
4. Ḥasan *ʿalā dhikrihiʾl-salām* (557–61/1162–6)
5. Nūr al-Dīn Muḥammad (561–607/1166–1210)
6. Jalāl al-Dīn Ḥasan (607–18/1210–21)
7. ʿAlāʾ al-Dīn Muḥammad (618–53/1221–55)
8. Rukn al-Dīn Khurshāh (653–4/1255–6)

The circumstances of the Nizārīs of the Alamūt period were drastically different from those faced by the Ismailis living in the Fatimid state. From early on, the Nizārī Ismailis were preoccupied with a revolutionary campaign and survival in an extremely hostile environment. Accordingly, they produced military commanders rather than learned theologians and jurists addressing different intellectual issues. Furthermore, adopting Persian as the religious language of their community, the Nizārīs of Persia and adjacent eastern lands did not have ready access to the Ismaili literature produced during the Fatimid times, although the Syrian Nizārīs using Arabic did preserve some of these earlier texts. Under such circumstances, the Persian Nizārīs did not evidently produce a substantial literature; and the bulk of their scanty writings was either destroyed in the Mongol invasions or perished soon afterwards during the Īlkhānid period. Syrian Nizārīs, too, produced a meagre literature during the Alamūt period. They were spared the Mongol catastrophe, but were eventually subdued by the Mamlūks, who permitted them to remain in their traditional strongholds. A good portion of the literature preserved or produced by the Syrian Nizārīs has been destroyed, in prolonged hostilities stretching to modern times, by their Nuṣayrī (ʿAlawī) neighbours.

Nevertheless, the Nizārī Ismailis did maintain a sophisticated outlook and a literary tradition, elaborating their teachings in response to changed circumstances of the Alamūt period. Ḥasan Ṣabbāḥ himself was a learned theologian, and he is credited with establishing an impressive library at Alamūt. Later, other major Nizārī fortresses in Persia and Syria came to be equipped with significant collections of books, documents and scientific instruments. The Nizārīs also extended their patronage of learning to outside scholars, including Sunnis, Twelver Shīʿīs and even non-Muslims.

In the doctrinal field, the Nizārīs from early on reaffirmed as their central teaching the old Shīʿī doctrine of *taʿlīm* or the necessity of authoritative teaching by the rightful imam of the time. This doctrine with various modifications provided the foundation for all the subsequent Nizārī teachings of the Alamūt period. With the all-important Nizārī emphasis placed on the teaching authority of the current imam, the fourth ruler of Alamūt proclaimed the *qiyāma* or resurrection, a controversial and ill-understood event. This declaration in 559/1164 made the Nizārī community spiritually and psychologically independent of the outside world, a world that was now considered spiritually irrelevant and non-existent. Having tired of their religio-political isolation, the sixth ruler of Alamūt, Jalāl al-Dīn Ḥasan, attempted his own daring rapprochement with the Sunni world, adopting the *sharīʿa* in its Sunni form. All these policies and their religious symbolisms were later explained by Naṣīr al-Dīn al-Ṭūsī, the renowned Muslim scholar who spent some three decades in the fortress communities of the Nizārīs and wrote several books on their teachings.

The Nizārī Ismailis, by and large, retained a degree of cohesion and sense of mission in the face of numerous crises and the persistent enmity of a majority of Muslims. Indeed, in addition to military campaigns, the Sunni Abbasid-Saljuq establishment also targeted the Nizārīs for a new round of polemical attacks, necessitated by their intellectual challenge as well as political threat. By the 620s/1220s, the Nizārī state of Persia had weakened as a result of prolonged struggles against too many formidable adversaries. The indecisive Nizārī policy towards the Mongols contributed to the eventual collapse of the Nizārī state in the wake of the Mongol invasions of Persia. At any rate, the surrender of the Alamūt fortress to the Mongols in 654/1256 brought to an end the tumultuous Alamūt period in Nizārī history.

ḤASAN ṢABBĀḤ AND THE REVOLT OF THE PERSIAN ISMAILIS

Our main source of information on Ḥasan Ṣabbāḥ, reflecting the contemporary Nizārī Ismaili tradition, is his already-noted biography entitled *Sargudhasht-i Sayyidnā*, an anonymous work which has not survived directly. But the *Sargudhasht*, together with other Persian

Nizārī chronicles of the Alamūt period, have been preserved fragmentarily in the Ismaili histories of Juwaynī, Rashīd al-Dīn and Kāshānī, who remain our major sources for the history of the Persian Nizārī state during the Alamūt period.[1] Ḥasan Ṣabbāḥ was born in the mid-440s/1050s in Qumm into a Twelver Shīʿī family. His father, ʿAlī b. Muḥammad al-Ṣabbāḥ al-Ḥimyarī, a Kūfan claiming Ḥimyarī Yamani origins, had settled down in Qumm, a traditionally Shīʿī town in central Persia. The Ṣabbāḥ family later moved to the nearby city of Rayy, another important centre of Shīʿī learning in Persia, where Ḥasan received his early religious education as a Twelver Shīʿī.

Since the middle of the 3rd/9th century, Rayy had been the centre of Ismaili *daʿwa* in the Jibāl. There, at the age of seventeen, Ḥasan was introduced to Ismaili doctrines by a certain Amīra Ḍarrāb, one of the several local *dāʿī*s. After receiving gradual instructions in Ismailism, Ḥasan was initiated and took the oath of allegiance (*ʿahd*) to the Ismaili imam of the time, al-Mustanṣir. Soon afterwards in 464/1072, Ḥasan was brought to the attention of Ibn ʿAṭṭāsh, the chief Ismaili *dāʿī* in Persia who was then staying in Rayy. Recognising Ḥasan's talents, the chief *dāʿī* appointed him to a post in the *daʿwa*. In 467/1074, Ibn ʿAṭṭāsh returned to his secret headquarters at Iṣfahān in the company of Ḥasan. Two years later in 469/1076, on Ibn ʿAṭṭāsh's recommendation, Ḥasan set off for the Fatimid capital to further his Ismaili education, as Nāṣir Khusraw had done some three decades earlier according to an established practice of the Fatimid *daʿwa*. By the time Ḥasan arrived in Cairo in Ṣafar 471/August 1078, Badr al-Jamālī had succceded al-Mu'ayyad fi'l-Dīn al-Shīrāzī as *dāʿī al-duʿāt* in addition to holding other important posts. Ḥasan spent some three years in Egypt, first in Cairo and then in Alexandria, evidently a base of opposition to Badr al-Jamālī. Almost nothing is known about Ḥasan's experiences in Egypt. It is certain, however, that he came into conflict with the all-powerful Badr, which may also explain Ḥasan's stay in Alexandria where he could not have received the expected Ismaili education. According to Nizārī sources used by our Persian historians, Ḥasan's conflict with Badr revolved around Nizār, al-Mustanṣir's heir-designate whose cause he was to uphold in due course.

Ḥasan seems to have learned important lessons in Egypt, which he took into account when developing a revolutionary strategy. By that time, the Persian Ismailis were aware of the declining fortunes of the Fatimid regime. The shrewd Ḥasan had witnessed the difficult situation of the caliph-imam at the very centre of the Fatimid state. He must have readily realised that the Fatimid regime, then under the effective control of Badr, lacked both the means and the resolve to assist the Persian Ismailis in their struggle against the Saljuqs, who were the major military power in the Near East. It was in recognition of such realities that Ḥasan Ṣabbāḥ eventually charted an independent course of action.

Upon returning to Persia, Ḥasan travelled extensively in the service of the *daʿwa* for some nine years. It was during this crucial period in his career that Ḥasan also formulated a revolutionary strategy and evaluated the military strength of the Saljuqs in different localities of Persia. By 480/1087, Ḥasan concentrated his attention on the general region of Daylam, in northern Persia, removed from the centres of Saljuq power in the central and western parts of the country. The mountainous region of Daylam had historically served as a safe refuge for ʿAlids. A stronghold of Zaydī Shīʿism, Daylam had already been penetrated also by Ismailism. Ḥasan was then clearly preparing for an open revolt against the Saljuqs, and needed a suitable site to establish his headquarters and base of operations. For this purpose, he eventually chose the inaccessible mountain fortress of Alamūt, situated in the Rūdbār region of Daylam, on a high rock in the central Alborz mountains.[2] At the time, the *daʿwa* in the Saljuq lands was still under the overall leadership of Ibn ʿAṭṭāsh, but Ḥasan had already embarked on an independent policy.

Ḥasan devised a detailed plan for the seizure of Alamūt, then held on behalf of the Saljuq sultan. Ḥasan, who was in due course appointed *dāʿī* of Daylam, now reinvigorated the *daʿwa* in northern Persia. He dispatched a number of subordinate *dāʿī*s to various districts around Alamūt to convert the local inhabitants. Ḥasan's activities were soon brought to the attention of Niẓām al-Mulk, the all-powerful vizier to the Great Saljuq Sultans Alp Arslān and Malik Shāh, who nurtured a deep hatred towards the Ismailis. However, the efforts of Niẓām al-Mulk to capture Ḥasan proved futile, and the *dāʿī* arrived safely in Rūdbār. On the eve of Wednesday 6 Rajab 483/4 September 1090, Ḥasan secretly entered the fortress of Alamūt. He disguised himself for a while as a teacher, using the pseudonym of Dihkhudā, instructing the children of Alamūt's garrison and infiltrating the area with his men. With his followers firmly installed in and around Alamūt, whose garrison had also been secretly converted, the castle fell readily into Ḥasan's hands; the date was the late autumn of 483/1090.

The seizure of Alamūt by Ḥasan Ṣabbāḥ initiated a new phase in the activities of the Persian Ismailis, who had hitherto operated clandestinely. It signalled the commencement of the armed revolt of the Persian Ismailis against the Saljuqs, also marking the effective foundation of what was to become an independent Nizārī Ismaili state.

Ḥasan Ṣabbāḥ seems to have had a complex set of religio-political motives for his revolt against the Saljuqs. As an Ismaili Shīʿī, he clearly could not tolerate the anti-Shīʿī policies of the Saljuqs, who as the new champions of Sunni Islam had sworn to uproot Fatimid Ismaili rule. Less conspicuously, Ḥasan's revolt was an expression of Persian "national" sentiments, which accounts for its early popular appeal and widespread success in Persia.

By the early decades of the 5th/11th century, a number of Turkish dynasties had appeared in the Iranian world. This trend towards the Turkish domination of the Iranian lands, initiated by the establishment of the Ghaznawid and Qarakhānid dynasties, climaxed under the Saljuqs who threatened the revival of Persian culture and sentiments. The revival of a specifically Perso-Islamic culture had been based on the sentiments of the Islamicised Persians, conscious of their Persian identity and cultural heritage in spite of centuries of Arab domination. This process, pioneered by the Ṣaffārids and maintained under the Sāmānids and the Būyids, had become quite irrevocable by the time of the Saljuqs when the conversion of the Persians to Islam was finally completed.[3] Niẓām al-Mulk himself, it will be recalled, wrote his *Siyāsat-nāma* for Sultan Malik Shāh in Persian.

At any rate, the Saljuq Turks were aliens in Persia and their rule was intensely detested by the Persians of various social classes. Anti-Saljuq sentiments were further aggravated by the anarchy and depredation caused in towns and villages by the Turks and their unruly soldiers, who were continuously attracted in new waves from Central Asia through Saljuq victories. Ḥasan Ṣabbāḥ himself resented the Turks and their rule over Persia. He referred to the Saljuq sultan as a mere ignorant Turk;[4] he is also reported to have said that the Turks were *jinn*.[5] It was, indeed, to the ultimate goal of uprooting Saljuq rule that Ḥasan dedicated himself and organised the Persian Ismailis into a formidable and highly disciplined revolutionary force. Henceforth, Persian Ismailis of different social backgrounds – as was fitting in a revolutionary movement – were to address each other as *rafīq* or comrade.

It is also significant to note that Ḥasan Ṣabbāḥ, as an expression of his Persian awareness and in spite of his intense Islamic piety, substituted Persian for Arabic as the religious language of the Ismailis of Persia. This was the first time that a major Muslim community had adopted Persian as its religious language. This also explains why the Persian-speaking (Nizārī) Ismaili communities of Persia, Afghanistan and Central Asia produced their literature entirely in Persian during the Alamūt period and later times.

The early success of the revolt led by Ḥasan Ṣabbāḥ in Persia was also rooted in certain economic grievances shared by the country's landless villagers and highlanders, as well as artisans and craftsmen, representing underprivileged social classes in Saljuq dominions. In Daylam and elsewhere, these masses were subject to the oppressive rule of numerous Saljuq *amīr*s who held and administered different localities as their *iqṭāʿ* on behalf of the sultan. The *amīr*s levied taxes on people who cultivated the land or lived under their jurisdiction, also maintaining local armies to assist the sultan as required. The Saljuq *amīr*s were often granted full jurisdiction over, and complete administrative control of, the districts which they held as their *iqṭāʿ*. For all intents and purposes, the Saljuq institution of *iqṭāʿ* led to the virtual subjection of the Persian peasantry by alien Turks. A variety of townspeople, too, including especially artisans, craftsmen and dispossessed lower classes, were dissatisfied with the Saljuq social order and the excessive taxes levied in both urban and rural areas. By contrast, those who became incorporated into Ismaili-held territories were treated more equitably in a society dedicated to establishing social justice.

No details are available on the actual tax system and the religious dues within the Ismaili territories. It is known, however, that the booty acquired in Ismaili campaigns was distributed equally among all; and the Ismailis viewed their participation in collective projects, such as improving the irrigation systems of particular localities or the construction of castles, as activities beneficial to the entire community. It is noteworthy that strict class strata and distinctions, as developed under the Saljuqs, did not exist among the Ismailis who referred to one another as comrade (*rafīq*). Any capable individual could rise to a leadership position as governor of a stronghold or chief *dāʿī* in a region. Kiyā Buzurg-Ummīd, and many other leading figures of the Persian Ismaili movement, hailed from modest backgrounds. Ḥasan Ṣabbāḥ by his own extremely austere lifestyle set an example for other Ismaili leaders, who were not accorded particular privileges as those enjoyed by Saljuq *amīr*s. In sum, it seems that income and wealth were distributed much more equitably in the Ismaili territories than in the Saljuq dominions. In addition, Ismaili lands were not subject to the alien rule of the Turks. All this contributed significantly to the early success and popularity of the revolt of the Persian Ismailis, whose support was initially concentrated in rural areas. They also received support, in both towns and rural areas, from those who may not have been necessarily Ismaili but sympathised with the revolt for a variety of already-noted political as well as socio-economic grievances against the established Saljuq order. Indeed, without widespread (non-Ismaili) support, the Persian Ismailis might not have been able to sustain their armed struggle against the Saljuqs for as long as they did.

Once installed at Alamūt, Ḥasan Ṣabbāḥ improved its fortifications and storage facilities to make it into a virtually impregnable castle. Alamūt was equipped to withstand long sieges. Ḥasan then extended his influence throughout Rūdbār and adjacent areas in Daylam, by winning more Ismaili converts and gaining possession of more castles, which were fortified systematically. Ḥasan's religio-political message evoked popular support among the Daylamis, highlanders and villagers already familiar with different forms of Shīʿism, including Ismailism. Ḥasan also attracted at least some of the remaining Khurramiyya in Ādharbāyjān and elsewhere who, as an expression of Persian sentiments, referred to themselves as Pārsiyān.[6] The Khurramiyya, or Khurramdīniyya, it may be recalled, were active in different parts of the Iranian world throughout Abbasid times, manifesting both anti-Arab and anti-Turkish sentiments. Be that as it may, a Saljuq *amīr* in the vicinity of Alamūt soon conducted a series of raids on the fortress. Henceforth, Persian Ismailis were drawn into an endless series of military encounters with the Saljuqs.[7]

In 484/1091, Ḥasan Ṣabbāḥ sent the *dāʿī* Ḥusayn Qā'inī to his native Quhistān in southeastern Khurāsān, to mobilise support. The people of Quhistān, at the time under the oppressive rule of a local Saljuq *amīr*, responded almost instantly and on a large scale. In what amounted to a popular uprising against the Saljuqs, they seized numerous strongholds as well as several major towns, including Tūn, Ṭabas, Qā'in and Zūzan. Quhistān became the second major territory, after Rūdbār, for the activities of the Persian Ismailis, led by a local leader designated from Alamūt and known as *muḥtasham*. In two regions, Rūdbār and Quhistān, Ḥasan had now founded an independent territorial state for the Persian Ismailis, challenging Saljuq hegemony. It was in recognition of growing Ismaili power that, in 485/1092, Sultan Malik Shāh and Niẓām al-Mulk sent major expeditions against Alamūt and the Ismaili strongholds in Quhistān. However, these military operations were soon terminated on Malik Shāh's death.

A decade-long civil war plagued the Saljuq empire on Sultan Malik Shāh's death in 485/1092. Sultan Barkiyāruq, the most prominent claimant to the Saljuq sultanate, devoted most of his time and energy to fighting his half-brother Muḥammad Tapar. Peace was not restored to the Saljuq dominions until Barkiyāruq's death in 498/1105, when Muḥammad Tapar emerged as the undisputed sultan while his brother Sanjar remained at Balkh as his viceroy in Khurāsān and other eastern regions. In this strife-ridden period of Saljuq history, with shifting alliances among various *amīrs*, Ḥasan Ṣabbāḥ found the much needed respite to consolidate and further extend his power to other parts of Persia.

They seized Girdkūh, and a number of lesser strongholds near Dāmghān, in medieval Qūmis. One of the chief Ismaili strongholds in Persia, Girdkūh was acquired through the efforts of Ra'īs Mu'ayyad al-Dīn Muẓaffar, originally an officer in Saljuq service who had been secretly converted to Ismailism by ʿAbd al-Malik b. ʿAṭṭāsh himself. Ra'īs Muẓaffar governed Girdkūh for a long time, rendering valuable services to the Ismaili cause in Persia. The Ismailis also came to possess several fortresses in Arrajān, in the border region between the provinces of Fārs and Khūzistān. There, they were led by the *dāʿī* Abū Ḥamza who, like Ḥasan himself, had spent some time in Egypt to further his Ismaili education. In Rūdbār, the Ismailis acquired more strongholds, including the key fortress of Lamasar, also called Lanbasar, to the west of Alamūt. Kiyā Buzurg-Ummīd seized Lamasar by assault in 489/1096, and stayed there as commander for more than twenty-five years until he was summoned to Alamūt to succeed Ḥasan Ṣabbāḥ. Buzurg-Ummīd, one of the most capable Ismaili leaders in Persia, transformed Lamasar into a major stronghold.

Meanwhile, the Ismailis acquired a growing number of supporters in Persian towns as well as among the Persians in the Saljuq armies. Encouraged by their successes, the Persian Ismailis now directed their attention closer to the seat of Saljuq power in Iṣfahān. In this area, they were led by Ibn ʿAṭṭāsh's son Aḥmad, who scored a major victory by gaining possession of the fortress of Shāhdiz in 494/1100. It is reported that Aḥmad converted some 30,000 persons in the Iṣfahān area, also collecting taxes to the detriment of the Saljuq treasury around Shāhdiz, which guarded the main routes to the Saljuq capital. The activities of Ḥasan Ṣabbāḥ and his immediate successors at Alamūt did not extend to Badakhshān and other parts of Central Asia.

The revolt of the Persian Ismailis soon acquired a distinctive pattern and method of struggle, adapted to the power structure of the Saljuq sultanate and other circumstances of the time. Ḥasan Ṣabbāḥ had recognised the decentralised nature of Saljuq rule as well as their much superior military power. After Malik Shāh, there was no longer a single all-powerful sultan to be uprooted by a large army, even if such an army could be mobilised by the Persian Ismailis and their sympathisers. Political and military power was now distributed locally among numerous *amīrs*, individuals who held *iqṭāʿ* assignments throughout the Saljuq empire. It was in recognition of these realities that Ḥasan designed a strategy to overwhelm the Saljuqs locality by locality, and from a multitude of impregnable strongholds.

Each Ismaili stronghold, normally a fortified mountain fortress, could be used as a local base of armed operations. The commanders of the major strongholds, appointed from Alamūt, generally enjoyed a large degree of local initiative, while every major Ismaili territory was placed under the overall leadership of a regional chief. The regional chiefs acted independently in the management of their affairs, although Alamūt continued to serve as the central co-ordinating headquarters of the Ismaili movement in Persia. All this contributed to the dynamism of the revolt, also enabling the local leaders to act swiftly and appropriately in response to local circumstances.

Ḥasan Ṣabbāḥ's adoption of assassination as an instrument for the attainment of military and political objectives was itself a response to the political decentralisation and military strength of the Saljuq order. In this, Ḥasan was merely resorting to a technique used previously by different groups, including some of the early Shīʿī *ghulāt* and the Khawārij. The Saljuqs themselves, as well as the Crusaders, assassinated their enemies in factional fighting. But Ḥasan did assign an important role to the selective assassination of prominent religio-political adversaries. Paradoxically, this policy became identified in a highly exaggerated manner with the Nizārī Ismailis of Persia and Syria, so that almost any assassination of any significance in the central Islamic lands during the Alamūt period was attributed to them. Ismaili assignments were carried out by their *fidāʾī*s, or *fidāwī*s, young self-sacrificing devotees who volunteered for such suicidal missions. The assassinations, normally conducted in public places, were daring acts with intimidating side effects. The *fidāʾī*s do not seem to have received training in languages and certain subjects, contrary to elaborate accounts found in the occidental chronicles of the Crusades and other European sources. In fact, the Crusaders and their western chroniclers were responsible for fabricating and disseminating a number of tales regarding the recruitment and training of the Ismaili *fidāʾī*s. From early on, the assassinations, whatever their real source, triggered massacres of the Ismailis, or of all suspected Ismailis in a particular town or district; and the massacres, in turn, provoked retaliatory assassinations.[8]

As the revolt of the Persian Ismailis spread successfully in Persia, the Fatimid caliph-imam al-Mustanṣir died in Cairo in 487/1094. As noted, the dispute over his succession split the Ismailis permanently into the Nizārī and Mustaʿlī factions. By then Ḥasan had emerged as leader of the Ismailis of Saljuq lands, eclipsing the *dāʿī* Ibn ʿAṭṭāsh. Nothing is known about the final years of Ibn ʿAṭṭāsh, although it is possible that he may have retired to Alamūt. At any rate, Ḥasan had been following an independent revolutionary policy for several years;

and the succession dispute provided an opportunity for him to sever relations with the Fatimid regime, weakened already by several decades of vizieral rule. Ḥasan lent his unconditional support to Nizār's cause and refused to recognise the authority of the *da'wa* headquarters in Cairo, now serving the Musta'lī Ismaili *da'wa*. By this decision, Ḥasan had in effect founded the independent Nizārī Ismaili *da'wa*, which survived the downfall of the Fatimid dynasty. An instructive parallel can be found in the efforts of the Ṣulayḥid queen al-Sayyida who established the independent Ṭayyibī *da'wa* in Yaman a few decades later. Ḥasan's decision was supported by all the Ismailis of Persia without any dissent, indicating his strong hold over the community.

Nizār, as noted, was executed a year after his father's death on al-Afḍal's order. It is a fact that Nizār did have male progeny, and some of them rose in revolts against the later Fatimids, claiming the caliphate and the imamate.[9] The last of these revolts was led in 556/1161 by a grandson of Nizār. Meanwhile, Ḥasan did not divulge the name of Nizār's successor to the imamate. It is possible that the Ismailis of Persia remained uninformed for quite some time of Nizār's tragic fate and continued awaiting his reappearance. As no Nizārī sources have survived from that early period, perceptions of contemporary Nizārīs of Persia on this matter remain obscure. At any rate, published numismatic evidence from the early Alamūt period shows that Nizār's own name and caliphal title, al-Muṣṭafā li-Dīn Allāh, was mentioned on coins minted at Alamūt for about seventy years after his death in 488/1095 and through the reign of the third lord of Alamūt, Muḥammad b. Buzurg-Ummīd (532–57/1138–62).[10] In the inscriptions of these rare Alamūt coins, Nizār's progeny are generally blessed anonymously.

The nascent Nizārī Ismailis were now left without an accessible imam. The Ismailis had already experienced a similar *dawr al-satr* in pre-Fatimid times, when the imam was hidden and inaccessible. And the absent imam, as already explained, had been represented by a *ḥujja*. The earliest Nizārīs lived through another *dawr al-satr*. It seems that soon after the schism of 487/1094, Ḥasan Ṣabbāḥ was recognised by the Nizārīs as the *ḥujja* of their inaccessible imam. On the basis of pre-Fatimid traditions, the Nizārīs now held that in the time of the imam's concealment his *ḥujja* would be his chief representative in the community. Indeed, in the *Haft bāb*, the earliest extant Nizārī treatise written around 596/1200, Ḥasan is reported to have predicted the imminent appearance of the imam-*qā'im* while he himself is given the rank of the *ḥujja* of that imam.[11]

Ḥasan's successors at Alamūt were regarded as *ḥujja*s of the hidden imam until the Nizārid imams themselves actually took charge of the affairs of their community, *da'wa* and state. According to the Nizārī traditions of the Alamūt period, as reported by Juwaynī and later Persian historians,[12] already in Ḥasan Ṣabbāḥ's time many Nizārīs held the view that a son or grandson of Nizār had been secretly brought from Egypt to Persia, and this Nizārid became the progenitor of the line of the Nizārī Ismaili imams who later emerged at Alamūt. The wide currency of this contemporary Nizārī tradition is attested to by the anti-Nizārī polemical epistle issued by the Fatimid caliph al-Āmir in 516/1122. In this epistle, aiming to discredit the claims of Nizār and his descendants to the imamate, al-Āmir found it necessary to ridicule the idea that a descendant of Nizār was then living secretly in Persia.[13]

THE DOCTRINE OF *TA'LĪM* AND CONSOLIDATION OF THE NIZĀRĪ STATE

It was under such circumstances that the outsiders from early on acquired the impression that the Persian (Nizārī) Ismailis had initiated a "new preaching" (*al-da'wa al-jadīda*) in contrast to the "old preaching" (*al-da'wa al-qadīma*) of Ismailis in Fatimid times. The "new preaching", conducted in Persian, made the Ismaili literature of earlier times, produced in Arabic (except for Nāṣir Khusraw's writings), inaccessible to the Persian Ismailis. As noted, a good share of the Arabic Ismaili literature was preserved by the Ṭayyibī Ismailis of Yaman, while the Syrian Nizārī Ismailis also preserved a small fraction. The "new preaching" did not represent any new doctrines; it was essentially a reformulation of an old Shī'ī doctrine of long standing among the Ismailis, namely, the doctrine of *ta'līm* or authoritative teaching by the imam.

In its fully developed form the reformulation of the doctrine of *ta'līm* is generally ascribed to Ḥasan Ṣabbāḥ, who was a learned theologian and also well grounded in philosophical thought. Ḥasan restated this doctrine, in a more vigorous form, in a theological treatise entitled *Chahār faṣl* (Arabic, *al-Fuṣūl al-arba'a*), or the *Four Chapters*. This treatise, originally written in Persian, has not survived directly, but it was seen and paraphrased by our Persian historians.[14] It has also been preserved fragmentarily, in Arabic translation, by Ḥasan's contemporary al-Shahrastānī (d. 548/1153) in his famous heresiographical work written around 521/1127.[15] A renowned theologian, al-Shahrastānī seems to have been very well informed about Ismaili teachings. He wrote several works bearing strong Ismaili imprints, and himself may have been an Ismaili.

The Shī'īs from early on had emphasised the necessity of a spiritual guide or imam to lead mankind along the right path. These guides, they had always held, were designated by divine command

and not by human choice as actually attempted by Sunni Muslims. For the Shīʿa, only the sinless and infallible ʿAlid imams, belonging to the *ahl al-bayt* and possessing special religious knowledge or *ʿilm*, were qualified to perform the spiritual functions of such guides or teachers. Ḥasan Ṣabbāḥ reformulated this Shīʿī doctrine in a series of four propositions. He aimed to show the inadequacy of human reason (*ʿaql*) by itself in enabling men to understand religious truths and to know God; and the need for a single authoritative teacher (*muʿallim-i ṣādiq*) to act as the spiritual guide of men, by contrast to a multiplicity of scholars (*ʿulamāʾ*) accepted as guides by Sunni Muslims. In a third proposition, Ḥasan established a logical basis for explaining the authority of the trustworthy teacher who would be none other than the Ismaili imam of the time. This imam, Ḥasan argued in a fourth proposition based on a dialectical principle, did not need to prove his authority or claim to the imamate by resorting to any proofs beyond himself or his own existence. In sum, Ḥasan argued that it is by virtue of his very existence that the true imam can fulfil man's need (for his authority), something that reasoning also corroborates. The doctrine of *taʿlīm*, emphasising the autonomous teaching authority of each imam in his own time, became the central doctrine of the early Nizārīs. It was due to the centrality and widespread impact of this doctrine that the Persian (Nizārī) Ismailis became known as the Taʿlīmiyya. It also provided the theological foundation of Nizārī teachings of the later Alamūt and, indeed, subsequent times. The doctrine of *taʿlīm* stressed absolute loyalty to the imam, and in his absence, to his full representative or *ḥujja*; and Ḥasan himself, as noted, was recognised as the first of such *ḥujja*s.

The intellectual challenge posed to the Sunni establishment by the doctrine of *taʿlīm*, which also refuted the legitimacy of the Abbasid caliph as the spiritual spokesman of Muslims, called forth the official reaction of the Abbasids and their Sunni scholars. Many Sunni theologians and jurists, led by al-Ghazālī, attacked the Ismaili doctrine of *taʿlīm*. As noted earlier, al-Ghazālī was in fact commissioned by the Abbasid caliph al-Mustaẓhir to write a treatise in refutation of the Ismāʿīliyya (Bāṭiniyya). As the most learned Sunni scholar of his time, al-Ghazālī produced several anti-Ismaili works, but he paid particular attention to refuting the doctrine of *taʿlīm* in his major anti-Ismaili treatise, *al-Mustaẓhirī*, which he wrote shortly before 488/1095. The Persian Ismailis, against whom *al-Mustaẓhirī* was written, did not respond to Sunni polemics. But an Ismaili response to al-Ghazālī was eventually provided in the more peaceful mountains of Yaman by a resident Ṭayyibī Ismaili *dāʿī*.[16]

Ismaili fortunes continued to rise in Persia during Sultan

Barkiyāruq's reign. Alarmed by the growing power of the Persian Ismailis, Barkiyāruq in western Persia and Sanjar in Khurāsān finally agreed in 494/1101 to deal more effectively, in their respective territories, with the Ismailis who now seriously undermined Saljuq rule. Despite new Saljuq offensives and massacres, however, Nizārī Ismailis managed to retain their strongholds and territories. By the time of Barkiyāruq's death in 498/1105, Ḥasan Ṣabbāḥ had already begun to extend his activities to Syria, reflecting his wider Islamic ambitions. A number of Persian emissaries, led by a *dāʿī* known as al-Ḥakīm al-Munajjim (d. 496/1103), were dispatched from Alamūt to Aleppo in northern Syria to organise the Ismailis and win new converts. The political fragmentation of Syria as well as diversity in the region's religious topography, which included different Shīʿī traditions, contributed to the spread of the Nizārī Ismaili *daʿwa*. As in Persia, Saljuq rule in Syria had caused many difficulties and was abhorred by Syrians, who also suffered from internal divisions. However, the success of the earliest Nizārī *dāʿī*s in northern Syria, under the protection of Riḍwān, Aleppo's opportunistic Saljuq ruler, proved short-lived. It was also in the course of their early campaigns in Syria that the Nizārīs came into contact with the Frankish troops of Tancred, the prince of Antioch, marking the first of the prolonged military and diplomatic encounters between the Syrian Nizārīs and the Crusaders. With the death of Riḍwān in 507/1113, the Nizārīs were severely persecuted in northern Syria.[17] Almost half a century of continuous effort was required before the Nizārīs finally succeeded, by the middle of the 6th/12th century, to gain possession of a network of permanent strongholds in Syria.

With the accession of Muḥammad Tapar (498–511/1105–18), marking the termination of dynastic disputes and factional fighting among the Saljuqs, the Nizārī fortunes were reversed. Barkiyāruq and Sanjar had already checked what had promised to be an Ismaili sweep through Saljuq dominions in Persia. Sultan Muḥammad now set out to deal even more effectively with the Nizārīs. He launched a series of major campaigns against them, in the process of which they lost most of their strongholds in the Zagros mountains and in Iraq. Sultan Muḥammad's main campaign against the Nizārīs was, however, directed at Shāhdiz, also known as Dizkūh. The sultan personally laid siege to Shāhdiz and eventually seized that castle. The *dāʿī* Aḥmad b. ʿAbd al-Malik b. ʿAṭṭāsh, who had fought the Saljuqs from tower to tower, was captured and executed. With the fall of Shāhdiz in 500/1107, the Nizārīs permanently lost their influence in the Iṣfahān region to the relief of the Saljuqs.[18]

Sultan Muḥammad Tapar also concerned himself with Rūdbār, the seat of Nizārī power in northern Persia, and its numerous fortresses. In eight consecutive years, the Saljuqs besieged Alamūt, where Ḥasan Ṣabbāḥ resided, Lamasar and other castles in Rūdbār, destroying the crops of the districts and engaging in sporadic battles with the Nizārīs. It was during this period that Ḥasan Ṣabbāḥ and many other Nizārī leaders sent their womenfolk to safer places. Ḥasan's wife and daughters were permanently sent to Girdkūh, where they earned a simple living as spinners. Ḥasan's resistance during these difficult years, when the Saljuqs received regular reinforcements, amazed the enemy. At any rate, despite their superior military power and prolonged war of attrition, the Saljuqs failed to take Alamūt by assault, and they broke camp on hearing the news of the sultan's death in 511/1118. Alamūt was once again saved from a dangerous situation.

On the death of Muḥammad Tapar, the Saljuqs were plunged into another period of dynastic disputes, providing a timely respite for the Nizārīs who did actually recover from some of their earlier setbacks. By the final years of Ḥasan's life, however, the anti-Saljuq revolt of the Nizārīs had lost its effectiveness, much in the same way that the Saljuqs had failed in their prolonged offensive campaigns to uproot the Persian Ismailis from their strongholds in Rūdbār, Qūmis and Quhistān. The Ismaili–Saljuq relations, as observed by Marshall Hodgson, had now in effect entered a new phase of "stalemate".

Feeling the end of his days, Ḥasan Ṣabbāḥ summoned his lieutenant at Lamasar, Kiyā Buzurg-Ummīd, and designated him as *dāʿī* of Daylam and his successor at Alamūt. At the same time, Ḥasan set up a council of advisers, comprised of three Nizārī dignitaries, to assist Buzurg-Ummīd in the affairs of the Nizārī state, community and *daʿwa* until such time as the imam himself would appear. Ḥasan died, after a brief illness, towards the end of Rabīʿ II 518/middle of June 1124. He was buried near the fortress of Alamūt; his mausoleum, where Buzurg-Ummīd and other Nizārī leaders were later buried, was destroyed by the Mongols in 654/1256.

Ḥasan Ṣabbāḥ was a remarkable organiser and political strategist in addition to being a learned theologian, philosopher and astronomer. He was held in great esteem by the Nizārī Ismailis who referred to him as Sayyidnā or "our master", and visited his grave as a shrine. He led an ascetic life and his lifestyle served to provide a role model for other Nizārī leaders, all engaged in revolutionary struggle. Our Persian historians have preserved several examples of his austere lifestyle and uncompromising values. During all the thirty-four years that Ḥasan spent at Alamūt, he is said never to have descended from the castle. He remained inside his modest quarters in that mountain fortress, committing the teachings of the *daʿwa* to writing and administering the affairs of his realm. It is reported that he observed the *sharīʿa* very closely, also imposing it on the community. In his time, nobody drank wine openly in the Alamūt valley, where the playing of musical instruments was also prohibited. He had both his sons executed, one for drinking wine, and the other on alleged complicity in the murder of the *dāʿī* Ḥusayn Qā'inī, which later proved unfounded. Ḥasan Ṣabbāḥ maintained a sense of purpose and dedication despite serious setbacks, and saw the independent Nizārī *daʿwa* and state he had founded through turbulent years. Possessing exceptional leadership qualities and charisma, Ḥasan's personality indeed offered a rallying point for other Nizārīs. More significantly, he provided a religio-political frame that was to serve as an appropriate response to the challenges of the time, enabling the Nizārīs to survive adversity in territories scattered from Syria to eastern Persia.

THE NIZĀRĪ–SALJUQ STALEMATE

By the final years of Ḥasan Ṣabbāḥ's life, the Nizārī Ismailis had failed in their general revolt against the Saljuqs. Despite their offensives against the Nizārīs, the Saljuqs, too, had failed to uproot the Nizārī fortress communities. Henceforth, the Nizārī–Saljuq relations were more of a stalemate. But the Nizārī revolt had succeeded on a local basis in several scattered territories, where they consolidated their positions, while the Saljuqs no longer conducted any large-scale offensives against them. In this period of stalemate, the Nizārī community transformed itself into an autonomous state, which now began to take its place as a principality within the Saljuq empire.

A native of Daylam, Kiyā Buzurg-Ummīd, too, was a capable commander and administrator. He maintained the policies of his predecessor at Alamūt, further expanding the frontiers of the Nizārī state. In 520/1126, two years after Buzurg-Ummīd's accession, the Saljuqs launched a series of attacks against Nizārī strongholds in Rūdbār and Quhistān, probably to test the capabilities of the new lord of Alamūt. However, the Nizārīs did not waver in resolve, and supported Ḥasan Ṣabbāḥ's successor without any dissent. They seized several new fortresses in Rūdbār, where they also continued to build castles, including Maymūndiz in the vicinity of Alamūt. The Nizārīs actually extended the limits of their Persian domains in this period. The Saljuqs could no longer hope to defeat them militarily, even though both parties engaged in entanglements of a more limited nature. The days of the great Saljuq offensives of Ḥasan Ṣabbāḥ's times had clearly passed. It was in recognition of the changed realities that Sultan Maḥmūd II (511–25/1118–31) found it expedient to enter into peace negotiations with Buzurg-Ummīd. Sultan Sanjar (d. 552/1157), too, had come to some sort of an understanding with the Nizārīs, sparing Quhistān of further Saljuq attacks. It is not surprising that the Nizārīs found more allies within the Saljuq camp, *amīrs* who could not maintain their own positions in particular regions without their assistance. As a result, a host of complex relations developed locally between the Nizārīs and the Saljuq *amīrs* to their mutual benefit.

The Nizārīs emerged as an important element in the local power politics of the Saljuq sultanate. They had, meanwhile, come to direct their attention increasingly to their immediate neighbours, in both Persia and later Syria. In the Caspian provinces of Daylam, the Zaydīs had persistently prevented the spread of the Ismaili form of Shīʿism. In 526/1132, the Nizārīs defeated Abū Hāshim ʿAlawī, who claimed the imamate of the Zaydīs in Daylam and had supporters as far as Khurāsān. In Daylam, the Nizārīs also confronted the recurring hostilities of the Bāwandids and other local dynasties of Ṭabaristān (Māzandarān), Gīlān and elsewhere. Alamūt also had regular entanglements with the nearby people of Qazwīn, mobilised by their Sunni *ʿulamāʾ*. The Nizārīs of Quhistān, too, were embroiled in prolonged military encounters with the neighbouring Naṣrid Maliks of Sīstān (or Nīmrūz), situated to the southeast of Quhistān.[19]

In the meantime, Syrian Nizārīs launched a new phase in operations after the debacle in Aleppo in 507/1113. They shifted their activities to Damascus and other localities in southern Syria. By 520/1126, Bahrām, another Persian *dāʿī* appointed from Alamūt, had been so successful that he began to preach the *daʿwa* openly in Damascus, where he established a *dār al-daʿwa* or "mission house". Enjoying the support of the local Būrid rulers of Damascus and southern Syria, Bahrām sent subordinate *dāʿīs* to different localities and won many converts among both the urban and rural populations. In southern Syria, too, however, Nizārī success proved short-lived. With the demise of Bahrām, killed in battle in 522/1128, and the death of their Būrid protector Ṭughtigīn in the same year, they were massacred in Damascus. These developments ushered in another period of disorganisation and obscure clandestine activities in the history of the Syrian Nizārī community.[20]

The Syrian Nizārīs succeeded, during the two decades following their tragic fate in Damascus, in finally acquiring a network of permanent strongholds in central Syria. During this period, the Ismailis adopted a new strategy and directed their activities away from major urban centres of Syria which had proved catastrophic. They now concentrated their efforts in the Jabal Bahrāʾ (present-day

Jabal Anṣāriyya), a mountainous region between Ḥamā and the Mediterranean coastline southwest of the Jabal al-Summāq, situated in central Syria with numerous castles possessed by various Muslim lords as well as the Crusaders. There, they came into possession of their first stronghold, Qadmūs, purchased from its Muslim owner in 527/1132–3. Soon afterwards, they acquired Kahf; and, in 535/1141, the Nizārīs seized Maṣyāf (or Maṣyād), their most important stronghold which usually served as the residence of the chief *dāʿī* of the Syrian Nizārīs. Around the same time, they seized several more fortresses, which became collectively known as the *qilāʿ al-daʿwa*, or the "fortresses of the mission".[21] The Nizārīs soon controlled a large part of the Jabal Bahrā', where they confronted the enmity of various local Sunni rulers as well as the Crusaders, active in adjacent territories belonging to the Latin states of Antioch and Tripoli.

Buzurg-Ummīd died in 532/1138, and was succeeded at Alamūt by his son Muḥammad. The Nizārī–Saljuq stalemate continued during Muḥammad's long reign (532–57/1138–62), when the Nizārīs further strengthened their positions in their main territories.[22] As a territorial power, however, the Nizārīs were now almost exclusively involved in petty quarrels and skirmishes with their immediate neighbours in Qazwīn, Sīstān and elsewhere, although they retained a great deal of dynamism and missionary zeal. In Muḥammad b. Buzurg-Ummīd's time, the Nizārī *dāʿīs* of Quhistān made major efforts to penetrate a new region, Ghūr, in present-day central Afghanistan; the Persian Nizārīs also extended their activities to Georgia (Gurjistān) and other Transcaucasian regions.

By the beginning of Muḥammad b. Buzurg-Ummīd's reign, the Nizārī state was firmly consolidated on a territorial basis. It had its own mint and central leadership at Alamūt. The Nizārī territories were separated from one another by long distances, stretching from Syria to eastern Persia, making communications difficult with Alamūt. Each Nizārī territory was placed under the leadership of a chief *dāʿī* appointed by Alamūt. And in addition to the general hostilities of the Saljuqs, the Nizārī territories incurred the persistent enmity of numerous local dynasties, including the Frankish invaders of the Near East. Nevertheless, the Nizārī Ismailis maintained a remarkable cohesion and their state manifested an astonishing stability. Having declared their independence from the Fatimid regime, which was now supporting Mustaʿlī Ismailism, the Nizārīs also maintained their independence amidst the hostile Saljuq empire. Highly disciplined and united in their mission, they acknowledged the supreme leadership of Alamūt, obeying without any dissenting voice the policies designed at that mountain fortress initially by the

Nizārī imam's representatives and, subsequently, by the imams themselves. The united Nizārīs remained dedicated to preparing the ground for the general rule of the Nizārī Ismaili imam. It was under such circumstances that the Nizārīs eagerly anticipated the appearance of their imam, who had not been accessible since Nizār's death in 488/1095.

PROCLAMATION OF *QIYĀMA* OR RESURRECTION

On Muḥammad b. Buzurg-Ummīd's death in 557/1162, his heir-designate, Ḥasan, succeeded to leadership at Alamūt. At the time, Ḥasan was believed to be Muḥammad b. Buzurg-Ummīd's son. At any rate, even before his accession, Ḥasan had acquired much popularity among the Nizārīs, some of whom seem to have considered him as the imam promised by Ḥasan Ṣabbāḥ. Before long, he was in fact acknowledged as an imam, the first Nizārī imam to manifest himself openly in the Alamūt period. Our Persian historians relate that Ḥasan was very learned in a variety of fields, including earlier Ismaili teachings, philosophical thought and Sufism. He was also well versed in Ismaili *ta'wīl* and its applications.

About two and a half years after his accession, Ḥasan summoned delegates from different Nizārī territories to Alamūt. Then, on 17 Ramaḍān 559/8 August 1164, as reported by our Persian historians, he organised a solemn ceremony in the public prayer ground at the foot of Alamūt to make an important announcement to the delegates assembled there. Ḥasan himself came down from the castle at noon and ascended a special pulpit erected for the occasion. He delivered a message to the audience which, he claimed, had been sent by the hidden imam who now had new instructions for the community. The imam of the time, Ḥasan declared, has sent you his blessings and compassion. He has called you, Ḥasan continued in a loud voice with his sword in hand, his special chosen servants. He has relieved you of the burdens of the *sharī'a* and has brought you to the *qiyāma* or resurrection. Ḥasan then delivered a *khuṭba* in Arabic, claiming that it represented the exact words of the imam. The *khuṭba*, translated instantly into Persian by the jurist Muḥammad Bustī, named Ḥasan not only as the imam's *dā'ī* and *ḥujja*, like his predecessors at Alamūt, but also as the imam's *khalīfa*, deputy or successor with plenary authority, a higher rank yet that was not defined at the time. The imam had also admonished his community to follow Ḥasan, obey his commands in all spiritual and temporal matters, and treat his word as that of the imam. After completing his address Ḥasan performed the two prostrations (*rak'at*) reserved for festive occasions. He declared that historic day the festival of resurrection (*'īd-i qiyāmat*), and invited all those present to share a variety of foods and drinks laid down for them. Henceforth, the 17th of Ramaḍān was celebrated each year by the Nizārīs as a day of rejoicing.

About two months later, in Dhu'l-Qa'da 559/October 1164, a similar ceremony was held at the castle of Mu'minābād, near Bīrjand, in Quhistān. The message and *khuṭba*, delivered earlier at Alamūt, were read by Ra'īs Muẓaffar, chief *dā'ī* in Quhistān. The *qiyāma* was now proclaimed, once again, for the Nizārīs of Quhistān, whose representatives had already participated in the Alamūt proceedings. But as far as Ḥasan's status was concerned, a significant new announcement was made to clarify the exact meaning of the title of *khalīfa*, which he had previously claimed. It was explained that Ḥasan was in fact God's caliph (*khalīfa*) on earth, in much the same way that the Fatimid caliph-imam al-Mustanṣir held that position in his time. In Syria, too, the *qiyāma* was announced somewhat later, though specific details are lacking.

Ḥasan's announcements at Alamūt and Mu'minābād, indeed, amounted to the proclamation of the *qiyāma* (Persian, *qiyāmat*), the long awaited Last Day when mankind would be judged and committed eternally to either Paradise or Hell. Relying heavily on Ismaili *ta'wīl* or esoteric exegesis, and drawing on earlier Ismaili teachings and traditions, however, the *qiyāma* was interpreted symbolically and spiritually for the living Nizārīs. It, in fact, meant nothing more than the manifestation of unveiled truth (*ḥaqīqa*) in the person of the Nizārī Ismaili imam. And as such, it was a spiritual resurrection reserved exclusively for Nizārīs wherever they existed. In other words, those who acknowledged the Nizārī imam were now capable of understanding the truth, or the esoteric essence of religion, and, therefore, Paradise was actualised for them in this very corporeal world. Like the Sufis, the Nizārīs were to rise to a spiritual level of existence, moving along a spiritual path, similarly to the *ṭarīqa* of the Sufis, from *ẓāhir* to *bāṭin*, from *sharī'a* to *ḥaqīqa*, or from the literal interpretation of the law to an understanding of its spiritual essence reflecting the eternal truths. It was evidently in this esoteric sense that the Nizārīs celebrated the end of earthly life. On the other hand, the "outsiders", those incapable of recognising the truth, were henceforth rendered spiritually non-existent. In line with earlier Ismaili teachings, the imam initiating the *qiyāma* would be the *qā'im al-qiyāma* or lord of the resurrection, a rank which in Ismaili religious hierarchy had always been higher than that of an ordinary imam; and his mission would be the *da'wat-i qiyāmat* or the *da'wa* of the resurrection.

The fourth lord of Alamūt, Ḥasan, to whom the Nizārīs referred with the expression *ʿalā dhikrihiʾl-salām* (on his mention be peace), as noted, had initially claimed to be only the *khalīfa* or deputy of the hidden imam, or *qāʾim* who had proclaimed the *qiyāma*. Subsequently, the rank of *khalīfa* was explicitly equated with God's caliph and identified with the rank held by al-Mustanṣir who had been an imam. In other words, Ḥasan *ʿalā dhikrihiʾl-salām* had in two stages claimed to have been the imam, and indeed the imam-*qāʾim*. Our Persian historians who had access to contemporary Alamūt documents report that after the proclamation of the *qiyāma*, Ḥasan in his various epistles (*fuṣūl*) and addresses did reiterate his position as imam and the *qāʾim* of the resurrection, though in appearance he had been considered to have been the son of Muḥammad b. Buzurg-Ummīd who was not an imam. At any rate, with the proclamation of the *qiyāma*, Ḥasan had also claimed the Nizārī imamate; and this claim was acknowledged unanimously by the entire Nizārī community.[23]

The declaration of the *qiyāma* in 559/1164 represents a controversial episode in Nizārī Ismaili history. Later, it also provided an ideal opportunity for Muslim enemies of the Nizārīs to misinterpret this declaration and its implications. From early on, even before the foundation of the Fatimid caliphate, the Ismailis had been accused of dispensing with the *sharīʿa*. The Sunni establishment had now found a unique chance for reasserting that accusation. However, the declaration of the *qiyāma* in Alamūt and Muʾminābād seems to have gone unnoticed for some time by the outside world. Contemporary Sunni chroniclers, including Ibn al-Athīr, do not mention the Nizārī *qiyāma*. All this implies that the Persian Nizārīs of the *qiyāma* times had not attracted the attention of other Muslims by a drastic change in lifestyle. It was, in fact, only after the fall of Alamūt that our Persian historians and the outside world in general became aware of the enigmatic event that had taken place almost a century earlier in 559/1164. Persian historians relate that in line with the circumstances expected in the *qiyāma* times, Ḥasan *ʿalā dhikrihiʾl-salām* had actually abrogated the *sharīʿa*, relieving his community of observing its commandments and prohibitions. In view of the fact that no contemporary Nizārī sources have survived, and other Muslim chronicles do not report any changes in the religious practices of the Nizārī community, it is rather difficult to judge as to how the *qiyāma* was perceived by the Nizārīs of Rūdbār, Quhistān and elsewhere. Indeed, there is no evidence suggesting that Nizārīs of the *qiyāma* period advocated a lawless society indulging in libertinism. Even Juwaynī, always free with his invectives on them, does not report any instance of libertinism in the Nizārī community of that period.

Doubtless, the Nizārī leadership now stressed the *bāṭin* and the inner spirituality of religion, rather than merely observing the *ẓāhir* or its literal meaning. The faithful were, henceforth, expected in the *qiyāma* times to pay greater attention to discovering the inner spiritual reality behind the positive law. And, as subsequent events in the history of the community indicate, the Nizārīs regarded themselves as specifically Shīʿī Ismaili Muslims, as this identity was understood by Nizārīs of medieval times, mostly villagers and mountain dwellers who since the time of Ḥasan Ṣabbāḥ were bound by the precepts of Ismaili Shīʿī law. For almost seven decades, the Nizārīs had obeyed the imam's chief representative or *ḥujja* while eagerly anticipating the imam's appearance. That expectation was now fulfilled. The authoritative teacher promised by Ḥasan Ṣabbāḥ had at long last made himself known; and it was now incumbent upon the faithful to obey his commands and follow his teachings. The *qiyāma* inaugurated a new era in the religious history of the early Nizārīs, who would henceforth have direct access to their imam.

In 561/1166, a year and a half after his proclamation of the *qiyāma*, Ḥasan *ʿalā dhikrihi'l-salām* was murdered mysteriously in the castle of Lamasar. He was succeeded by his son Nūr al-Dīn Muḥammad, who devoted his long and peaceful reign (561–607/1166–1210) to a systematic elaboration and refinement of the doctrine of *qiyāma*.[24] In his teachings, Nūr al-Dīn Muḥammad assigned a central role to the imam, and, more specifically, to the present imam. Exaltation of the autonomous teaching authority of the present Nizārī imam over those of the previous imams, which had already been taught according to Ḥasan Ṣabbāḥ's doctrine of *taʿlīm*, became the central feature of Nizārī Ismaili thought. The doctrine of *qiyāma*, as expounded by Nūr al-Dīn Muḥammad, implied a complete personal transformation of the Nizārīs who, henceforth, were expected to perceive the imam in his true spiritual reality. The attainment of this vision required metaphysical transcendence of the person of the imam so as to enable the believer to see the unveiled truth. This perception of the universe and the imam of the time would lead the believer to the realm of ultimate reality, the *ḥaqīqa*. In this realm of spiritual existence, the believers would turn from the *ẓāhirī* world of appearances to a *bāṭinī* world of unchangeable truths, the common message of all the Abrahamic world religions. As noted earlier, the doctrine of *qiyāma*, drawing on earlier religious traditions, introduced a further element in the cyclical history of the Nizārī Ismailis in the form of the figure of imam-*qā'im*, the imam inaugurating the era of *qiyāma*. Nūr al-Dīn Muḥammad identified the present Nizārī imam with the figure of imam-*qā'im*, also making every Nizārī imam potentially a *qā'im*.

In the era of *qiyāma*, the hierarchical ranks of the *da'wa*, whatever they may have been in its simplified Alamūt organisation, faded away. In the spiritual world of resurrection, when the spiritual reality of the imam-*qā'im* would be perceivable by believers, there would no longer be any need for ranks intervening between him and his followers. In the *qiyāma*, therefore, there would remain only three idealised categories of persons, representing different levels of existence among mankind defined in terms of their relationships with the Nizārī imam. There are the "people of opposition" (*ahl-i taḍādd*), comprised of all those outside the Nizārī community. These opponents, who do not acknowledge the Nizārī imam, exist only in the realm of appearances (*ẓāhir*); they are spiritually non-existent and irrelevant in the era of the *qiyāma*. Secondly, there are the ordinary followers of the Nizārī imam, designated as the "people of gradation" (*ahl-i tarattub*), representing the elite of mankind. These Nizārīs have penetrated the *sharī'a*, extending their perception from its literal to its inner meaning. However, they have found access to only partial truth, as they still do not fully understand the *bāṭin*. As a result, the ordinary Nizārīs merely find partial salvation in the earthly *qiyāma*. Finally, there are the "people of union" (*ahl-i vaḥdat*), the Nizārī super-elite or the *akhaṣṣ-i khāṣṣ*, who perceive the imam in his true spiritual reality. They have arrived at the realm of the *ḥaqīqa*, in a sense the *bāṭin* behind the ordinary *bāṭin*, where they find full, as opposed to partial, truth. Only the "people of union" are resurrected and spiritually existent in the *qiyāma*; and, therefore, they alone enjoy full, eternal salvation in the paradisal state actualised for them in this world. It seems that the difficult and privileged state of the "people of union" was attainable by only a few, if any; ordinary Nizārīs had to be content with understanding the *sharī'a* and its inner significance, or the positive law and its spirituality, as interpreted by Ismaili *ta'wīl*.

Nūr al-Dīn Muḥammad's teachings, and the demanding conditions for attaining the state of the "people of union" serve to underlie the difficulties and dilemmas confronted by the Nizārīs of the *qiyāma* times. All these complex doctrinal developments were, however, ignored by the later anti-Nizārī sources, which hastily and simplistically equated the declaration of the spiritual *qiyāma* with the literal abrogation of the *sharī'a*. Nūr al-Dīn Muḥammad also explicitly affirmed the Nizārid genealogy of his father and, therefore, of himself. He explained that his father, Ḥasan, was in fact imam also by physical descent, as he was the son of a descendant of Nizār b. al-Mustanṣir who had earlier found refuge in the Alamūt district. This claim, put forth earlier by Ḥasan himself, was fully acknowledged by the Nizārīs who recognised the lords of Alamūt, beginning with Ḥasan *ʿalā dhikrihiʾl-salām*, as their imams. There were evidently alternative versions of Ḥasan's Nizārid ancestry, as reported by Juwaynī and other Persian historians. With the declaration of the *qiyāma*, the *dawr al-satr*, or the period of concealment, also came to an end.

In the meantime, Syrian Nizārīs had entered into an important phase of their history coinciding with the career of Rāshid al-Dīn Sinān, their greatest chief *dāʿī*.[25] Sinān was born in the 520s/1126–35 into an Imāmī family near Baṣra, where he was converted to Nizārī Ismailism. Subsequently, he went to Alamūt to further his Ismaili studies. There, he became a close companion of Muḥammad b. Buzurg-Ummīd's heir apparent Ḥasan. It was, in fact, Ḥasan *ʿalā dhikrihiʾl-salām* who soon after his accession in 557/1162 sent Sinān to Syria, then ruled by the Zangid Nūr al-Dīn. Sinān stayed for some time in the castle of Kahf, endearing himself to the Nizārī community in Syria. Before long, he was appointed by Alamūt to lead the Syrian Nizārīs. Thereupon, he devoted himself to reorganising and strengthening the Syrian Nizārī *daʿwa*, also fortifying the Nizārī castles and acquiring more strongholds in the Jabal Bahrāʾ. He also established a corps of *fidāʾī*s, more generally referred to in Syria as *fidāwī*s or *fidāwiyya*. As noted, it was the actual or alleged missions of the Nizārī *fidāʾī*s that provided the basis for the imaginative tales circulating in the Crusader circles of the Near East and Europe. In these legends, Sinān was referred to as the "Old Man of the Mountain", a designation applied later by Marco Polo and others also to the lords of Alamūt.

Sinān was a skilful strategist and a master of the art of diplomacy. Aiming to safeguard the Syrian Nizārī community, he entered into an intricate web of shifting alliances with the major neighbouring powers and rulers, especially the Crusaders, the Zangids and Saladin. As a result, he played a prominent role in the regional politics of Syria and managed to maintain the independence of his community under difficult circumstances. When Sinān assumed power, Nūr al-Dīn Zangī, and Saladin who soon uprooted Fatimid rule, posed greater threats to the Syrian Nizārīs than the Crusaders who had been fighting them sporadically. Therefore, initially Sinān established friendly relations with the Crusaders and their Latin states. In fact, in 569/1173, he sent an embassy to Amalric I, king of the Latin state of Jerusalem. Before long, Sinān came to confront the enmity of Saladin, then leading the Muslim holy war against the Crusaders. At the time, Saladin harboured expansionist designs on Syria, and the Nizārī principality. In retaliation, Sinān entered into a temporary alliance with the Zangids of Aleppo and Mawṣil, equally threatened by Saladin's ambitions. It was during this period, 570–1/1174–6, that Sinān dispatched teams of *fidā'īs* to kill Saladin on two occasions without success.[26] In the aftermath of these attempts Saladin invaded the Nizārī territory and laid seige to the castle of Maṣyāf. But hostilities soon ceased between Saladin and Sinān, who had evidently reached some sort of a permanent truce.

Later, relations once again deteriorated between the Syrian Nizārīs and the Crusaders, while the Nizārīs continued to fight the Templars and the Hospitallers, Frankish military orders which often acted independently in the Latin East. In 537/1142, the Hospitallers had come into possession of the famous Crusader fortress of Krak des Chevaliers (Ḥisn al-Akrād) at the southern end of the Jabal Bahrā' in proximity to Nizārī castles. These military orders also intermittently exacted tribute from the Nizārī community. At any rate, the murder of Conrad of Montferrat, king of Jerusalem, in 588/1192 by two assassins who had disguised themselves as Christian monks was attributed to Sinān, among other instigators. In particular, Ibn al-Athīr and other sources hostile to Saladin claim that the latter had asked Sinān to arrange for the murder of Conrad as well as Richard I (1189–99), nicknamed the Lion Heart, king of England who was then in the Holy Land. Other Muslim sources, and some occidental ones, name Richard himself as the instigator of this murder, which is reported in almost every occidental chronicle of the Third Crusade (1189–92) as well as by many Muslim historians.

It fell upon Sinān to announce the *qiyāma* to the Syrian Nizārīs soon after 559/1164. Sinān evidently propagated his own version of the doctrine of *qiyāma*, which did not acquire deep roots in the Syrian community. He drew particularly on the popular Shī'ī and other local traditions circulating in Syria, including certain teachings associated more closely with the local Nuṣayrīs. There are also indications that Sinān's teaching of the doctrine of *qiyāma* was misunderstood by a faction of the community, especially some of those living outside the main Nizārī territory in the Jabal Bahrā'. Sinān personally dealt with the refractories who called themselves al-Ṣufāt, the Pure, ending their antinomian activities.

Sinān enjoyed unprecedented popularity within the Syrian Nizārī community. He was, in fact, the only one of the Syrian *dā'īs* to act somewhat independently of Alamūt. However, there is no evidence suggesting, as claimed by certain non-Ismaili sources,[27] that he was ever acknowledged as imam by the Syrian Nizārīs, who were sometimes referred to as Sinānīs by outsiders.[28] At any rate, Rāshid al-Dīn Sinān led the Syrian Nizārīs for almost three decades to the peak of their power and fame, and through his carefully selected alliances and skilled diplomacy, safeguarded the independence of the community in the most turbulent and challenging period of their medieval history. Sinān died in the castle of Kahf in 589/1193 or, less probably, a year earlier.[29]

Meanwhile, the sultanate of the Great Saljuqs had been disintegrating following Sanjar's death in 552/1157. A number of Turkish dynasties overtook formerly Saljuq dominions. At the same time, a new power based in Khwārazm, the region of the lower Oxus in Central Asia, emerged with great political ambitions. The hereditary rule of Khwārazm had earlier passed into the hands of a Turkish dynasty acting as Saljuq vassals and adopting the region's traditional regnal title of Khwārazm Shāh. After Sanjar, the Khwārazm Shāhs asserted their independence and expanded their new empire westward into Persia, clearing away the remnants of Saljuq rule. The collapse of the Saljuqs also led to an Abbasid revival. With the accession of al-Nāṣir (575–622/1180–1225), the Abbasid caliph emerged as a central figure in Muslim war and diplomacy. One of the major concerns of al-Nāṣir was to restore the religious unity of Islam with the Abbasid caliph acting as its real, and not merely titular, head. Subsequent decades in the history of the Nizārīs of the Alamūt period should be studied within this context of changing political realities and aspirations.

As successors to Saljuqs, and faced with the same predicaments, the Khwārazm Shāhs soon engaged in hostile relations with the Nizārīs of Rūdbār and elsewhere in Persia. The Persian Nizārīs retained their traditional petty skirmishes with their neighbours in the Caspian provinces. In Quhistān, they had military encounters with the Ghūrids and the Naṣrid Maliks of Sīstān. Having reigned longer than any other lord of Alamūt, Nūr al-Dīn Muḥammad died in 607/1210. He was succeeded by his son Ḥasan who, according to the prevalent custom at Alamūt, carried the honorific title of Jalāl al-Dīn. The sixth lord of Alamūt moved to proclaim his religious policy, no less daring than his grandfather's declaration of the *qiyāma*.

RAPPROCHEMENT WITH SUNNI ISLAM AND AL-ṬŪSĪ'S INTERPRETATIONS

Jalāl al-Dīn Ḥasan wearied of the isolation of the Nizārī community from the outside world; he desired to establish better relations with Sunni Muslims and their rulers. These sentiments may have been shared by others in the Nizārī community. At any rate, the Persian historians relate that he communicated his new ideas to a number of Sunni Muslim leaders prior to his accession, after which he publicly repudiated the doctrine of *qiyāma* and ordered his followers to observe the *sharī'a* in its Sunni form.[30] The new lord of Alamūt then sent messengers to the caliph al-Nāṣir, Muḥammad Khwārazm Shāh and other Sunni rulers, informing them of his new policy. The Nizārīs entered into yet another phase of their history, a phase that lasted until the fall of Alamūt.

Jalāl al-Dīn Ḥasan did his utmost to convince the outside world of his new policy and to end the isolation of his community. He invited Sunni scholars belonging to the Shāfiʿī *madhhab* to instruct his people, also permitting Sunni observers to remove any books they deemed "heretical" from the library at Alamūt. In 608/1211, the caliph al-Nāṣir acknowledged the Nizārī leader's rapprochement with Sunni Islam and issued a decree to that effect. Henceforth, the rights of Jalāl al-Dīn Ḥasan to Nizārī territories were officially recognised for the first time by the Abbasid caliph, with all that this endorsement implied for Sunni Muslims. It is significant that all Nizārīs, true to their Alamūt tradition, accepted Jalāl al-Dīn's reform without opposition, regarding him as the imam who guided his community and contextualised the interpretation of the *sharīʿa* as he saw fit. As it was explained later, the Nizārīs viewed their imam's declarations as a reimposition of *taqiyya*, which had been lifted in the *qiyāma* times. The observance of *taqiyya* could now be taken to imply any type of accommodation to the outside world as decreed by the infallible imam.

Jalāl al-Dīn Ḥasan's daring rapprochement with Sunni Muslims had obvious advantages for the Nizārī community, who had been marginalised as "heretics" for several decades. He changed all that by aligning himself with the spiritual head of Sunni Islam and situating his community at the very heart of contemporary Muslim affairs. Above all, he now won territorial security for his state as well as peace and amnesty for his community. Truce seemed to have been finally established between the Nizārīs and other Muslims. The Ghūrid attacks against the Nizārīs of Quhistān came to an end. And in Syria, where the Nizārīs faced renewed Frankish hostilities, they received timely assistance from the Ayyūbids. Consequently, the Nizārī imam actively joined the caliph al-Nāṣir's alliances.

The centrality of the Nizārīs in the regional power structure is well attested to by the fact that in 610/1213 the Nizārī imam personally led his army to join forces with Muẓaffar al-Dīn Özbeg (607–22/1210–25), the last Eldigüzid ruler of Ādharbāyjān and one of al-Nāṣir's major allies. Muẓaffar al-Dīn was then engaged in a campaign against a rebellious lieutenant. In appreciation of the Nizārī role in this campaign, the imam was given the towns of Abhar and Zanjān with their environs. In addition to enhancing the caliphal alliances, these regional pacts also bore further benefits for the Sunni community at large. By the end of Jalāl al-Dīn's reign, when the Mongols had already crossed the Oxus, many Sunnis fleeing Khurāsān and other eastern regions, found refuge in the Nizārī towns and fortress communities of Quhistān, where they were treated most lavishly by the Nizārī *muḥtashams*. A keen observer of political realities, Jalāl al-Dīn Ḥasan was also quick in recognising the impending danger of the Mongols; he was evidently the first Muslim ruler to engage them in negotiations. Jalāl al-Dīn Ḥasan died in 618/1221, and was succeeded by his only son 'Alā' al-Dīn Muḥammad, then only nine years of age.[31]

Intellectual life flourished in the reign of 'Alā' al-Dīn Muḥammad (618–53/1221–55). Politically, too, this was an eventful period for all Muslims. The vizier to Jalāl al-Dīn Ḥasan was reinstated in his post and managed the affairs of the Nizārī state for a while. He maintained amicable relations with the Sunni–Abbasid establishment, and Nizārīs continued to appear in Sunni guise throughout 'Alā' al-Dīn Muḥammad's reign. Gradually the Sunni *sharī'a* was less enforced within the community and Nizārī traditions associated with *qiyāma* were revived.

Nizārī teachings, as noted, had undergone a number of changes or reformulations since Ḥasan Ṣabbāḥ's time, some of which must have been rather perplexing to the rank and file of the community. There is evidence suggesting that the Nizārī leadership in 'Alā' al-Dīn Muḥammad's time made a conscious and sustained effort to explain the different doctrinal declarations and religious policies of the lords of Alamūt. As a result, the earlier teachings were interpreted comprehensively within a coherent doctrinal framework. In a sense, this was an intellectual endeavour for the internal benefit of the community, aiming to provide satisfactory explanations for the seemingly contradictory policies adopted at Alamūt.

The intellectual life of the community now received a special impetus from the continuing influx of outside scholars who fled the Mongol invasions, taking refuge in Nizārī strongholds. These scholars, availing themselves of the Nizārī libraries and patronage of learning, and free to maintain their religious convictions, invigorated intellectual endeavours. A few of them, notably al-Ṭūsī, also made major contributions to the Nizārī Ismaili thought of the late Alamūt period.

One of the most learned Muslim scholars, Naṣīr al-Dīn Abū Ja'far Muḥammad b. Muḥammad al-Ṭūsī was born into a Twelver Shī'ī family in 597/1201. In his youth, around 624/1227, he entered the service of Nāṣir al-Dīn 'Abd al-Raḥīm b. Abī Manṣūr (d. 655/1257), the Nizārī *muḥtasham* in Quhistān, himself a learned man. During his long residence in Quhistān, al-Ṭūsī developed a close friendship with his patron, the Nizārī *muḥtasham*. In recognition of this relationship, al-Ṭūsī dedicated both of his great works on ethics, the *Akhlāq-i Nāṣirī* and the *Akhlāq-i muḥtashamī*, to his Nizārī patron, the *muḥtasham* Nāṣir al-Dīn. Later, al-Ṭūsī went to Alamūt and enjoyed the munificence of the Nizārī imam himself until the surrender of Alamūt to the Mongols. Still later, on the fall of Alamūt, al-Ṭūsī became a trusted adviser to the Mongol conqueror, Hülegü, who built a renowned observatory for him at Marāgha in Ādharbāyjān. Al-Ṭūsī also served Abaqa, Hülegü's successor in the Mongol Īlkhānid dynasty, continuing with his scientific and philosophical enquiries. Having also served as vizier to the Īlkhānids, he died in Baghdad in 672/1274.

Thus, al-Ṭūsī spent some three decades, the most productive period of his life, in the Nizārī strongholds of Persia. During this period he wrote numerous treatises on astronomy, theology, philosophy and many other subjects. The *Rawḍat al-taslīm* (*Meadow of Submission*), his major Ismaili work; the *Sayr va sulūk* (*Contemplation and Action*), his spiritual autobiography in which al-Ṭūsī explains how he came to acknowledge the teaching authority of the Nizārī imam, and a few shorter treatises bearing an Ismaili imprint, also date from that period. The study of al-Ṭūsī's "true" religious affiliation has preoccupied a number of his modern biographers.[32] Taking into account the circumstances of al-Ṭūsī's career, his contributions to Ismaili thought, his long stay among the Nizārīs, and the latter's generally liberal policy towards non-Ismaili scholars living among them, it is safe to assume that al-Ṭūsī willingly embraced Ismailism sometime during his association with Nizārīs. There is no reason to believe that he was detained in the Nizārī strongholds against his will, or that he was ever coerced into conversion, an unprecedented episode in the annals of Ismaili history. However, al-Ṭūsī did revert to Twelver Shīʿism upon joining the Mongols, whose patronage he then sought.

At any event, al-Ṭūsī made important contributions to Nizārī thought of his time. As noted, the teachings of the Alamūt period were explained in ʿAlāʾ al-Dīn Muḥammad's reign by a number of scholars. But it is primarily through al-Ṭūsī's extant Ismaili works that we have a detailed exposition of Nizārī thought as it developed during the *qiyāma* and its aftermath. Al-Ṭūsī provided an integrated theological frame for contextualising the policy declarations of the different lords of Alamūt. He sought to demonstrate that these seemingly contradictory policies partook, in effect, of a singular spiritual reality, since each infallible imam acted in accordance with the exigencies of his own time. In the process, al-Ṭūsī, and presumably others whose writings have not survived, expounded an adjusted doctrine which may be called the *satr* doctrine.[33]

Qiyāma, al-Ṭūsī explained, was not necessarily a final eschatological event in the history of mankind but a transitory condition of life, when the veil of *taqiyya* would be removed so as to make the unveiled truth accessible. Thus, the identification between *sharīʿa* and *taqiyya*, tacitly implied by the teachings of Ḥasan *ʿalā dhikrihiʾl-salām*, was explicitly confirmed by al-Ṭūsī, who also identified *qiyāma* with *ḥaqīqa*.[34] As a result, the imposition of the Sunni *sharīʿa* by Jalāl al-Dīn Ḥasan was presented as a return to *taqiyya*, and to a new period of *satr* or concealment, when the truth (*ḥaqīqa*) would be once again concealed in the *bāṭin* of religion. The condition of *qiyāma* could, in principle, be granted by the current Nizārī imam to mankind or to its elite at any time, because every imam was potentially also an imam-*qāʾim*. As a corollary, human life could alternate, at the will of the imam, between periods of *qiyāma*, when reality is manifest, and *satr*, when it would be concealed. It was in this sense that Ḥasan *ʿalā dhikrihiʾl-salām* had introduced a period of *qiyāma* while his grandson terminated that period, initiating a new period of *satr* which required the observance of *taqiyya*. Al-Ṭūsī clearly allows for such alterations by stating that each prophetic era associated with the *ẓāhir* of the *sharīʿa* is a period of *satr*, whilst that of an imam-*qāʾim*, who reveals the truths of religious laws, is one of *qiyāma* and *dawr-i kashf* or era of manifestation.[35]

In the current cycle of the sacred history of mankind, however, it was still expected that the full *qiyāma*, or the Great Resurrection (*qiyāmat-i qiyāmāt*), would occur at the end of the final millennial era after Adam, that is, at the end of the sixth era initiated by the Prophet Muḥammad. The Great Resurrection would inaugurate the final, seventh era in the history of mankind. In the meantime, in the current era of Islam (which was an era of *satr* like those initiated by all preceding prophets), and in special honour of the Prophet Muḥammad's greatness, periods of *satr* and *qiyāma* could alternate at the discretion of each current Nizārī imam. In the Nizārī teachings of the late Alamūt period, the term *satr* was, thus, redefined. It implied the concealment of the religious truths and the true spiritual reality of the imam, and not the hiddenness of the physical person of the imam, as had been the case in the pre-Fatimid and early Alamūt times. According to al-Ṭūsī, such a period of *satr* and *taqiyya* had started with the advent of Jalāl al-Dīn Ḥasan, even though he and his successor were manifest and accessible.[36]

The Nizārī Ismaili teachings of the late Alamūt period brought them even closer to the esoteric traditions more widely associated with Sufism, also making it possible for them to maintain a distinct identity and spiritual independence under changing circumstances.

These teachings allowed post-Alamūt Nizārīs to survive independently of the state support they had enjoyed in the Alamūt period. The same teachings and traditions allowed the Nizārīs to adopt the guise of Sufism among other forms of *taqiyya* as self-protection in the turbulent centuries following the fall of Alamūt.

THE FINAL DECADES

Early in ʿAlāʾ al-Dīn Muḥammad's reign the eastern Iranian world experienced a foretaste of the Mongol catastrophe. ʿAlāʾ al-Dīn's accession at Alamūt in 618/1221 followed immediately the first Mongol conquests in Transoxania, sealing the fate of the short-lived empire of the Khwārazm Shāhs. By the time of Chingiz Khan's death in 624/1227, the Mongols had already destroyed Marw, Nīshāpūr and much of Khurāsān. It was in the aftermath of these early Mongol invasions that an increasing number of refugees, including many Sunni scholars of Khurāsān, found asylum in the Nizārī towns and fortresses of Quhistān.

It seems that Jalāl al-Dīn Ḥasan's earlier negotiations with the Mongols had paid off; his secret emissaries had evidently met with Chingiz Khan himself in 618/1221 informing him of the Nizārī imam's desire for peace. The Mongols did not attack the Nizārīs of Quhistān for some time. Life among the Nizārīs of Quhistān and the benevolence of their *muḥtasham*s, Shihāb al-Dīn and his successor Shams al-Dīn, is vividly narrated by Jūzjānī, the Ghūrid historian and official who visited Quhistān several times during 621–3/1224–6 on diplomatic missions.[37] Enjoying their precious security and flourishing trade, Nizārī influence now stretched to the internal affairs of Sīstān, then beset by dynastic strifes. In the wake of the disintegration of the Khwārazmian empire, the Nizārīs seized Dāmghān as well as a number of fortresses in Qūmis, Ṭārum and elsewhere in Persia. Thus, they actually expanded their territories in Persia, as Alamūt continued to maintain friendly relations with the caliph in Baghdad and the Mongol Great Khan. On the other hand, relations between Alamūt and the Khwārazmians, who had replaced the Saljuqs as the Nizārīs' foremost enemy, remained characterised by warfare and diplomacy until Jalāl al-Dīn Mengübirti, the last Khwārazm Shāh, was defeated at the hands of the Mongols and murdered in 628/1231.

Nizārī fortunes in Persia rapidly reversed after the collapse of the Khwārazmian empire, as they were now forced to confront the Mongols directly. In 644/1246, ʿAlāʾ al-Dīn Muḥammad dispatched his ambassadors to Mongolia on the occasion of the Great Khan Güyük's enthronement, carrying a message of peace from their imam. However, Güyük was not to be pacified as he intended to conquer all the territories in Persia which were not yet in Mongol hands.[38] He duly dismissed the Nizārī emissaries with contempt. Henceforth, Mongol–Nizārī relations deteriorated beyond repair.

Güyük did not live to accomplish his designs of conquest, taken up by his successor Möngke (649–58/1251–60). When Möngke decided to complete the Mongol conquests of western Asia, he assigned first priority to the destruction of the Nizārī Ismaili state, and the Abbasid caliphate. In 650/1252, he entrusted this mission to his brother Hülegü, who took some four years to prepare for the campaigns. Meanwhile, he sent an advance army to join forces with the Mongol garrisons stationed in Persia and attack Nizārī strongholds in Quhistān. By 651/1253, the Mongols had destroyed several Nizārī towns and strongholds, also laying siege to Girdkūh, a protracted one as we shall see.

As the Mongols attacked the Nizārī territories in Persia incessantly, 'Alā' al-Dīn Muḥammad was found murdered under enigmatic circumstances on the last day of Shawwāl 653/1 December 1255. He was succeeded by his eldest son Rukn al-Dīn Khurshāh, who would rule for exactly one year as the last lord of Alamūt.[39] The youthful Khurshāh was drawn into a complex, and ultimately futile, series of negotiations with the Mongols, especially after Hülegü's arrival in Khurāsān in Rabī' I 654/April 1256. Khurshāh was urged to submit personally and surrender his strongholds, while the Nizārī imam for his part resorted to delaying tactics. Indeed, the sources are rather ambiguous on Rukn al-Dīn's policy towards the invading Mongols. Vacillating between surrender and resistance, he seems to have inclined towards a compromise, perhaps hoping to save at least the major strongholds from Mongol wrath.

At any rate, by Sha'bān 654/September 1256, Hülegü attacked the seat of Nizārī power, ordering the main Mongol armies in Persia to converge on the Alamūt district. On 18 Shawwāl 654/8 November 1256, Hülegü encamped on a hilltop facing the fortress of Maymūndiz, where Rukn al-Dīn Khurshāh was staying. After the failure of a last round of negotiations and some intense fighting, the Nizārī imam was finally forced to surrender. On 29 Shawwāl 654/19 November 1256, Khurshāh descended from Maymūndiz in the company of Naṣīr al-Dīn al-Ṭūsī, his vizier Mu'ayyad al-Dīn, and other Nizārī dignitaries. The fate of the Nizārī state of Persia was sealed.

Whilst in Mongol captivity, Khurshāh issued a general order to his commanders to surrender the Nizārī strongholds. The Mongols seized some forty castles in Rūdbār in this manner, demolishing them after taking their garrisons into custody. The commanders of several major strongholds, notably Alamūt, Lamasar and Girdkūh, did not surrender immediately, perhaps thinking that the imam had acted under duress. Alamūt, too, surrendered at the end of Dhu'l-Qaʿda 654/December 1256, while Lamasar held out for another year. Girdkūh remained the last Nizārī outpost in Persia; its garrison finally yielded from want of clothing in 669/1270. Juwaynī, who participated in the truce negotiations with the Nizārīs on behalf of Hülegü, has left a valuable description of Alamūt and its library before that majestic fortress was destroyed.

Khurshāh was treated hospitably by the Mongols as long as he was of some use to them. Upon the surrender of the bulk of Nizārī strongholds in Persia, however, Hülegü granted Khurshāh's desire for a visit to the court of the Great Khan in Mongolia. On 1 Rabīʿ I 655/9 March 1257, the imam set out on that fateful journey. Möngke apparently refused to see Khurshāh in Karakorum on the pretext that he still had not delivered Lamasar and Girdkūh. On the return journey, the last lord of Alamūt was murdered by his Mongol guards somewhere in central Mongolia. By then, the Mongols had put to the sword all Persian Nizārīs in their custody. Thousands perished in Quhistān and elsewhere, adding immeasurably to the tragic end of the Persian Nizārī Ismaili state of the Alamūt period.

In the meantime, the Nizārīs of Syria had been led by other *dāʿīs* after Rāshid al-Dīn Sinān. During this period, the authority of Alamūt was once again restored over the Syrian Nizārī community. From the time of Jalāl al-Dīn Ḥasan's rapprochement with Sunni Islam, relations between the Syrian Nizārīs and their Ayyūbid neighbours improved significantly. Sporadic skirmishes as well as negotiations continued with the Franks who still held the Syrian coastline. The last important encounter between the Nizārīs and the Crusaders related to extended diplomatic dealings with Louis IX, the French king better known as St Louis (d. 1270), leader of the Seventh Crusade (1248–54). Joinville, the king's biographer and secretary who participated in these negotiations, has preserved valuable details on the embassies exchanged during the early 1250s between St Louis and the Old Man of the Mountain.[40] It was in the course of these encounters that an Arabic-speaking friar met the chief *dāʿī* of the Syrian Nizārīs, probably Tāj al-Dīn whose name is inscribed at Maṣyāf, to discuss religious matters.

The collapse of the Nizārī state in Persia must have shocked the Syrian Nizārīs, as they could no longer count on Alamūt's support. Soon, they too were threatened by the Mongols who, after seizing Baghdad and killing the Abbasid caliph in 656/1258, had proceeded to Syria. By the time the Mongols entered Damascus in 658/1260, Syrian Nizārīs were stricken by internal strife, originating in leadership rivalries among their *dāʿīs*. However, the Mongols were soon expelled from Syria by Baybars, the Mamlūk sultan who succeeded the Ayyūbids as the dominant power in Egypt and Syria.

The Nizārīs collaborated with the Mamlūks and other Muslim rulers in uprooting the Mongols from Syria, also developing friendly relations with Sultan Baybars. But Baybars from early on resorted to various measures for gaining the submission of the Nizārī strongholds in the Jabal Bahrā'. Beginning in 665/1267, the political independence of the Syrian Nizārīs was compromised as Sultan Baybars encroached on their sovereignty and exacted tributes from them. In fact, the Syrian Nizārīs were now effectively incorporated into the Mamlūk state, and it did not take long before they lost their nominal independence as well. Soon, Baybars himself was appointing and dismissing chief *dāʿīs* for Syrian Nizārīs.[41] After the failure of a late attempt to resist Baybars, the Nizārī castles submitted in rapid succession to the Mamlūk sultan. Kahf was the last Nizārī outpost in Syria to fall in 671/1273. The Nizārīs were, however, permitted to remain in their traditional abodes under the watchful eyes of Mamlūk commanders. The Nizārī Ismailis survived in Syria in a semi-autonomous manner as loyal subjects of the Mamlūks and their successors.

By the time of the Mongol invasions, the Nizārī Ismailis were no longer a power to be reckoned with as in the days of Ḥasan Ṣabbāḥ and Rāshid al-Dīn Sinān. With the demise of their state in Persia and Mamlūk reduction of their Syrian strongholds, the Nizārīs irrevocably lost their independence and political prominence. They now entered a new and often obscure phase of their history, surviving precariously and secretly in numerous scattered communities.

NOTES

1. Our primary sources for Ḥasan Ṣabbāḥ's life and career, all drawing on the Nizārī work entitled *Sargudhasht-i Sayyidnā*, are ʿAlā' al-Dīn ʿAṭā-Malik Juwaynī, *Ta'rīkh-i jahān-gushāy*, ed. M. Qazwīnī (Leiden and London, 1912–37), vol. 3, pp. 186–216; English trans. John A. Boyle, *The History of the World-Conqueror* (Manchester, 1958), vol. 2, pp. 666–83; Rashīd al-Dīn Faḍl Allāh, *Jāmiʿ al-tawārīkh: qismat-i Ismāʿīliyān va Fāṭimiyān va Nizāriyān va dāʿīyān va rafīqān*, ed. M. T. Dānishpazhūh and M. Mudarrisī Zanjānī (Tehran, 1338/1959), pp. 97–137; Abu'l-Qāsim ʿAbd Allāh b. ʿAlī Kāshānī, *Zubdat al-tawārīkh: bakhsh-i Fāṭimiyān va Nizāriyān*, ed. M. T. Dānishpazhūh (2nd edn, Tehran, 1366/1987), pp. 133–72. For modern studies on Ḥasan Ṣabbāḥ, see Marshall G. S. Hodgson, *The Order of Assassins* (The Hague, 1955), pp. 41–98, and his "The Ismāʿīlī State", in *The Cambridge History of Iran*: Volume 5, *The Saljuq and Mongol Periods*, ed. J. A. Boyle (Cambridge, 1968), pp. 424–49; B. Lewis, *The Assassins* (London, 1967), pp. 38–63, 145–8; Daftary, *The Ismāʿīlīs*, pp. 324–71, 669–81, and his "Ḥasan-i

Ṣabbāḥ and the Origins of the Nizārī Isma'ili Movement", in Daftary (ed.), *Mediaeval Isma'ili History*, pp. 181–204.

2. On Alamūt and its environs, see W. Ivanow, *Alamūt and Lamasar: Two Mediaeval Ismaili Strongholds in Iran* (Tehran, 1960), pp. 1–11, 30–59; P. Willey, *The Castles of the Assassins* (London, 1963), pp. 204–26, and B. Hourcade, "Alamūt", EIR, vol. 1, pp. 797–801.
3. Professor C. E. Bosworth has studied the revival of Persian culture under Arab and Turkish rule in numerous works; see, for instance, his "The Development of Persian Culture under the Early Ghaznavids", *Iran, Journal of the British Institute of Persian Studies*, 6 (1968), pp. 33–44, reprinted in his *The Medieval History of Iran, Afghanistan and Central Asia* (London, 1977), article XVIII, and his *The History of Saffarids of Sistan and the Maliks of Nimruz (247/861 to 949/1542–3)* (Costa Mesa, Calif., and New York, 1994), pp. 168–80. See also S. M. Stern, "Ya'qūb the Coppersmith and Persian National Sentiments", in C. E. Bosworth (ed.), *Iran and Islam, in Memory of the Late Vladimir Minorsky* (Edinburgh, 1971), pp. 535–55, reprinted in his *History and Culture*, article VI.
4. Rashīd al-Dīn, p. 112, and Kāshānī, p. 148.
5. *Haft bāb-i Bābā Sayyidnā*, ed. W. Ivanow, in his *Two Early Ismaili Treatises* (Bombay, 1933), p. 30; English trans. M. G. S. Hodgson, in his *Order*, p. 314.
6. Rashīd al-Dīn, pp. 149–53; Kāshānī, pp. 186–90, and Madelung, *Religious Trends in Early Islamic Iran*, pp. 9–12.
7. For an interesting survey of the Muslim chroniclers' treatment of the Ismaili–Saljuq military encounters, and their general anti-Ismaili biases, see Carole Hillenbrand, "The Power Struggle between the Saljuqs and the Isma'ilis of Alamūt, 487–518/1094–1124: The Saljuq Perspective", in Daftary, *Mediaeval Isma'ili History*, pp. 205–20.
8. Ẓahīr al-Dīn Nīshāpūrī, *Saljūq-nāma* (Tehran, 1332/1953), pp. 40–1; Muḥammad b. 'Alī al-Rāwandī, *Rāḥat al-ṣudūr wa-āyat al-surūr*, ed. M. Iqbāl (London, 1921), pp. 157–8, and Ḥamd Allāh Mustawfī Qazwīnī, *Ta'rīkh-i guzīda*, ed. 'Abd al-Ḥusayn Navā'ī (Tehran, 1339/1960), pp. 445–6.
9. On the revolts of these Nizārids, who were mostly based in the Maghrib, see Ibn Ẓāfir, *Akhbār al-duwal al-munqaṭi'a*, ed. A. Ferré (Cairo, 1972), pp. 97, 111; al-Maqrīzī, *Itti'āẓ*. vol. 3, pp. 147, 186, 246; Ibn al-Qalānisī, *Dhayl ta'rīkh Dimashq*, ed. H. F. Amedroz (Leiden, 1908), p. 302; ed. S. Zakkār (Damascus, 1983), pp. 469–70; Ibn Muyassar, *Akhbār*, p. 139; Ibn Taghrībirdī, *al-Nujūm al-zāhira* (1348–91/1929–72), vol. 5, pp. 282, 339, and the anonymous *Bustān al-jāmi'*, ed. Claude Cahen, in his "Une Chronique Syrienne du VIe/XIIe siècle: Le Bustān al-Jāmi'", *Bulletin d'Etudes Orientales*, 7–8 (1937–8), p. 127.
10. P. Casanova, "Monnaie des Assassins de Perse", *Revue Numismatique*, 3 série, 11 (1893), pp. 343–52, and G. C. Miles, "Coins of the Assassins of Alamūt", *Orientalia Lovaniensia Periodica*, 3 (1972), pp. 155–62.
11. *Haft bāb-i Bābā Sayyidnā*, pp. 21–2; tr. Hodgson, in his *Order*, pp. 301–2.
12. Juwaynī, *Ta'rīkh*, vol. 3, pp. 180–1, 231–7; tr. Boyle, vol. 2, pp. 663, 691–5; Rashīd al-Dīn, pp. 79, 166–8, and Kāshānī, pp. 115, 202–4.

13. Al-Āmir bi-Aḥkām Allāh, *al-Hidāya al-Āmiriyya*, pp. 23–4, reprinted in al-Shayyāl (ed.), *Majmū'at al-wathā'iq*, pp. 226–7. See also Ibn Muyassar, *Akhbār*, pp. 99–101, 103.
14. Juwaynī, *Ta'rīkh*, vol. 3, pp. 195–9; tr. Boyle, vol. 2, pp. 671–3; Rashīd al-Dīn, pp. 105–7, and Kāshānī, pp. 142–3.
15. Abu'l-Fatḥ Muḥammad b. 'Abd al-Karīm al-Shahrastānī, *Kitāb al-milal wa'l-niḥal*, ed. W. Cureton (London, 1842–6), pp. 150–2; ed. 'A. M. al-Wakīl (Cairo, 1968), vol. 1, pp. 195–8; partial English trans. A. K. Kazi and J. G. Flynn, *Muslim Sects and Divisions* (London, 1984), pp. 167–70, also by Hodgson, in his *Order*, pp. 325–8; French trans. D. Gimaret et al., *Livre des religions et des sectes* (Louvain, 1986–93), vol. 1, pp. 560–5. See also Hodgson, *Order*, pp. 51–61, and his "Ismā'īlī State", pp. 433–7.
16. The fifth *dā'ī muṭlaq* of the Ṭayyibīs, 'Alī b. Muḥammad b. al-Walīd (d. 612/1215), provided a detailed response to *al-Mustaẓhirī*, refuting al-Ghazālī's attacks point by point, in his *Dāmigh al-bāṭil*, ed. M. Ghālib (Beirut, 1982), 2 vols. See also H. Corbin, "The Ismā'īlī Response to the Polemic of Ghazālī", in S. H. Nasr (ed.), *Ismā'īlī Contributions to Islamic Culture* (Tehran, 1977), pp. 69–98, and his *Itineraire d'un enseignement* (Tehran, 1993), pp. 150–3.
17. On the opening phase of the Nizārī *da'wa* in Syria, see B. Lewis, "The Ismā'īlites and the Assassins", in K. M. Setton (ed.), *A History of the Crusades*: Volume 1, *The First Hundred Years*, ed. M. W. Baldwin (2nd edn, Madison, Wis., 1969), pp. 99–114, and his *The Assassins*, pp. 97–104; see also Nasseh A. Mirza, *Syrian Ismailism* (Richmond, Surrey, 1997), pp. 6–15.
18. Rashīd al-Dīn, pp. 120–2; Kāshānī, pp. 156–7; Ẓahīr al-Dīn Nīshāpūrī, *Saljūq-nāma*, pp. 41–2; al-Rāwandī, *Rāḥat al-ṣudūr*, pp. 158–61, and Ibn al-Athīr, *al-Kāmil*, vol. 10, pp. 299–302. See also Ibn al-Qalānisī, *Dhayl*, ed. Amedroz, pp. 151–6; ed. Zakkār, pp. 244–50, containing also the text of the victory statement issued on that occasion; C. O. Minasian, *Shah Diz of Isma'ili Fame: Its Siege and Destruction* (London, 1971), pp. 17–39, 52–62, and F. Daftary, "Dezkūh", EIR, vol. 7, p. 354.
19. Relations between the Nizārīs of Quhistān and their neighbours in Sīstān are treated at great length in the anonymous local chronicle entitled *Ta'rīkh-i Sīstān*, ed. M. T. Bahār (Tehran, 1314/1935); ed. J. Mudarris Ṣādiqī (Tehran, 1373/1994); English trans. M. Gold, *The Tārikh-e Sistān* (Rome, 1976). See also Bosworth, *History of the Saffarids*, pp. 387–410, and his "The Isma'ilis of Quhistān and the Maliks of Nīmrūz or Sīstān", in Daftary, *Mediaeval Isma'ili History*, pp. 221–9.
20. Complete information on the succession of Nizārī *dā'īs* in Syria during the Alamūt period is lacking. For a provisional list, see C. E. Bosworth, *The New Islamic Dynasties* (Edinburgh, 1996), pp. 68–9.
21. The Ismaili fortresses of Syria, which are much better preserved than in Persia, have not been systematically studied in modern times. For some information on these fortresses, and their valuable epigraphs, see Max van Berchem, "Epigraphie des Assassins de Syrie", *Journal Asiatique*, 9 série, 9 (1897), pp. 453–501, reprinted in his *Opera Minora* (Geneva, 1978), vol, 1, pp. 453–501, and P. Thorau , "Die Burgen der Assassinen in Syrien und ihre Einnahme durch sultan Baibars", WO, 18 (1987), pp. 132–58; see also Lewis,

"Ismā'īlites and the Assassins", pp. 119–20, and E. Honigmann and N. Elisséeff, "Maṣyād", EI2, vol. 6, pp. 789–92.

22. For the events of the Nizārī state under Buzurg-Ummīd and his son Muḥammad, see Juwaynī, *Ta'rīkh*, vol. 3, pp. 216–22; tr. Boyle, vol. 2, pp. 683–6; Rashīd al-Dīn, pp. 137–61; Kāshānī, pp. 172–99, and W. Madelung, "Bozorg-Omīd", EIR, vol. 4, p. 429.

23. On the reign of Ḥasan *'alā dhikrihi'l-salām* and his declaration of the *qiyāma*, see Juwaynī, *Ta'rīkh*, vol. 3, pp. 222–39; tr. Boyle, vol. 2, pp. 686–97; Rashīd al-Dīn, pp. 162–70; Kāshānī, pp. 199–208; Abū Isḥāq Quhistānī, *Haft bāb*, ed. and tr. W. Ivanow (Bombay, 1959), text pp. 19, 24, 38–9, 40–2, 43–4, 46–7, 53, 58, 65, translation pp. 19, 23, 38, 40–2, 43–4, 46–7, 53–4, 58, 65; Hodgson, *Order*, pp. 146–59; Lewis, *The Assassins*, pp. 70–5; Poonawala, *Biobibliography*, pp. 257–8, and Daftary, *The Ismā'īlīs*, pp. 385–91.

24. The doctrine of *qiyāma*, as expounded under Nūr al-Dīn Muḥammad, is contained in the *Haft bāb-i Bābā Sayyidnā*, pp. 4–42, a Nizārī treatise wrongly attributed to Ḥasan Ṣabbāḥ; English trans., in Hodgson, *Order*, pp. 279–324. The doctrine of *qiyāma*, with various modifications, is also represented in the Ismaili writings of Naṣīr al-Dīn al-Ṭūsī, Abū Isḥāq Quhistānī and Khayrkhwāh-i Harātī. For the best modern exposition of this doctrine, see Hodgson, *Order*, pp. 160–80. More recently, Christian Jambet produced a phenomenological account of this event in his *La Grande résurrection d'Alamût* (Lagrasse, 1990). On Nūr al-Dīn Muḥammad's reign, see Juwaynī, *Ta'rīkh*, vol. 3, pp. 240–2; tr. Boyle, vol. 2, pp. 697–9; Rashīd al-Dīn, pp. 170–3; Kāshānī, pp. 208–14; Hodgson, *Order*, pp. 180–4, 210–17, and Daftary, "Nūr al-Dīn Muḥammad II", EI2, vol. 8, pp. 133–4.

25. The chief Nizārī source on Sinān's life is a hagiographical work attributed to the Syrian *dā'ī* Abū Firās Shihāb al-Dīn al-Maynaqī (fl. 10th/16th century) entitled *Faṣl min al-lafẓ al-sharīf*, ed. and tr. S. Guyard in his "Un Grand maître des Assassins au temps de Saladin", *Journal Asiatique*, 7 série, 9 (1877), pp. 387–489. Among non-Ismaili sources, the most important biographical account of Sinān was contained in Ibn al-'Adīm's still undiscovered volume of his *Bughyat al-ṭalab*. This biography, as preserved in later recensions, is edited and translated into English by B. Lewis in his "Kamāl al-Dīn's Biography of Rāšid al-Dīn Sinān", *Arabica*, 13 (1966), pp. 225–67, reprinted in his *Studies*, article X. See also Lewis, "Ismā'īlites and the Assassins", pp. 120–7, and his *The Assassins*, pp. 110–18; Hodgson, *Order*, pp. 185–209; Poonawala, *Biobibliography*, pp. 289–90; Mirza, *Syrian Ismailism*, pp. 22–39; Daftary, *Assassin Legends*, pp. 67–74, 94ff., and his "Rāshid al-Dīn Sinān", EI2, vol. 8, pp. 442–3.

26. On these attempts on Saladin's life, see Abū Shāma, *Kitāb al-rawḍatayn*, vol. 1, pp. 239–40, 258; Ibn Faḍl Allāh al-'Umarī, *Masālik al-abṣār fī mamālik al-amṣār*, selections ed. and tr. by Eva R. Lundquist as *Saladin and the Crusaders* (Lund, 1992), pp. 24–6, 32–4; see als B. Lewis, "Saladin and the Assassins", BSOAS, 15 (1953), pp. 239–45, reprinted in his *Studies*, article IX, where further references to the sources are given, and Malcolm C. Lyons and D. E. P. Jackson, *Saladin: The Politics of the Holy War* (Cambridge, 1982), pp. 87–8, 99, 105–6, 108–9.

27. See, for instance, S. Guyard, *Fragments relatifs à la doctrine des Ismaélîs* (Paris, 1874), text pp. 17–19, 66–9, 193–5, translation pp. 99–101, 204–9, 275–84; Ibn Faḍl Allāh al-ʿUmarī, *Masālik al-abṣār fī mamālik al-amṣār*, ed. A. Fu'ād Sayyid (Cairo, 1985), pp. 77–8, and Hodgson, *Order*, pp. 199–201.
28. Ibn Khallikān, *Ibn Khallikan's Biographical Dictionary*, tr. W. MacGuckin de Slane (Paris, 1842–71), vol. 3, p. 340, and Taqī al-Dīn Aḥmad al-Maqrīzī, *Kitāb al-sulūk*, partial English translation as *A History of the Ayyūbid Sultans of Egypt*, tr. Ronald J. C. Broadhurst (Boston, 1980), p. 55.
29. Ibn al-ʿAdīm, in Lewis, "Kamāl al-Dīn's Biography", pp. 230, 261; al-Qalqashandī, *Ṣubḥ*, vol. 1, p. 122; Ibn Taghrībirdī, *al-Nujūm*, vol. 6, p. 117, and John G. Phillips, "Mashhad Rāshid al-Dīn Sinān: A 13th Century Ismāʿīlī Monument in the Syrian Jabal Anṣārīya", JRAS (1984), pp. 19–37.
30. On Jalāl al-Dīn Ḥasan and his religious policy, see Juwaynī, *Ta'rīkh*, vol. 3, pp. 243–9; tr. Boyle, vol. 2, pp. 699–704; Rashīd al-Dīn, pp. 174–8; Kāshānī, pp. 214–17; Hodgson, *Order*, pp. 217–25; his "Ismāʿīlī State", pp. 468–72; Lewis, *The Assassins*, pp. 78–81, and Daftary, *The Ismāʿīlīs*, pp. 404–7.
31. Juwaynī, *Ta'rīkh*, vol. 3, pp. 249–59; tr. Boyle, vol. 2, pp. 704–12; Rashīd al-Dīn, pp. 178–84; Kāshānī, pp. 218–24; Hodgson, *Order*, pp. 225–7, 244–6, 250–262, and Lewis, *The Assassins*, pp. 82–91.
32. On Naṣīr al-Dīn al-Ṭūsī's Ismaili writings and the controversy surrounding his religious affiliation, see M. Mudarrisī Zanjānī, *Sargudhasht va ʿaqā'id-i falsafī-yi Khwāja Naṣīr al-Dīn Ṭūsī* (Tehran, 1335/1956), pp. 27–34, 54–6, 125–30; M. T. Mudarris Raḍavī, *Aḥvāl va āthār-i ... al-Ṭūsī* (2nd edn, Tehran, 1354/1975), pp. 3–16, 83–93; Mīnuvī's introduction to al-Ṭūsī's *Akhlāq-i Nāṣirī*, ed. M. Mīnuvī and ʿA. Ḥaydarī (2nd edn, Tehran 1356/1977), pp. 14–32; Hodgson, *Order*, pp. 239–43; Poonawala, *Biobibliography*, pp. 260–3; W. Madelung, "Naṣīr ad-Dīn Ṭūsī's Ethics between Philosophy, Shiʿism, and Sufism", in R. G. Hovannisian (ed.), *Ethics in Islam* (Malibu, Calif., 1985), pp. 85–101, and H. Dabashi, "The Philosopher/Vizier: Khwāja Naṣīr al-Dīn al-Ṭūsī and the Ismaʿilis", in Daftary, *Mediaeval Ismaʿili History*, pp. 231–45.
33. Naṣīr al-Dīn al-Ṭūsī's exposition of Nizārī thought of the Alamūt period may be found in his *Rawḍat al-taslīm*, ed. and tr. W. Ivanow (Leiden, 1950); French trans. Christian Jambet, *La Convocation d'Alamût: Somme de philosophie Ismaélienne* (Lagrasse, 1996). Al-Ṭūsī's *Sayr va sulūk*, in M. T. Mudarris Raḍavī (ed.), *Majmūʿa-yi rasā'il ... al-Ṭūsī* (Tehran, 1335/1956), pp. 36–55; ed. and tr. S. J. Badakhchani as *Contemplation and Action* (London, 1998), is also relevant here. See also Hodgson, *Order*, pp. 225–38; his "Ismāʿīlī State", pp. 472–6, and Daftary, *The Ismāʿīlīs*, pp. 407–12.
34. For reiteration of these ideas in post-Alamūt Nizārī writings, see Abū Isḥāq Quhistānī, *Haft bāb*, text pp. 38, 43, translation pp. 38–9, 43, and Khayrkhwāh-i Harātī, *Taṣnīfāt*, ed. W. Ivanow (Tehran, 1961), pp. 18–19.
35. Al-Ṭūsī, *Rawḍat al-taslīm*, ed. Ivanow, text p. 61, translation pp. 67–8; tr. Jambet, p. 214.
36. Ibid., text p. 110, translation p. 126; tr. Jambet, pp. 290–1.
37. Minhāj al-Dīn ʿUthmān b. Sirāj Jūzjānī, *Ṭabaqāt-i Nāṣirī*, ed. ʿAbd

al-Ḥayy Ḥabībī (2nd edn, Kabul, 1342–3/1963–4), vol. 2, pp. 182–5, 186–8; English trans. Henry G. Raverty, *The Ṭabaḳāt-i-Nāṣirī: A General History of the Muhammadan Dynasties of Asia* (London, 1881–99), vol. 2, pp. 1197–1205, 1212–14.

38. Juwaynī, *Ta'rīkh*, vol. 1, pp. 211–12; tr. Boyle, vol. 1, pp. 256–7.

39. On Rukn al-Dīn's brief reign and the Mongol operations against the Persian Nizārīs, see Juwaynī, *Ta'rīkh*, vol. 3, pp. 259–78; tr. Boyle, vol. 2, pp. 712–25; Rashīd al-Dīn, pp. 185–95, and Kāshānī, pp. 224–33. Hülegü's expedition against the Nizārīs is also covered separately in Juwaynī, *Ta'rīkh*, vol. 3, pp. 106–42; tr. Boyle, vol. 2, pp. 618–40, and in Rashīd al-Dīn's history of Hülegü: *Jāmi' al-tawārīkh*, vol. 3, ed. A. A. Alizade (Baku, 1957), pp. 24ff., 27–38. See also Hodgson, *Order*, pp. 263–71; Lewis, *The Assassins*, pp. 91–6; J. A. Boyle, "The Ismā'īlīs and the Mongol Invasion", in Nasr (ed.), *Ismā'īlī Contributions*, pp. 7–22; Daftary, *The Ismā'īlīs*, pp. 416ff., 421–30, and his "Rukn al-Dīn Khurshāh", EI2, vol. 8, pp. 598–9.

40. Jean de Joinville, *Memoirs of John Lord de Joinville*, tr. J. Johnes (Hafod, 1807), vol. 1, pp. 194–7, and Daftary, *Assassins Legends*, pp. 79–82.

41. On the final years of the Syrian Nizārīs, until their subjugation by the Mamlūks, see Ibn Muyassar, *Akhbār*, p. 102; Ibn Shaddād, *Ta'rīkh al-Malik al-Ẓāhir*, ed. A. Ḥuṭayṭ (Wiesbaden, 1983), pp. 37, 60, 88, 268–9, 323, 327, 358; Ibn Faḍl Allāh al-'Umarī, *Masālik al-abṣār*, ed. Sayyid, pp. 77, 132–3; al-Qalqashandī, *Ṣubḥ*, vol. 1, p. 121, vol. 4, pp. 146–7 and vol. 13, p. 245; Ibn al-Dawādārī, *Kanz al-durar*, vol. 8, ed. U. Haarmann (Cairo, 1971), pp. 84–5, 157–8; S. Fatima Sadeque, *Baybars I of Egypt* (Dacca, 1956), text pp. 45, 70–1, translation pp. 138–9, 171–2; A. A. Khowaiter, *Baibars the First: His Endeavours and Achievements* (London, 1978), pp. 118–26; P. Thorau, *The Lion of Egypt*, tr. P. M. Holt (London, 1992), pp. 147, 164, 169, 176, 194, 201–3, 208; Lewis, *The Assassins*, pp. 121–4, and Mirza, *Syrian Ismailism*, pp. 57–68.

5

Later Developments: Continuity and Modernisation

This final chapter will present a brief survey of the main developments and trends in the history of Ismaili communities during the post-Alamūt period, from the fall of Alamūt in 654/1256 till the 1990s. It will focus mainly on the majoritarian Nizārī branch of Ismailism. In this period, several Nizārī communities developed in various regions and, more or less, independently of one another. These communities, scattered widely from Syria to Persia, Central Asia and India, elaborated a diversity of religious and literary traditions in different languages. The Ṭayyibī Musta'lī Ismailis had continued to be centred in Yaman with a growing subsidiary Bohra community in Gujarāt. In time, the Bohra community overshadowed the Ṭayyibīs of Yaman, while both communities preserved a good portion of the Ismaili literature of the Fatimid times. In this chapter we shall also discuss aspects of the modern history of the Ṭayyibī Ismailis.

POST-ALAMŪT PATTERNS AND RESEARCH PROBLEMS

The first five centuries after the fall of Alamūt represent the longest obscure phase in the entire history of the Ismailis. Many aspects of their activities and thought in this period are still not sufficiently studied, and the situation is exacerbated by a paucity of primary sources. A variety of factors, related to the very nature of post-Alamūt Ismailism, have combined to create special research problems here. In the aftermath of the destruction of their state, the Nizārīs were completely deprived of the centralised leadership they had enjoyed during the Alamūt period. The Nizārī imamate itself continued in the progeny of the last lord of Alamūt, Rukn al-Dīn Khurshāh. But the imams remained in hiding and inaccessible to their followers for about two centuries. Under the circumstances, various Nizārī communities, as noted, developed locally and more or less in isolation from one another, each community elaborating separate religious and literary traditions. The communities of Central Asia and India expanded significantly, gradually overshadowing their co-religionists in the traditional Nizārī abodes, namely, Persia and Syria. The origins and early formation of the religious traditions of the Nizārī Khojas of the Indian subcontinent are among the least understood areas of post-Alamūt Ismailism.

More complex research difficulties arise from the widespread adoption of *taqiyya* or precautionary dissimulation by the Nizārīs of different regions. During much of their post-Alamūt history, until modern times, the Nizārīs were obliged to dissimulate rather strictly to safeguard themselves against persecution. To that end, they not only concealed their beliefs and literature, but actually resorted to Sufi, Twelver Shīʿī, Sunni and Hindu disguises in the midst of hostile surroundings in the Iranian world and the Indian subcontinent. It is important here to distinguish between short-term or temporary *taqiyya* practices used traditionally by Ismailis and Twelver Shīʿīs and their long-term applications that acquired near permanency among certain Nizārī communities during the post-Alamūt period. The latter phenomenon, with its lasting consequences, has not sufficiently attracted the attention of modern scholars. It is a truism that extended dissimulating practices under different guises would in time lead to irrevocable influences on the traditions and indeed the very religious identity of the community. In time, these influences might be manifested in different forms, ranging from total acculturation or full assimilation of Nizārīs of a specific locality into a community chosen initially as a dissimulating cover, to various degrees of interfacing between "Nizārī" and "other" traditions without the actual loss of Nizārī identity. Risks of complete assimilation or total disintegration were particularly high during the early post-Alamūt centuries when the scattered Nizārīs were deprived of any form of central leadership, including especially the guidance of their imams, who have provided throughout their history the most important single source for a cohesive identity in the midst of fluid circumstances. Even after the Nizārī imams emerged in Anjudān in central Persia, in the middle of the 9th/15th century, initiating the Anjudān revival in Nizārī history, many isolated Nizārī groups may have failed to establish links with the imam's headquarters or with his regional representatives. In time, many such groups must have disappeared in various ways, contributing to the decline in the overall size of the Nizārī population from the time of the Mongol massacres until the early Anjudān times.

All in all, the dissimulating practices of the Nizārīs have made it very difficult, if not impossible, to distinguish between the traditions developed indigenously by the Nizārīs of a particular community or region and those resulting from the long-term observance of *taqiyya* and extended interaction with "other" traditions. It is not surprising that the dissimulating Nizārīs should not have generally attracted the attention of historians. Indeed, for several post-Alamūt centuries, only a handful of local histories contain sporadic references to the

Nizārīs. The difficulties of studying post-Alamūt Nizārī Ismailism are further aggravated by the fact that, as in Alamūt times, the Nizārīs produced few religious texts; while upon the demise of their state, they were unable to maintain their earlier interest in historiography of any kind.

In the light of these problems, and gaps in our knowledge, the findings of modern scholarship on post-Alamūt Ismailism should be generally treated as provisional. Further progress here would ultimately depend on acquiring a better understanding of the history as well as the religious and literary traditions of major Nizārī communities of the post-Alamūt period, especially those in Central Asia and the Indian subcontinent where the bulk of Nizārīs resided by the early modern times. Only then would it be possible to compile a coherent and connected history of post-Alamūt Ismailism in its myriad dimensions.

Modern scholarship, following the pioneering studies of W. Ivanow, has distinguished three main periods in the history of post-Alamūt Nizārī Ismailism, namely an obscure early period covering the first two centuries after the fall of Alamūt; the Anjudān revival, from the middle of the 9th/15th century until the end of the 12th/18th century, and the modern period, dating to the 13th/19th century. Our discussion has been organised on the basis of this classification, with due consideration to certain major regional developments in post-Alamūt Ismailism.

EARLY POST-ALAMŪT CENTURIES AND NIZĀRĪ RELATIONS WITH SUFISM

The Mongols demolished Alamūt and numerous other fortresses in Persia, also massacring large numbers of Nizārīs in northern Persia and Quhistān. These events in 654/1256 signalled the demise of the Nizārī Ismaili state. The news of the execution of Rukn al-Dīn Khurshāh, the last lord of Alamūt and twenty-seventh Nizārī imam, in Mongolia in 655/1257 must have dealt another devastating blow to the Nizārīs. However, despite the claims of Juwaynī,[1] who served Hülegü and was an eyewitness to the Mongol destruction of Alamūt and its famous library, Persian Ismailis survived the downfall of their state and mountainous strongholds. Many Persian Nizārīs who had survived the Mongol swords migrated to adjacent lands in Afghanistan, Central Asia and Sind in the Indian subcontinent, where Ismaili communities already existed. Other Nizārī groups, isolated in remote places or in towns outside their traditional territories in Persia, soon either disintegrated or were assimilated into the religiously dominant communities of their milieu.

The centralised *da'wa* organisation and the direct leadership of

Nizārī imams who had hitherto ruled from Alamūt were also bygone. Under the circumstances, scattered Nizārī communities outside of Syria resorted once again to a strict observance of *taqiyya*. This was particularly the case with the Persian Nizārīs who lived clandestinely outside their traditional fortress communities. It is important to bear in mind that the observance of *taqiyya* in this period, marked by an absence of a viable central leadership apparatus, was not imposed on the community. Deeply rooted in their Imāmī teachings and communal practices, it was a measure adopted by the Nizārīs on their own initiative and as necessitated by the exigencies of the time. The Nizārīs were rather experienced in adopting different external guises as required to safeguard themselves. For a while during the Alamūt period, they had even adopted the *sharī'a* in its Sunni form. Many Nizārī groups in the eastern Iranian world, where Sunnism prevailed, now probably disguised themselves once again as Sunnis.

According to Nizārī tradition, a group of their dignitaries had managed, before the fall of Alamūt, to hide Rukn al-Dīn Khurshāh's minor son Shams al-Dīn Muḥammad, who soon afterwards in 655/1257 succeeded to the imamate.[2] Subsequently, the youthful imam was taken to Ādharbāyjān, where he lived secretly as an embroiderer, hence his nickname of Zardūz. Certain allusions in the still unpublished versified *Safar-nāma* (*Travelogue*) of Nizārī Quhistānī (d. 720/1320), the first post-Alamūt Nizārī Ismaili poet, indicate that he actually met the imam in Ādharbāyjān, possibly in Tabrīz, in 678/1280. Tabrīz, it may be noted, was then the capital of Abaqa (663–81/1265–82), Hülegü's son and successor in the Īlkhānid dynasty. Shams al-Dīn, synonymous in legendary Ismaili accounts with Shams-i Tabrīz, the spiritual guide of Mawlānā Jalāl al-Dīn Rūmī (d. 672/1273), died around 710/1310. A little-known dispute over his succession split the line of Nizārī imams and their following into what became known as the Qāsim-Shāhī and Muḥammad-Shāhī branches.[3] This schism provided another serious blow to the Nizārī Ismailis. The Muḥammad-Shāhī line of imams initially seems to have enjoyed special prominence in northern Persia and Central Asia; their seat was transferred to India in the early decades of the 10th/16th century, and by the end of the 12th/18th century this line was extinct. On the other hand, the Qāsim-Shāhī branch has persisted to our times, accounting for modern Nizārī Ismaili population in its entirety. The last four Qāsim-Shāhī Nizārī imams have enjoyed international prominence under the hereditary title of Aga Khan. Paucity of information does not permit us always to differentiate accurately between rival Nizārī communities in the early post-Alamūt period. It remains true, however, that all Nizārī Ismailis dissimulated in Persia and adjacent lands.

It was in the early post-Alamūt times that Persian Nizārīs, as part of their dissimulating practices, disguised themselves under the mantle of Sufism, without actually establishing formal affiliations with any one of the Sufi orders or *ṭarīqa*s then spreading in Mongol Persia. The origins and early development of this phenomenon remain very obscure. The practice soon seems to have gained wide currency among the Nizārīs of different regions. The earliest recorded manifestation of it is found in the writings of the Nizārī poet Ḥakīm Saʿd al-Dīn b. Shams al-Dīn, better known as Nizārī Quhistānī.[4] In fact, he may have been the very first post-Alamūt Nizārī author to have chosen the poetic and Sufi forms of expression for concealing Ismaili ideas, a model adopted by many later Nizārī authors in Persia, Afghanistan and Central Asia.

The Nizārīs of Quhistān never recovered from the Mongol onslaught, which left all of Khurāsān in ruins. They survived clandestinely in villages around Bīrjand, Qā'in and other towns of Quhistān formerly in their possession.[5] Nizārī the poet was born in 645/1247 in Bīrjand into a landowning family. His father, a poet himself, had lost much of his wealth in the Mongol invasions of Khurāsān. Quhistān was now incorporated into the territories of the Mongol Īlkhānids who ruled over Persia until the middle of the 8th/14th century. For a few decades after the demise of the Ismaili strongholds in Quhistān, however, the Mongols allotted Quhistān to the Sunni Karts, their vassals. The Karts soon extended their influence throughout eastern Khurāsān and northern Afghanistan from their seat in Harāt. In his youth, Nizārī Quhistānī evidently served in the administration of the founder of the Kart dynasty, Shams al-Dīn Muḥammad I (643–76/1245–77), and his successors. With their rising political fortunes the Mihrabānid Maliks of neighbouring Sīstān (or Nīmrūz), themselves originally vassals of the Mongols, extended their influence throughout Quhistān. The Mihrabānids, in fact, had succeeded the Karts in eastern Persia; they also managed to subdue, at least temporarily, the intermittent ravaging activities of various Turco-Mongol bands in Sīstān and Quhistān. By 688/1289, the Mihrabānid Malik Naṣīr al-Dīn Muḥammad (653–718/1255–1318) had conquered all of Quhistān, which he then gave as an appanage for his son Shams al-Dīn ʿAlī.[6] Nizārī Quhistānī served for a while at the court and chancery of Shams al-Dīn ʿAlī, governor of Quhistān until his untimely demise in battle in 706/1306. Nizārī panegyrised this Mihrabānid prince, referring to him also as Shams-i Dīn Shāh-i Nīmrūz ʿAlī and ʿAlī Shāh.

Eventually, Nizārī Quhistānī lost the favour of his Mihrabānid patron, who dismissed him from his posts and confiscated his properties. The poet's subsequent efforts to regain the prince's goodwill proved futile; and his lamentable situation remained unchanged when the governorship of Quhistān passed to Shams al-Dīn ʿAlī's son Tāj al-Dīn. He died destitute in 720/1320 in his native Bīrjand where his mausoleum still remains.

Nizārī's persecution was probably related to his Ismaili faith and the failure of his *taqiyya* practices in a highly hostile Sunni milieu. Belonging to a family whose Ismaili affiliation was a known fact before the coming of the Mongols, Nizārī may thus have found it particularly difficult to conceal his identity in later life. Indeed, he does refer frequently to the intrigues of his enemies and the fact that he had been considered a *mulḥid* or heretic. Be that as it may, Nizārī – who occasionally refers to himself as a *dāʿī* perhaps metaphorically – discreetly praises the imam of the time in many of his poems, with countless references to Ismaili idioms and terminologies like *ẓāhir*, *bāṭin*, *ta'wīl*, *qiyāma* and *qā'im*. He is also the first Nizārī to use Sufi terminology such as *khānaqāh*, *darwīsh* (dervish), *ʿārif* (gnostic), *qalandar* (wandering dervish), as well as *pīr* and *murshid*, terms used by Sufis in reference to their spiritual guide.[7] Nizārī's works, which have not yet been studied adequately, are unequivocally Shīʿī in outlook, emphasising the veneration of the *ahl al-bayt*, the ʿAlids, and the necessity of the imam's teaching and guidance, as well as ideas more specifically associated with the Ismailis, including especially the Nizārīs of the Alamūt period. In the latter category, mention may be made of his spiritual interpretation of the *qiyāma*, Paradise and Hell.

In early post-Alamūt times, the Nizārīs were more successful in regrouping in Daylam, where they remained active throughout the Īlkhānid and Tīmūrid periods. Soon after the Mongol invasions, various local dynasties emerged in the Caspian provinces; and this political fragmentation provided suitable opportunities for the Nizārīs who made periodic attempts to regain control of Alamūt and Lamasar, also winning several local rulers of northern Persia to their side. For instance, some of the Kūshayjī *amīr*s, including Kiyā Sayf al-Dīn who by 770/1368 controlled much of Daylam, adhered to Nizārī Ismailism.[8] In time, Kiyā Sayf al-Dīn encountered the animosity of Sayyid ʿAlī Kiyā (d. 791/1389), founder of a local Zaydī dynasty who ruled over Daylamān and adjacent territories until 1000/1592 when the region was seized by the Safawids. The Zaydī *amīr* Sayyid ʿAlī eventually defeated Kiyā Sayf al-Dīn and then, in 781/1379, persecuted the local Nizārīs.

Meanwhile, a certain Nizārī leader known as Khudāwand Muḥammad appeared in Daylam where he played an active part in local conflicts and alliances. Khudāwand Muḥammad, who may perhaps be identified with Muḥammad b. Mu'min Shāh (d. 807/1404), the twenty-seventh Muḥammad-Shāhī Nizārī imam, united the Nizārīs of northern Persia and established his leadership at Alamūt for a while.[9] Later, the Zaydī Sayyid ʿAlī Kiyā, then the most powerful ruler of Daylamān, besieged Alamūt and forced Khudāwand Muḥammad to surrender the castle which, like other major fortresses of Daylam formerly in Nizārī possession, had been partially restored and used by the Mongols themselves. Khudāwand Muḥammad was given safe-conduct and sought refuge with Tīmūr (771–807/1370–1405), founder of the Tīmūrid dynasty of Persia and Transoxania, who later exiled him to Sulṭāniyya. Subsequently, the Zaydī rulers of Lāhījān controlled Alamūt and dealt severe blows to the Nizārīs of Daylam. Only a few isolated Nizārī groups survived in northern Persia through the 10th/16th century. By then, the Caspian provinces, too, had been incorporated into Safawid dominions and their inhabitants embraced Twelver Shīʿism. The Safawids used Alamūt for a while as a state prison for the rebellious princes of their household before that historic fortress was permanently abandoned.

The Ismailis of Badakhshān and other parts of Central Asia, as noted, had essentially remained outside the Nizārī–Mustaʿlī schism and the confines of the Nizārī state in Persia. In fact, not much is known about the Ismaili history of Central Asia between the time of Nāṣir Khusraw and the Mongol invasions. The region had not completely embraced Islam until Alamūt times. Central Asian Ismailis, as well as many who still adhered to ancient Iranian religions, evidently acknowledged the Nizārī imamate during the late Alamūt period as a result of the activities of *dāʿīs* sent from Quhistān. This is essentially corroborated by the local traditions of the Badakhshānī Nizārīs, who place the initiation of the Nizārī *daʿwa* in Badakhshān earlier in the middle of the 6th/12th century.[10] The first of these *dāʿīs*, a certain Sayyid Shāh Malang, established his rule in Shughnān, one of the major districts of Badakhshān. He was followed by a second *dāʿī*, Mīr Sayyid Ḥasan Shāh Khāmūsh. These *dāʿīs* founded dynasties of *pīrs* and *mīrs* who ruled over Shughnān, Rūshān and adjacent districts of Badakhshān in the upper Oxus region until modern times. That entire region of Central Asia, protected by the Pamirs and the Hindu Kush mountains, escaped the Mongol debacle, but was incorporated into the Tīmūrid empire in the middle of the 9th/15th century. Subsequently, Badakhshān was conquered by the Özbegs, whose rule was persistently resisted by different local dynasties, including the lesser Tīmūrids and the Ismaili *mīrs* of Shughnān. In 913/1507, Shāh Raḍī al-Dīn b. Ṭāhir, a Muḥammad-Shāhī Nizārī imam, arrived in Badakhshān from his original base of operations in eastern Persia. He established his rule over a part of Badakhshān with the help of his local followers. Shāh Raḍī al-Dīn was killed in battle in 915/1509, and thereupon the Badakhshānī Nizārīs, then belonging to the Muḥammad-Shāhī branch, were severely persecuted by the local Tīmūrid *amīrs*.[11]

By the middle of the 9th/15th century, Ismaili–Sufi relations had become well established in the Iranian world. In the early post-Alamūt centuries, as noted, the Nizārīs dissimulated under the cloak of Sufism. This is clearly attested by the fact that the meagre literary output of the Nizārīs of Persia and Central Asia dating to that period is permeated with Sufi terminology as well as ideas closely associated with Sufism. At the same time, however, the Sufis themselves used the *bāṭinī ta'wīl* or esoteric exegesis and teachings more widely ascribed to the Ismailis. Indeed, a coalescence had now emerged between Persian Sufism and Nizārī Ismailism, two independent esoteric traditions in Islam. The use of Persian as the religious language of the Persian-speaking Nizārīs had facilitated the Ismaili–Sufi literary relations. At any rate, it is because of this very coalescence, still less understood from the Sufi side, that it is often impossible to ascertain whether a certain post-Alamūt Persian treatise was written by a Nizārī author influenced by Sufism, or that it was produced in Sufi milieus exposed to Ismaili teachings.

As an early instance of this Ismaili–Sufi interaction, mention may be made of the celebrated Sufi treatise entitled *Gulshan-i rāz* (*The Rose-Garden of Mystery*) written by Nizārī Quhistānī's contemporary Maḥmūd Shabistarī (d. after 740/1339), and its later commentary by an anonymous Nizārī author. A relatively obscure Sufi master from Ādharbāyjān, Maḥmūd Shabistarī composed the *Gulshan-i rāz*, a *mathnawī* containing some one thousand couplets, in response to a number of questions put to him on Sufi teachings, clearly revealing his familiarity with certain Ismaili doctrines. This treatise is very popular in Sufi circles, and, consequently, many commentaries have been written on it. However, the Nizārīs of Persia and Central Asia have generally claimed the *Gulshan-i rāz* as part of their literary heritage. This explains why it was later commented upon in Persian by a Nizārī author.[12] The authorship of this partial commentary, comprised of Ismaili interpretations or *ta'wīlāt* of selected passages of the *Gulshan*, may possibly be attributed to Shāh Ṭāhir (d. c. 952/1545), the most famous imam of the Muḥammad-Shāhī line, who did in fact write an exegetical treatise entitled *Sharḥ-i gulshan-i rāz*.

Similarly, owing to their close relations with Sufism in post-Alamūt times, the Persian-speaking Nizārīs have regarded some of the greatest mystic poets of Persia as their co-religionists and selections of their works have been preserved particularly in the private libraries of the Nizārīs of Badakhshān. Among such poets, mention may be made of Sanā'ī, Farīd al-Dīn ʿAṭṭār, Jalāl al-Dīn Rūmī as well as Sufi personalities and lesser poets like Qāsim al-Anwār (d. c. 837/1433).[13] Central Asian Nizārīs also consider ʿAzīz al-Dīn Nasafī (d. c. 661/1262), the celebrated local Sufi master, as a co-religionist, and they have preserved his Sufi treatise entitled *Zubdat al-ḥaqā'iq* as an Ismaili work.[14] The Nizārī Ismailis of Persia, Afghanistan and Central Asia use verses of the mystical poets of the Iranian world in their religious ceremonies, which are often akin to Sufi-like *dhikr* incantations.

By the 9th/15th century, and possibly earlier, the dissimulating Persian Ismailis had adopted visible aspects of the Sufi way of life. Thus, the Nizārī imams, who were still obliged to hide their identity, appeared to outsiders as Sufi masters or *pīr*s, while their followers adopted the typically Sufi guise of disciples or *murīd*s, a term used earlier by Nizārī Quhistānī. The Nizārī success in practising *taqiyya* in the general guise of Sufism would not have been so readily possible if these two esoteric traditions in Islam did not share close affinities and common doctrinal grounds. The Sufis, too, had from early on developed their own *bāṭinī* tradition based on a distinction between the *ẓāhir* and the *bāṭin* dimensions of religion, the *sharīʿa* and its inner meaning. With the Nizārī declaration of *qiyāma* or resurrection in 559/1164, even greater affinities were established between Nizārī Ismailism and Sufism.

The proclamation of *qiyāma*, as noted, implied a complete personal transformation of the Nizārīs who, henceforth, were expected to see nothing but their imam. However, the imam had to be seen in his true spiritual reality. Only then would the believer be enabled to view the world from the imam's perspective, and lead a genuine spiritual and ethical life in paradise on earth. This worldview, in fact, led the individual to a third level of existence, a world of *bāṭin* behind the *bāṭin*, the ultimate reality or *ḥaqīqa*, distinguishable from the worlds of *sharīʿa* and its *bāṭin* as interpreted by ordinary Ismaili *ta'wīl*. In the Nizārī teachings of the Alamūt period, as noted, *qiyāma* was identified with *ḥaqīqa*, a realm of spiritual experience akin to the *ḥaqīqa* of the Sufi inner experience. The Nizārīs who attained that level of existence were expected to lead a spiritual life; and the Nizārī imam would serve for his followers as a Sufi *pīr* or *shaykh* did for his *murīd*s or disciples. In both situations, by focusing their devotion on the imam or the Sufi master, the followers or disciples (*murīd*s) could be made to transcend the limitations of their own separate selves. However, the Nizārī imam was much more than a Sufi master, the latter being one among a multitude of such guides at any time.

For the Ismailis, the imam was a single cosmic individual who summed up in his person the entire reality of existence; the perfect microcosm for whom a lesser guide or a Sufi *pīr* could not substitute. The ontological position of the Nizārī Ismaili imam, as representative of cosmic reality, was also analogous to that of the "perfect man" (*al-insān al-kāmil*) of the Sufis, though again the latter could not offer a full equivalent of the imam, in the knowledge of whose inner reality the post-*qiyāma* Nizārīs shared a joint spiritual communion.

The Twelver Shīʿīs, representing another minority community in predominantly Sunni Persia, developed their own intellectual rapport with Sufism in pre-Safawid Persia. The earliest instance of this non-Ismaili Shīʿī–Sufi collaboration is reflected in the writings of Sayyid Ḥaydar Āmulī, the learned Twelver theologian and gnostic (*ʿārif*) from Māzandarān who died after 787/1385. Influenced by the teachings of Ibn al-ʿArabī (d. 638/1240), one of the greatest Sufis of Islam whom the Nizārīs also rank among their famous co-religionists, Ḥaydar Āmulī amalgamated Shīʿī theology with certain gnostic-mystical traditions, also emphasising the common grounds of Shīʿism and Sufism. According to him, a Muslim who combines *sharīʿa* with *ḥaqīqa* and *ṭarīqa*, the spiritual path followed by Sufis, is not only a believer but a believer put to the test (*al-muʾmin al-mumtaḥan*). Such a Muslim, at once true Shīʿī and gnostic, would preserve a balance between the *ẓāhir* (*sharīʿa*) and the *bāṭin* (*ḥaqīqa*), avoiding both the excessively literalist interpretations of Islam undertaken by jurists and the antinomian tendencies of the radical groups such as the Shīʿī *ghulāt*.[15] Aspects of this interaction between Twelver Shīʿism and gnosis (*ʿirfān*), in combination with different philosophical (theosophical) traditions, later culminated in the works of Mīr Dāmād (d. 1040/1630), Mullā Ṣadrā (d. 1050/1640) and other Shīʿī gnostic theosophers belonging to the so-called "school of Iṣfahān". It may be noted in passing that with the persecution of Sufis in early Safawid times, the advocates of mystical experience used the term gnosis or *ʿirfān* in preference to Sufism (*taṣawwuf*).

Meanwhile, certain developments in the religio-political ambience of post-Mongol Persia made for better opportunities for the activities of the Nizārīs, and a number of Shīʿī-related movements, as well as general Ismaili–Sufi interactions. Īlkhānid rule in Persia effectively ended with Abū Saʿīd (716–36/1316–35) who made peace with the Mamlūks over Syria. By contrast to the Nizārīs of the Iranian world, the Syrian Nizārīs, as noted, openly maintained their identity. They remained in their traditional strongholds, as reported by Ibn Baṭṭūṭa who visited them in 726/1326; and they were closely watched by the Mamlūks who sporadically used them in their designs against the

Īlkhānids of Persia.[16] Persia was politically fragmented with the demise of the Mongol Īlkhānids. In this turbulent period lasting until the advent of the Safawids, excepting the reigns of Tīmūr and his son Shāh Rukh (d. 850/1447), parts of Persia and adjacent lands were ruled by a number of local dynasties, including the minor Īlkhānids, the Muẓaffarids, the Jalāyirids, the Sarbadārids, the later Tīmūrids, and finally the Qara Qoyunlu and the Aq Qoyunlu Turkmen rulers. The Nizārīs, along with certain other Shīʿī and related movements with millenarian aspirations, such as those of the Sarbadārids and the Ḥurūfiyya, as well as a number of Sufi orders, now found a suitable respite to organise or reorganise themselves during the 8th/14th and 9th/15th centuries. It was under such circumstances that the Nizārī imams emerged at Anjudān.

The political fragmentation of Persia proved favourable to a rising tide of Shīʿī tendencies rendering the country's religious milieu conducive to the activities of the Nizārīs and other crypto-Shīʿī or Shīʿī-related movements. Some of these movements, especially the radical ones with political designs and possessing millenarian or Mahdist aspirations, as those organised by the Ḥurūfiyya and their Nuqṭawī (or Pisīkhānī) offshoot, were extremely popular. It is interesting to note that a majority of the leaders of these movements in predominantly Sunni Persia hailed from Shīʿī–Sufi backgrounds. However, the Shīʿism that was then spreading in Persia was of a new form. Instead of propagating Twelver or any other particular school of Shīʿism, it was of a popular type infused with Sufi ideas and disseminated mainly through Sufi orders. Marshall Hodgson designated this popular Shīʿī phenomenon, which ultimately culminated in Safawid Shīʿism, as "*ṭarīqah* Shīʿism".[17] It is significant to recall that most of the Sufi orders in question, formed during the early post-Alamūt period, remained outwardly Sunni in pre-Safawid Persia. But they were, at the same time, particularly devoted to ʿAlī b. Abī Ṭālib and the *ahl al-bayt*, acknowledging ʿAlī's spiritual guidance and including him at the head of their *silsilas* or chains of spiritual masters.

In this atmosphere of religious eclecticism, ʿAlid loyalism espoused by Shīʿī movements, as well as the Sunni-centred Sufi orders, gradually became more widespread. As a result, Shīʿī elements began, in a unique manner, to be superimposed on Sunni Islam. The late Claude Cahen referred to this curious phenomenon as the "Shīʿitisation of Sunnism", as opposed to the systematic propagation of Shīʿism of any specific school.[18] The Nizārī Ismailis found it both convenient and pragmatic increasingly to seek refuge under the "politically correct" mantle of Sufism, with which they also shared many esoteric precepts. At the same time, the religious topography of Persia was remoulded by this *ṭarīqa*-diffused Shīʿī–Sunni syncretism, preparing the ground for the adoption of Shīʿism as the religion of the land under the Safawids. Among the Sufi orders that played a key role in spreading ʿAlid loyalism and Shī'ī sentiments in pre-Safawid Persia, mention should be made of the Nūrbakhshiyya, the Niʿmat Allāhiyya and the Ṣafawiyya. All these *ṭarīqa*s eventually became fully Shīʿī. The Ṣafawī *ṭarīqa*, with its strong military organisation, played the most direct role in the "Shīʿitisation" of Persia. It was, indeed, the Ṣafawī *shaykh* or master who ascended the throne of Persia in 907/1501 as Shāh Ismāʿīl, and adopted Twelver Shīʿism as the state religion of his dominions.

THE ANJUDĀN REVIVAL IN NIZĀRĪ HISTORY

The Nizārī Ismailis and their imams were quite successful in their *taqiyya* practices in Persia during the early post-Alamūt period. As a result, there is a paucity of information on the imams succeeding Shams al-Dīn Muḥammad. It is a fact, however, that the Nizārī imamate was handed down in two parallel lines amongst the descendants of Shams al-Dīn Muḥammad. By the middle of the 9th/15th century, the Nizārī imams of the Qāsim-Shāhī line emerged in Anjudān in the guise of Sufi *pīr*s. Anjudān, situated in central Persia in the vicinity of Maḥallāt and Qumm, remained the seat of the Qāsim-Shāhī Nizārī imams and their *daʿwa* activities for more than two centuries. Anjudān was evidently chosen carefully; the locality had a central position removed from the main seats of the Sunni dynasties ruling over Persia. It was also in proximity to the cities of Qumm and Kāshān, traditional centres of Shīʿī learning in Persia. Additionally, it was home to an Ismaili community before the imams permanently settled there. Indeed, the Persian chroniclers of Tīmūr's reign refer to Nizārī activities there, also mentioning an expedition led by Tīmūr himself in 795/1393 against the Nizārīs of Anjudān who by then must have attracted sufficient attention.[19]

Islām Shāh, a contemporary of Tīmūr and Khudāwand Muḥammad, may have been the first Qāsim-Shāhī imam to have settled in Anjudān. It is, however, with his grandson, Mustanṣir bi'llāh (II), who succeeded to the imamate around 868/1463, that the Qāsim-Shāhī Nizārī imams became definitely established in the locality, initiating the Anjudān revival in Nizārī Ismailism. The mausoleum of Mustanṣir bi'llāh, who died in 885/1480, is still preserved in Anjudān, where several other imams were later buried.[20] It is interesting to note that the modern-day inhabitants of Anjudān remain completely ignorant of the Ismaili history of the area; they believe that the (Nizārī) dignitaries buried in their village were actually Twelver Shīʿī

Sayyids, indicative perhaps of the lasting success of the Nizārīs' *taqiyya* practices.

By the beginning of the Anjudān period, the Nizārī imams, like the leaders of certain other religious communities and movements, took advantage of the changing religio-political climate of Persia, characterised by political fragmentation and spread of ʿAlid loyalism and Shīʿī tendencies through a number of Sufi orders. Under these circumstances, the imams, while still hiding their identity, reorganised and reinvigorated their *daʿwa* not only to win new converts but also to reassert their central authority over the various Nizārī communities, especially those situated in Central Asia and India. These communities had been led, after the fall of Alamūt, by hereditary dynasties of *pīr*s and *mīr*s. The *pīr*s, functioning as chief *dāʿī*s in particular regions, had indeed become powerful and autonomous figures. They also enjoyed a great deal of financial independence, as they rarely forwarded the religious dues collected in their communities to the imams whose whereabouts were secret. For all these reasons, the imams of the Anjudān period devoted much of their attention to circumscribing the position of *pīr*s in the Indian subcontinent and elsewhere, on occasions replacing them with their loyal appointees. This policy seems to have been initiated by Mustanṣir bi'llāh who dispatched a number of trusted *dāʿī*s to various localities in Persia, Afghanistan and Central Asia. His successors retained this policy, also periodically summoning the regional *dāʿī*s to the *daʿwa* headquarters in Anjudān. The *dāʿī*s now received their instructions directly from the imam, to whom they regularly delivered the religious dues collected on his behalf.

The Anjudān period also witnessed a revival in the literary activities of the Nizārīs, especially in Persia. The earliest results of this literary revival, representing the first Nizārī doctrinal works of the post-Alamūt period, were produced in Persian by Abū Isḥāq Quhistānī, who flourished in the second half of the 9th/15th century, and Khayrkhwāh-i Harātī, who died after 960/1553. Muḥammad Riḍā b. Sulṭān Ḥusayn Ghūriyānī Harātī, better known as Khayrkhwāh-i Harātī, was a prolific writer and a poet. He was also appointed by the imam of the time to succeed his father as a local *dāʿī* or *pīr* in his native western Afghanistan. Khayrkhwāh's writings are of great historical value in explaining not only the Nizārī doctrines of the time, but also for containing unique details on the contemporary organisation and leadership structure of the community.[21] Khayrkhwāh, who was summoned to Anjudān by the imam, describes how the *dāʿī*s of Khurāsān and other regions arrived there during his stay, bringing the religious dues of their communities. The imam had by then clearly asserted his leadership over the outlying Nizārī communities in Badakhshān, Sind and elsewhere.

In the early Anjudān period, the Nizārīs adopted a new communal organisation, which played a key role in reasserting and rearticulating (at least secretly) their religious identity. The emergence of the imams and their accessibility to the community through the intermediacy of trusted agents or *dāʿīs* was instrumental in this development. Before the Anjudān revival, and even afterwards for a while, many Nizārī groups had disintegrated or acquired new identities owing to a lack of contact with their imam or his representatives. But the Nizārīs still found it necessary, in predominantly Sunni Persia, to practise *taqiyya* in the guise of Sufism. It was thus customary for the imams to adopt Sufi names, starting with Mustanṣir bi'llāh (II), known as Shāh Qalandar. In addition, the Nizārī imams often added, similarly to Sufi masters, terms such as Shāh and ʿAlī to their names. For all practical purposes, the Persian Nizārīs now appeared as a Sufi *ṭarīqa*; and they continued to use the master-disciple (*murshid-murīd*) terminology of the Sufis. To the outsiders, the Nizārī imam living in Anjudān appeared as a Sufi *murshid*, *pīr* or *shaykh*. They were also regarded as pious ʿAlid Sayyids, descendants of the Prophet. Similarly, the ordinary Nizārīs acted as the imam's *murīd*s, guided along a spiritual path or *ṭarīqa* to *ḥaqīqa* by their spiritual master, very much like a Sufi order. With ʿAlid loyalism and Shīʿī tendencies spreading through Sufi orders whose members were actually Sunnis, the Nizārīs' veneration of ʿAlī and other early ʿAlid imams did not pose any danger of divulging their true identity. The variegated influences of some of these medieval *taqiyya* practices have left an indelible mark on the historical development of the Nizārī community in the post-Anjudān centuries. For instance, they still refer to themselves as their imam's *murīd*s and the word *ṭarīqa* itself has been retained in reference to the Ismaili form and interpretation of Islam.

In the context of Nizārī–Sufi relations during the early Anjudān period, precious evidence is preserved in a book entitled *Pandiyāt-i jawānmardī* (*Admonitions on Spiritual Chivalry*), on the religious admonitions of the Imam Mustanṣir bi'llāh (II).[22] These sermons, addressed to true believers (*mu'mins*) and to those seeking high standards of ethical behaviour and spiritual chivalry, were compiled and written in Persian during the imamate of Mustanṣir bi'llāh's son and successor ʿAbd al-Salām Shāh. The Nizārī Khojas, who have preserved a Gujarātī (Khojkī) version of the *Pandiyāt* maintain that this book was sent to them as guidance by the imam of the time. Manuscripts of the Persian text of the *Pandiyāt* are still preserved by the Nizārīs of Badakhshān, Hunza and other northern areas of Pakistan.

In the *Pandiyāt*, the Nizārīs are referred to by Sufi expressions such as *ahl-i ḥaqq* and *ahl-i ḥaqīqat*, or the "people of the truth", while the imam is designated as *pīr*, *murshid* or *quṭb*. Permeated with ideas widely associated with Sufism, the imam's admonitions start with the *sharī'at-ṭarīqat-ḥaqīqat* categorisation of the Sufis, describing *ḥaqīqat* as the *bāṭin* of *sharī'at* which would be attainable by the faithful through following the spiritual path or *ṭarīqat*. In line with the Nizārī teachings of the time, rooted essentially in the doctrine of *qiyāma* propounded in the Alamūt period, the *Pandiyāt* further explains that *ḥaqīqat* essentially consists of recognising the spiritual reality of the imam of the time. The acknowledgement of the current imam and obeying his commands are stressed throughout the *Pandiyāt*, which equally emphasises the duty of the believers to pay their religious dues regularly to the imam of the time. The same admonitions are reiterated in the writings of Khayrkhwāh-i Harātī. By his time, in the 10th/16th century, the term *pīr*, the Persian equivalent of the Arabic *shaykh*, had acquired widespread currency among Nizārī Ismailis; it was applied to *dā'īs* of different ranks as well as the imam himself. Subsequently, this term fell into disuse in Persia, but it was retained in the Nizārī communities of Central Asia and India.

The Nizārīs of the Anjudān period once again possessed a secret *da'wa* organisation. As before, the *da'wa* hierarchy was headed by the imam. The contemporary Qāsim-Shāhī Nizārī texts mention five lower ranks in the *da'wa* hierarchy.[23] The imam was followed by a single *ḥujja*, normally residing at the headquarters of the *da'wa* near the imam. He acted as the administrative head of the *da'wa* and the imam's chief assistant. There was, then, a single category of *dā'ī*, a missionary at large, mainly responsible for periodic inspections of different communities and reporting their situation to the *da'wa* headquarters and conveying the instructions of the imam and his *ḥujja* to local leaders. The next lower rank in the hierarchy was that of *mu'allim* or teacher who was normally in charge of *da'wa* activities in a particular community or region, now again referred to as *jazīra*. The *mu'allims* were appointed by the *ḥujja*, with the approval of the imam who thus ensured the appointment of trusted persons to the post. Every *mu'allim*, in turn, was assisted by two categories of *ma'dhūn*; the senior one, *ma'dhūn-i akbar*, was permitted to teach the Nizārī doctrines and to convert anyone on his own initiative, while the junior assistant or *ma'dhūn-i aṣghar* could perform these tasks only with the *mu'allim*'s permission. The ordinary initiates, as in earlier times, were known as *mustajībs*. By the 10th/16th century, the term *pīr*, as noted, came to be generally used in reference to the imam and the higher ranks in the *daʿwa* hierarchy, notably *ḥujja*, *dāʿī* and *muʿallim*.

The Qāsim-Shāhī Nizārīs of the Anjudān period essentially retained the teachings of the Alamūt times, especially as elaborated after the declaration of *qiyāma*. The Ismaili writings of the Fatimid period, preserved in the Ṭayyibī Mustaʿlī collections of Yaman, were now no longer available to the Nizārīs of Persia and adjacent lands. As a result, the Nizārīs did not maintain any systematic interest in cosmology or cyclical history, subjects elaborated in the Ṭayyibī writings of medieval times. However, some of the *daʿwa* terminologies of the Fatimid period, such as *jazīra*, and certain *daʿwa* ranks like *ma'dhūn* were revived and used by the Nizārīs, presumably through the writings of Nāṣir Khusraw preserved in Badakhshān. Greatly influenced by Nāṣir Khusraw, the Badakhshānī Nizārīs also retained, at least in the early Anjudān period, some of the pre-Alamūt interest of the Ismailis in cosmology.[24]

The current imam retained his central importance in the Nizārī doctrine of the Anjudān period, and the recognition of his true spiritual reality remained the prime concern of the Nizārīs, whose religious quest was defined afresh around the attainment of that knowledge.[25] This knowledge, as in Alamūt times, required a spiritual journey from the apparent *ẓāhirī* world to the hidden *bāṭinī* world of *ḥaqīqa*; from an understanding of the apparent meaning of the *sharīʿa* to the truths concealed in its *bāṭin*, and as interpreted by the person of the current imam.

The Nizārīs of the Anjudān period, too, distinguished three categories of men:[26] *ahl-i taḍādd*, all non-Nizārīs representing the opponents of the imam; *ahl-i tarattub*, now also called *ahl-i ḥaqq* or *ḥaqīqat*, the Nizārīs themselves who, in turn, were divided into the "strong", comprised of the holders of the *daʿwa* ranks below the *ḥujja*, and the "weak", represented by the ordinary members of the community. Finally, there was the *ahl-i vaḥdat* category consisting of the person of *ḥujja* alone. It seems that only the *ḥujja* had truly entered the spiritual realm of *ḥaqīqa*. The Nizārīs of the Alamūt period had held that even in the time of *satr* and *taqiyya*, *ḥaqīqa* could be accessible to a few members of the community. But in Anjudān times, that elite group was reduced to one person, the *ḥujja*, the closest associate of the imam who was normally selected from among his relatives. The role of the *ḥujja*, already stressed by Naṣīr al-Dīn al-Ṭūsī, had now acquired even greater importance in Nizārī doctrine, second only to that of the imam. Some of these ideas, propounded by Khayrkhwāh, may not necessarily have been incorporated into the general Nizārī teachings of the Anjudān period.[27]

In the meantime, the advent of the Safawids and the proclamation of Twelver Shīʿism as the state religion of the Safawid realm in 907/1501 promised yet more favourable opportunities for the activities of the Nizārīs and other Shīʿī movements in Persia. The Nizārī Ismailis did, in fact, reduce the intensity of their *taqiyya* practices during the initial decades of Safawid rule. As a result, the religious identity of the Persian Nizārīs became somewhat better known for the first time in the post-Alamūt period, even though they still continued to use the *murshid-murīd* dyad and other Sufi terms. The new optimism of the Nizārīs proved short-lived, however, as the Safawids and their *sharīʿa*-minded *ʿulamāʾ* soon adopted a vigorous persecutionary policy against all popular forms of Sufism and those Shīʿī or Shīʿī-related movements which fell outside the confines of state-sponsored Twelver Shīʿism.[28] This policy was used even against the Qizilbāsh, the Turkmen Sufi soldiers who had brought the Safawids to power. Most of the Sufi orders of Persia were, in fact, extirpated in the reign of Shāh Ismāʿīl (907–30/1501–24), with the major exceptions of the Niʿmat Allāhiyya and a few other *ṭarīqa*s which rapidly lost their earlier importance. Meanwhile, Persia had embarked on a process of conversion to Twelver Shīʿism through the efforts of a number of jurists brought in from Iraq and elsewhere.

Engaged in more overt activities, the Nizārīs, too, attracted the attention of the early Safawids and their *ʿulamāʾ*, and received their share of persecutions. Shāh Ismāʿīl persecuted Shāh Ṭāhir al-Ḥusaynī, the most famous imam of the Muḥammad-Shāhī Nizārī line.[29] Shāh Ṭāhir was a learned theologian and had attained much popularity thanks to his learning and piety. But Shāh Ṭāhir's expanding religious following in Persia proved intolerable to the Safawid ruler and his Twelver scholars, who accused him of heretical teachings and conspiracy against the monarch. In the event, Shāh Ismāʿīl issued an order for the execution of Shāh Ṭāhir. However, the latter succeeded in fleeing to India in 926/1520. In 928/1522, he settled permanently in the Deccan and rendered valuable diplomatic services to the Niẓām-Shāhs of Aḥmadnagar. There, Shāh Ṭāhir was appointed as the most trusted adviser to Burhān Niẓām-Shāh (915–61/1509–54), on whose request he also held weekly lectures on different religious subjects for large audiences. It is interesting to note that from early on in India, Shāh Ṭāhir advocated Twelver Shīʿism, which he had adopted in Persia obviously as a form of disguise. Twelver Shīʿism was also more acceptable to the Muslim rulers of India who were generally interested in cultivating friendly relations with the Safawids. These factors explain why Shāh Ṭāhir wrote several commentaries on the theological works of well-known Twelver scholars.

Shāh Ṭāhir achieved his greatest religious success in the Deccan when Burhān Niẓām-Shāh, after his own conversion, proclaimed Twelver Shīʿism as the official religion of his state in 944/1537. This event was, of course, rejoiced at the Safawid court in Persia. Subsequently, Shāh Ṭāhir's son and future successor, Ḥaydar, was dispatched on a goodwill mission to the Safawid capital in Persia. Shāh Ṭāhir died around 952/1545. His successors, too, observed *taqiyya* in India mainly in the form of Twelver Shīʿism. In this connection it is interesting to point out that in the *Lamaʿāt al-ṭāhirīn*, one of a few extant Muḥammad-Shāhī Nizārī treatises composed in the Deccan around 1110/1698, the author clearly hides his Ismaili ideas under the covers of Twelver Shīʿī as well as Sufi expressions; he eulogises the Ithnāʿasharī imams whilst also alluding to the Nizārī imams of the Muḥammad-Shāhī line.

Meanwhile, the second Safawid monarch, Shāh Ṭahmāsp (930–84/1524–76), persecuted the Qāsim-Shāhī Nizārīs of Anjudān and their thirty-sixth imam, Murād Mīrzā.[30] This imam was evidently active politically, possibly in collaboration with the Nuqṭawiyya, an obscure Shīʿī-related religio-political movement and an offshoot of the Ḥurūfiyya, severely repressed by the Safawids.[31] Murād Mīrzā, who had a large following in Persia as well as in Sind and elsewhere in India, was eventually captured and executed in 981/1574 on Shāh Ṭahmāsp's order.

After Shāh Ṭahmāsp, the Safawids were drawn into their own dynastic disputes lasting a decade. This provided a timely respite for the Nizārīs, and other (non-Twelver) religious communities, who had survived the earlier persecutions. Order was restored to the Safawid state by Shāh ʿAbbās I (995–1038/1587–1629), who led Safawid Persia to the peak of its glory. By then, the Persian Nizārīs had successfully adopted a second tactical disguise, namely, Twelver Shīʿism enforced by the Safawids. Shāh Ṭāhir may have been the earliest Nizārī leader to have conceived of this new form of dissimulation, which could readily be adopted by the Nizārīs who shared the same early ʿAlid heritage and Imāmī Shīʿī traditions with the Twelvers. At any rate, Shāh ʿAbbās did not persecute the Nizārīs; and their imams, in fact, enjoyed friendly relations with the Safawids. Khalīl Allāh, Murād Mīrzā's successor as the thirty-seventh imam of the Qāsim-Shāhī Nizārīs, known also under the Sufi name of Dhu'l-Faqār ʿAlī, was married to a Safawid princess, possibly a sister of Shāh ʿAbbās.

The success of the Nizārīs in dissimulating as Twelvers is clearly attested to by an epigraph, recovered by the author in Anjudān in 1976. This epigraph reproduces the text of a royal decree issued by Shāh ʿAbbās I in Rajab 1036/March–April 1627. According to this edict, addressed to Amīr Khalīl Allāh Anjudānī (the contemporary Nizārī imam), the Shīʿa of Anjudān, referred to as Ithnāʿasharīs, like other Twelver Shīʿīs around Qumm, were exempted from paying certain taxes. Amīr Khalīl Allāh, according to his epitaph in Anjudān, died in 1043/1634. This imam and his successor, Nūr al-Dahr ʿAlī (d. 1082/1671), were eulogised by their contemporary Nizārī poet Khākī Khurāsānī who personally visited Anjudān.[32] Khākī also refers to the success of the Nizārī *daʿwa* in central Persia and Khurāsān as well as in Multan and other parts of India. The Nizārī imams in Persia, by now solely of the Qāsim-Shāhī line, continued to practise *taqiyya* under the double guises of Sufism and Twelver Shīʿism, though the Sufi cover seems to have been increasingly eclipsed by that of Twelver Shīʿism. Nūr al-Dahr's successor, Shāh Khalīl Allāh II (d. 1090/1680), was the last imam of his line to reside in Anjudān. By the closing decades of the 11th/17th century, the Anjudān revival had clearly bore fruit. The Qāsim-Shāhī Nizārī *daʿwa* had gained the allegiance of the Nizārī majoritarian community at the expense of the Muḥammad-Shāhīs. At the same time, the Nizārī *daʿwa* had spread successfully in Central Asia and several regions of the Indian subcontinent.

THE KHOJAS AND SATPANTH ISMAILISM

The Nizārī Ismaili *daʿwa* was introduced into the Indian subcontinent during the first half of the 7th/13th century, or possibly earlier in the Alamūt period. The matter remains rather obscure owing to paucity of reliable historical information on the subject. It was evidently only during the late Alamūt period that the central Nizārī leadership made systematic efforts to extend the *daʿwa* activities to Badakhshān and Sind, regions which had remained outside the confines of the Nizārī state. At any rate, for the earliest phase of Nizārī activities in India we have to rely almost exclusively on the traditional accounts of the Nizārīs of the Indian subcontinent, the Khojas, as expressed in their indigenous religious literature, the *ginān*s. The Nizārī Khojas, it may be added, have always acknowledged the imams of the Qāsim-Shāhī Nizārī line.

The term *ginān* (*gnān*) seems to have been derived from the Sanskrit word *jñāna* meaning sacred knowledge or wisdom. The *ginān*s have attained a very special status within the Nizārī Khoja community. Composed in a number of Indic languages and dialects of Sind, Panjāb and Gujarāt, these hymn-like poems vary in length from four to over a thousand verses. The *ginān*s were transmitted orally for several centuries before they were recorded mainly in the Khojkī script developed in Sind by the Khoja community. Much controversy surrounds the authorship of the *ginān*s, generally ascribed to a few early missionaries, or *pīr*s as *dāʿī*s were called in the Indian subcontinent. The *ginān* literature contains a diversity of missionary, mystical, mythological, didactic, cosmological and eschatological themes; many *ginān*s contain ethical and moral instructions for the conduct of religious life and guiding the spiritual quest of the believer. As an oral tradition, some *ginān*s also relate anachronistic, hagiographic and legendary accounts of the activities of *pīr*s and their converts and as such, they are not generally reliable as historical sources of information. Be that as it may, the *ginān*s have continued to occupy a central role in the religious life and rituals of the Nizārī Khojas, as they are held to contain the teachings of their *pīr*s.[33]

According to the traditional accounts of the Nizārī Khojas, a certain Pīr Satgur Nūr was the first Nizārī missionary sent from Daylam to Gujarāt. There, in Patan, he converted the local Rājput king, Siddharāja Jayasingh (487–527/1094–1133), who is also reported to have been converted to Ṭayyibī Mustaʿlī Ismailism but actually died a devout Hindu. Before long, Pīr Satgur converted all the inhabitants of Patan, which now became known as Pīrna Patan or "the *pīr*'s city". The dates mentioned for this missionary's arrival in Gujarāt vary widely from the time of the Fatimid caliph-imam al-Mustanṣir to the middle of the 6th/12th century. There is no evidence attesting to the success of the Nizārī *daʿwa* in Gujarāt until after the 7th/13th century, when the Ṭayyibī *daʿwa* led from Yaman was already well established there.[34]

The earliest Nizārī missionaries operating in India, whoever they may have been, apparently concentrated their efforts in Sind (modern-day Panjāb in Pakistan), where Ismailism had persisted clandestinely since the Fatimid times in Multan and elsewhere. Pīr Shams al-Dīn is the earliest figure specifically associated in the *ginān* literature with the commencement of Nizārī activities in Sind. An obscure missionary clouded in numerous legends, Pīr Shams has been identified also with Shams-i Tabrīz.[35] In some of the many *ginān*s attributed to him, Qāsim Shāh, Imam Shams al-Dīn Muḥammad's son and successor in the Qāsim-Shāhī line, is named as his contemporary imam. On that basis, Pīr Shams seems to have flourished around the middle of the 8th/14th century. In other *ginān*s, the activities of Pīr Shams are placed some two centuries earlier. At any rate, he was apparently active particularly in Ucch and Multan, where his mausoleum is preserved under the name of Shāh Shams al-Dīn Sabzawārī. After Pīr Shams, the Nizārī *daʿwa* continued to be preached secretly in Sind by his descendants during the early post-Alamūt centuries. It may be noted that Sind was ruled from around 752/1351 by the Sunni

Sammas in succession to the Sūmras who adhered to Ismailism. The Sūmras themselves had ruled from Thatta for almost three centuries from 443/1051, and they probably acknowledged the Nizārī *da'wa* before the end of the Alamūt period. By the time of Pīr Ṣadr al-Dīn, a great-grandson of Pīr Shams, the *pīr*s in India had established a hereditary dynasty without regular contacts with the Nizārī imams, who were yet to assert their leadership.

Pīr Ṣadr al-Dīn consolidated and organised the *da'wa* in India. He is, in fact, considered to have been the founder of the Nizārī Khoja community in the Indian subcontinent; he has also been credited with the authorship of the largest number of *ginān*s. According to ginanic evidence, he died sometime between the middle of the 8th/14th and the beginning of the 9th/15th century, shortly before the Anjudān revival. His shrine is located near Ucch, to the south of Multan. Ṣadr al-Dīn converted large numbers of Hindus from the Lohana trading caste and gave them the title of Khoja, derived from the Persian word *khwāja*, an honorary title meaning lord or master corresponding to the Hindi term *thākur* by which the Hindu Lohanas were addressed. Pīr Ṣadr al-Dīn is also reputed to have built the first *jamā'at-khāna* (literally, community house), in Kotri, Sind, for the religious and communal activities of the Khojas. In time, he successfully preached the *da'wa* in Panjāb and Kashmir, where he built more *jamā'at-khāna*s. For all practical purposes, Ṣadr al-Dīn laid the foundations of the Nizārī communal organisation in India where the Nizārīs became generally designated as Khojas. The specific form of Nizārī-related Ismailism that developed in India became known as Satpanth (*sat panth*) or the "true path" (to salvation); a term used by Khojas and throughout their *ginān*s.

Ṣadr al-Dīn was succeeded as *pīr* by his son Ḥasan Kabīr al-Dīn. He, too, travelled widely and reportedly visited his contemporary Nizārī imam, Mustanṣir bi'llāh (II), in Anjudān. Pīr Ḥasan converted numerous Hindus and eventually settled in Ucch, which served as the seat of the Satpanth *da'wa* in India. His mausoleum still remains outside of Ucch and is locally known as Ḥasan Daryā. It is interesting to note that this *pīr* is reported to have been affiliated with the Suhrawardī Sufi order, which was at the time prevalent in western and northern India. In fact, Pīr Ḥasan Kabīr al-Dīn's name appears in the list of the spiritual masters of the Suhrawardī *ṭarīqa*.[36] Indeed, the available evidence reveals that in India, too, the Nizārīs developed close relations with Sufism. Multan and Ucch in Sind, in addition to serving as centres of Satpanth Ismaili missionary activities, were the headquarters of the Suhrawardī and Qādirī Sufi orders. The Suhrawardiyya, it may be noted, was the most important Sufi order of

Sind during the 7–8th/13–14th centuries, while the Qādirīs began to acquire prominence in the 9th/15th century. The same doctrinal affinities that existed between Persian Ismailism and Sufism also existed between Satpanth Ismailism and Sufism in India. As a result, close relations developed between these two esoteric traditions in the Indian subcontinent, especially in Sind where both Sufism and Satpanth Ismailism had deep roots. The adoption of Sufi terminology, such as *murshid* and *murīd*, by the Nizārī Khoja community as well as strong parallels between the poetic and mystical expressions found in the *ginān*s and in Sufi poetry composed in Panjābī and Sindhi facilitated the Satpanth–Sufi relations.

Thus, the Nizārī Khojas were able to represent themselves for extended periods as one of the many mystically oriented communities of Sind, where such communities and groups existed among both the predominantly Sunni Muslim as well as Hindu milieus. This enabled the Khojas to blend more readily into the religious, cultural and social structure of Sind, attracting less attention as Ismailis and escaping persecution by Sind's Sunni rulers. However, the *pīr*s and their Khoja followers may not have consciously and explicitly developed their Sufi connections for *taqiyya* purposes. The Nizārī Khojas, by contrast to the situation of the contemporary Nizārī Ismailis of Persia, were already safeguarded against Sunni persecution by their Hindu elements which, as we shall see, were component parts of their traditions. More cannot be said in our present state of knowledge on Ismaili–Sufi relations in the Indian subcontinent. It is clear, however, that these relations did exist and developed over time, also explaining why a *pīr* of the Khoja community was recognised as one of the *pīr*s of the Suhrawardī Sufi order while several of the early Satpanth *pīr*s are still generally regarded as Sufi masters and saints of Sunni persuasion in the subcontinent.

Close relations between the Khojas and Sufis of India in post-Alamūt times are also attested to by a lengthy didactic poem in medieval Hindustani known as *Būjh Nirañjan* (*Knowledge of the One*). As Ali Asani has shown in his meticulous study,[37] this long poem about the mystical path actually originated in Qādirī Sufi circles of Sind and then entered the *ginān* literature of the Khojas, who attribute it to Pīr Ṣadr al-Dīn. That the *Būjh Nirañjan* is considered by the Khojas to be an expression of Satpanth Ismailism, even though it does not contain any specifically Ismaili elements, is due to the fact that its mystical themes and terms readily lent themselves to Ismaili interpretations.

After Pīr Ḥasan Kabīr al-Dīn, the Khojas were set back by internal dissensions which eventually split their hitherto unified community. The Nizārī imams of the Anjudān period made systematic efforts to control the hereditary authority of the *pīrs* and other local dynasties of various Nizārī communities. This may explain why the imam appointed Ḥasan Kabīr al-Dīn's brother Tāj al-Dīn, rather than one of his numerous sons, to succeed him as *pīr*. This appointment displeased Ḥasan Kabīr al-Dīn's sons who plotted against their uncle, the new *pīr*. Tāj al-Dīn visited the imam in Persia and delivered to him the religious dues, the *dassondh* or tithe, collected from the Khoja community. Pīr Tāj al-Dīn evidently died towards the end of the 9th/15th century. Subsequently, Imām al-Dīn ʿAbd al-Raḥīm, better known as Imām Shāh, one of Ḥasan Kabīr al-Dīn's sons, attempted in vain to become *pīr* in Sind. Weary of the incessant leadership quarrels among Imām Shāh and his many brothers, and aiming to assert his own direct control, however, the imam decided not to appoint any more *pīrs*. Meanwhile Imām Shāh, who had evidently remained loyal to the imam, migrated to Gujarāt, where he converted local Hindus to Satpanth Ismailism. Imām Shāh died in 919/1513 in Pirana, the town founded by himself near Aḥmadābād, where his shrine is located.

The Nizārī imams, as noted, did not appoint any new *pīrs* to the leadership of the Khojas after Pīr Tāj al-Dīn. Instead, a book of guidance, namely, the already-noted *Pandiyāt-i jawānmardī*, was sent to them. This book, containing the admonitions of the Imam Mustanṣir bi'llāh of Anjudān, came to occupy the twenty-sixth place, after Tāj al-Dīn, in the traditional lists of *pīrs* compiled by the Nizārī Khojas.[38] The *Pandiyāt*, translated into Gujarātī and written in the Khojkī script, appears to have reached Sind by the middle of the 10th/16th century. By then, the Nizārī imam had asserted his control over the Khoja community. Henceforth, the Nizārī Khojas, who now greatly outnumbered the Persian Nizārīs, embarked on periodic journeys to Anjudān to visit the imam.[39]

On Imām Shāh's death, his son Nar Muḥammad seceded from the Nizārī Khoja community and founded an independent sect known as the Imām-Shāhīs, named after his father.[40] He now claimed the imamate for himself, and retrospectively for Imām Shāh, by claiming to represent the incarnation of the imam, a concept very familiar to a Hindu milieu and also to the contemporary Khojas. However, a majority of the Khojas of Gujarāt remained loyal to the Nizārī imam and his *daʿwa*. On Nar Muḥammad's death in 940/1533, the Imām-Shāhīs split into several groups following different *pīrs*. The Imām-Shāhīs, who produced their own version of the *ginān*s, soon denied any connections with Ismailism. They, in fact, claimed that their early *pīrs*, until Ḥasan Kabīr al-Dīn, were Twelver Shīʿīs. The adherents of this syncretic sect, subdivided into a number of groupings and concentrated in the rural communities of Gujarāt and Khandesh, today consider themselves chiefly Twelver Shīʿīs or Sunnis without any distinct memories of their Ismaili past.

In the meantime, the Nizārī imams had evidently appointed one more *pīr*, after Tāj al-Dīn (and the *Pandiyāt-i jawānmardī*). This *pīr*, named Dādū, was dispatched to Sind in the second half of the 10th/16th century, with a special mission to prevent the reversion of the Nizārī Khojas to Hinduism or their conversion to Sunnism, the dominant religions of the contemporary Indo-Muslim society. Under obscure circumstances, Dādū was later obliged to flee from Sind together with many Sindhi Khojas. He settled in Jamnagar (Navanagar) in Gujarāt, and later moved to Bhuj, where he died in 1001/1593. Dādū played an important role in strengthening relations between the Khoja community and the Nizārī *daʿwa* headquarters in Anjudān. Henceforth, the imams attempted to retain and strengthen their direct control over the Khojas in the subcontinent. With Dādū, whose name does not appear in the later lists of *pīr*s, or possibly Tāj al-Dīn, the line of *pīr*s definitely came to an end. The imams now maintained their contacts with the Khoja community through functionaries referred to as *wakīl*s or *bābā*s, representatives with less authority compared to the *pīr*s.

The origins and early development of the particular form of Ismailism known as Satpanth, and its religious literature, the *ginān*s, remain obscure. In particular, it is not known whether Satpanth Ismailism as it developed in the Indian subcontinent had resulted from the conversion policies of the early *pīr*s, who operated in Sind from the 7th/13th century, or whether it represented a tradition that had evolved gradually over several centuries from the Fatimid times, with the Nizārī missionaries adapting their preaching to an existing situation and religious mould. Ismailism, as noted, had survived in a subdued form in Sind since the collapse of the Ismaili principality of Multan and the persecutions of Sultan Maḥmūd of Ghazna at the beginning of the 5th/11th century. However, nothing is known about its particular form while the Ismailis of Sind and surrounding areas evidently remained outside the Nizārī–Mustaʿlī boundaries until later Alamūt times, very much akin to the situation of the Central Asian Ismailis. Under the circumstances, modern scholars of Satpanth, beginning with Ivanow,[41] have generally attributed the mixed, Hindu–Muslim, interfacing of this Ismaili tradition to the preaching strategy of the *pīr*s who are held to have designed suitable Hindu-oriented policies for the purpose of converting the Hindus to Ismailism. According to this view, not satisfactorily substantiable on the basis of available evidence, Satpanth Ismailism is said to have evolved primarily as a result of the ingenious conversion policies of *pīrs*, who aimed to make their preaching understandable and attractive to a Hindu audience.

Satpanth Ismailism, whatever the circumstances surrounding its origins, represents an indigenous tradition reflecting certain historical, social, cultural and political circumstances prevailing in medieval Indian subcontinent, especially in Sind and other areas of northern India. The background to Satpanth (in terms of its specific concepts and thematic admixtures) may very well have already existed by the time the Nizārī missionaries or *pīrs* became active in Sind in the latter decades of the Alamūt period; and the *pīrs* may indeed have drawn inspiration from, and adapted their policies to, an existing situation.

Be that as it may, the Nizārī *da'wa* was reinvigorated in Sind by a succession of *pīrs*, culminating in the successes of the Anjudān period when the imams took more direct charge of the affairs of the Nizārī Khoja community. On the evidence of the *ginān*s, the *pīrs* did attempt ingeniously to maximise the appeal of their message in a Hindu ambience, for the Nizārī *da'wa* in India was addressed mainly to the rural, and largely uneducated, lower castes. Therefore, the *pīrs* from early on turned to Indian vernaculars, rather than Arabic and Persian used by the educated classes, in order to enhance the effectiveness and spread of their message. For the same reason, the *pīrs* also used Hindu idioms and mythology, interfacing their Islamic and Ismaili tenets with myths, images and symbols already familiar to the Hindus. In other words, the *pīrs* adopted a strategy of accommodating indigenous religious mores and concepts, a strategy of acculturation that proved very successful and won masses of converts from among Sind's lower castes. In time, Satpanth Ismailism developed its own set of themes and theological concepts emanating from an interfacing of Hinduism with Ismaili Islam and a number of other traditions and mystical movements prevalent in Indo-Muslim milieus of India, including Sufism, Tantrism and the Bhakti tradition.

The Hindu cover of the Nizārī Khojas, as expressed by Hindu elements in their Satpanth tradition, in addition to inducing conversions, served *taqiyya* purposes and made the Khojas less conspicuous in their predominantly Hindu and Sunni Muslim environments. This, of course, protected the Khojas against certain persecution at the hands of Sind's Sunni rulers, who could not tolerate Shī'ī Ismailism. In a sense, then, Satpanth Ismailism represented a complex form of dissimulation and acculturation adapted to the religious, social, cultural and political realities of the Indian subcontinent. In this context, dissimulation meant something much more than the concealment of true identity or superficial adoption of an exterior guise. It involved, as Tazim Kassam has argued,[42] the creative application of *taqiyya* through a complex process of indigenisation, adhesion and syncretism. All this explains why the Satpanth tradition of the Nizārī Khojas of the subcontinent differs significantly from the Nizārī traditions developed in Central Asia, Persia and Syria.

Satpanth Ismailism did not, however, always evolve smoothly, coherently or successfully in India. We have already noted the secession of the Imām-Shāhīs who drifted away variously from their Ismaili origins. It was also in recognition of such difficulties that the Nizārī imam in Persia entrusted Pīr Dādū with the mission of preaching among those Khojas who had evidently reverted to Hinduism. Recent research has shown that some communities which originally may have adhered to Satpanth Ismailism did, in fact, revert to Hinduism. This phenomenon seems to have occurred in the case of the Kāmaḍ (or Kāmaḍiyya) of Rajasthan, the untouchable worshippers of a deified saint known as Ramdev Pīr.[43] Cut off from the religious centres of Satpanth in Ucch and Multan, and perhaps originally converted only in a superficial or incomplete manner, the Kāmaḍ went through a process of "re-Hinduisation", redefining their identity. In the event, they completely rejected or forgot their Satpanth Ismaili heritage, while their devotional poems are replete with Ismaili references. As a different example of shifting identities, it may be noted that many isolated Persian Nizārī groups dissimulating as Twelver Shīʿīs eventually became fully integrated into their predominantly Twelver Shīʿī environment.

The Satpanth tradition drew on a multitude of indigenous concepts and motifs prevalent in the Indo-Muslim context of the subcontinent. As a result, the spread of this form of Ismailism was facilitated in India, also providing a protective shield for the Khoja converts. The teachings of Satpanth Ismailism are abundantly reflected in the *ginān* literature.[44] As noted, the *pīr*s had transformed Hindu mythology and motifs into narratives propounding their Ismaili teachings. In particular, they expounded within a Hindu framework the doctrine of the imamate as held by the Nizārī Ismailis of the post-*qiyāma* times. This found expression in an important *ginān* entitled *Dasa Avatāra*, which has been recorded in three separate versions attributed to Pīr Shams al-Dīn, Pīr Ṣadr al-Dīn and Imām Shāh.[45] The *Dasa Avatāra*, which like other *ginān*s with strong Hindu influences is no longer in usage in the Nizārī Khoja community, presents the imam as the long-awaited saviour within a Vaishnavite framework concerning the ten descents (*dasa avatāra*) of the Hindu deity Vishnu through the ages. While the *pīr*s condemned idol worship, a variety of symbolic correspondences and equivalences were established in some *ginān*s between Hindu and Islamic concepts and figures, facilitating the transformation of the religious identity of the converts from Hinduism to Satpanth Ismailism.

The *pīr*s taught that it was only through the recognition of the "true path" (*sat panth*) that their converts would be liberated from the Hindu cycles of rebirth and attain salvation in Paradise. The Qur'an was represented as the last of the Vedas or sacred scriptures, whose true meaning was known only to the *pīr*s representing the imams. The *ginān*s, indeed, portray the *pīr* as the "true guide" (*sat guru*) who can lead the faithful in their spiritual quest, in order to attain knowledge of the imam and the true path to salvation. All this explains the particular reverence the Nizārī Khojas hold for their *pīr*s and their teachings as expounded in the *ginān*s.

THE BOHRAS AND ṬAYYIBĪ ISMAILISM

We have already discussed the origins and early history of the Ṭayyibīs, who remain the sole representatives of Musta'lī Ismailism. In this section, we shall briefly survey the later history of this minority Ismaili community in Yaman and the Indian subcontinent, from the time of their second *dā'ī muṭlaq*, Ibrāhīm al-Ḥāmidī (d. 557/1162), to the 1990s.[46] In the absence of imams, the Ṭayyibī *da'wa* and community remained under the leadership of a *dā'ī muṭlaq*, a position that was held by Ibrāhīm al-Ḥāmidī's descendants until 605/1209. The third *dā'ī*, Ḥātim b. Ibrāhīm al-Ḥāmidī, successfully spread the Ṭayyibī *da'wa* in the mountainous region of Ḥarāz, to the southwest of Ṣan'ā', with its several towns and fortresses. There, with the support of different clans of Banū Hamdān, the *dā'ī* seized a number of fortresses, including Ḥuṭayb situated on one of the peaks of the Shibām mountain. Henceforth, Ḥarāz served as the main stronghold of the Ṭayyibī *da'wa* in Yaman.

The Ṭayyibīs preserved a good portion of the Ismaili literature of the Fatimid period. The *dā'ī* Ḥātim also resumed the Fatimid traditions of teaching and delivered regular lectures (*majālis*) on a variety of subjects in Ḥuṭayb, the headquarters of the *da'wa*. There, he also provided instructions for his subordinate *dā'ī*s in Yaman as well as in India. Ḥātim b. Ibrāhīm died in 596/1119 and was buried under the fortress of Ḥuṭayb, where his grave is still piously visited by Ṭayyibī pilgrims. Starting with the fifth *dā'ī*, 'Alī b. Muḥammad b. al-Walīd (605–12/1209–15), the position of *dā'ī muṭlaq* remained essentially in the hands of the Banu'l-Walīd al-Anf family of Quraysh for almost three centuries until 946/1539. 'Alī b. Muḥammad was a learned scholar and a prolific writer, and his works, including especially the

Tāj al-ʿaqāʾid and the *Kitāb al-dhakīra*, are important for understanding the Ṭayyibī *ḥaqāʾiq* system.

In the doctrinal domain, the Ṭayyibīs maintained the Fatimid Ismaili traditions, including the earlier interests in cosmology and cyclical history. These concerns, in fact, provided the basis of the Ṭayyibī gnostic, esoteric *ḥaqāʾiq* system with its distinctive eschatological and salvational themes. From early on, the Ṭayyibīs also used al-Qāḍī al-Nuʿmān's *Daʿāʾim al-Islām* as their most authoritative legal compendium; this text has retained its juridical importance for the Ṭayyibīs of Yaman and India down to modern times. The *daʿwa* organisation of the Ṭayyibīs drew on the Fatimid antecedents with certain modifications and simplifications dictated by the changed realities of Yaman. The Ṭayyibī Ismaili imam remained in concealment since al-Ṭayyib himself, along with his *bāb* and *ḥujja*s. Under the circumstances, the executive head of the *daʿwa* hierarchy in Yaman was designated as *al-dāʿī al-muṭlaq*, a *dāʿī* enjoying absolute authority within the community. As the highest representative of the hidden imam, the *dāʿī muṭlaq* was entitled to the obedience and submission of the Ṭayyibīs. As in the case of the imams, every *dāʿī* appointed his successor by the rule of *naṣṣ*; and the position was normally handed down on a hereditary basis. The Ṭayyibī *dāʿī*s in Yaman were among the most educated members of their community; many of them became outstanding scholars producing the bulk of the Ṭayyibī literature on esoteric subjects.[47] The *dāʿī muṭlaq* was assisted in the affairs of the *daʿwa* by several subordinate *dāʿī*s designated as *maʾdhūn* and *mukāsir*. The Ṭayyibī *daʿwa* generally retained, on a much reduced scale, the traditions of the Fatimid *daʿwa* in terms of initiation, secrecy and education of the initiates, though few specific details are available.

The Ṭayyibī *dāʿī*s maintained peaceful relations with various local dynasties of Yaman, including the Rasūlids and the Ṭāhirids. By contrast, encounters between the Ṭayyibīs and the Zaydīs, who were led by their own imams, were frequently marred by open warfare. There is no evidence suggesting that the Ṭayyibī *daʿwa* was then active in any region outside Yaman and India. The Yamani *dāʿī*s, meanwhile, maintained close relations with the Ṭayyibī community of Gujarāt. In fact, the Ṭayyibī *daʿwa* in India remained under the strict supervision of the *dāʿī muṭlaq* and the *daʿwa* headquarters in Yaman until the second half of the 10th/16th century. During this long period, the head of the Ṭayyibī *daʿwa* in India, locally known as *wālī*, was regularly appointed by the *dāʿī muṭlaq*. The *wālī*, too, had his own hierarchy of assistants and subordinate *dāʿī*s in India, about which there is little information.

The Ismaili community of western India, adhering to the Ṭayyibī Musta'lī *da'wa*, grew steadily since the arrival of the first Yamani *dā'ī*, 'Abd Allāh, in 460/1067. He and his successors preached the *da'wa* successfully among the Hindus of Gujarāt from their original base in Khambhat (modern-day Cambay). The early *da'wa*, as noted, spread in Gujarāt under the supervision of the Ṣulayḥids of Yaman. In western India, the Ismaili converts, mostly of Hindu descent, were known as Bohrās (Bohorās). The *da'wa* originally spread among the urban artisans and traders of Gujarāt, a rich province owing to its commercial and maritime relations with other shores of the Indian Ocean. It is generally held that the word *bohrā* (*bohorā*) is derived from the Gujarātī term *vohorvū* meaning "to trade". The term was evidently applied to the Ṭayyibī Musta'lī Ismailis of Gujarāt because they originally belonged to a trading community. According to another etymological explanation, these Ismailis were designated as Bohras because they had been converted from the Hindu caste of Vohra. At any rate, the Ṭayyibī *dā'īs* succeeded in converting large numbers in Cambay, Patan, Sidhpūr and later in Aḥmadābād, where the Indian headquarters of the *da'wa* was established.

By contrast to the Nizārī Khojas of Sind who were frequently persecuted by the local Sunni rulers, the Ṭayyibīs of Gujarāt were not harassed by the region's Hindu rulers. The latter evidently did not feel endangered by the Ṭayyibī *da'wa* in their midst. As a result, the Ṭayyibī community expanded without encountering serious difficulties until the Muslim conquest of Gujarāt in 697/1298, when the main local Hindu dynasty (the Vaghelas of Anahilwāra) was uprooted. Thus, the local Ṭayyibī *dā'īs*, unlike the Nizārī *pīrs* in Sind, were not obliged to dissimulate. Later, when *taqiyya* was required in Gujarāt, it was adopted in the form of Sunni Islam. All this provides further explanation as to why Hindu–Muslim interfacing is absent from the religious literature of the Ismaili Bohra community. This literature, as noted, was based on the earlier heritage of the Fatimid and Yamani Ṭayyibī Ismailis. Henceforth, the *da'wa* activities in western India became scrutinised by the region's Muslim governors appointed by the rulers of the Delhi sultanate. The situation of the Ismaili Bohras deteriorated seriously when Ẓafar Khān (793–806/1391–1403) established the independent sultanate of Gujarāt. The reign of the Sunni sultans of Gujarāt effectively ended in 980/1572 when the region was annexed by Akbar to the Mughal empire.

Ẓafar Khān was the first ruler of Gujarāt to suppress Shī'ism. The Ismailis, too, began to be widely persecuted from the time of Ẓafar Khān's grandson, Aḥmad Shāh I (814–46/1411–42), who built a new capital at Aḥmadābād, replacing Anahilwāra. Henceforth, the Ismaili

Bohras were obliged to observe *taqiyya* in the guise of Sunnism. It was during Aḥmad Shāh's oppressive rule that many Ismaili Bohras converted to Sunni Islam. At the same time, a dispute between the Ṭayyibī *wālī* and a dissident Ismaili Bohra led to further Sunni conversions and secessions from the community. According to some accounts, more than half of the community now seceded and became Sunni.[48] These developments once again serve to show how, under specific circumstances, extended dissimulation may lead to intensive and incremental acculturation, and ultimately to complete assimilation. It was only after the establishment of Mughal rule that the Bohra community enjoyed a certain degree of religious freedom.

The twenty-third *dāʿī muṭlaq*, Muḥammad b. al-Ḥasan al-Walīd, was the last of the *dāʿī*s from Banu'l-Walīd al-Anf as well as the last Yamani *dāʿī* to lead the undivided Ṭayyibī Ismailis of Yaman and India. Upon his death in 946/1539, the headship of the community passed to an Indian from Sidhpūr, Yūsuf b. Sulaymān. By then, it was customary for talented Bohras to receive their Ismaili education in Yaman; these visits also enhanced the religious and literary links between the Yamani and Indian factions of the community. Yūsuf b. Sulaymān was one such Bohra selected by the *wālī* to study in Yaman. It was in recognition of Yūsuf's learning that the twenty-third *dāʿī* nominated him as his successor. Yūsuf, the first Indian *dāʿī muṭlaq*, eventually settled in Yaman, and when he died in 974/1567 the headquarters of the Ṭayyibī *daʿwa* was transferred by his successor, Jalāl b. Ḥasan, another Indian, to Aḥmadābād. By then, despite prolonged persecutions and secessions, the Ṭayyibī Bohras of India greatly outnumbered their co-religionists in Yaman, preparing the ground for a new phase in the history of Ṭayyibī Ismailism.

Meanwhile, the Ṭayyibīs of Yaman had been experiencing their own difficulties under Ottoman rule, extended to cover southern Arabia in 923/1517. At the same time, the Zaydīs, the traditional enemies of the Yamani Ismailis, had practically exterminated the Banu'l-Walīd. It was under such circumstances that the Ṭayyibī *daʿwa* headquarters was moved to Gujarāt, where the *dāʿī*s could count on the religious tolerance of the Mughal emperors. Thus ended the Yamani phase of unified Ṭayyibī Ismailism.

Jalāl b. Ḥasan, the twenty-fifth *dāʿī*, died in 975/1567 soon after his accession to leadership, and was succeeded by Dā'ūd b. ʿAjabshāh. During his leadership Akbar annexed Gujarāt to the Mughal empire. The *dāʿī* personally visited Akbar in Agra in 981/1573, inducing the emperor to instruct his officials in Gujarāt to accord religious freedom to the Bohras. Dā'ūd also revitalised the community and its organisation, restoring the Ṭayyibī religious practices which had been abandoned for a long time in India owing to persecution. On the death of Dā'ūd b. ʿAjabshāh, the twenty-sixth *dāʿī*, in 997/1589, his succession was disputed causing the Dā'ūdī-Sulaymānī schism in the Ṭayyibī community. Dā'ūd b. ʿAjabshāh was succeeded in India by Dā'ūd Burhān al-Dīn b. Quṭbshāh, his deputy in Gujarāt. A few years later, however, Sulaymān b. Ḥasan al-Hindī, grandson of the *dāʿī* Yūsuf b. Sulaymān and the deceased *dāʿī*'s deputy in Yaman, claimed the succession for himself, and returned to India to prove his case. The dispute was, in fact, brought in 1005/1597 before Akbar in Lahore, but the emperor's intercession failed to resolve it. This dispute, with its Indian and Yamani rivalry undertones, led to a permanent split in the Ṭayyibī *dāʿwa* and community, further weakening this branch of Ismailism.[49]

The great majority of Ṭayyibīs, represented by Bohras, acknowledged Dā'ūd Burhān al-Dīn (d. 1021/1612) as their new, twenty-seventh *dāʿī*; they became known as Dā'ūdīs. A small faction of the Yamani Ṭayyibīs, too, supported the Dā'ūdī cause. On the other hand, a minority of the Ṭayyibīs, accounting for the bulk of the community in Yaman and a small number in India, recognised Sulaymān b. Ḥasan as their new *dāʿī*. These Ṭayyibīs, designated as Sulaymānīs, are a small minority within the Ṭayyibī Mustaʿlī community. Henceforth, the Dā'ūdīs and Sulaymānīs followed separate lines of *dāʿī*s. The Dā'ūdī *dāʿī*s continued to reside in India, while the headquarters of the Sulaymānī *daʿwa* remained in Yaman.[50]

Subsequently, the Dā'ūdī Bohras were further subdivided in India because of periodic challenges laid to the authority of their *dāʿī muṭlaq*. In 1034/1624, as one such instance, ʿAlī b. Ibrāhīm founded the ʿAliyya splinter group who established their own line of *dāʿī*s. At present, the ʿAliyya are a small community centred in Baroda, Gujarāt. Meanwhile, the main Dā'ūdī community continued to grow and prosper, as they were not molested by the Mughal emperors and their governors in Gujarāt. Strictly adhering to the Ḥanafī school of Sunnism, and pursuing zealous religious policies of his own, Awrangzīb was the only member of the Mughal dynasty to adopt anti-Shīʿī measures, and persecute the Ismailis and other Shīʿī Muslims as "heretics" during his long reign (1068–1118/1658–1707). Even before his accession, while briefly governor of Gujarāt, Awrangzīb widely persecuted the local Ismailis. He arrested the thirty-second *dāʿī*, Quṭbkhān Quṭb al-Dīn, and had him convicted of heresy in a Sunni court; the *dāʿī* was then executed in 1056/1646 on Awrangzīb's order. The Ismaili Bohras turned the mausoleum of their martyred *dāʿī* in Aḥmadābād into a shrine. As part of Awrangzīb's persecutions, the religious rituals and practices of the Ismaili Bohras were banned, their mosques were placed in the charge of Sunni custodians, and they were subjected to heavy punitive taxes. Once again, the Ismaili Bohras were pressured into converting to Sunni Islam, while they also resorted to *taqiyya* practices. After Awrangzīb, whose reign was also marred by persecutionary measures against non-Muslims, the Bohra community was generally permitted to develop freely and peacefully. The seat of the Dā'ūdī *da'wa* had, meanwhile, been transferred from Aḥmadābād to Jamnagar, and Burhānpūr had become another important Dā'ūdī Bohra stronghold outside of Gujarāt.

It was in the time of their fortieth *dā'ī*, Hibat Allāh al-Mu'ayyad fi'l-Dīn (1168–93/1754–79), coinciding with the early decades of British rule over India, that the Dā'ūdīs witnessed yet another dissident movement. The leaders of this movement were Ismā'īl b. 'Abd al-Rasūl al-Majdū', author of the famous catalogue of Ismaili literature, and his son Hibat Allāh who claimed to have established contact with the hidden Ṭayyibī imam. Hibat Allāh acquired some following in Ujjain, then the seat of the Dā'ūdī *da'wa*, and elsewhere; they became known as Hiptias (Hibtias) after his name.[51]

In 1200/1785, the headquarters of the Dā'ūdī *da'wa* was transferred to Sūrat, then under British control and a safe refuge. There, the forty-third *dā'ī*, 'Abd 'Alī Sayf al-Dīn (1213–32/1798–1817), founded a seminary known as Sayfī Dars (also Jāmi'a Sayfiyya) for the education of Dā'ūdī scholars and community functionaries. This institution, with a later branch in Bombay, has continued to serve as a centre of traditional Islamic and Ismaili learning for the Dā'ūdī Bohras. With the consolidation of British rule in India in the early decades of the 13th/19th century, the Indian Ismailis, from a variety of Bohra and Khoja communities, were no longer subjected to official persecutions.

Since 1232/1817, the office of *dā'ī muṭlaq* of the Dā'ūdī Ṭayyibī Bohras has remained in the progeny of Shaykh Jīwānjī Awrangābādī. But the Dā'ūdī community experienced incessant internal strife and discord brought about by oppositions to the *dā'ī*'s authority. In particular, the controversial circumstances surrounding the succession to the forty-sixth *dā'ī*, Muḥammad Badr al-Dīn who died suddenly in 1256/1840 without having openly designated his successor, caused a deep rift in the community. In the event, a group of the Dā'ūdī *'ulamā'* appointed 'Abd al-Qādir Najm al-Dīn, related to the deceased *dā'ī*, to act as the caretaker and administrator (*nāẓim*) of the *da'wa*. 'Abd al-Qādir's subsequent assumption of the title of *dā'ī muṭlaq* aggravated the situation and led to the formation of a permanent opposition movement to the *dā'ī*. 'Abd al-Qādir enforced his authority during his long leadership (1256–1302/1840–85), but only at the cost of irrevocable dissensions in the community.

A new era in the modern history of the Dā'ūdī Bohras began with their fifty-first *dā'ī*, Ṭāhir Sayf al-Dīn (1333–85/1915–65), who led the community longer than any of his predecessors. In his time the Dā'ūdīs were clearly polarised between his traditionally-minded supporters and a number of reformist groups. The latter have campaigned for secular education and individual rights as well as the democratisation of institutions of the Dā'ūdī *da'wa* and the financial accountability of the *dā'ī muṭlaq* to the community. By the 1960s, the reformist groups had established a united front called Pragati Mandal (Progressive Group).[52] However, Ṭāhir Sayf al-Dīn successfully established his absolute authority over all religious and secular affairs of the community, also laying claims to sinlessness and infallibility (*'isma*), traditional attributes and prerogatives of the imams. The *dā'ī* appointed members of his large family to high positions within the *da'wa* organisation, and enforced policies including excommunication, to ensure the unwavering obedience of the Dā'ūdīs. He also established direct control over all communal endowments and financial resources. The present *dā'ī muṭlaq*, Muḥammad Burhān al-Dīn b. Ṭāhir Sayf al-Dīn, succeeded to his position as fifty-second in the series in 1385/1965.

The *dā'ī muṭlaq* is the supreme head of the Dā'ūdī *da'wa* organisation. For all practical purposes, the *dā'ī*, addressed as Sayyidnā Ṣāḥib, is a substitute for the hidden Ṭayyibī imam. The *dā'ī*'s chief assistant, or *ma'dhūn*, is chosen from among his close relatives and he normally succeeds to the position of *dā'ī muṭlaq*. The *dā'ī* also nominates one *mukāsir*, again a relative, to act as the *ma'dhūn*'s assistant. Next, there are the *mashāyikh* (singular, *shaykh*), usually eighteen in number, selected from among the learned members of the community. The *mashāyikh* officiate at the larger Dā'ūdī centres. Finally, the *dā'ī* appoints his own *'āmil*s or agents, the lowest rank in the *da'wa* hierarchy, to every Dā'ūdī community exceeding fifty families. The *'āmil* acts as the local leader of the Dā'ūdīs, performing various ceremonies. He is also responsible for collecting the religious dues and sending them to the *dā'ī*'s central headquarters. The *'āmil*s administer to every Dā'ūdī on attaining the age of fifteen an oath of allegiance (*mīthāq*) to the Ṭayyibī imams and their *dā'ī*s; the oath now includes unconditional obedience to the *dā'ī muṭlaq*. Indeed, every concern and activity of Bohras requires the *dā'ī*'s consent. This also applies to academic and research activities. In particular, the study of the so-called esoteric Ismaili texts cannot be undertaken without the *dā'ī*'s personal consent, which is difficult to obtain.

Centuries of persecution and forced conversion to Sunnism have taken their toll on the Ismaili Bohras of India. The total Dā'ūdī population is currently estimated at around only 700,000 persons. More than half of the Dā'ūdī Bohras live in Gujarāt. The largest single Dā'ūdī Bohra community is situated in Bombay (c. 60,000 persons). Since the 1920s, Bombay has also served as the permanent seat of the Dā'ūdī *dā'ī muṭlaq* and the central administration of his *da'wa* organisation, designated officially as the *"Dawat-i Hadiyah"*. Other important urban centres of the Dā'ūdī Bohras in India are located in Dohad, Udaipur, Ujjain, Sūrat, Aḥmadābād and Sidhpūr. Outside India, the largest Dā'ūdī community is settled in Karachi (c. 30,000 persons). In Yaman, the Dā'ūdīs represent a small minority, not exceeding 5,000; they live mainly in the Ḥarāz region and especially among the Banū Muqātil.

The Ṭayyibī Bohras, along with the Nizārī Khojas, were among the earliest Asian communities to settle in East Africa.[53] Their settlement was particularly encouraged during the early decades of the 13th/19th century by Sultan Sayyid Sa'īd (1220–73/1806–56), of the Āl Bū Sa'īd dynasty of 'Umān and Zanzibar. Aiming to develop the commercial basis of his African dominions, the sultan encouraged the emigration of Indian traders to Zanzibar, where they were accorded religious freedom. After the Khojas, the Ismaili Bohra emigrants from western India constituted the largest Asian community of Zanzibar. Asian emigration increased after Sultan Sa'īd permanently transferred his capital in 1256/1840 from Muscat to Zanzibar. In time, the Indian Ismailis moved from Zanzibar to the growing urban centres of the East African coastline. By 1970, some 20,000 Ismaili Bohras lived in Kenya, Tanzania and Uganda. Since then, most of the East African Bohras as well as Khojas have been obliged to emigrate and settle in the West and elsewhere owing to the anti-Asian policies of certain African regimes.

In the aftermath of the Dā'ūdī–Sulaymānī schism, the Yamani Ṭayyibīs lent their overwhelming support to the Sulaymānī cause. Sulaymānī *dā'īs*, too, have followed one another by the rule of *naṣṣ*. Since the time of their thirtieth *dā'ī muṭlaq*, Ibrāhīm b. Muḥammad b. al-Fahd al-Makramī (1088–94/1677–83), Sulaymānī leadership has remained hereditary, with few exceptions, in the same Makramī family. Unlike the Dā'ūdīs, the Sulaymānīs are not plagued by succession disputes and, consequently, their community is unified. The Sulaymānī Makramī *dā'īs* established their headquarters in Badr, Najrān, in northeastern Yaman. They ruled independently over Najrān with the military support of the local Banū Yām. The *dā'īs* had numerous hostile encounters with the Zaydī imams, but managed to hold their own; they even succeeded in regaining a foothold in Ḥarāz. In the second half of the 13th/19th century, however, the Ottomans ended the political prominence of the Sulaymānī *dāʿī*s in Yaman. In the twentieth century, the political influence of the *dāʿī*s was further curtailed by the rising power of the Saʿūdī family. Najrān, the seat of the Makramī *dāʿī*s, was in fact annexed by Saudi Arabia in 1353/1934. The present *dāʿī muṭlaq*, the forty-ninth in the series, al-Sharafī al-Ḥusayn b. al-Ḥasan al-Makramī, succeeded to office in 1396/1976, and is living in Saudi Arabia.

At present, the Sulaymānī Ṭayyibī Ismailis of Yaman number around 100,000 persons. They live mainly in the northern districts of Yaman and on the border region with Saudi Arabia. Besides the Banū Yām of Najrān, there are small Sulaymānī communities in Ḥarāz. The Sulaymānī as dictinct from the Dā'ūdī Bohras of India represent a small and diminishing community of a few thousand, scattered in Bombay, Baroda, Aḥmadābād and Ḥaydarābād. The Sulaymānīs have a simple *dāʿwa* organisation; their *dāʿī*, addressed as Sayyidnā, personally looks after the affairs of the community with the help of a few assistants, designated as *ma'dhūn* and *mukāsir*. The Sulaymānī *daʿwa* has traditionally been active in three regions (*jazā'ir*), namely, Yaman itself, Hind (India) and Sind (Pakistan). The *dāʿī* appoints his agents (*ʿāmils*) to the main Sulaymānī districts of Yaman, and has a chief representative or *manṣūb* in India, at the Sulaymānī headquarters in Baroda; he also supervises the affairs of the small Sulaymānī Bohra community of Pakistan.

The Sulaymānīs, too, withhold their literature from outsiders. The Ismaili texts of the pre-Fatimid, Fatimid and Yamani periods until the Dā'ūdī-Sulaymānī schism, are accepted by both of the Ṭayyibī Mustaʿlī branches. After the schism, the Dā'ūdīs and Sulaymānīs produced separate literatures, mostly of a polemical nature defending or refuting the claims of various *dāʿī*s.[54] There are certain differences between the traditions of the Arabic-speaking Yamani Sulaymānīs and the Dā'ūdī Bohras who use a form of the Gujarātī language. The Bohras incorporated many Hindu customs in their marriage and other ceremonies. The Sulaymānī leadership has been more progressive than its Dā'ūdī counterpart. In particular, the small Sulaymānī Bohra community of the subcontinent has allowed itself a certain degree of social change, secularisation and modernisation.

MODERN DEVELOPMENTS IN THE NIZĀRĪ COMMUNITY

In this final section we shall present highlights of the modern history of the Nizārī Ismailis, focusing on developments from the middle of the nineteenth century, and on the modernisation policies of the recent imams. A thorough treatment of this subject would require much better information than is currently available on modern developments in a number of Nizārī communities, especially those situated in Iran, Afghanistan, Central Asia, the Indo-Pakistan subcontinent, Syria and East Africa.

Shāh Khalīl Allāh (II) was the last of the Qāsim-Shāhī Nizārī imams to reside in Anjudān. By then, the *daʿwa* of this majority Nizārī line had proved successful particularly in Afghanistan and Central Asia, as well as in the Indian subcontinent. On the other hand, the fortunes of the Muḥammad-Shāhī imams, who lived in Aḥmadnagar and later in Awrangābād, had rapidly declined. In Persia, the majority of the Muḥammad-Shāhīs, distanced from their imams, converted to Twelver Shīʿism, originally adopted as a form of *taqiyya*. The Muḥammad-Shāhī communities of Badakhshān and India, too, rapidly disappeared in the course of the 12th/18th century. In Badakhshān, they switched their allegiance mainly to the Qāsim-Shāhī line. By the middle of the 13th/19th century, Muḥammad-Shāhī Nizārīs were found only in Syria, where their small community still exists. Our discussion here, unless otherwise stated, refers to the Nizārī Ismaili imams of the Qāsim-Shāhī line and their followers.

Shāh Khalīl Allāh II died in 1090/1680 and was succeeded by his son Shāh Nizār. By his time, the imams had acquired widespread influence in Anjudān and its surroundings in central Persia. At an unknown date in his imamate (1090–1134/1680–1722), Shāh Nizār transferred the *daʿwa* headquarters to the nearby village of Kahak, ending the Anjudān period in the Nizārī Ismaili imamate. The imams maintained a foothold in Kahak for more than a century. Shāh Nizār died in 1134/1722, according to his tombstone in Kahak, now a small Ithnāʿasharī village with a population of around 500 persons. Shāh Nizār's mausoleum, where his successor Sayyid ʿAlī and other family members are also buried, may have been part of the original residence of the imams in Kahak. It is interesting to note that this necropolis also contains several graves with Khojkī inscriptions, testimonies to visits by Nizārī Khojas from the subcontinent to see their imam. Kahak is indeed cited in some *ginān*s as the abode of the Ismaili imams.

By the middle of the 12th/18th century, the imams moved to Shahr-i Bābak in the province of Kirmān. In the unsettled conditions prevailing after the Afghan invasion of Persia and the downfall of the Safawids in 1135/1722, the Khoja travellers, who journeyed to see their imam, were often plundered and killed before they could reach Kahak.[55] Consequently, the imams moved their headquarters to Shahr-i Bābak in southeastern Persia, closer to the route of the Indian pilgrims. By then, the centre of gravity of the Nizārī community had clearly shifted towards the Khojas, both in terms of their numbers and financial resources. In Persia, as a result of persecutions and dissimulation, many Nizārī Ismailis had converted to Twelver Shī'ism, especially in the urban areas. With the improved flow of funds from India, the forty-second imam, Ḥasan 'Alī, acquired extensive properties in Shahr-i Bābak as well as in the city of Kirmān. He was also the first Nizārī imam to abandon the traditional *taqiyya* practices. He became actively involved in the affairs of Kirmān, establishing close relations with the province's Afshārid ruler Shāh Rukh (1160–72/1747–59).

The forty-fourth imam, Abu'l-Ḥasan 'Alī, rose to political prominence in Kirmān.[56] He was appointed to the governorship of the province by Karīm Khān Zand (1164–93/1751–79), founder of another short-lived dynasty in Persia. This imam played a decisive role in the local politics of Kirmān during the turbulent period when Āghā Muḥammad Khān (1193–1212/1779–97), the future founder of the Qājār dynasty, challenged Zand rule in various Persian provinces. Imam Abu'l-Ḥasan 'Alī, the popular governor of Kirmān, ruled autonomously over that province, even after Karīm Khān Zand's death in 1193/1779. It was in his time that the Ni'mat Allāhī Sufi order was revived in Persia by its contemporary master Riḍā 'Alī Shāh (d. 1214/1799), who like his predecessors lived in the Deccan. This Sufi *ṭarīqa* spread rapidly in Kirmān, where the shrine of their founder Shāh Ni'mat Allāh Walī (d. 834/1431) is preserved in Māhān. The arrival of prominent Ni'mat Allāhī Sufis in Kirmān also revived erstwhile ties between this Sufi order and the Nizārī Ismaili imams.[57] Abu'l-Ḥasan 'Alī died in 1206/1792 and was succeeded in the Ismaili imamate by his son Shāh Khalīl Allāh (III).

Soon after his accession, instability in Kirmān urged Shāh Khalīl Allāh to move temporarily to Kahak. However, his stay in the ancestral locality lasted about two decades before he settled in Yazd in 1230/1815. The choice of Yazd, too, situated on the route to Balūchistān and Sind, was dictated apparently by concern for the safe passage of the Khoja travellers to Persia. It was in Yazd that the imam was enmeshed in certain disputes and religious rivalries between his followers and the local Twelver leaders. In 1232/1817, he was murdered, together with several of his followers, including a Khoja *murīd*, in a mob attack on his house.

Shāh Khalīl Allāh (III) was married to a relative, Bībī Sarkāra (d. 1267/1851), who bore him the successor to the Ismaili imamate, Ḥasan 'Alī Shāh, in 1219/1804. Bībī Sarkāra's father and brother, Muḥammad Ṣādiq Maḥallātī (Ṣidq 'Alī Shāh) and 'Izzat 'Alī Shāh, were prominent Ni'mat Allāhī Sufis, in close relations with Zayn al-

ʿĀbidīn Shīrwānī (d. 1253/1837), who carried the Sufi name of Mast ʿAlī Shāh and became the spiritual master (*quṭb*) of the chief branch of the Niʿmat Allāhī *ṭarīqa*. Close associations between the family of the Ismaili imam and various Niʿmat Allāhī leading personalities, including Raḥmat ʿAlī Shāh (d. 1278/1861), Munawwar ʿAlī Shāh (d. 1301/1884), Ṣafī ʿAlī Shāh (d. 1316/1898) and Maʿṣūm ʿAlī Shāh (d. 1344/1926), author of the famous Sufi work entitled *Ṭarāʾiq al-ḥaqāʾiq*, were re-enacted throughout the nineteenth century.[58]

Ḥasan ʿAlī Shāh was only thirteen when he succeeded his father as the forty-sixth Nizārī Ismaili imam.[59] On the murder of Shāh Khalīl Allāh, his widow went to Tehran to the court of the Qājār monarch, Fatḥ ʿAlī Shāh (1212–50/1797–1834), seeking justice for her husband and children. She was eventually successful. The instigators of the imam's murder were punished after a fashion, and the monarch appointed Ḥasan ʿAlī Shāh to the governorship of Qumm, also giving him properties in nearby Maḥallāt. In addition, Fatḥ ʿAlī Shāh gave one of his daughters, Sarv-i Jahān Khānum, in marriage to the youthful imam, and bestowed upon him the honorific title (*laqab*) of Āghā Khān meaning lord and master. Henceforth, Ḥasan ʿAlī Shāh was known in Persia as Āghā Khān Maḥallātī, because of his royal title and the family's deep roots in Maḥallāt and its environs (Anjudān, Kahak and Qumm); and the title of Āghā Khān (Aga Khan) was inherited by his successors to the Ismaili imamate.

Āghā Khān I lived a quiet life in Persia, honoured and respected at the Qājār court for the remainder of Fatḥ ʿAlī Shāh's reign. By then, the Ismaili imam also gathered a fighting force in Maḥallāt. The next Qājār monarch, Muḥammad Shāh, appointed the imam to the governorship of Kirmān in 1251/1835, soon after his accession to the throne of Persia. Kirmān was then in constant turmoil because of incessant raids by Afghan and Balūchī bands and rebellious activities of certain Qājār princes. The imam soon restored order to Kirmān, with the support of the local Khurāsānī and ʿAṭāʾ Allāhī tribesmen among his local followers. However, his governorship was short-lived, and he was dismissed from that post in 1252/1837 under obscure circumstances rooted in the enmity of the powerful chief minister, Ḥājjī Mīrzā Āqāsī. Āghā Khān's dismissal led to prolonged confrontations between the imam and the Qājār government, deteriorating into a series of military encounters in 1256/1840.[60] The Ismaili forces were eventually defeated decisively in a major battle in Kirmān in 1257/1841, and the imam was obliged to flee to neighbouring Afghanistan. This marked the end of the Persian period of the Nizārī Ismaili imamate which had lasted some seven centuries since the Alamūt times.

Accompanied by a large retinue, Āghā Khān I arrived in the summer of 1257/1841 in Qandahār, then besieged by an Anglo-Indian army. Henceforth, a close association developed between the Ismaili imam and the British Raj. In Qandahār, the imam received deputations from his followers in Badakhshān and Sind; the Ismaili communities of these regions now strove to establish more direct contacts with their imam. With the defeat of the British forces in Kābul and Qandahār, Āghā Khān proceeded to Sind in 1258/1842. There, his cavalry assisted in the annexation of Sind to British India in 1259/1843. In Sind, Āghā Khān stayed in Jerruk, where his house is still preserved. For his services, Āghā Khān was awarded an annual pension from General Sir Charles Napier (1782–1853), the conqueror of Sind who maintained friendly relations with the imam.[61]

From the time of his arrival in Sind, Āghā Khān I revived contact with his Khoja followers, who were now seeing their imam for the first time. In 1260/1844, the imam left Sind and after spending a year at Kathiawar in Gujarāt with his followers, he arrived in Bombay in 1262/1846. British intercessions for the imam's return to his Persian homeland, as was his personal desire, failed. After a brief stay in Calcutta, the Ismaili imam settled permanently in Bombay in 1265/1848, which marks the commencement of the modern period of Nizārī Ismaili history.

Āghā Khān I was the first Ismaili imam of his line to live in India. The Nizārī Khojas, representing a large community for several centuries, were finally able to receive the imam in their midst. The remittance of their religious dues, too, could henceforth take place in a more regular and orderly fashion. The imam soon established elaborate headquarters and residences in Bombay, Poona and Bangalore. He attended the chief *jamā'at-khāna* in Bombay on special religious occasions, and also held regular *durbar* (Persian, *darbār*) giving audiences at his residence, the Aga Hall, to his followers who came in large numbers to receive his blessings. Āghā Khān I spent the last three decades of his life and long imamate in Bombay.

As the spiritual head of a Muslim community, Āghā Khān I received the protection of the British establishment in India, which strengthened and stabilised his position. Nevertheless, he initially encountered some serious difficulties in establishing his religious authority. The Nizārī Khojas of the Indian subcontinent were left without a *pīr* for quite a long time. Satpanth Ismailism, as noted, was influenced by Hindu elements, while the Khojas were also obliged to dissimulate for long periods as Sunnis or Twelver Shī'īs. In the settlement of their legal affairs, too, the Khojas, like certain other Indian Muslims, had often resorted to Hindu customs rather than the provisions of Islamic law, especially in matters relating to inheritance. The above factors were hardly conducive to the formation of a lucid and strong sense of religious identity. In fact, dissident groups emerged intermittently, claiming Sunni or Ithnāʿasharī heritage for the Khoja community

It was under such circumstances that Āghā Khān I launched a widespread campaign for defining and delineating the particular religious identity of his Khoja following. In 1861, the imam circulated a document that specified the religious beliefs and practices of the Nizārī Ismailis, requesting every Khoja to sign it. The signatories were, in effect, asked to pledge their loyalty to the imam and to their Shīʿī Ismaili Muslim faith as interpreted by him. This document, a landmark in asserting Nizārī Ismaili identity, was circulated in Bombay and elsewhere. The bulk of the Ismaili Khojas complied. However, a small dissident group persisted in challenging Āghā Khān's authority and refused to acknowledge the Ismaili identity of their community. Matters came to a head in 1866 when the dissident Khojas brought their case before the Bombay High Court. In the course of the prolonged hearings of this so-called "Aga Khan Case", the imam produced a variety of documents on the history of the community and his leadership mandate. A detailed judgement was finally rendered against the plaintiffs and in favour of the Ismaili imam on all counts.[62] This judgement legally established in British India the status of Āghā Khān's Khoja followers as a community of "Shia Imami Ismailis", also recognising Āghā Khān as the spiritual head of that community and heir in lineal descent to the imams of the Alamūt period.[63] Furthermore, this historic judgement confirmed his rights to all customary dues collected from the Khojas, including the *dassondh* or tithe. The authority of Āghā Khān, addressed by his Khoja followers as Sarkār Ṣāḥib and Pīr Salāmat, was never again challenged seriously in the subcontinent or elsewhere.

Āghā Khān I gradually succeeded in exerting control over the Nizārī Khojas through their traditional communal organisation. He personally appointed the officers of the major Khoja congregations. These officers included a *mukhi* (pronounced *mukī)*, who normally acted as the social and religious head of any local Khoja community, and his assistant, called *kamadia* (pronounced *kāmriyā*). Every Khoja community (*jamāʿat*) of a certain size had its own *mukhi* and *kamadia*, with clearly defined duties, including the collection of the religious dues, and presiding over religious ceremonies in the *jamāʿat-khāna* or congregation house. The Nizārī Ismailis are still organised according to this traditional structure; and the terms *mukhi* and *kamadia*, derived from Sanskrit words, and *jamāʿat-khāna* were in time adopted by all non-Khoja Nizārī Ismaili communities as well. Āghā Khān I also encouraged a revival of literary activities among the Ismailis. Foremost among the pioneers of this revival was his eldest grandson, Shihāb al-Dīn Shāh (d. 1302/1884), who composed a few treatises in Persian on ethical and mystical aspects of Nizārī teachings.[64]

Ḥasan ʿAlī Shāh, Āghā Khān I, the forty-sixth Nizārī Ismaili imam, died after an eventful imamate of sixty-four years, in 1298/1881. He was buried in the Mazagaon area of Bombay where his mausoleum stands as an impressive monument next to an old *jamāʿat-khāna*. Āghā Khān I was succeeded by his eldest son Āqā ʿAlī Shāh, his sole son by his Qājār spouse. The forty-seventh imam was born in 1246/1830 in Maḥallāt, Persia, where he spent his youthful years. Āqā ʿAlī Shāh eventually arrived in Bombay in 1269/1853 and, henceforth, regularly visited different Khoja communities, especially in Gujarāt and Sind. He also lived for some time in Karachi, where his future successor Sulṭān Muḥammad Shāh was born in 1294/1877.

Āqā ʿAlī Shāh led the Nizārī Ismailis for a brief four-year period, during which time he concentrated mainly on improving the educational and welfare standards of the Nizārīs. He also made special efforts to collect the *ginān*s circulating in the community, by charging a group of his followers with the task of locating and acquiring the relevant manuscripts. Āghā Khān II was an accomplished sportsman and hunter; he died in 1302/1885 of pneumonia contracted on a day's hunt near Poona, and was buried in the family mausoleum in Najaf, Iraq.

Āqā ʿAlī Shāh was succeeded by his sole surviving son, Sulṭān Muḥammad Shāh, who led the Nizārī Ismailis as their forty-eighth imam for seventy-two years, longer than any of his predecessors. He became well known as a Muslim reformer and statesman owing to his prominent role in Indo-Muslim as well as international affairs. His life and achievements are, therefore, amply documented.[65]

Sulṭān Muḥammad Shāh, Aga Khan III, was installed to the Ismaili imamate in official ceremonies in Bombay in 1302/1885 when he was only eight years old. He grew up under the close supervision of his capable mother, Shams al-Mulūk (d. 1356/1938), a granddaughter of Fatḥ ʿAlī Shāh of Persia, while his paternal uncle Āqā Jangī Shāh (d. 1314/1896) was designated as his guardian. Aga Khan III received a rigorous traditional education in Bombay, which included Arabic and Persian as well as exposure to English language and literature. In 1898, the Ismaili imam paid his first visit to Europe, where he later established his permanent residence. Sulṭān Muḥammad Shāh maintained close relations with the British throughout his life and received numerous honours from that government. This relationship brought immense benefits to his followers in India and Africa who lived under British imperial rule.

From early on, Aga Khan III concerned himself with the affairs of his followers, especially the Nizārī communities of the subcontinent and East Africa. In time, these concerns evolved in the form of specific policies and programmes. In 1899, he made the first of his visits to his followers in East Africa. The Nizārī Khojas had emigrated regularly from western India to Zanzibar, where they established their earliest settlement and *jamā'at-khāna*. The emigration of Nizārī Khojas and other Asians to Zanzibar increased significantly during 1840–70, a period of economic prosperity and improved trading and commercial opportunities in the island. By World War I, Nizārī Khoja settlements existed also in many of the urban centres of the East African mainland, including especially Mombasa, Dar-es-Salaam, Nairobi and Kampala.

In 1905, while the imam was in East Africa, a suit was filed against him in the Bombay High Court by some members of his family. The court's ruling against the plaintiffs, led by Aga Khan's cousin Ḥājjī Bībī, reiterated the imam's status within his family and community. This ruling had a number of wider implications as well; in particular, it further delineated the identity of the Nizārī Ismailis and distinguished them from the Twelver Shī'īs. Henceforth, Aga Khan III made systematic efforts to set his followers' identity apart from the Twelver Shī'īs as well as the Sunnis. His religious policy, thus, centred for quite some time around asserting or reasserting the Nizārī Ismaili identity of his followers, who were also urged to respect the traditions of other Muslim communities. This identity was spelled out in the constitutions that the imam promulgated for his followers in different regions, the first of which was issued in Zanzibar in 1905. This policy soon put a stop to occasional secessions by dissident groups as well as the absorption of the Ismailis into their surrounding Sunni and Twelver Shī'ī communities, rooted in the age old *taqiyya* practices.

In the meantime, the Ismaili imam was increasingly concerned with reform policies that would benefit not only his followers but other Muslims as well. He campaigned for a variety of educational reforms and played a leading role in the transformation of the Muhammadan Anglo-Oriental College at Aligarh into a leading university; he also became one of the founders of the All-India Muslim League. At the same time, Aga Khan III was drawn into Indian affairs and effectively participated in the crucial discussions that led to the eventual independence of India and Pakistan from British rule. During World War I, the imam set forth his ideas on the future of India in a book.[66] Later in the 1930s, he represented the Muslims of India at the Round Table Conferences in London, discussing India's destiny with other eminent participants such as Mahatma Gandhi and Muhammad Ali Jinnah, founder of the state of Pakistan. Aga Khan III's involvement in international affairs culminated in his election in 1937 as president of the League of Nations in Geneva for a session. By then, the Ismaili imam had already celebrated his golden jubilee in 1935, marking the fiftieth anniversary of his imamate.

Simultaneously with defining and delineating their Ismaili identity, Aga Khan III worked vigorously for consolidating and reorganising his followers into a modern Muslim community with high standards of education, health and social well-being. The implementation of his reforms, however, required suitable institutions and administrative organisations. The development of a new communal network, thus, became one of the imam's major tasks, to which he devoted much of his time and financial resources over several decades.

In 1905, Aga Khan III issued a set of written rules and regulations which, in effect, comprised the first constitution for his community in East Africa. This constitution, and those issued later for other regions, also represented the personal law of the community, dealing especially with matters related to inheritance, marriage, divorce, guardianship and so on.[67] The constitution of 1905, initiating Aga Khan III's institutional and modernisation policies, also foresaw a new administrative organisation in the form of a hierarchy of councils for the Nizārī Ismailis of East Africa. Subsequently, similar constitutions, with council systems of administration and their affiliated bodies, were developed for the Ismaili communities of India and Pakistan. The constitutions specified the powers and functions of different categories of national, regional and local councils. The officeholders in the council system were appointed by the imam for limited periods and they did not draw any salaries. In fact, Aga Khan III successfully encouraged the undertaking of voluntary public service within his community, which was an established tradition. The Ismaili constitutions were revised periodically to account for changes in the political and socio-economic circumstances of different communities. It may be noted that Aga Khan III from around 1910 also introduced certain changes in the religious rituals and practices of his followers, emphasising their spirituality and esoteric significance. These changes also served to distinguish further the Nizārī Ismailis from the Twelver Shīʿīs, especially in Persia and the subcontinent where the Ismailis had either dissimulated as Twelvers or had interfaced with them for extended periods. These measures also safeguarded the separate identity of the Nizārī Ismailis who were at the same time experiencing modernisation.

In his reforms, Aga Khan III drew on the court decisions in Bombay, which had set his Khoja followers apart from those Khojas who preferred to join the Sunni or Ithnāʿasharī communities. At the same time, these decisions had clarified the imam's status in respect to his followers, and communal properties and revenues. The deep devotion of the Ismailis to their imam, referred to as Mawlana Hazir Imam, "our lord, the living and present imam", made all of Aga Khan III's reform measures readily acceptable to his followers, even when changes in religious rituals were at stake. The figure of the imam, as the religious and administrative head of the community, was central to all the Ismaili constitutions; he was the sole person empowered to change or revise the constitutions. Aga Khan III remained in close contact with his followers, and guided them through his oral and written directives or *farmān*s, yet another communal mechanism for introducing reforms.[68]

Aga Khan III's modernisation policies may indeed be traced through his *farmān*s and speeches on spiritual matters, on education, social welfare and female emancipation and on matters related to religious tolerance, personal conduct and co-operative economic enterprises. In particular, the education of Ismailis, both male and female at different levels, and their health standards, as well as the participation of women in communal affairs, received high priorities in the imam's reforms. Aga Khan III used the religious dues and other offerings submitted to him, and the funds collected at various jubilee celebrations, to finance his modernisation policies. To the same end, he created a variety of institutions with their benefits accruing not only to his own followers but to non-Ismailis as well. He founded and maintained a large network of schools, vocational institutions, libraries, sports and recreational clubs, dispensaries and hospitals in East Africa, the Indo-Pakistan subcontinent and elsewhere.[69]

By the early decades of the twentieth century, the non-Khoja Nizārī Ismailis had, by and large, lost their earlier predominance. In Syria, the Nizārī Ismailis had mainly acknowledged the Muḥammad-Shāhī (or Mu'minī) line of imams while remaining loyal subjects of the Ottomans. They also had periodic entanglements with their Nuṣayrī (ʿAlawī) neighbours, who often occupied their fortresses and destroyed their literature. In the early 1840s, a local Ismaili leader in Qadmūs successfully petitioned the Ottoman authorities for permission to restore Salamiyya, then in ruins, for the settlement of the Syrian Ismailis. This initiated a new era in the modern history of the Syrian community. Meanwhile, since 1210/1796, the Syrian Nizārīs of the Muḥammad-Shāhī line had not heard from their imam, Muḥammad al-Bāqir, who like his predecessors lived in India. As their search to locate the imam proved futile, in 1304/1887 the bulk of the Syrian Muḥammad-Shāhīs transferred their allegiance to the Qāsim-Shāhī line, then represented by Aga Khan III. These Ismailis, currently numbering to around 80,000, live in Salamiyya and its surrounding villages. However, an Ismaili minority, centred in Maṣyāf and Qadmūs, remained loyal to the Muḥammad-Shāhī line, and are still awaiting the reappearance of their hidden imam. Numbering around 15,000 persons, these Ismailis (locally known as the Jaʿfariyya) are today the sole remnants of the Muḥammad-Shāhī Nizārīs; ʿĀrif Tāmir, editor of numerous Ismaili texts, was their foremost scholar.[70]

In Persia, the Nizārīs were left without effective leadership upon the departure of Āghā Khān I in 1257/1841. The scattered and small Ismaili communities of Persia once again resorted to strict dissimulation in the guise of Twelver Shīʿism, Persia's official religion. Later, Āghā Khān I designated from Bombay a certain Mīrzā Ḥasan from the village of Sidih in southern Khurāsān to oversee the affairs of his Persian followers. Upon Mīrzā Ḥasan's death around 1305/1887, his privileged position was taken over by his son Murād Mīrzā. By his time the Persian Ismailis no longer had any direct contacts with their imam, and Murād Mīrzā now displayed leadership aspirations of his own. In particular, he claimed the rank of *ḥujja* and demanded the absolute obedience of the community. In 1908, Murād Mīrzā sided with the plaintiffs in the Ḥājjī Bībī Case against Aga Khan III, whose leadership he was then challenging. Subsequently, Murād Mīrzā recognised Ṣamad Shāh, Ḥājjī Bībī's son, as an imam. This claim was accepted by a faction of the Ismailis of southern Khurāsān, known as Murād Mīrzā'īs. By the 1920s, Ṣamad Shāh had reconciled his own differences with the imam, who sent him on a mission to Hunza. But the dissident Murād Mīrzā'īs never reverted to the main Nizārī Ismaili community. By the 1940s, most of the Murād Mīrzā'īs of Sidih and its environs, then led by Murād Mīrzā's daughter Bībī Ṭalʿat, had converted to Twelver Shīʿism.

In the meantime, Aga Khan III attempted to establish his own control over the Persian community through Muḥammad b. Zayn al-ʿĀbidīn, better known as Fidā'ī Khurāsānī, the most learned Persian Ismaili of the time. Fidā'ī Khurāsānī travelled to Bombay three times during 1313–24/ 1896–1906 to see the imam, and was appointed by him as the *muʿallim* or teacher in charge of the religious affairs of the Persian Ismailis. Fidā'ī Khurāsānī regularly visited the Ismailis of different localities in Persia, explaining their heritage and winning their renewed allegiance to Aga Khan III. He also conveyed the imam's instructions on the practices of the faith, engendered to assert and protect the communal identity. The Persian Nizārīs had hitherto observed their religious rituals mainly in the fashion of, and in company with, the Twelver Shīʿīs. They were now requested to set themselves apart from the Twelvers, reaffirming their own identity as a separate religious community like the Nizārī Khojas. As one such measure, they recited the entire list of their imams at the conclusion of their daily prayers. They were also discouraged from joining the Twelvers in their mosques or on special religious occasions. By the time of Fidā'ī Khurāsānī's death in 1342/1923, Aga Khan III had established his authority over the Persian community.

Aga Khan III extended, in a limited manner, his modernisation policies to Persia, especially in the field of education. In Khurāsān, where the bulk of the community is concentrated in modern times, a policy of a school for every Ismaili village was successfully undertaken. At present, there are about 30,000 Nizārī Ismailis living in Persia (Iran), with almost half in the province of Khurāsān. Other Persian Nizārī communities are located in Tehran, Maḥallāt and its surrounding villages, as well as in the cities of Kirmān, Shahr-i Bābak, Sīrjān, Yazd and their environs. In many villages, their inhabitants, often related to one another, continue to belong to both the Ismaili and Twelver Shīʿī communities, a product of centuries of dissimulation practices and assimilation into the dominant religious community of the region.[71]

Not much is available on the modern histories of the Nizārī Ismailis of Afghanistan and Central Asia as well as the communities located in the northern areas of Pakistan. The Ismailis of these mountainous regions, living in the midst of the prohibitive Pamirs, the Hindu Kush and the Karakorum ranges, have been isolated historically from other Ismaili communities. Until recently, they were also deprived of regular contacts with their imam or his appointed representatives. As a result, the Ismailis of Central Asia and surrounding areas developed rather autonomously under the local leadership of their *khalīfa*s, the more learned members of their community who officiate at religious ceremonies. These Ismailis, concentrated in Badakhshān, elaborated an indigenous literary tradition, centred on the writings of highly revered Nāṣir Khusraw, as well as certain indigenous rituals such as the *chirāgh-rawshan* rite for the dead. The bulk of extant Nizārī Ismaili literature, as noted, has been secretly preserved in numerous private collections in Badakhshān.

The Nizārī Ismailis of Badakhshān account for the bulk of the Ismailis of Afghanistan and Central Asia; their predominant language is Persian, with Tajik which is its Central Asian variant. In the course of the nineteenth century, the northern portion of Badakhshān was annexed to various Central Asian Khanates, but the greater part of that region came under the increasing control of imperial Russia, with the British extending their hegemony over Badakhshān proper in the Afghan territories. These political realities were officially recognised in 1895 when an Anglo-Russian boundary commission handed the region on the right bank of the Panj, a major upper headwater of Āmū Daryā (Oxus), to the Khanate of Bukhārā, then controlled by Russians, while designating the left bank as Afghan territory, with Fayḍābād as its chief town. Aga Khan III found it difficult to establish direct contacts with his followers in Badakhshān; unsurmountable difficulties exacerbated by the incorporation of Central Asia into the Soviet Union. Aga Khan III's last contact with his Central Asian followers was probably in 1923 through a Nizārī Khoja dignitary, (Pīr) Sabz ʿAlī (d. 1938), dispatched there as his emissary. In 1925, the Soviet government created the Autonomous Region of Gorno-Badakhshān, with its capital at Khorog, as a province of the Socialist Soviet Republic of Tajikistan. Until the dissolution of the Soviet Union in 1991, Tajikistan's Ismailis were completely cut off from their imam, and they were not permitted to practise their faith due to anti-religious policies of the Soviet regime.[72]

In some of the areas now situated in northern Pakistan, such as Chitral and Gilgit, small Ismaili communities have existed, probably dating from the Anjudān period. In Hunza, too, now accounting for the largest Nizārī Ismaili community of northern Pakistan (c. 50,000), Ismailism seems to have originally spread at the same time. However, the people of Hunza reverted to Twelver Shīʿism sometime before the 13th/19th century. Nizārī Ismailism was reintroduced to Hunza during the early decades of the nineteenth century by *dāʿī*s coming from neighbouring Badakhshān.[73] Hunza was ruled independently for several centuries until 1974 when the region became part of the federal state of Pakistan, by a family of *mīr*s who had their seat in Baltit (now Karīmābād). Salīm Khān (d. 1239/1823) was the first *mīr* of Hunza to convert to Nizārī Ismailism. Later in 1254/1838, in the reign of his son and successor Mīr Ghaẓanfar, the entire population of Hunza was converted by Badakhshānī *dāʿī*s, who also trained local *khalīfa*s to instruct the converts in Ismaili doctrines. Henceforth, the people of Hunza referred to themselves as Mawlā'īs, because they were followers of the Ismaili imam addressed by them as Mawlā. Hunza, along with Nagir, Chitral and other adjoining districts, was annexed to British India in 1891. Subsequently, Aga Khan III established close relations with Mīr Ṣafdar Khān (1886–1931) and his successors.[74] The imam's emissary Sabz ʿAlī also visited Hunza, where he set up *jamāʿat-khāna*s in 1923. The Nizārīs of Hunza have a selection of the Ismaili texts preserved by their co-religionists in Badakhshān, and participate in more or less identical religious rituals.

Small Nizārī communities exist also in Yārkand and Kāshghar, in Sinkiang province of China, about whose history no specific details are available. The Turkish-speaking Ismailis of China have not been permitted by the country's Communist regime to communicate with the outside world.

Sir Sulṭān Muḥammad Shāh, Aga Khan III, the forty-eighth imam of the Nizārī Ismailis, was indeed very successful in his modernisation policies. As a spiritual leader and Muslim reformer, he responded to the challenges of a rapidly changing world and made it possible for his followers in different countries to live in the twentieth century as a progressive community with a distinct Islamic identity. A full appreciation of his reforms and achievements is beyond the scope of this study. Aga Khan III died in his villa near Geneva in 1376/1957, and was later buried in a permanent mausoleum at Aswan, overlooking the Nile, in Egypt. Sulṭān Muḥammad Shāh was married four times, and survived by two sons, Prince Aly Khan (1911-60) and Prince Sadruddin (b. 1933). He stipulated in his will and testament that owing to the changing conditions of the world the Ismailis would be better served if their next imam were a person brought up and educated in more recent times. Consequently, he designated his grandson Karim, Aly Khan's son, as his successor to the imamate.

Mawlana Hazir Imam Shah Karim al-Husayni, as he is addressed by his followers, is the forty-ninth and the present imam of the Nizārī Ismailis, and the fourth imam to carry the title of Aga Khan. He is internationally known as His Highness Prince Karim Aga Khan IV. Born in 1936 in Geneva, Aga Khan IV was educated at Le Rosey, an exclusive school in Switzerland, and Harvard University, from where he graduated in 1959 with a degree in Islamic history.

The present Ismaili imam has continued and substantially expanded the modernisation policies of his grandfather, also developing a multitude of new programmes and institutions of his own for the benefit of his community. At the same time, he has concerned himself with a variety of social, developmental and cultural issues which are of wider interest to the Muslims and the Third World countries. By 1997, when the Ismailis celebrated the fortieth anniversary of his imamate, Aga Khan IV had established an impressive record of achievement not only as the Ismaili imam but also as a Muslim leader deeply aware of the demands and dilemmas of modernity, and dedicated to promoting a better understanding of Islamic civilisation with its diversity of expressions and interpretations.

Aga Khan IV closely supervises the spiritual and secular affairs of his community. He regularly visits his followers in different parts of Asia, Africa, Europe and North America, and guides them through his *farmāns*. He maintained the elaborate council system of communal administration developed by his grandfather, also extending it to new territories in Europe, the United States and Canada in recognition of the large-scale emigration of his followers from East Africa and the subcontinent to the West since the 1970s. High standards of education and significant business acumen have made for a ready integration of these Ismaili migrants into the economic life of their adopted homelands. Sulṭān Muḥammad Shāh had issued separate constitutions for his Khoja followers in East Africa, India and Pakistan. A new chapter was initiated in the "constitutional" history of the community in 1986, when their imam promulgated a universal document entitled "The Constitution of the Shia Imami Ismaili Muslims", for all his followers throughout the world. After affirming the fundamental creeds of Islam, the preamble to the 1986 constitution emphasises the imam's *taʿlīm* or teaching which is required for guiding the community along the path of spiritual enlightenment as well as improved material life. On the basis of this constitution, a uniform system of councils with affiliated bodies is now operative in some fourteen regions of the world where the Nizārī Ismailis are concentrated, including India, Pakistan, Syria, Kenya, Tanzania, France, Portugal, the United Kingdom, Canada and the United States.

The council system has not yet been extended to certain Ismaili communities including the Persian-speaking *jamāʿats* of Iran, Afghanistan and Tajikistan. These latter communities are administered through alternative systems based on special committees. In recent years, particular attention has been paid to the religious and socio-economic affairs of the Ismailis of Badakhshān in Tajikistan, who emerged from their forced isolation in 1991 in the aftermath of the establishment of independent Central Asian republics. Numbering around 200,000 persons, the Ismailis of Tajikistan had the opportunity of seeing their imam for the first time in 1995. By then, Aga Khan IV's humanitarian and developmental aid to Tajik Badakhshān, through his Pamir Relief and Development Programme, had already saved the region from imminent economic catastrophe. The Badakhshānī Ismailis, severely repressed under the Soviets, gathered in tens of thousands to renew their allegiance to their imam in Shughnān, Rūshān and other districts of the Gorno-Badakhshān province of the Republic of Tajikistan.

The Nizārī Ismailis have maintained their traditional pattern of social and religious organisation in terms of local communities (*jamāʿats*), with their *jamāʿat-khānas*. The communal affairs of each local *jamāʿat* have continued to be under the jurisdiction of a *mukhi* and a *kamadia*, now acting as treasurer. These functionaries officiate on various special occasions, such as marriage ceremonies and funeral rites, as well as the daily communal prayers. They also collect the religious dues. From the time of Aga Khan III, religious matters of general interest to the community, including especially the religious education of the Nizārī Ismailis, have been entrusted to special bodies, originally called Ismailia Associations. Designated as Ismaili Tariqah and Religious Education Boards (ITREB) since 1987 with their own national, regional and local hierarchies, they are responsible also for the distribution of religious literature, including the school curricula developed for Ismaili pupils throughout the world.

Modern Nizārī Ismailis do not engage in proselytisation activities; and the *daʿwa* organisation is, therefore, no longer in place. However, the community does have religious functionaries, designated as teacher (*muʿallim*) and preacher (*wāʿiẓ*), who perform the vital tasks of providing religious education for members of the community and delivering sermons on special occasions.

Aga Khan IV has also initiated many new policies, programmes and projects for the socio-economic and educational benefits of his followers as well as the non-Ismaili populations of certain regions in Africa and Asia. To that end, and building on foundations laid by his grandfather, he has created a complex institutional network, generally referred to as the Aga Khan Development Network (AKDN). Implementing projects related to social, economic and cultural development, the AKDN disburses on the average $100 million per annum on its non-profit activities.

In the area of social development, the imam's network has been particularly active in East Africa, Central Asia, Pakistan and India in projects for health, education and housing services, and rural development. Many of these are promoted or financed through the Aga Khan Foundation established in 1967. While Aga Khan III pioneered modern educational reforms in his community, his grandson has built upon that central interest of the Ismaili imamate and extended it to higher education and educational institutions. In this connection, mention should be made of the Institute of Ismaili Studies, founded in London in 1977 for the promotion of general Islamic and Ismaili studies, and the Aga Khan University, with faculties of medicine, nursing and education, and an affiliated hospital, inaugurated in Karachi in 1985. The present imam has also encouraged young Ismailis to aim for a balanced spiritual and worldly life, and to acquire specialised education and achieve academic excellence, thus preparing his followers for the meritocratic world of the twenty-first century. In the economic development field, too, Aga Khan IV has sponsored many projects and services. Activities in this general area, ranging from self-help finance and insurance services to industrial ventures and tourism promotion, are placed under the overall charge of the Aga Khan Fund for Economic Development.

The present Ismaili imam has devoted much of his time and resources to promoting a better understanding of Islam, not only as a religion but as a major world civilisation with its diversity of social, intellectual and cultural traditions. To that end, he has launched innovative programmes for the preservation and regeneration of the cultural heritages of the Muslim societies. The apex institution here is the Aga Khan Trust for Culture, which was set up in 1988 in Geneva for promoting awareness of the importance of the built environment in both historic and contemporary contexts, and for pursuing excellence in architecture. The Trust's mandate now covers the Aga Khan Award for Architecture, founded in 1977 to recognise and encourage outstanding architectural achievements in different Muslim environments; the Aga Khan Program for Islamic Architecture, established in 1979 at Harvard University and the Massachusetts Institute of Technology (MIT), to educate architects and planners to cater to the needs of modern Muslim societies; and the Historic Cities Support Program launched in the early 1990s to promote the conservation and restoration of buildings and public spaces in historic Muslim cities, such as Cairo and Zanzibar. Aga Khan IV takes a personal interest in the operations of all his institutions, and regulates their activities through his Secretariat at Aiglemont, near Paris.[75]

The Nizārī Ismailis, a Muslim minority scattered in many countries, experienced repression and religious persecution almost uninterruptedly from the fall of Alamūt until recent times. Thus, they often resorted to extensive and extended dissimulating practices, disguising themselves as Sufis, Twelver Shī'īs, Sunnis or even Hindus. That the Nizārīs survived at all and emerged in modern times as a progressive community with a distinct identity attests to the resiliency of their traditions as well as their adaptability under the capable and foresighted leadership of their recent imams, the Aga Khans.

NOTES

1. Juwaynī, *Ta'rīkh*, vol. 3, pp. 277–8; tr. Boyle, vol. 2, pp. 724–5.
2. F. Daftary, "Shams al-Dīn Muḥammad", EI2, vol. 9, pp. 295–6.
3. W. Ivanow, "A Forgotten Branch of the Ismailis", JRAS (1938), pp. 57–79; 'Ārif Tāmir, "Furū' al-shajara al-Ismā'īliyya al-Imāmiyya", *al-Mashriq*, 51 (1957), pp. 581–612, and Daftary, *The Ismā'īlīs*, pp. 446ff., 451–2.
4. Tch. Baradin, "Ḥakīm Nizārī-yi Quhistānī", *Farhang-i Īrān Zamīn*, 6 (1337/1958), pp. 178–203; 'Alī Riḍā Mujtahidzāda, "Sa'd al-milla wa'l-dīn Nizārī Quhistānī", *Revue de la Faculté des Lettres de Meched*, 2 (1345/1966), pp. 71–100, 298–315; Z. Ṣafā, *Ta'rīkh-i*

adabiyyāt dar Īrān (Tehran, 1342– /1963–), vol. 3, part 2, pp. 731–45; Ch. G. Baiburdi, *Zhizn i tvorchestvo Nizārī-Persidskogo poeta* (Moscow, 1966); Persian trans. M. Ṣadrī, *Zindigī va āthār-i Nizārī* (Tehran, 1370/1991); Poonawala, *Biobibliography*, pp. 263–7, and J. T. P. de Bruijn, "Nizārī Ḳuhistānī", EI2, vol. 8, pp. 83–4.

5. For some of the earliest historical references to the Nizārīs of Quhistān in the immediate aftermath of the Mongol conquests, see Sayf b. Muḥammad al-Harawī, *Ta'rīkh nāma-yi Harāt*, ed. M. Z. al-Ṣiddīqī (Calcutta, 1944), pp. 267–8, 302.
6. *Ta'rīkh-i Sīstān*, ed. Bahār, pp. 406, 407, 408; tr. Gold, pp. 331, 332, 333. For an excellent summary description of Quhistān's political situation at this time, see Bosworth, *History of the Saffarids*, pp. 410–24, 429–40.
7. These references may be found in Nizārī Quhistānī's *Dīwān*, ed. M. Muṣaffā (Tehran, 1371–3/1992–4), vol. 1, pp. 583–4, 617, 632–3, 634–5, 642–3, 660, 674–5, 724–5, 753–4, 795, 860, 866, 880, 881, 966–8, 994–5, 1083, 1137, 1219, 1224, 1271–2, 1292, 1315, 1359–60, and elsewhere in his poetry.
8. Ẓahīr al-Dīn Mar'ashī, *Ta'rīkh-i Gīlān va Daylamistān*, ed. M. Sutūda (Tehran, 1347/1968), pp. 66–8.
9. Ibid., pp. 52–66, 69–70, 81 ff., 89, 121, 123–30.
10. Badakhshī and Surkh Afsar, *Ta'rīkh-i Badakhshān*, ed. Boldyrev, pp. 227–53, and Muḥammad-Zāda and Shāh-Zāda, *Ta'rīkh-i Badakhshān*, pp. 87–94; A. A. Semenov, *Istorya Shughnana* (Tashkent, 1916), and C. E. Bosworth, "Shughnān", EI2, vol. 9, pp. 495–6.
11. Mīrzā Muḥammad Ḥaydar Dughlāt, *A History of the Moghuls of Central Asia*, ed. and tr. N. Elias and E. Denison Ross (2nd edn, London, 1898), pp. 217–21, and V. V. Barthold, *Guzīda-yi maqālāt-i taḥqīqī*, tr. K. Kishāvarz (Tehran, 1358/1979), pp. 326 ff., and his "Badakhshān", EI2, vol. 1, pp. 851–4.
12. This anonymous Nizārī commentary entitled *Ba'ḍī az ta'wīlāt-i gulshan-i rāz* has been edited with French translation by Corbin in his *Trilogie Ismaélienne*, text pp. 131–61, translation pp. 1–174.
13. See, for instance, Fidā'ī Khurāsānī, *Hidāyat al-mu'minīn*, pp. 113–16, and W. Ivanow's introduction to his edition of the *Chirāgh-nāma*, a Sufi poem preserved in the Nizārī community of Badakhshān, published in *Revue Iranienne d'Anthropologie*, 3 (1959), pp. 53–70, English summary pp. 13–17.
14. Berthels and Baqoev, *Alphabetic Catalogue*, pp. 63–4, 81–2. Nasafī's *Zubdat al-ḥaqā'iq* has been included in a collection of Ismaili works recovered and edited from Badakhshān under the title of *Panj risāla dar bayān-i āfāq va anfus*, ed. A. E. Berthels (Moscow, 1970), pp. 91–207.
15. Ḥaydar Āmulī, *Jāmi' al-asrār*, ed. H. Corbin and O. Yahya in a collection entitled *La Philosophie Shī'ite* (Tehran and Paris, 1969), pp. 47, 116–17, 216–17, 220–2, 238, 388, 611 ff. See also Corbin, *History of Islamic Philosophy*, pp. 332–5; S. H. Nasr, "Le Shī'isme et le Soufisme", in *Le Shī'isme Imāmite* (Paris, 1970), pp. 215–33, and his *Sufi Essays* (London, 1972), pp. 104–20.
16. Ibn Baṭṭūṭa, *The Travels of Ibn Baṭṭūṭa*, tr. H. A. R. Gibb and C. F. Beckingham (Cambridge, 1958–94), vol. 1, pp. 106–7, 108–9; Ibn Faḍl Allāh al-'Umarī, *Masālik al-abṣār*, pp. 77, 132–3; al-Qalqashandī, *Ṣubḥ*, vol. 4, pp. 146, 202, vol. 13, p. 245, and Charles Melville,

"Sometimes by the Sword, Sometimes by the Dagger: The Role of the Isma'ilis in Mamlūk–Mongol Relations in the 8th/14th Century", in Daftary, *Mediaeval Isma'ili History*, pp. 247–63.

17. Marshall G. S. Hodgson, *The Venture of Islam: Conscience and History in a World Civilization* (Chicago, 1974), vol. 2, pp. 493 ff.
18. Claude Cahen, "Le Problème du Shī'isme dans l'Asie Mineure Turque préottomane", in *Le Shī'isme Imāmite*, pp. 118 ff. See also M. Molé, "Les Kubrawiya entre Sunnisme et Shiisme aux huitième et neuvième siècles de l'hégire", *Revue d'Etudes Islamiques*, 29 (1961), pp. 61–142; S. Amir Arjomand, *The Shadow of God and the Hidden Imam* (Chicago, 1984), pp. 66–84, and Halm, *Shiism*, pp. 71–83.
19. Niẓām al-Dīn Shāmī, *Ẓafar-nāma*, ed. F. Tauer (Prague, 1937–56), vol. 1, p. 136, and Sharaf al-Dīn 'Alī Yazdī, *Ẓafar-nāma*, ed. A. Urunbayev (Tashkent, 1972), p. 500.
20. On Anjudān and its Nizārī antiquities, see W. Ivanow, "Tombs of Some Persian Ismaili Imams", *Journal of the Bombay Branch of the Royal Asiatic Society*, NS, 14 (1938), pp. 49–62, and F. Daftary, "Anjedān", EIR, vol. 2, p. 77.
21. In particular, see Khayrkhwāh, *Risāla*, in his *Taṣnīfāt*, pp. 1–75.
22. *Pandiyāt-i jawānmardī*, ed. and tr. W. Ivanow (Leiden, 1953). See also Ivanow, *Ismaili Literature*, pp. 139–40, and Poonawala, *Biobibliography*, p. 268.
23. *Pandiyāt-i jawānmardī*, text pp. 41 ff., 62 ff., translation pp. 25 ff., 39 ff.; Abū Isḥāq Quhistānī, *Haft bāb*, text pp. 49–50, 59, translation pp. 49–50, 59; Khayrkhwāh-i Harātī, *Kalām-i pīr*, ed. and tr. W. Ivanow (Bombay, 1935), text pp. 44, 76–7, 93–4, 101, 110, translation pp. 37, 72, 88, 97, 106, and his *Taṣnīfāt*, pp. 3, 23, 58, 113 ff.
24. For the best expression of these intellectual interests among the Badakhshānī Nizārīs of the early Anjudān period, see Sayyid Suhrāb Valī Badakhshānī, *Sī va shish ṣaḥīfa*, ed. H. Ujāqī (Tehran, 1961), a treatise written in 856/1452. See also F. Daftary, "Badakhshānī, Sayyid Suhrāb Valī", *The Persian Encyclopaedia of Islam*, B, Fascicule 7 (Tehran, 1996), p. 1132.
25. Abū Isḥāq Quhistānī, *Haft bāb*, text pp. 19–20, 37, 53, 58, 67, translation pp. 19–20, 37–8, 53–4, 58, 67–8; Khayrkhwāh, *Kalām-i pīr*, text pp. 46, 72–3, 86, 95–6, 100, 104, 107, 114–16, translation pp. 38–9, 67–9, 80, 91, 96, 100, 103, 111–12, and his *Taṣnīfāt*, pp. 18 ff.; see also Imām Qulī Khākī Khurāsānī, *Dīwān*, ed. W. Ivanow (Bombay, 1933), pp. 12, 14, 19, 33, 44–5, 49, 55, 56, 58, 61, 62, 64, 66, 68, 69, 75, 103, 106, 115–18, 124–5.
26. Abū Isḥāq Quhistānī, *Haft bāb*, text pp. 21–2, 48, translation pp. 20–1, 48; Khayrkhwāh, *Kalām-i pīr*, text pp. 48, 92, 106 ff., translation pp. 40–1, 86–7, 103ff.; also his *Taṣnīfāt*, pp. 2–3, 18, 22, 86, 89–90, 92–3, 116 ff., and his *Faṣl dar bayān-i shinākht-i imām*, ed. W. Ivanow (3rd edn, Tehran, 1960), pp. 6–7, 9, 11 ff., 29–31, 32–6; English trans. W. Ivanow, *On the Recognition of the Imam* (2nd edn, Bombay, 1947), pp. 22–3, 25–6, 28 ff., 45–6, 48–52; Badakhshānī, *Sī*, pp. 35, 62–3, 64, 66, and Khākī Khurāsānī, *Dīwān*, pp. 84–5.
27. See the following works of Khayrkhwāh: *Taṣnīfāt*, pp. 20, 26, 52, 77, 78, 82, 89–90, 100, 102, 116, 120, *Kalām-i pīr*, text pp. 58, 94, translation pp. 52, 88, and *Faṣl*, pp. 9, 11, 13, 21–2; tr. Ivanow, pp. 25–6, 28, 30, 36–7.
28. Arjomand, *Shadow of God*, pp. 109–21, 160–87, and K. Babayan,

"Sufis, Dervishes and Mullas: The Controversy over Spiritual and Temporal Domination in Seventeenth-Century Iran", in Charles Melville (ed.), *Safavid Persia* (London, 1996), pp. 117–38.

29. On Shāh Ṭāhir, see Muḥammad Qāsim Hindū Shāh Astarābādī, better known as Firishta, *Ta'rīkh-i Firishta*, ed. J. Briggs (Bombay, 1832), vol. 2, pp. 213–31; 'Alī b. 'Azīz Ṭabāṭabā, *Burhān-i ma'āthir* (Hyderabad, 1936), pp. 251–70, 274ff., 281ff., 291, 308, 314, 324–6, 338–9, 361, 381, 433, 448–50, 452–4, 502–3, 505, 525, 557, 584; al-Qāḍī Nūr Allāh al-Shūshtarī, *Majālis al-mu'minīn* (Tehran, 1375–6/1955–6), vol. 2, pp. 234–40; Ivanow, "A Forgotten Branch", pp. 57ff.; Ṣafā, *Ta'rīkh-i adabiyyāt*, vol. 5, part 2, pp. 662–70; Poonawala, *Biobibliography*, pp. 271–5, and his "Shāh Ṭāhir", EI2, vol. 9, pp. 200–1.
30. *Ta'rīkh-i alfī*, cited in Ṣ. Kiyā, *Nuqṭawiyān yā Pisīkhāniyān* (Tehran, 1320/1941), pp. 36–7, and Qāḍī Aḥmad al-Qummī, *Khulāṣat al-tawārīkh*, ed. I. Ishrāqī (Tehran, 1359–63/1980–4), vol. 1, pp. 582–4.
31. Arjomand, *Shadow of God*, pp. 71–4, 198–9; Ṣafā, *Ta'rīkh-i adabiyyāt*, vol. 4, pp. 61–6; A. Amanat, "The Nuqṭawī Movement of Maḥmūd Pisīkhānī and his Persian Cycle of Mystical-Materialism", in Daftary, *Mediaeval Isma'ili History*, pp. 281–97, and H. Algar, "Nuḳtawiyya", EI2, vol. 8, pp. 114–17.
32. Khākī Khurāsānī, *Dīwān*, pp. 9, 10, 12, 17, 19, 20ff., 31, 54, 66ff., 76, 95, 101, 104.
33. Ali S. Asani, "The Ismaili *Ginān*s as Devotional Literature", in R. S. McGregor (ed.), *Devotional Literature in South Asia* (Cambridge, 1992), pp. 101–12; his "The Isma'ili *Ginān*s: Reflections on Authority and Authorship", in Daftary, *Mediaeval Isma'ili History*, pp. 265–80, and C. Shackle and Z. Moir, *Ismaili Hymns from South Asia: An Introduction to the Ginans* (London, 1992), especially pp. 3–54. See also W. Madelung, "Khōdja", EI2, vol. 5, pp. 25–7.
34. The ginanic tradition on the commencement and early history of the Nizārī *da'wa* in the Indian subcontinent is analysed in A. Nanji, *The Nizārī Ismā'īlī Tradition in the Indo-Pakistan Subcontinent* (Delmar, NY, 1978), pp. 50–96; see also S. Mujtaba Ali, *The Origins of the Khojāhs and their Religious Life Today* (Würzburg, 1936), pp. 39–44; W. Ivanow, "Satpanth", in W. Ivanow (ed.), *Collectanea*, vol. 1 (Leiden, 1948), pp. 1–19; John N. Hollister, *The Shi'a of India* (London, 1953), pp. 339–62; S. C. Misra, *Muslim Communities in Gujarat* (Bombay, 1964), pp. 10–12, 54–65, and I. Poonawala, "Nūr Satgur", EI2, vol. 8, pp. 125–6.
35. Tazim R. Kassam, *Songs of Wisdom and Circles of Dance: Hymns of the Satpanth Ismā'īlī Muslim Saint, Pīr Shams* (Albany, NY, 1995), pp. 75–116; see also W. Ivanow, "Shums Tabrez of Multan", in S. M. Abdullah (ed.), *Professor Muḥammad Shafi' Presentation Volume* (Lahore, 1955), pp. 109–18, and I. Poonawala, "Pīr Shams or Shams al-Dīn", EI2, vol. 8, p. 307.
36. John A. Subhan, *Sufism, its Saints and Shrines* (revised edn, Lucknow, 1960), p. 359.
37. Ali S. Asani, *The Būjh Nirañjan: An Ismaili Mystical Poem* (Cambridge, Mass., 1991).
38. Nanji, *Nizārī Ismā'īlī Tradition*, pp. 139–41.
39. Khayrkhwāh, *Taṣnīfāt*, pp. 54, 60–1.

40. On this schism and the later history of the Imām-Shāhīs, also known as Satpanthīs and Momnas, see W. Ivanow, "The Sect of Imam Shah in Gujrat", *Journal of the Bombay Branch of the Royal Asiatic Society*, NS, 12 (1936), pp. 19–70, and A. A. A. Fyzee, "Imām Shāh", EI2, vol. 3, p. 1163.
41. Ivanow, "Satpanth", pp. 19–28, and Kassam, *Songs of Wisdom*, pp. 9–26, where the author sums up her personal impressions of modern Satpanth studies.
42. Kassam, *Songs of Wisdom*, pp. 62–74.
43. See the following works of Dominique-Sila Khan: "L'Origine Ismaélienne du culte Hindou de Ramdeo Pir", *Revue de l'Histoire des Religions*, 210 (1993), pp. 27–47; "The Kāmaḍ of Rajasthan – Priests of a Forgotten Tradition", JRAS (1996), pp. 29–68, and *Conversions and Shifting Identities: Ramdev Pir and the Ismailis in Rajasthan* (Delhi, 1997). See Also Françoise Mallison, "Hinduism as Seen by the Nizārī Ismā'īlī Missionaries of Western India: The Evidence of the Ginān", in G. D. Sontheimer and H. Kulke (eds), *Hinduism Reconsidered* (Delhi, 1989), pp. 93–103, and her "La Secte Ismaélienne des Nizārī ou Satpanthī en Inde: Hétérodoxie Hindoue ou Musulmane?", in S. Bouez (ed.), *Ascèse et Renoncement en Inde* (Paris, 1992), pp. 105–13.
44. For a wide selection of *ginān*s in English translation, see V. N. Hooda, "Some Specimens of Satpanth Literature", in W. Ivanow, *Collectanea*, vol. 1, pp. 55–137; Shackle and Moir, *Ismaili Hymns*, pp. 62–141, Kassam, *Songs of Wisdom*, pp. 163–370, and Asani, *Būjh Nirañjan*, pp. 120–92. The corpus of the *ginān* literature is comprised of some one thousand separate poems. For some listings of the *ginān*s, see Ivanow, *Ismaili Literature*, pp. 174–81; Poonawala, *Biobibliography*, pp. 298–311, and Ali S. Asani, *The Harvard Collection of Ismaili Literature in Indic Languages* (Boston, 1992).
45. Nanji, *Nizārī Ismā'īlī Tradition*, pp. 99–130, 144–5, and Gulshan Khakee, "The Dasa Avatāra of the Satpanthi Ismailis and Imam Shahis of Indo-Pakistan" (Ph.D. thesis, Harvard University, 1972).
46. This section is largely based on my *The Ismā'īlīs*, pp. 286–323, 663–9, where the relevant references are cited.
47. See Poonawala, *Biobibliography*, pp. 133–77.
48. These developments are narrated in the traditional Bohra histories, such as Muḥammad 'Alī b. Mullā Jīwābhā'ī, *Mawsim-i bahār* (Bombay, 1301–11/1884–93), vol. 3, pp. 117–27. See also Ḥasan 'Alī Ismā'īljī, Badrispresswala, *Akhbār al-du'āt al-akramīn* (Rajkot, 1937), pp. 61–6; Najm al-Ghanī Khān, *Madhāhib al-Islām* (Lucknow, 1924), pp. 316–17; Mulla Abdul Husain, *Gulzare Daudi, for the Bohras of India* (Ahmedabad, 1920), pp. 45–6, and Misra, *Muslim Communities*, pp. 22–3.
49. On this schism, see Muḥammad 'Alī, *Mawsim-i bahār*, vol. 3, pp. 169–259; Ismā'īljī, *Akhbār*, pp. 110–12, Najm al-Ghanī Khān, *Madhāhib*, pp. 312–14; Abdul Husain, *Gulzare Daudi*, p. 46; Misra, *Muslim Communities*, pp. 27–31, and A. A. Engineer, *The Bohras* (New Delhi, 1980), pp. 117–22.
50. Lists of the Dā'ūdī and Sulaymānī *dā'ī*s may be found in Abdul Husain, *Gulzare Daudi*, pp. 39–43; Hollister, *Shī'a of India*, pp. 266–7, 274–5; Poonawala, *Biobibliography*, pp. 364–9, and Daftary, *The Ismā'īlīs*, pp. 555–7.

51. Ismāʿīl b. ʿAbd al-Rasūl al-Majdūʿ, *Fihrirst al-kutub wa'l-rasā'il*, ed. ʿA. N. Munzavī (Tehran, 1966), pp. 108–9, 119; Muḥammad ʿAlī, *Mawsim-i bahār*, vol. 3, pp. 440–526; Misra, *Muslim Communities*, pp. 41–2; Ivanow, *Ismaili Literature*, pp. 93–4, and Poonawala, *Biobibliography*, pp. 13, 204–6.
52. For more details, see Engineer, *Bohras*, pp. 165–281, 303–23.
53. On the Ismailis of East Africa, see H. M. Amiji, "The Asian Communities", in J. Kritzeck and W. H. Lewis (eds), *Islam in Africa* (New York, 1969), pp. 141–81, and his "The Bohras of East Africa", *Journal of Religion in Africa*, 7 (1975), pp. 27–61; see also Robert G. Gregory, *India and East Africa* (Oxford, 1971), especially pp. 17–45, and N. King, "Toward a History of the Ismāʿīlīs in East Africa", in I. R al-Fārūqī (ed.), *Essays in Islamic and Comparative Studies* (Washington, DC, 1982), pp. 67–83.
54. Poonawala, *Biobibliography*, pp. 184–250.
55. Muḥammad Kāẓim Marwī, *ʿĀlamārā-yi Nādirī*, ed. N. D. Miklukho-Maklai (Moscow 1960–6), vol. 1, pp. 438, 549ff., and Aḥmad ʿAlī Khān Vazīrī, *Ta'rīkh-i Kirmān*, ed. M. I. Bāstānī Pārīzī (2nd edn, Tehran 1352/1973), p. 542.
56. A detailed account of this imam and his governorship is contained in Vazīrī, *Ta'rīkh*, pp. 543–65. Briefer references to the Imam Abu'l-Ḥasan ʿAlī, also known as Sayyid Abu'l-Ḥasan Kahakī, are found in a number of chronicles of the Zand and Qājār periods of Persian history; see, for instance, ʿAlī Riḍā b. ʿAbd al-Karīm Shīrāzī, *Ta'rīkh-i Zandiyya*, ed. E. Beer (Leiden, 1888), pp. 52–6; Riḍā Qulī Khān Hidāyat, *Rawḍat al-ṣafā-yi Nāṣirī* (Tehran, 1339/1960), vol. 9, pp. 250, 252, 255, and Muḥammad Ḥasan Khān Iʿtimād al-Salṭana, *Ta'rīkh-i muntaẓam-i Nāṣirī* (Tehran, 1298–1300/1881–3), vol. 3, pp. 53–4.
57. Vazīrī, *Ta'rīkh*, pp. 556–60; Muḥammad Maʿṣūm Shīrāzī, Maʿṣūm ʿAlī Shāh, *Ṭarā'iq al-ḥaqā'iq*, ed. M. J. Maḥjūb (Tehran, 1339–45/1960–6), vol. 3, pp. 170–92, and N. Pourjavady and P. L. Wilson, "Ismāʿīlīs and Niʿmatullāhīs", *Studia Islamica*, 41 (1975), pp. 113–35.
58. Maʿṣūm ʿAlī Shāh, *Ṭarā'iq*, vol. 3, pp. 190, 209, 263–4, 328, 399, 413, 434, 445–6, 528, 561; his *Tuḥfat al-ḥaramayn* (Bombay, 1306/1889), pp. 292–8; M. Humāyūnī, *Ta'rīkh-i silsilihā-yi Niʿmat Allāhiyya* (Tehran, 1358/1979), pp. 194, 259, 267–70, 277–9, 285–7, 289, and Daftary, *The Ismāʿīlīs*, pp. 503–4, 506–7, 517–18.
59. On Ḥasan ʿAlī Shāh, Āghā Khān I, see his autobiography entitled *ʿIbrat-afzā* (Bombay, 1278/1862); ed. Ḥ. Kūhī Kirmānī (Tehran, 1325/1946), containing the events of his youth and disputes with the Persian government; see also Fidā'ī Khurāsānī, *Hidāyat al-mu'minīn*, pp. 146–76; N. M. Dumasia, *A Brief History of the Aga Khan* (Bombay, 1903), pp. 66–95; also his *The Aga Khan and his Ancestors* (Bombay, 1939), pp. 25–59; H. Algar, "Maḥallātī, Āghā Khān", EI2, vol. 5, pp. 1221–2, and Daftary, *The Ismāʿīlīs*, pp. 504–16, 717–20, where references to the sources and studies are cited.
60. For details, see Āghā Khān I's *ʿIbrat-afzā*, Bombay, pp. 8–49; Tehran, pp. 9–56. See also Hidāyat, *Rawḍat al-ṣafā*, vol. 10, pp. 169, 249–53, 259–61; Muḥammad Taqī Lisān al-Mulk Sipihr, *Nāsikh al-tawārīkh: Ta'rīkh-i Qājāriyya*, ed. M. B. Bihbūdī (Tehran, 1344/1965), vol. 2, pp. 248, 334–5, 350–6, 358–60, 364; Iʿtimād al-Salṭana, *Ta'rīkh-i muntaẓam*, vol. 3, pp. 165, 167, 173–4, 175–6, 177; Vazīrī,

Ta'rīkh, pp. 602–4, 608–13, and H. Algar, "The Revolt of Āghā Khān Maḥallātī and the Transference of the Ismā'īlī Imamate to India", *Studia Islamica*, 29 (1969), pp. 61–81.

61. Āghā Khān, *'Ibrat-afzā*, Bombay, pp. 52ff.; Tehran, pp. 59ff., and the following works of William F. P. Napier: *The Conquest of Scinde* (London, 1845), vol. 2, pp. 369, 372, 404–5; *History of General Sir Charles Napier's Administration of Scinde* (London, 1851), pp. 75–6, and *The Life and Opinions of General Sir Charles James Napier* (London, 1857), vol. 2, p. 342, and vol. 3, pp. 45, 127. See also H. T. Lambrick, *Sir Charles Napier and Sind* (Oxford, 1952), pp. 157ff., and Priscilla Napier, *I have Sind: Charles Napier in India, 1841–1844* (Salisbury, Wiltshire, 1990), pp. 155–6, 177, 239, 242, 259–60.
62. Asaf A. A. Fyzee, *Cases in the Muhammadan Law of India and Pakistan* (Oxford, 1965), pp. 504–49.
63. For lists of the Nizārī Ismaili imams, see Poonawala, *Biobibliography*, pp. 371–3, and Daftary, *The Ismā'īlīs*, pp. 553–4.
64. Ivanow, *Ismaili Literature*, pp. 149–50, Poonawala, *Biobibliography*, pp. 283–4, and Daftary, "Shihāb al-Dīn al-Ḥusaynī", EI2, vol. 9, p. 435.
65. Aga Khan III has left a valuable account of his life, career, and aspirations in his memoirs entitled *The Memoirs of Aga Khan: World Enough and Time* (London, 1954). Amongst the biographies of this imam mention may be made of Dumasia, *The Aga Khan*, pp. 62–338; Sirdar Ikbal Ali Shah, *The Prince Aga Khan: An Authentic Life Story* (London, 1933); S. Jackson, *The Aga Khan* (London, 1952); H. J. Greenwall, *His Highness the Aga Khan: Imam of the Ismailis* (London, 1952), and W. Frischauer, *The Aga Khans* (London, 1970).
66. Aga Khan, Sulṭān Muḥammad Shāh, *India in Transition: A Study in Political Evolution* (Bombay, 1918).
67. See J. D. Anderson, "The Isma'ili Khojas of East Africa: A New Constitution and Personal Law for the Community", *Middle Eastern Studies*, 1 (1964), pp. 21–39; Daftary, *The Ismā'īlīs*, pp. 523–30, and Biancamaria Scarcia Amoretti, "Controcorrente? Caso della comunità Khogia di Zanzibar", *Oriente Moderno*, NS, 14 (1995), pp. 153–70.
68. Numerous collections of Aga Khan III's *farmān*s exist in the Institute of Ismaili Studies Library, London, and elsewhere in the Nizārī Ismaili community. See, for instance, *Kalām-i Imām-i Mubīn*: *Holy Firmans of Mowlana Hazar Imam Sultan Mahomed Shah the Aga Khan* (Bombay, 1950); Sherali Alidina and Kassim Ali, comp., *Precious Pearls: Firman Mubarak of Hazar Imam Mowlana Sultan Mahomed Shah* (Karachi, 1954), and A. K. Adatia and N. Q. King, "Some East African Firmans of H. H. Aga Khan III", *Journal of Religion in Africa*, 2 (1969), pp. 179–91. See also Aga Khan III, *Selected Speeches and Writings of Sir Sultan Muhammad Shah*, ed. K. K. Aziz (London, 1998), 2 vols.
69. For further details on Aga Khan III's reforms and modernisation philosophy, see his *Memoirs*, pp. 169–91; A. Nanji, "Modernization and Change in the Nizārī Ismaili Community in East Africa – A Perspective", *Journal of Religion in Africa*, 6 (1974), pp. 123–39; M. Boivin, "The Reform of Islam in Ismaili Shī'ism from 1885 to 1957", in F. N. Delvoye (ed.), *Confluence of Cultures* (New Delhi,

1994), pp. 121–39, and his "Shiʿisme Ismaélien et modernité chez Sultan Muhammad Shah Aga Khan (1877–1957)" (doctoral thesis, Université de la Sorbonne Nouvelle, Paris III, 1993), 3 vols.

70. See Tāmir, "Furūʿ al-shajara", pp. 590–3, 597–8; M. Ghaleb, *The Ismailis of Syria* (Beirut, 1970), pp. 149–72; Norman N. Lewis, "The Ismaʿilis of Syria Today", *Royal Central Asian Journal*, 39 (1952), pp. 69–77; also his *Nomads and Settlers in Syria and Jordan, 1800–1980* (Cambridge, 1987), pp. 58–67, and Dick Douwes and N. N. Lewis, "The Trials of Syrian Ismaʿilis in the First Decade of the 20th Century", IJMES, 21 (1989), pp. 215–32.

71. On the conditions of the Persian Ismailis in modern times, see W. Ivanow, "Ismailitica", *Memoirs of the Asiatic Society of Bengal*, 8 (1922), pp. 50–8; Daftary, *The Ismāʿīlīs*, pp. 534–44; Maryam Moezzi, "Ismāʿīliyān-i Īrān" (master's thesis, Dānishgāh-i Firdawsī, Mashhad, 1372/1993); Rafique H. Keshavjee, "The Quest for Gnosis and the Call of History: Modernization among the Ismailis of Iran" (Ph.D. thesis, Harvard University, 1981), and his *Mysticism and the Plurality of Meaning: The Case of the Ismailis of Rural Iran* (London, 1998).

72. Aga Khan, *Memoirs*, p. 183; A. Nanji, "Sabz ʿAlī", EI2, vol. 8, p. 694, and Y. Bregel, "Central Asia: vii. In the 12th–13th/18th–19th Centuries", EIR, vol. 5, pp. 193–205.

73. Qudrat Allāh Beg, *Ta'rīkh-i ʿahd-i ʿatīq-i riyāsat-i Hunza* (Baltit, 1980), vol. 1, pp. 140–1, 173–8, 304–5, and W. Holzwarth, *Die Ismailiten in Nordpakistan* (Berlin, 1994), especially pp. 19–78.

74. Qudrat Allāh Beg, *Ta'rīkh*, pp. 332–6, 362–5.

75. A full account of Aga Khan IV's modernisation policies and achievements remains to be written. Much relevant information may be found in the imam's *farmāns*, and speeches delivered over the years on a number of special occasions, as well as in a variety of publications by different institutions within the Aga Khan Development Network. For some overviews, see Frischauer, *The Aga Khans*, pp. 206–72; A. Thobani, *Islam's Quiet Revolutionary: The Story of Aga Khan IV* (New York, 1993), and Paul J. Kaiser, *Culture, Transnationalism, and Civil Society: Aga Khan Social Service Initiatives in Tanzania* (Westport, Connecticut, 1996).

Glossary

Listings in the glossary are selected terms and names appearing frequently in the text. The meanings given often refer to the technical and religious senses of the words as adopted especially by the Ismailis. The abbreviated forms "pl." and "lit." mean "plural" and "literally", respectively.

adhān: Muslim call to prayer. There are slight differences between the Sunni and Shīʿī calls to prayer made five times a day.

ahl al-bayt: lit., people of the house; members of the household of the Prophet Muḥammad, including especially, besides the Prophet, ʿAlī, Fāṭima, al-Ḥasan, al-Ḥusayn, and their progeny.

ʿAlids: descendants of ʿAlī b. Abī Ṭālib, cousin and son-in-law of the Prophet and also the first Shīʿī imam. Descendants of ʿAlī and Fāṭima, the Prophet's daughter, through their sons al-Ḥasan and al-Ḥusayn are also called Ḥasanids and Ḥusaynids, comprising the Fatimid ʿAlids.

ʿālim (pl., *ʿulamāʾ*): a scholar in Islamic religious sciences.

amīr (pl., *umarāʾ*): commander, prince; also the title used by many independent rulers.

amr: the divine command or volition.

ʿaql: intellect, reason.

ʿawāmm (or *ʿāmma*): the common people, in distinction from the *khawāṣṣ* (q.v.).

bāb: lit., gate; the Ismaili religious term for the administrative head of the *daʿwa* (q.v.); in the Fatimid *daʿwa* hierarchy, the highest rank after imam; the equivalent of the term *dāʿī al-duʿāt* (q.v.) mentioned mainly in non-Ismaili sources.

Banū Hāshim: *see* Hāshimids.

bāṭin: the inward, hidden, or esoteric meaning behind the literal wording of sacred texts and religious prescriptions, notably the Qur'an and the *sharīʿa* (q.v.), in distinction from the *ẓāhir* (q.v.).

dāʿī (pl., *duʿāt*): lit., summoner; a religious missionary or propagandist, especially among the Ismailis; a high rank in the *daʿwa* (q.v.) hierarchy of the Ismailis.

dāʿī al-duʿāt: chief *dāʿī*; the administrative head of the *daʿwa* (q.v.); *see bāb*.

dāʿī muṭlaq: *dāʿī* with absolute authority; highest rank in the Ṭayyibī Mustaʿlī *daʿwa* (q.v.); also the chief *dāʿī* (q.v.) acting as the administrative head of the (Dāʾūdī and Sulaymānī) Ṭayyibī *daʿwa* organisation.

daʿwa: mission; in the religio-political sense, *daʿwa* is the invitation or call to adopt the cause of an individual or family claiming the right to the imamate; it also refers to the hierarchy of ranks, sometimes called *ḥudūd*, within the particular religious organisation developed for this purpose, especially among the Ismailis.

dawla: state, dynasty.

dawr: era, cycle of history; the Ismailis held that the religious history of mankind proceeded through seven *dawr*s, each one initiated by a speaker or *nāṭiq* (q.v.).

faqīh (pl., *fuqahā'*): an exponent of *fiqh* or Islamic jurisprudence; a Muslim jurist in general.

Fatimids: descendants of ʿAlī b. Abī Ṭālib and Fāṭima, the Prophet's daughter, corresponding to Ḥasanid and Ḥusaynid ʿAlids (q.v.); also the name of the Ismaili dynasty of caliph-imams from 297/909 to 567/1171.

fidā'ī (or *fidāwī*): one who offers his life for a cause; a term used particularly for the special Nizārī Ismaili devotees of the Alamūt period who risked their lives in the service of their community.

fuqahā': *see faqīh*.

ghulāt (pl. of *ghālī*): exaggerators, extremists; a term of disapproval for individuals accused of exaggeration in religion and in respect to the imams. Criteria for defining "exaggeration" changed over time, but almost all early Shīʿī groups had their *ghulāt* activists.

ginān: a general term, derived from a Sanskrit word meaning contemplative or sacred knowledge, used in reference to the indigenous religious literatures of the Nizārī Khojas and some other communities of South Asia. Composed in a number of Indic languages, the hymn-like *ginān*s are recorded mainly in the Khojkī script.

ḥadīth: a report, sometimes translated as Tradition, relating an action or saying of the Prophet. For the Shīʿī communities, it also refers to the actions and sayings of their imams. Muslims regard *ḥadīth* as a source of Islamic law, second in importance only to the Qur'an.

ḥaqā'iq (pl. of *ḥaqīqa*): truths; as a technical term the *ḥaqā'iq* are the unchangeable truths contained in the *bāṭin* (q.v.); it also refers to the Ismaili gnostic system of thought.

Hāshimids: descendants of the Prophet's ancestor Hāshim b. ʿAbd Manāf, the eponym of Banū Hāshim. The chief Hāshimid branches were the ʿAlids (q.v.) and the ʿAbbasids, descendants of the Prophet's uncle al-ʿAbbās.

ḥujja: proof or the presentation of proof. The application of the term, in the sense of the proof of God's presence on earth, was systematised by the Imāmī Shīʿīs to designate the category of prophets and imams. The *ḥujja* was also a high rank in the Fatimid *daʿwa* (q.v.) hierarchy; in theory there were twelve such *ḥujja*s, each one in charge of a separate *daʿwa* region called *jazīra* (lit., island). For the Nizārī Ismailis, the term generally denoted the chief representative of the imam.

ilḥād: deviation from the right religious path; heresy in religion. A person accused of *ilḥād* is called *mulḥid* (pl., *malāḥida*).

ʿilm: religious knowledge. The Shīʿa held that every imam possessed a special knowledge, *ʿilm*, which was divinely inspired and transmitted through the *naṣṣ* (q.v.) of the previous imam.

iqṭāʿ: an administrative grant of land or of its revenue to an individual, in recompense for service.

jamāʿat-khāna: lit., community house; congregation place, with a special prayer hall, used by Nizārī Ismailis for their religious, communal and cultural activities.

kalima: the divine word, logos.

kashf: manifestation, unveiling; in Ismaili thought, it was used in reference to a period, called *dawr al-kashf*, when the imams were manifest, or when the *ḥaqā'iq* (q.v.) would no longer be hidden in the *bāṭin* (q.v.), in distinction from *satr* (q.v.).

khawāṣṣ (or *khāṣṣa*): the elite, the privileged people, in distinction from the *ʿawāmm* (q.v.).

khuṭba: an address or sermon delivered at the Friday midday public prayers in the mosque; since it includes a prayer for the acknowledged ruler, mention in the *khuṭba* is a mark of sovereignty in Islam.

madhhab: a system or school of religious law in Islam.

ma'dhūn: lit., licentiate, a rank in the Ismaili *da'wa* (q.v.) hierarchy following that of *dā'ī* (q.v.); also used generically in reference to the assistant of the *dā'ī*.

Mahdi: the rightly guided one; a name applied to the restorer of religion and justice who will appear and rule before the end of the world. A figure of profound eschatological significance in Islam; belief in the coming of the Mahdi from the Prophet's household, *ahl al-bayt* (q.v.), became a central aspect of early Shī'ī teachings. In Shī'ī usage, the Mahdi was commonly given the epithet of the *qā'im* (q.v.), 'riser', denoting a member of the *ahl al-bayt* who would rise and restore true Islam and justice on earth. In Twelver and Ismaili usage, the term *qā'im* widely replaced that of Mahdi.

muḥtasham: a title used during the Alamūt period in reference to the chief or governor of the Nizārī Ismailis in Quhistān, eastern Persia.

murīd: disciple; specifically, disciple of a Sufi master; member of a Sufi order in general; also used in reference to the ordinary Nizārī Ismailis in Persia and elsewhere during the post-Alamūt period.

mustajīb: lit., respondent; a term denoting an ordinary Ismaili initiate.

nafs: soul.

naṣṣ: explicit designation by an imam of his successor, under divine guidance.

nāṭiq (pl., *nuṭaqā'*): speaker; in early Ismaili thought, a speaking or law-announcing prophet who brings a new religious law (*sharī'a*), abrogating the previous law and initiating a new era, *dawr* (q.v.), in the religious history of mankind.

pīr: the Persian equivalent of the Arabic word *shaykh* in the sense of a spiritual guide or Sufi master, qualified to lead disciples, *murīd*s (q.v.), on the mystical path, *ṭarīqa* (q.v.), to truth (*ḥaqīqa*); also used in reference to the Nizārī imam and the holders of the highest ranks in the *da'wa* (q.v.) hierarchy of the Nizārī Ismailis of the post-Alamūt period.

qāḍī (pl., *quḍāt*): a religious judge administering Islamic law.

qāḍī al-quḍāt: chief *qāḍī*; the highest judiciary officer of the Fatimid state.

qā'im: 'riser'; the eschatological Mahdi (q.v.).

qiyāma: resurrection and the Last Day, when mankind would be judged and committed forever to either Paradise or Hell. In Ismaili thought, it was also used in reference to the end of any partial cycle in the history of mankind. The Nizārī Ismailis of the Alamūt period interpreted the *qiyāma* esoterically as the manifestation of the unveiled truth (*ḥaqīqa*) in the spiritual reality of the current imam, who was also called the *qā'im* (q.v.) of the *qiyāma*.

satr: concealment, veiling; in Ismaili thought, it was used in reference to a period, called *dawr al-satr*, when the imams were hidden from the eyes of their followers, or when the *ḥaqā'iq* (q.v.) were concealed in the *bāṭin* (q.v.), in distinction from *kashf* (q.v.).

sharī'a: the sacred law of Islam.

Sufi: an exponent of Sufism (*taṣawwuf*); the commonest term for that aspect of Islam that is based on the mystical life; hence, it denotes a Muslim mystic.

ta'līm: teaching, instruction; in Shī'ī thought, authoritative teaching in religion which could be carried out only by an imam in every age after the Prophet.

taqiyya: precautionary dissimulation of one's true religious beliefs, especially in time of danger; used especially by the Twelver (Ithnāʿasharī) and Ismaili Shīʿīs.

ṭarīqa: path; the mystical, spiritual path followed by Sufis; also any one of the organised Sufi orders. It is also used by Nizārī Ismailis of today in reference to their interpretation of Islam.

ta'wīl: the educing of the inner, original meaning from the literal wording or apparent meaning of a text or a ritual religious prescription; as a technical term among the Shīʿa, particularly the Ismailis, it denotes the method of educing the *bāṭin* (q.v.) from the *ẓāhir* (q.v.). It was used extensively by the Ismailis for the symbolic or esoteric interpretation of the Qur'an and the *sharīʿa* (q.v.). Translated also as hermeneutic or spiritual exegesis, *ta'wīl* may be distinguished from *tafsīr*, the external or philological exegesis of the Qur'an.

ʿulamā': *see ʿālim.*

umma: any people as followers of a particular religion or prophet; in particular, the Muslims as forming a single religious community.

vizier: see *wazīr*.

waṣī (pl., *awṣiyā'*): legatee; also the immediate successor to a prophet; in this sense, it was the function of *awṣiyā'* to explain and interpret the messages brought by prophets.

wazīr: a high officer of state, usually a civilian. The power and status of the office varied greatly in different periods and under different Muslim dynasties.

ẓāhir: the outward, literal, or exoteric meaning of sacred texts and religious prescriptions, notably the Qur'an and the *sharīʿa* (q.v.), in distinction from the *bāṭin* (q.v.).

Select Bibliography

The bibliography includes some basic works of reference and a selection of published sources and studies. The abbreviations used in the bibliography are the same as those used in the notes to the individual chapters. See Note on Transliteration, Dates and Abbreviations for a list of these abbreviations.

Abū Isḥāq Quhistānī. *Haft bāb*, ed. and English tr. W. Ivanow. Bombay, 1959

Abu-Izzeddin, Nejla M. *The Druzes: A New Study of their History, Faith and Society*. Leiden, 1993

Abū Shāma, Shihāb al-Dīn b. Ismā'īl. *Kitāb al-rawḍatayn fī akhbār al-dawlatayn*. Cairo, 1287–8/1870–1

Aga Khan, Sulṭān Muḥammad Shāh. *The Memoirs of Aga Khan: World Enough and Time*. London, 1954. French trans. J. Fillion, *Mémoires*. Paris, 1955

Algar, Hamid. "The Revolt of Āghā Khān Maḥallātī and the Transference of the Ismā'īlī Imamate to India", *Studia Islamica*, 29 (1969), pp. 55–81

Ali, S. Mujtaba. *The Origins of the Khojāhs and their Religious Life Today*. Würzburg, 1936

Amiji, Hatim M. "The Asian Communities", in J. Kritzeck and W. H. Lewis (eds), *Islam in Africa*. New York, 1969, pp. 141–81

al-Āmir bi-Aḥkām Allāh, Abū 'Alī al-Manṣūr. *al-Hidāya al-Āmiriyya*, ed. Asaf A. A. Fyzee. Bombay, etc., 1938, reprinted in al-Shayyāl (ed.), *Majmū'at al-wathā'iq*, pp. 203–30

'Arīb b. Sa'd al-Qurṭubī. *Ṣilat ta'rīkh al-Ṭabarī*, ed. M. J. de Goeje. Leiden, 1897

Arjomand, Said Amir. *The Shadow of God and the Hidden Imam*. Chicago, 1984

Asani, Ali S. "The Ginān Literature of the Ismailis of Indo-Pakistan: Its Origins, Characteristics and Themes", in D. L. Eck and F. Mallison (eds), *Devotion Divine: Bhakti Traditions from the Regions of India*. Groningen and Paris, 1991, pp. 1–18

Asani, Ali S. "The Ismaili *Gināns* as Devotional Literature", in R. S. McGregor (ed.), *Devotional Literature in South Asia*. Cambridge, 1992, pp. 101–12

Asani, Ali S. "The Isma'ili *Gināns*: Reflections on Authority and Authorship", in Daftary (ed.), *Mediaeval Isma'ili History*, pp. 265–80

Badakhshānī, Sayyid Suhrāb Valī. *Sī va shish ṣaḥīfa*, ed. H. Ujāqī. Tehran, 1961

Badakhshī, Mīrzā Sang Muḥammad and Surkh Afsar, Mīrzā Faḍl 'Alī Beg. *Ta'rīkh-i Badakhshān*, ed. A. N. Boldyrev. Leningrad, 1959; ed. M. Sutūda. Tehran, 1367/1988

al-Baghdādī, Abū Manṣūr 'Abd al-Qāhir b. Ṭāhir. *al-Farq bayn al-firaq*, ed. M. Badr. Cairo, 1328/1910. English trans. under the title *Moslem Schisms and Sects*, part I, tr. K. C. Seelye. New York, 1919; part II, tr. A. S. Halkin. Tel Aviv, 1935

Baiburdi, Chengiz G. *Zhizn i tvorchestvo Nizārī-Persidskogo poeta*. Moscow, 1966. Persian trans. M. Ṣadrī, *Zindigī va āthār-i Nizārī*. Tehran, 1370/1991

Barthold, Vasilii V. *Turkestan down to the Mongol Invasion*, ed. C. E. Bosworth. 3rd edn, London, 1968

Berchem, Max van. "Epigraphie des Assassins de Syrie", *Journal Asiatique*, 9 série, 9 (1897), pp. 453–501, reprinted in his *Opera Minora*. Geneva, 1978, vol. 1, pp. 453–501

Berthels, Andrei E. *Nasir-i Khosrov i ismailizm*. Moscow, 1959. Persian trans. Y. Āriyanpūr, *Nāṣir Khusraw va Ismāʿīliyān*. Tehran, 1346/1967

Berthels, Andrei and Baqoev, M. *Alphabetic Catalogue of Manuscripts Found by 1959–1963 Expedition in Gorno-Badakhshan Autonomous Region*, ed. B. G. Gafurov and A. M. Mirzoev. Moscow, 1967

Bianquis, Thierry. "La Prise du pouvoir par les Fatimides en Egypte (357–363/968–974)", *Annales Islamologiques*, 11 (1972), pp. 49–108

Bianquis, Thierry. *Damas et la Syrie sous la domination Fatimide, 359–468/969–1076*. Damascus, 1986–9

Bosworth, C. Edmund. *The History of the Saffarids of Sistan and the Maliks of Nimruz (247/861 to 949/1542–3)*. Costa Mesa, Calif., and New York, 1994

Bosworth, C. Edmund. *The New Islamic Dynasties: A Chronological and Genealogical Manual*. Edinburgh, 1996

Bosworth, C. Edmund. "The Ismaʿilis of Quhistān and the Maliks of Nīmrūz or Sīstān", in Daftary (ed.), *Mediaeval Ismaʿili History*, pp. 221–9

Brett, Michael. "The Realm of the Imām, the Fāṭimids in the Tenth Century", BSOAS, 59 (1996), pp. 431–49

Bryer, David R. W. "The Origins of the Druze Religion", *Der Islam*, 52 (1975), pp. 47–84, 239–62, and 53 (1976), pp. 5–27

The Cambridge History of Iran: Volume 4, *The Period from the Arab Invasion to the Saljuqs*, ed. R. N. Frye. Cambridge, 1975

The Cambridge History of Iran: Volume 5, *The Saljuq and Mongol Periods*, ed. J. A. Boyle. Cambridge, 1968

Canard, Marius. *Miscellanea Orientalia*. London, 1973

Canard, Marius. "Fāṭimids", EI2, vol. 2, pp. 850–62

Corbin, Henry. "Rituel Sabéen et exégèse Ismaélienne du rituel", *Eranos Jahrbuch*, 19 (1950), pp. 181–246. English trans. in H. Corbin, *Temple and Contemplation*, tr. P. Sherrard. London, 1986, pp. 132–82

Corbin, Henry (ed. and tr.) *Trilogie Ismaélienne*. Tehran and Paris, 1961

Corbin, Henry. "Herméneutique spirituelle comparée: I. Swedenborg. II. Gnose Ismaélienne", *Eranos Jahrbuch*, 33 (1964), pp. 71–176, reprinted in H. Corbin, *Face de Dieu, face de l'homme*. Paris, 1983, pp. 41–162. English trans. in H. Corbin, *Swedenborg and Esoteric Islam*, tr. L. Fox. West Chester, PA, 1995, pp. 35–149

Corbin, Henry. "L'Initiation Ismaélienne ou l'ésotérisme et le Verbe", *Eranos Jahrbuch*, 39 (1970), pp. 41–142, reprinted in H. Corbin, *L'Homme et son ange*. Paris, 1983, pp. 81–205

Corbin, Henry. "Nāṣir-i Khusrau and Iranian Ismāʿīlism", in *The Cambridge History of Iran*: Volume 4, pp. 520–42, 689–90

Corbin, Henry. *Cyclical Time and Ismaili Gnosis*, tr. R. Manheim and J. W. Morris. London, 1983

Corbin, Henry. *History of Islamic Philosophy*, tr. L. Sherrard. London, 1993

Dabashi, Hamid. "The Philosopher/Vizier: Khwāja Naṣīr al-Dīn al-Ṭūsī and the Ismaʿilis", in Daftary (ed.), *Mediaeval Ismaʿili History*, pp. 231–45

Dachraoui, Farhat. *Le Califat Fatimide au Maghreb, 296–365 H./909–975 Jc.* Tunis, 1981

Daftary, Farhad. *The Ismāʿīlīs: Their History and Doctrines*. Cambridge, 1990. Persian trans. F. Badra'ī, *Ta'rīkh va ʿaqā'id-i Ismāʿīliyya*. Tehran, 1375/1996

Daftary, Farhad. "The Earliest Ismāʿīlīs", *Arabica*, 38 (1991), pp. 214–45

Daftary, Farhad. "Persian Historiography of the Early Nizārī Ismāʿīlīs", *Iran, Journal of the British Institute of Persian Studies*, 30 (1992), pp. 91–7

Daftary, Farhad. "A Major Schism in the Early Ismāʿīlī Movement", *Studia Islamica*, 77 (1993), pp. 123–39

Daftary, Farhad. *The Assassin Legends: Myths of the Ismaʿilis*. London, 1994. Persian trans. F. Badra'ī, *Afsānihā-yi ḥashāshīn*. Tehran, 1376/1997

Daftary, Farhad (ed.). *Mediaeval Ismaʿili History and Thought*. Cambridge, 1996

Daftary, Farhad. "Ḥasan-i Ṣabbāḥ and the Origins of the Nizārī Ismaʿili Movement", in his *Mediaeval Ismaʿili History*, pp. 181–204

Daftary, Farhad. "Diversity in Islam: Communities of Interpretation", in Azim A. Nanji (ed.), *The Muslim Almanac*. Detroit, 1996, pp. 161–73

Daftary, Farhad. "Sayyida Ḥurra: The Ismāʿīlī Ṣulayḥid Queen of Yemen", in Gavin R. G. Hambly (ed.), *Women in the Medieval Islamic World*. New York, 1998, pp. 117–30

Daftary, Farhad. "Carmatians", EIR, vol. 4, pp. 823–32

Daftary, Farhad. "Dāʿī", EIR, vol. 6, pp. 590–3

Dumasia, Naoroji M. *The Aga Khan and his Ancestors*. Bombay, 1939

Encyclopaedia Iranica, ed. E. Yarshater. London, 1982–

The Encyclopaedia of Islam, ed. H. A. R. Gibb et al. New edn, Leiden and London, 1960–

Fidā'ī Khurāsānī, Muḥammad b. Zayn al-ʿĀbidīn. *Kitāb-i hidāyat al-mu'minīn al-ṭālibīn*, ed. A. A. Semenov. Moscow, 1959; reprinted, Tehran, 1362/1983

Filippani-Ronconi, Pio. *Ismaeliti ed 'Assassini'*. Milan, 1973

Frischauer, Willi. *The Aga Khans*. London, 1970

Fyzee, Asaf A. A. "Qadi an-Nuʿman: The Fatimid Jurist and Author", JRAS (1934), pp. 1–32

Fyzee, Asaf A. A. *Compendium of Fatimid Law*. Simla, 1969

Fyzee, Asaf A. A. "Bohorās", EI2, vol. 1, pp. 1254–5

Gacek, Adam. *Catalogue of Arabic Manuscripts in the Library of the Institute of Ismaili Studies*. London, 1984–5

Guyard, Stanislas. "Un Grand maître des Assassins au temps de Saladin", *Journal Asiatique*, 7 série, 9 (1877), pp. 324–489

Haft bāb-i Bābā Sayyidnā, ed. W. Ivanow, in his *Two Early Ismaili Treatises*. Bombay, 1933, pp. 4–44. English trans. Hodgson, in his *Order of Assassins*, pp. 279–324

Halm, Heinz. *Kosmologie und Heilslehre der frühen Ismāʿīlīya: Eine Studie zur islamischen Gnosis*. Wiesbaden, 1978

Halm, Heinz. "Die Söhne Zikrawaihs und das erste fatimidische Kalifat (290/903)", WO, 10 (1979), pp. 30–53

Halm, Heinz. "Les Fatimides à Salamya", *Revue des Etudes Islamiques*, 54 (1986), pp. 133–49

Halm, Heinz. *Shiism*, tr. J. Watson. Edinburgh, 1991

Halm, Heinz. *The Empire of the Mahdi: The Rise of the Fatimids*, tr. M. Bonner. Leiden, 1996

Halm, Heinz. "The Cosmology of the Pre-Fatimid Ismāʿīliyya", in Daftary (ed.), *Mediaeval Ismaʿili History*, pp. 75–83

Halm, Heinz. "The Isma'ili Oath of Allegiance (*'ahd*) and the 'Sessions of Wisdom' (*majālis al-ḥikma*) in Fatimid Times", in Daftary (ed.), *Mediaeval Isma'ili History*, pp. 91–115
Halm, Heinz. *The Fatimids and their Traditions of Learning*. London, 1997
Halm, Heinz. "Bāṭenīya", EIR, vol. 3, pp. 861–3
Hamdani, Abbas. "The Dā'ī Ḥātim Ibn Ibrāhīm al-Ḥāmidī (d. 596H/1199AD) and his Book *Tuḥfat al-Qulūb*", *Oriens*, 23–4 (1970–1), pp. 258–300
Hamdani, Abbas. "Evolution of the Organisational Structure of the Fāṭimī Da'wah", *Arabian Studies*, 3 (1976), pp. 85–114
Hamdani, Abbas. "The Ṭayyibī-Fāṭimid Community of the Yaman at the Time of the Ayyūbid Conquest of Southern Arabia", *Arabian Studies*, 7 (1985), pp. 151–60
Hamdani, Abbas. "Faṭimid History and Historians", in M. J. L. Young et al. (eds), *Religion, Learning and Science in the 'Abbasid Period*. Cambridge, 1990, pp. 234–47, 535–6
Hamdani, Abbas and de Blois, F. "A Re-Examination of al-Mahdī's Letter to the Yemenites on the Genealogy of the Fatimid Caliphs", JRAS (1983), pp. 173–207
al-Hamdānī, Ḥusayn F. *al-Ṣulayḥiyyūn wa'l-ḥaraka al-Fāṭimiyya fi'l-Yaman*. Cairo, 1955
al-Hamdānī, Ḥusayn F. *On the Genealogy of Fatimid Caliphs*. Cairo, 1958
al-Ḥāmidī, Ibrāhīm b. al-Ḥusayn. *Kitāb kanz al-walad*, ed. M. Ghālib. Wiesbaden, 1971
Hillenbrand, Carole. "The Power Struggle between the Saljuqs and the Isma'ilis of Alamūt, 487–518/1094–1124: The Saljuq Perspective", in Daftary (ed.), *Mediaeval Isma'ili History*, pp. 205–20
Hodgson, Marshall G. S. *The Order of Assassins: The Struggle of the Early Nizārī Ismā'īlīs against the Islamic World*. The Hague, 1955. Persian trans. F. Badra'ī, *Firqa-yi Ismā'īliyya*. 2nd edn, Tehran, 1369/1990
Hodgson, Marshall G. S. "The Ismā'īlī State", in *The Cambridge History of Iran*: Volume 5, pp. 422–82
Hodgson, Marshall G. S. "Durūz", EI2, vol. 2, pp. 631–4
Hollister, John N. *The Shi'a of India*. London, 1953
Holzwarth, Wolfgang. *Die Ismailiten in Nordpakistan*. Berlin, 1994
Hunzai, Faquir M. and Kassam, K. (eds and trans). *Shimmering Light: An Anthology of Ismaili Poetry*. London, 1996
Ibn al-Athīr, 'Izz al-Dīn 'Alī b. Muḥammad. *al-Kāmil fi'l-ta'rīkh*, ed. C. J. Tornberg. Leiden, 1851–76
Ibn al-Dawādārī, Abū Bakr b. 'Abd Allāh. *Kanz al-durar*, vol. 6, ed. Ṣ. al-Munajjid. Cairo, 1961
Ibn Faḍl Allāh al-'Umarī, Shihāb al-Dīn Aḥmad. *Masālik al-abṣār fī mamālik al-amṣār*, ed. A. Fu'ād Sayyid. Cairo, 1985
Ibn Ḥawqal, Abu'l-Qāsim b. 'Alī. *Kitāb ṣūrat al-arḍ*, ed. J. H. Kramers. 2nd edn, Leiden, 1938–9. French trans. J. H. Kramers and G. Wiet, *Configuration de la terre*. Paris, 1964
Ibn 'Idhārī al-Marrākushī, Abu'l-'Abbās Aḥmad b. Muḥammad. *al-Bayān al-mughrib*, ed. G. S. Colin and E. Lévi-Provençal. New edn, Leiden, 1948–51
Ibn Isfandiyār, Muḥammad b. al-Ḥasan. *Ta'rīkh-i Ṭabaristān*, ed. 'Abbās Iqbāl. Tehran, 1320/1941. Abridged English trans. E. G. Browne, *An Abridged Translation of the History of Ṭabaristān*. Leiden and London, 1905
Ibn Mālik al-Ḥammādī al-Yamānī, Abū 'Abd Allāh Muḥammad. *Kashf asrār*

al-Bāṭiniyya wa-akhbār al-Qarāmiṭa, ed. M. Z. al-Kawtharī. Cairo, 1357/1939
Ibn Ma'mūn al-Baṭā'iḥī, Jamāl al-Dīn Abū 'Alī Mūsā. *Nuṣūs min akhbār Miṣr*, ed. A. Fu'ād Sayyid. Cairo, 1983
Ibn Muyassar, Tāj al-Dīn Muḥammad b. 'Alī. *Akhbār Miṣr*, ed. A. Fu'ād Sayyid. Cairo, 1981
Ibn al-Nadīm, Abu'l-Faraj Muḥammad b. Isḥāq al-Warrāq. *Kitāb al-fihrist*, ed. M. R. Tajaddud. 2nd edn, Tehran, 1973. English trans. B. Dodge, *The Fihrist of al-Nadīm*. New York, 1970
Ibn al-Qalānisī, Abū Ya'lā Ḥamza b. Asad. *Dhayl ta'rīkh Dimashq*, ed. H. F. Amedroz. Leiden, 1908; ed. S. Zakkār. Damascus, 1983. French trans. Roger Le Tourneau, *Damas de 1075 à 1154*. Damascus, 1952
Ibn Taghrībirdī, Jamāl al-Dīn Abu'l-Maḥāsin Yūsuf. *al-Nujūm al-zāhira fī mulūk Miṣr wa'l-Qāhira*. Cairo, 1348–91/1929–72
Ibn al-Ṭuwayr, Abū Muḥammad al-Murtaḍā. *Nuzhat al-muqlatayn fī akhbār al-dawlatayn*, ed. A. Fu'ād Sayyid. Beirut, 1992
Ibn Ẓāfir, Jamāl al-Dīn 'Alī b. Abī Manṣūr al-Azdī. *Akhbār al-duwal al-munqaṭi'a*, ed. A. Ferré. Cairo, 1972
Idrīs 'Imād al-Dīn b. al-Ḥasan. *'Uyūn al-akhbār wa-funūn al-āthār*, vols 4–6, ed. M. Ghālib. Beirut, 1973–84
Idrīs 'Imād al-Dīn b. al-Ḥasan. *Ta'rīkh al-khulafā' al-Fāṭimiyyīn bi'l-Maghrib* (=*'Uyūn al-akhbār*, vol. 5 and part of vol. 6), ed. M. al-Ya'lāwī. Beirut, 1985
Idrīs 'Imād al-Dīn b. al-Ḥasan. *Zahr al-ma'ānī*, ed. M. Ghālib. Beirut, 1991
al-Imad, Leila S. *The Fatimid Vizierate, 969–1172*. Berlin, 1990
Ivanow, Wladimir. "The Sect of Imam Shah in Gujrat", *Journal of the Bombay Branch of the Royal Asiatic Society*, NS, 12 (1936), pp. 19–70
Ivanow, Wladimir. *Ismaili Tradition Concerning the Rise of the Fatimids*. London, etc., 1942
Ivanow, Wladimir. *The Alleged Founder of Ismailism*. Bombay, 1946
Ivanow, Wladimir. "Satpanth", in W. Ivanow (ed.), *Collectanea*, vol. 1. Leiden, 1948, pp. 1–54
Ivanow, Wladimir. *Studies in Early Persian Ismailism*. 2nd edn, Bombay, 1955
Ivanow, Wladimir. *Problems in Nasir-i Khusraw's Biography*. Bombay, 1956
Ivanow, Wladimir. *Alamut and Lamasar: Two Mediaeval Ismaili Strongholds in Iran*. Tehran, 1960
Ivanow, Wladimir. *Ismaili Literature: A Bibliographical Survey*. Tehran, 1963
Ja'far b. Manṣūr al-Yaman. *Kitāb al-kashf*, ed. R. Strothmann. London, etc., 1952
Ja'far b. Manṣūr al-Yaman. *Sarā'ir wa-asrār al-nuṭaqā'*, ed. M. Ghālib. Beirut, 1984
Jambet, Christian. *La Grande résurrection d'Alamût*. Lagrasse, 1990
al-Jawdharī, Abū 'Alī Manṣūr al-'Azīzī. *Sīrat al-ustādh Jawdhar*, ed. M. Kāmil Ḥusayn and M. 'A. Sha'īra. Cairo, 1954. French trans. M. Canard, *Vie de l'ustadh Jaudhar*. Algiers, 1958
Juwaynī, 'Alā' al-Dīn 'Aṭā-Malik b. Muḥammad. *Ta'rīkh-i jahān-gushāy*, ed. M. Qazwīnī. Leiden and London, 1912–37. English trans. John A. Boyle, *The History of the World-Conqueror*. Manchester, 1958; reprinted, Manchester and Paris, 1997
Kāshānī, Abu'l-Qāsim 'Abd Allāh b. 'Alī. *Zubdat al-tawārīkh: bakhsh-i Fāṭimiyān va Nizāriyān*, ed. M. T. Dānishpazhūh. 2nd edn, Tehran, 1366/1987
Kassam, Tazim R. *Songs of Wisdom and Circles of Dance: Hymns of the Satpanth Ismā'īlī Muslim Saint, Pīr Shams*. Albany, NY, 1995

Kay, Henry C. (ed. and tr.). *Yaman, its Early Mediaeval History*. London, 1892
Khākī Khurāsānī, Imām Qulī. *Dīwān*, ed. W. Ivanow. Bombay, 1933
Khan, Dominique-Sila. *Conversions and Shifting Identities: Ramdev Pir and the Ismailis in Rajasthan*. Delhi, 1997
Khayrkhwāh-i Harātī, Muḥammad Riḍā b. Sulṭān Ḥusayn. *Faṣl dar bayān-i shinākht-i imām*, ed. W. Ivanow. 3rd edn, Tehran, 1960. English trans. W. Ivanow, *On the Recognition of the Imam*. 2nd edn, Bombay, 1947
Khayrkhwāh-i Harātī, Muḥammad Riḍā b. Sulṭān Ḥusayn. *Kalām-i pīr*, ed. and English tr. W. Ivanow. Bombay, 1935
Khayrkhwāh-i Harātī, Muḥammad Riḍā b. Sulṭān Ḥusayn. *Taṣnīfāt*, ed. W. Ivanow. Tehran, 1961
al-Kirmānī, Ḥamīd al-Dīn Aḥmad b. ʿAbd Allāh. *Kitāb al-riyāḍ*, ed. ʿĀrif Tāmir. Beirut, 1960
al-Kirmānī, Ḥamīd al-Dīn Aḥmad b. ʿAbd Allāh. *Majmūʿat al-rasāʾil al-Kirmānī*, ed. M. Ghālib. Beirut, 1983
al-Kirmānī, Ḥamīd al-Dīn Aḥmad b. ʿAbd Allāh. *Rāḥat al-ʿaql*, ed. M. Kāmil Ḥusayn and M. Muṣṭafā Ḥilmī. Leiden and Cairo, 1953; ed. M. Ghālib. Beirut, 1967. Russian trans. A. V. Smirnov, *Uspokoenie Razuma*. Moscow, 1995
Kitāb al-ʿālim waʾl-ghulām, ed. M. Ghālib, in his *Arbaʿ kutub ḥaqqāniyya*. Beirut, 1983, pp. 13–75. Abridged English trans. W. Ivanow, "The Book of the Teacher and the Pupil", in his *Studies*, pp. 61–86
Klemm, Verena. *Die Mission des fāṭimidischen Agenten al-Muʾayyad fī d-dīn in Šīrāz*. Frankfurt, etc., 1989
Kohlberg, Etan. *Belief and Law in Imāmī Shīʿism*. Aldershot, 1991
Köhler, Bärbel. *Die Wissenschaft unter den ägyptischen Fatimiden*. Hildesheim, 1994
Kraus, Paul. *Alchemie, Ketzerei, Apokryphen im frühen Islam*, ed. R. Brague. Hildesheim, 1994
Lev, Yaacov. *State and Society in Fatimid Egypt*. Leiden, 1991
Lewis, Bernard. "Sources for the History of the Syrian Assassins", *Speculum*, 27 (1952), pp. 475–89, reprinted in his *Studies*, article VIII
Lewis, Bernard. "Kamāl al-Dīn's Biography of Rāšid al-Dīn Sinān", *Arabica*, 13 (1966), pp. 225–67, reprinted in his *Studies*, article X
Lewis, Bernard. *The Assassins: A Radical Sect in Islam*. London, 1967. Persian trans. F. Badraʾī, *Fidāʾīyān-i Ismāʿīlī*. Tehran, 1348/1969. French trans. A. Pélissier, *Les Assassins: Terrorisme et politique dans l'Islam médiéval*. Paris, 1982
Lewis, Bernard. "The Ismāʿīlites and the Assassins", in K. M. Setton (ed.), *A History of the Crusades*: Volume I, *The First Hundred Years*, ed. M. W. Baldwin. 2nd edn, Madison, Wis., 1969, pp. 99–132
Lewis, Bernard. *Studies in Classical and Ottoman Islam (7th–16th Centuries)*. London, 1976
Lokhandwalla, Shamoon T. "The Bohras, a Muslim Community of Gujarat", *Studia Islamica*, 3 (1955), pp. 117–35
Madelung, Wilferd. "Fatimiden und Baḥrainqarmaṭen", *Der Islam*, 34 (1959), pp. 34–88. English trans., "The Fatimids and the Qarmaṭīs of Baḥrayn", in Daftary (ed.), *Mediaeval Ismaʿili History*, pp. 21–73
Madelung, Wilferd. "Das Imamat in der frühen ismailitischen Lehre", *Der Islam*, 37 (1961), pp. 43–135
Madelung, Wilferd. "The Sources of Ismāʿīlī Law", *Journal of Near Eastern Studies*, 35 (1976), pp. 29–40, reprinted in his *Religious Schools*, article XVIII

Madelung, Wilferd. "Aspects of Ismāʿīlī Theology: The Prophetic Chain and the God Beyond Being", in S. H. Nasr (ed.), *Ismāʿīlī Contributions to Islamic Culture*. Tehran, 1977, pp. 51–65, reprinted in his *Religious Schools*, article XVII

Madelung, Wilferd. *Religious Schools and Sects in Medieval Islam*. London, 1985

Madelung, Wilferd. *Religious Trends in Early Islamic Iran*. Albany, NY, 1988

Madelung, Wilferd. "Cosmogony and Cosmology: vi. In Ismaʿilism", EIR, vol. 6, pp. 322–6

Madelung, Wilferd. "Ismāʿīliyya", EI2, vol. 4, pp. 198–206

Madelung, Wilferd. "Ḳarmaṭī", EI2, vol. 4, pp. 660–5

Madelung, Wilferd. "Khōdja", EI2, vol. 5, pp. 25–7

Madelung, Wilferd. "Shīʿa", EI2, vol. 9, pp. 420–4

al-Maqrīzī, Taqī al-Dīn Aḥmad b. ʿAlī. *Ittiʿāẓ al-ḥunafāʾ bi-akhbār al-aʾimma al-Fāṭimiyyīn al-khulafāʾ*, ed. J. al-Shayyāl and M. Ḥ. M. Aḥmad. Cairo, 1967–73

al-Maqrīzī, Taqī al-Dīn Aḥmad b. ʿAlī. *Kitāb al-mawāʿiẓ wa'l-iʿtibār bi-dhikr al-khiṭaṭ wa'l-āthār*. Būlāq, 1270/1853–4; ed. A. Fu'ād Sayyid. London, 1995

Marquet, Yves. "Ikhwān al-Ṣafā'", EI2, vol. 3, pp. 1071–6

Miles, George C. "Coins of the Assassins of Alamūt", *Orientalia Lovaniensia Periodica*, 3 (1972), pp. 155–62

Mirza, Nasseh A. *Syrian Ismailism*. Richmond, Surrey, 1997

Miskawayh, Abū ʿAlī Aḥmad b. Muḥammad. *Tajārib al-umam*, ed. and English tr. H. F. Amedroz and D. S. Margoliouth under the title *The Eclipse of the ʿAbbasid Caliphate*. Oxford, 1920–1

Misra, Satish C. *Muslim Communities in Gujarat*. Bombay, 1964

al-Mu'ayyad fi'l-Dīn al-Shīrāzī, Abū Naṣr Hibat Allāh b. Abī ʿImrān Mūsā. *al-Majālis al-Mu'ayyadiyya*, vols 1 and 3, ed. M. Ghālib. Beirut, 1974–84; vols 1 and 2, ed. Ḥātim Ḥamīd al-Dīn. Bombay, 1395–1407/1975–86

al-Mu'ayyad fi'l-Dīn al-Shīrāzī, Abū Naṣr Hibat Allāh b. Abī ʿImrān Mūsā. *Sīrat al-Mu'ayyad fi'l-Dīn dāʿī al-duʿāt*, ed. M. Kāmil Ḥusayn. Cairo, 1949

al-Musabbiḥī, ʿIzz al-Mulk Muḥammad b. ʿUbayd Allāh. *Akhbār Miṣr*, ed. A. Fu'ād Sayyid et al. Cairo, 1978–84

al-Mustanṣir bi'llāh, Abū Tamīm Maʿadd. *al-Sijillāt al-Mustanṣiriyya*, ed. ʿA. Mājid. Cairo, 1954

Nanji, Azim. "Modernization and Change in the Nizārī Ismaili Community in East Africa – A Perspective", *Journal of Religion in Africa*, 6 (1974), pp. 123–39

Nanji, Azim. "An Ismāʿīlī Theory of *Walāyah* in the *Daʿā'im al-Islām* of Qāḍī al-Nuʿmān", in D. P. Little (ed.), *Essays on Islamic Civilization Presented to Niyazi Berkes*. Leiden, 1976, pp. 260–73

Nanji, Azim. *The Nizārī Ismāʿīlī Tradition in the Indo-Pakistan Subcontinent*. Delmar, NY, 1978

Nanji, Azim. "Ismāʿīlism", in S. H. Nasr (ed.), *Islamic Spirituality: Foundations*. London, 1987, pp. 179–98, 432–3

Nanji, Azim. "Ismāʿīlī Philosophy", in S. H. Nasr and O. Leaman (eds), *History of Islamic Philosophy*. London, 1996, vol. 1, pp. 144–54

Nāṣir Khusraw. *Dīwān*, ed. M. Mīnuvī and M. Muḥaqqiq. Tehran, 1353/1974. Partial English trans. P. L. Wilson and G. R. Aavani, *Forty Poems from the Divan*. Tehran, 1977; partial English trans. in Annemarie Schimmel, *Make a Shield from Wisdom*. London, 1993

Nāṣir Khusraw. *Gushāyish va rahāyish*, ed. S. Nafīsī. Leiden, 1950; Italian trans. P. Filippani-Ronconi, *Il libro dello scioglimento e della liberazione*. Naples, 1959; ed. and English tr. F. M. Hunzai, *Knowledge and Liberation*. London, 1998

Nāṣir Khusraw. *Jāmiʿ al-ḥikmatayn*, ed. H. Corbin and M. Muʿīn. Tehran and Paris, 1953. French trans. I. de Gastines, *Le Livre réunissant les deux sagesses*. Paris, 1990

Nāṣir Khusraw. *Safar-nāma*, ed. and French tr. Charles Schefer. Paris, 1881; ed. M. Dabīr Siyāqī. 5th edn, Tehran, 1356/1977. English trans. W. M. Thackston, Jr., *Nāṣer-e Khosraw's Book of Travels (Safarnāma)*. Albany, NY, 1986. German trans. U. von Melzer, *Safarnāme: Das Reisetagebuch des persischen Dichters Nāṣir-i Ḫusrau*, ed. M. Mayerhofer. Graz, 1993

Nāṣir Khusraw. *Shish faṣl*, ed. and English tr. W. Ivanow. Leiden, 1949

Nāṣir Khusraw. *Wajh-i dīn*, ed. G. R. Aʿvānī. Tehran, 1977

al-Nawbakhtī, Abū Muḥammad al-Ḥasan b. Mūsā. *Kitāb firaq al-Shīʿa*, ed. H. Ritter. Istanbul, 1931

Netton, Ian R. *Allāh Transcendent: Studies in the Structure and Semiotics of Islamic Philosophy, Theology and Cosmology*. London, 1989

al-Nīsābūrī, Aḥmad b. Ibrāhīm. *Istitār al-imām*, ed. W. Ivanow, in *Bulletin of the Faculty of Arts, University of Egypt*, 4, part 2 (1936), pp. 93–107. English trans. Ivanow, in his *Ismaili Tradition*, pp. 157–83

Niẓām al-Mulk, Abū ʿAlī al-Ḥasan b. ʿAlī al-Ṭūsī. *Siyar al-mulūk (Siyāsat-nāma)*, ed. H. Darke. 2nd edn, Tehran, 1347/1968. English trans. H. Darke, *The Book of Government or Rules for Kings*. 2nd edn, London, 1978

al-Nuʿmān b. Muḥammad, al-Qāḍī Abū Ḥanīfa. *Daʿāʾim al-Islām*, ed. Asaf A. A. Fyzee. Cairo, 1951–61. Persian trans. ʿAbd Allāh Umīdvār, *Tarjuma-yi kitāb-i daʿāʾim al-Islām*. Tehran, 1372/1993

al-Nuʿmān b. Muḥammad, al-Qāḍī Abū Ḥanīfa. *Iftitāḥ al-daʿwa*, ed. W. al-Qāḍī. Beirut, 1970; ed. F. Dachraoui. Tunis, 1975

al-Nuʿmān b. Muḥammad, al-Qāḍī Abū Ḥanīfa. *Kitāb al-majālis wa'l-musāyarāt*, ed. al-Ḥabīb al-Faqī et al. Tunis, 1978

al-Nuʿmān b. Muḥammad, al-Qāḍī Abū Ḥanīfa. *Sharḥ al-akhbār*, ed. S. M. al-Ḥusaynī al-Jalālī. Qumm, 1409–12/1988–92

al-Nuʿmān b. Muḥammad, al-Qāḍī Abū Ḥanīfa. *Ta'wīl al-daʿāʾim*, ed. M. Ḥ. al-Aʿẓamī. Cairo, 1967–72

al-Nuwayrī, Shihāb al-Dīn Aḥmad b. ʿAbd al-Wahhāb. *Nihāyat al-arab fī funūn al-adab*, vol. 25, ed. M. J. ʿA. al-Ḥīnī et al. Cairo, 1984

Pandiyāt-i jawānmardī, ed. and English tr. W. Ivanow. Leiden, 1953

Poonawala, Ismail K. "Al-Qāḍī al-Nuʿmān's Works and the Sources", BSOAS, 36 (1973), pp. 109–15

Poonawala, Ismail K. "A Reconsideration of al-Qāḍī al-Nuʿmān's *Madhhab*", BSOAS, 37 (1974), pp. 572–9

Poonawala, Ismail K. *Biobibliography of Ismāʿīlī Literature*. Malibu, Calif., 1977

Poonawala, Ismail K. "Al-Qāḍī al-Nuʿmān and Ismaʿili Jurisprudence", in Daftary (ed.), *Mediaeval Ismaʿili History*, pp. 117–43

Pourjavady, Nasrollah and Wilson, Peter L. "Ismāʿīlīs and Niʿmatullāhīs", *Studia Islamica*, 41 (1975), pp. 113–35

al-Qalqashandī, Shihāb al-Dīn Aḥmad b. ʿAlī. *Ṣubḥ al-aʿshā fī ṣināʿat al-inshāʾ*. Cairo, 1331–8/1913–20

al-Qummī, Saʿd b. ʿAbd Allāh al-Ashʿarī. *Kitāb al-maqālāt wa'l-firaq*, ed. M. J. Mashkūr. Tehran, 1963

Rashīd al-Dīn Ṭabīb, Faḍl Allāh b. 'Imād al-Dawla Abi'l-Khayr. *Jāmi' al-tawārīkh: qismat-i Ismā'īliyān va Fāṭimiyān va Nizāriyān va dā'īyān va rafīqān*, ed. M. T. Dānishpazhūh and M. Mudarrisī Zanjānī. Tehran, 1338/1959
al-Rāzī, Abū Ḥātim Aḥmad b. Ḥamdān. *A'lām al-nubuwwa*, ed. Ṣ. al-Ṣāwī and G. R. A'vānī. Tehran, 1977. Partial French trans. F. Brion, in his "Philosophie et révélation", *Bulletin de Philosophie Médiévale*, 28 (1986), pp. 134–62
Sanders, Paula. *Ritual, Politics, and the City in Fatimid Cairo*. Albany, NY, 1994
Sayyid, A. Fu'ād. "Lumières nouvelles sur quelques sources de l'histoire Fatimide en Egypte", *Annales Islamologiques*, 13 (1977), pp. 1–41
Sayyid, A. Fu'ād. *al-Dawla al-Fāṭimiyya fī Miṣr: tafsīr jadīd*. Cairo, 1992
Shackle, Christopher and Moir, Zawahir. *Ismaili Hymns from South Asia: An Introduction to the Ginans*. London, 1992
al-Shahrastānī, Abu'l-Fatḥ Muḥammad b. 'Abd al-Karīm. *Kitāb al-milal wa'l-niḥal*, ed. W. Cureton. London, 1842–6; ed. 'A. M. al-Wakīl. Cairo, 1968. Partial English trans. A. K. Kazi and J. G. Flynn, *Muslim Sects and Divisions*. London, 1984. French trans. D. Gimaret et al., *Livre des religions et des sectes*. Louvain, 1986–93
al-Shayyāl, Jamāl al-Dīn (ed.). *Majmū'at al-wathā'iq al-Fāṭimiyya*. Cairo, 1958
Shihāb al-Dīn Shāh al-Ḥusaynī. *Khiṭābāt-i 'āliya*, ed. H. Ujāqī. Bombay, 1963
Shihāb al-Dīn Shāh al-Ḥusaynī. *Risāla dar ḥaqīqat-i dīn*, ed. W. Ivanow. Bombay, 1947. English trans. W. Ivanow, *True Meaning of Religion*. 2nd edn, Bombay, 1947
al-Sijistānī, Abū Ya'qūb Isḥāq b. Aḥmad. *Kashf al-maḥjūb*, ed. H. Corbin. Tehran and Paris, 1949. French trans. H. Corbin, *Le Dévoilement des choses cachées*. Lagrasse, 1988
al-Sijistānī, Abū Ya'qūb Isḥāq b. Aḥmad. *Kitāb al-yanābī'*, ed. and French tr. Corbin, in his *Trilogie Ismaélienne*, text pp. 1–97, translation pp. 1–127. English trans. Walker, *The Book of Wellsprings*, in his *The Wellsprings of Wisdom*, pp. 37–111
Smet, Daniel de. *La Quiétude de l'intellect: Néoplatonisme et gnose Ismaélienne dans l'œuvre de Ḥamīd ad-Dīn al-Kirmānī (Xe/XIe s.)*. Louvain, 1995
Stern, Samuel M. "Ismā'īlī Propaganda and Fatimid Rule in Sind", *Islamic Culture*, 23 (1949), pp. 298–307, reprinted in his *Studies*, pp. 177–88
Stern, Samuel M. "The Epistle of the Fatimid Caliph al-Āmir (al-Hidāya al-Āmiriyya) – its Date and its Purpose", JRAS (1950), pp. 20–31, reprinted in his *History and Culture*, article X
Stern, Samuel M. "The Succession to the Fatimid Imam al-Āmir, the Claims of the Later Fatimids to the Imamate, and the Rise of Ṭayyibī Ismailism", *Oriens*, 4 (1951), pp. 193–255, reprinted in his *History and Culture*, article XI
Stern, Samuel M. "Heterodox Ismā'īlism at the Time of al-Mu'izz", BSOAS, 17 (1955), pp. 10–33, reprinted in his *Studies*, pp. 257–88
Stern, Samuel M. "The Early Ismā'īlī Missionaries in North-West Persia and in Khurāsān and Transoxania", BSOAS, 23 (1960), pp. 56–90, reprinted in his *Studies*, pp. 189–233
Stern, Samuel M. "Cairo as the Centre of the Ismā'īlī Movement", in *Colloque international sur l'histoire du Caire*. Cairo, 1972, pp. 437–50, reprinted in his *Studies*, pp. 234–56
Stern, Samuel M. *Studies in Early Ismā'īlism*. Jerusalem and Leiden, 1983
Stern, Samuel M. *History and Culture in the Medieval Muslim World*. London, 1984

Stroeva, Ludmila V. *Gosudarstvo ismailitov v Irane v XI–XIII vv.* Moscow, 1978. Persian trans. P. Munzavī, *Ta'rīkh-i Ismā'īliyān dar Īrān.* Tehran, 1371/1992

Strothmann, Rudolf (ed.). *Gnosis Texte der Ismailiten.* Göttingen, 1943

al-Ṭabarī, Abū Ja'far Muḥammad b. Jarīr. *Ta'rīkh al-rusul wa'l-mulūk*, ed. M. J. de Goeje et al., 3 series. Leiden, 1879–1901. English trans. by various scholars as *The History of al-Ṭabarī.* Albany, NY, 1985–

Tāmir, 'Ārif. "Furū' al-shajara al-Ismā'īliyya al-Imāmiyya", *al-Mashriq*, 51 (1957), pp. 581–612

Ta'rīkh-i Sīstān, ed. M. T. Bahār. Tehran, 1314/1935; ed. J. Mudarris Ṣādiqī. Tehran, 1373/1994. English trans. M. Gold, *The Tārikh-e Sistān.* Rome, 1976

al-Ṭūsī, Naṣīr al-Dīn Muḥammad b. Muḥammad. *Rawḍat al-taslīm*, ed. and English tr. W. Ivanow. Leiden, 1950. French trans. Christian Jambet, *La Convocation d'Alamût: Somme de philosophie Ismaélienne.* Lagrasse, 1996

Vazīrī, Aḥmad 'Alī Khān. *Ta'rīkh-i Kirmān*, ed. M. I. Bāstānī Pārīzī. 2nd edn, Tehran, 1352/1973

Vermeulen, U. and Smet, D. de (eds). *Egypt and Syria in the Fatimid, Ayyubid and Mamluk Eras.* Louvain, 1995

al-Walīd, 'Alī b. Muḥammad. *Kitāb al-dhakīra fi'l-ḥaqīqa*, ed. M. Ḥ. al-A'ẓamī. Beirut, 1971

al-Walīd, 'Alī b. Muḥammad. *Tāj al-'aqā'id*, ed. 'Ārif Tāmir. Beirut, 1967. Summary English trans. W. Ivanow, *A Creed of the Fatimids.* Bombay, 1936

Walker, Paul E. "Eternal Cosmos and the Womb of History: Time in Early Ismaili Thought", IJMES, 9 (1978), pp. 355–66

Walker, Paul E. *Early Philosophical Shiism: The Ismaili Neoplatonism of Abū Ya'qūb al-Sijistānī.* Cambridge, 1993

Walker, Paul E. "The Ismaili Da'wa in the Reign of the Fatimid Caliph al-Ḥākim", *Journal of the American Research Center in Egypt*, 30 (1993), pp. 161–82

Walker, Paul E. *The Wellsprings of Wisdom: A Study of Abū Ya'qūb al-Sijistānī's Kitāb al-Yanābī'.* Salt Lake City, 1994

Walker, Paul E. "Succession to Rule in the Shiite Caliphate", *Journal of the American Research Center in Egypt*, 32 (1995), pp. 239–64

Walker, Paul E. *Abū Ya'qūb al-Sijistānī: Intellectual Missionary.* London, 1996

al-Yamānī, Muḥammad b. Muḥammad. *Sīrat al-Ḥājib Ja'far b. 'Alī*, ed. W. Ivanow, in *Bulletin of the Faculty of Arts, University of Egypt*, 4, part 2 (1936), pp. 107–33. English trans. Ivanow, in his *Ismaili Tradition*, pp. 184–223. French trans. M. Canard, "L'Autobiographie d'un chambellan du Mahdī 'Obeidallāh le Fāṭimide", *Hespéris*, 39 (1952), pp. 279–324, reprinted in Canard, *Miscellanea Orientalia*, article V

Zāhid 'Alī. *Hamārī Ismā'īlī madhhab.* Hyderabad, 1373/1954

Zakkār, Suhayl (ed.). *Akhbār al-Qarāmiṭa.* 2nd edn, Damascus, 1982

Index